Spanish
for
Law
Enforcement
Personnel

Second Edition

William C. Harvey, M.S.

BARRON'S

Special thanks to the men and women of the
Santa Ana Police Department in Orange County, California

About the Author

William C. Harvey is founder of Language Services Institute, a highly successful conversation Spanish program aimed specifically at meeting the needs of today's busy adult learner. For the past 12 years he has taught Spanish and ESL (English as a Second Language) in school districts and community colleges, as well as in private industry. He has also traveled extensively throughout the West Coast giving workshops and seminars to teachers and professional organizations. Mr. Harvey holds a bachelor's degree in Spanish and a master's degree in Bilingual-Bicultural Education from Cal State University, Fullerton, where he received the "Project of the Year" award for his work in ESL Curriculum Development.

He currently has several books published by Barron's including *Spanish for Gringos, Inglés para Latinos, Household Spanish*, and *Spanish for Health Care Professionals*.

© Copyright 2007, 1996 by William C. Harvey.
Drawings © Copyright 1996 by Barron's Educational Series, Inc.

All inquiries should be addressed to:
Barron's Educational Series, Inc.
250 Wireless Boulevard
Hauppauge, New York 11788
www.barronseduc.com

ISBN-13: 978-0-7641-3751-8 (book only)
ISBN-10: 0-7641-3751-4 (book only)
ISBN-13: 978-0-7641-9365-1 (book and CD package)
ISBN-10: 978-0-7641-9365-1 (book and CD package)

Library of Congress Catalog Card Number 2006048821

Library of Congress Cataloging-in-Publication Data
Harvey, William C.
   Spanish for law enforcement personnel / William C. Harvey. — 2nd ed.
      p. cm.
   ISBN-10: 0-7641-3751-4 (alk. paper)
   ISBN-13: 978-0-7641-3751-8 (alk. paper)
   1. Spanish language—Conversation and phrase books (for police) I. Title.

   PC4120.P64H37 2008
   468.3′4210243632—dc22   2006048821

Printed in the United States of America
9 8 7 6 5 4 3 2 1

TABLE OF CONTENTS

A LITTLE BACKGROUND

I grew up in Southern California, and have experienced firsthand the rapid growth of a Spanish-speaking community. Years ago, when I was first picking up Spanish as a student in high school, the only real practice I had was with my co-workers at a local Mexican restaurant. Today, as a Spanish instructor who travels throughout the country, I find that there is more Spanish being spoken in the United States than ever before.

This rapid increase in the number of Spanish speakers has left a tremendous impact on America's law enforcement agencies. In cities everywhere, officials are struggling to meet the needs of the non-English-speaking Hispanic community. But it is difficult to serve and protect the public when language and culture barriers interfere with basic communication.

Spanish for Law Enforcement Personnel teaches readers how to participate in everyday conversations with Spanish speakers, while at the same time guiding them through a variety of police-related activities. More importantly, this guidebook helps law enforcement personnel understand and appreciate various aspects of the Hispanic culture.

To find a specific skill or list of vocabulary, simply use the Table of Contents. Individual words can be found in the English-Spanish and Spanish-English glossary at the end of the book.

A Closer Look

Chapter One is a general introduction to the Spanish language, while Chapters Two through Seven focus on individual professional skills. Each chapter is divided into a variety of topical categories, which all tie into the chapter title or theme. To get the most out of this book, try focusing on the icons provided below. They can be helpful when you are working on a specific skill or topic of interest. Simply scan the pages for the corresponding icon, and read up on whatever you need:

 A MIS ORDENES (*ah mees 'ohr-deh-nehs*) means "at my command," and provides insights on how to use command words.

 TEMAS CULTURALES (*'teh-mahs kool-too-'rah-lehs*) is, yes, you guessed, "cultural subjects." Different races with different cultural backgrounds may lead to misunderstandings. Check this icon for help.

 ACCIÓN (*ahk-see-'ohn*) clearly means "action." This segment covers verbs and the impressive sentences you can build with them.

 INFORMACIÓN PRIVADA (*een-fohr-mah-see-'ohn pree-'vah-dah*) signifies "inside, or private, information." Here we cover details related to language usage.

GRANDES HABILIDADES (*'grahn-dehs ah-bee-lee-'dah-dehs*) we translate as "super skills"! Additional verbal forms and constructions are shown here.

 REPASO (*reh-'pah-soh*) is "review." Here you make sure that you remembered what you learned.

After reading through the first chapter, skim the following material until you come to a specialized vocabulary list that interests you. Notice how each Spanish word includes an English pronunciation guide. Say the word at least twice and then fit it into one of the suggested grammatical patterns. If you need help with the grammar, new skills are presented toward the end of each chapter.

One method for practice is to read key parts of a chapter with notecards and a pen in hand. Copy down those words, expressions, or command phrases that you will be needing soon, and carry the card around as a reference tool. You can also print everything out from a computer, or use color-coded index cards, and then laminate them for protection. Be as creative as you like. The key is to learn Spanish at your own pace. There's a lot of information here, and no two *Spanish for Law Enforcement Personnel* students are exactly the same. Find out a system that works best for you, and just go for it!

Face the Facts

Contrary to popular belief, learning a new language does not have to include repetition drills, written exercises, or dialog memorization. In fact, most "traditional" techniques often do more harm than good. Studies have shown that Spanish is acquired more readily when the following guidelines are taken into consideration:

- Avoid focusing too much on grammar rules and pronunciation practice.
- Study when you have the desire and feel relaxed.
- Learn those Spanish words that are similar to English in form and meaning.
- Seek opportunities to practice your new skills with non-English speaking Hispanics.
- Listen to the language first, and allow Spanish words to emerge naturally.
- Begin by using simple commands or expressions, since messages can be sent with only a few key words.
- Acquire those words and phrases that relate to real-life experiences.

Learning Spanish does not have to be a stressful experience. This guidebook is for law enforcement officials who want training to be effective, simple, and fun. So relax, *Spanish for Law Enforcement Personnel* is really **no problema** (*noh proh-'bleh-mah*) at all.

CHAPTER ONE
Capítulo Uno
(kah-'pee-too-loh 'oo-noh)

BASIC TRAINING
Entrenamiento básico
(ehn-treh-nah-mee-'ehn-toh 'bah-see-koh)

SOUND SECRETS
Los secretos de los sonidos *(lohs seh-'kreh-tohs deh lohs soh-'nee-dohs)*

You will be glad to know that your poor pronunciation won't interfere much with your communication. The Spanish-speaking public is quite forgiving and, in general, many of the sounds are the same in both languages.

The primary sounds to remember are the vowels, which, unlike their equivalents in English, are pronounced the way they are written:

a *(ah)*   as in palm
e *(eh)*   as in pet
i *(ee)*   as in peep
o *(oh)*   as in poke
u *(oo)*   as in pool

Become familiar with these five sounds as soon as possible, and remember that they are always pronounced the same. Also, don't forget to practice the rest of the sounds in Spanish. Some of these letters might give you a little trouble:

Spanish Letter	English Sound
c (after an e or i)	s as in Sally (**cigarro**) *(see-'gah-rroh)*
g (after an e or i)	h as in Harry (**Geraldo**) *(heh-'rahl-doh)*
h	silent, like k in knife (**hola**) *('oh-lah)*
j	h as in hot (**Julio**) *('hoo-lee-oh)*
ll	y as in yellow (**tortilla**) *(tohr-'tee-yah)*
ñ	ny as in canyon (**señorita**) *(seh-nyoh-'ree-tah)*
rr	the "rolled" r sound (**burro**) *('boo-rroh)*
z	s as in son (**Sánchez**) *('sahn-chehs)*

Although some dialects may vary slightly, the rest of the letters in Spanish are similar to their equivalents in English:

b **bueno** *('bweh-noh)*
d **dinero** *(dee-'neh-roh)*
f **foto** *('foh-toh)*
l **linda** *('leen-dah)*
m **mucho** *('moo-choh)*
n **nada** *('nah-dah)*

p **policía** *(poh-lee-'see-ah)*
r **rancho** *('rahn-choh)*
s **sí** *(see)*
t **taco** *('tah-koh)*
x **extra** *('ehk-strah)*

Now, read the following words aloud and remember that *each letter* needs to be pronounced the way it was introduced earlier. Can you guess at their meanings?

amigo *(ah-'mee-goh)*
arresto *(ah-'rreh-stoh)*
carro *('kah-rroh)*
español *(ehs-pah-'nyohl)*
excelente *(ehk-seh-'lehn-teh)*
general *(heh-neh-'rahl)*
grande *('grahn-deh)*
hombre *('ohm-breh)*

macho *('mah-choh)*
pistola *(pee-'stoh-lah)*
pollo *('poh-yoh)*
poquito *(poh-'kee-toh)*
plaza *('plah-sah)*
reporte *(reh-'pohr-teh)*
señor *(seh-'nyohr)*
vino *('vee-noh)*

Yo excelente policía, bueno, macho y amigo, ¡oh sí!

INFORMACIÓN PRIVADA

➤ Any part of a word with an accent mark (´) needs to be pronounced LOUDER and with more emphasis (e.g., **policía**). If there's no accent mark, say the last part of the word louder and with more emphasis (e.g., **señor**). For words ending in a vowel, or in **n** or **s**, the next to the last part of the word is stressed (e.g., **reporte**, *reh-'pohr-teh)*.

➤ In some cases, the letter **u** doesn't make the "oo" sound; for example, **guitarra** *(gee-'tah-rrah)* or **guerra** *('geh-rrah)*.

➤ Several words in English are spelled the same in Spanish, and they usually have the same meaning. But, watch out! They are NOT pronounced the same way!

color *(koh-'lohr)*
chocolate *(choh-koh-'lah-teh)*
doctor *(dohk-'tohr)*
final *(fee-'nahl)*

hospital *(oh-spee-'tahl)*
idea *(ee-'deh-ah)*
natural *(nah-too-'rahl)*
terror *(teh-'rrohr)*

HOW DO YOU WRITE IT?

¿Cómo se escribe? *('koh-moh seh eh-'skree-beh)*

In the world of law enforcement, there are occasions when the best way to communicate is through the written word. In those cases, you may have to depend on your spelling skills in Spanish. Fortunately, the language is spelled the way it is pronounced. So, if you know your alphabet in Spanish, you are in pretty good shape.

a *(ah)*	**n** *('eh-neh)*
b *(beh 'grahn-deh)*	**ñ** *('eh-nyeh)*
c *(seh)*	**o** *(oh)*
ch *(cheh)*	**p** *(peh)*
d *(deh)*	**q** *(koo)*
e *(eh)*	**r** *('eh-reh)*
f *('eh-feh)*	**rr** *('eh-rreh)*
g *(heh)*	**s** *('eh-seh)*
h *('ah-cheh)*	**t** *(teh)*
i *(ee)*	**u** *(oo)*
j *('ho-tah)*	**v** *(veh-'chee-kah)*
k *(kah)*	**w** *(veh-'doh-bleh)*
l *('el-leh)*	**x** *('eh-kees)*
ll *('eh-yeh)*	**y** *(ee-gree-'eh-gah)*
m *('eh-meh)*	**z** *('seh-tah)*

EASY EXPRESSIONS

Expresiones fáciles *(eh-spreh-see-'oh-nehs 'fah-see-lehs)*

What better way to open up in Spanish than to mutter a few common greetings or courteous expressions! Although there are other phrases with similar meanings, these will do fine for now. As you read each word in Spanish, try to focus on those new sounds you have just learned:

And you?	**¿Y usted?** *(ee oo-'stehd)*
Bye!	**¡Adiós!** *(ah-dee-'ohs)*
Excuse me!	**¡Con permiso!** *('kohn 'pehr-mee-soh)*
Fine	**Bien** *('bee·ehn)*
Go ahead!	**¡Pase!** *('pah-seh)*
Good	**Bueno** *('bweh-noh)*
Good afternoon	**Buenas tardes** *('bweh-nahs 'tahr-dehs)*
Good evening/Good night	**Buenas noches** *('bweh-nahs 'noh-chehs)*

Good morning	**Buenos días** ('bweh-nohs 'dee-ahs)
Hi!	**¡Hola!** ('oh-lah)
How are you?	**¿Cómo está?** ('koh-moh eh-'stah)
How's it going?	**¿Qué tal?** (keh tahl)
I'm sorry!	**¡Lo siento!** (loh see-'ehn-toh)
May I come in?	**¿Se puede?** (seh 'pweh-deh)
May I help you?	**¿Puedo ayudarle?** ('pweh-doh ah-yoo-'dahr-leh)
Nice to meet you!	**¡Mucho gusto!** ('moo-choh 'goo-stoh)
Not bad	**Así-así** (ah-'see ah-'see)
OK	**Regular** (reh-goo-'lahr)
Please	**Por favor** (pohr fah-'vohr)
Same here	**Igualmente** (ee-gwahl-'mehn-teh)
Thank you	**Gracias** ('grah-see-ahs)
Very well	**Muy bien** ('moo·ee 'bee·'ehn)
What happened?	**¿Qué pasó?** (keh pah-'soh)
What's happening?	**¿Qué pasa?** (keh 'pah-sah)
You're welcome	**De nada** (deh 'nah-dah)

INFORMACIÓN PRIVADA

➤ The upside down exclamation point (¡) (for exclamations) and question mark (¿) (for questions) are found at the beginning of sentences, and must be used when you write in Spanish.

➤ Scan these other "excuse me" phrases:

Excuse me! (if you cough or sneeze) **¡Perdón!** (pehr-'dohn)
Excuse me! (if you need someone's attention) **¡Disculpe!** (dee-'skool-peh)
Attention! (if it's an announcement to a crowd) **¡Atención!** (ah-tehn-see-'ohn)

Friendly greetings may involve more than just an exchange of simple expresions. Healthy touch is an active part of many cultures, and in Latin America, **cariño** *(kah-'ree-nyoh)* (affection) is openly displayed between family and friends. Hugs, kisses, embraces, and handshakes abound, so don't be startled by all the physical contact!

MORE EXPRESSIONS!
¡Más expresiones! *(mahs ehk-spreh-see-'oh-nehs)*

Bless you!	**¡Salud!** *(sah-'lood)*
Congratulations!	**¡Felicitaciones!** *(feh-lee-see-tah-see-'oh-nehs)*
Go with God!	**¡Vaya con Dios!** *('vah-yah kohn dee-'ohs)*
Good luck!	**¡Buena suerte!** *('bweh-nah 'swehr-teh)*
Happy Birthday!	**¡Feliz cumpleaños!** *(feh-'lees koom-pleh-'ah-nyohs)*
Have a nice day!	**¡Que le vaya bien!** *(keh leh 'vah-yah bee-'ehn)*
I'll be right back!	**¡Ahora vengo!** *(ah-'oh-rah 'vehn-goh)*
I'm leaving now!	**¡Ya me voy!** *(yah meh 'voh-ee)*
Ready?	**¿Listo?** *('lee-stoh)*
See you later!	**¡Hasta luego!** *('ahs-tah loo-'eh-goh)*
Take it easy!	**¡Cúidese bien!** *('kwee-deh-seh bee-'ehn)*
Welcome!	**¡Bienvenidos!** *(bee-ehn-veh-'nee-dohs)*
Wow!	**¡Caramba!** *(kah-'rahm-bah)*

INFORMACIÓN PRIVADA

➤ Although Spanish expressions and words may differ slightly from region to region, the material in this guidebook is general enough to be understood by all Hispanics worldwide.

➤ Bear in mind that most idiomatic expressions cannot be translated word for word. Therefore, it's best to memorize each phrase as one long string of individual sounds.

TEMAS CULTURALES

Friendly greetings in Spanish are used all day long. Being courteous is the key to establishing trust in the Hispanic community. Throughout most cultures everywhere, a sincere smile and a kind word can lead to respect and complete cooperation.

At times, you may need to refer to the cultural differences between the United States and other Spanish-speaking countries. In terms of greetings and friendly exchanges, these topics might emerge:

courtesy	**la cortesía** *(lah kohr-teh-'see-ah)*
custom	**la costumbre** *(lah koh-'stoom-breh)*
formality	**la formalidad** *(lah fohr-mah-lee-'dahd)*
honor	**el honor** *(ehl oh-'nohr)*
respect	**el respeto** *(ehl reh-'speh-toh)*
tradition	**la tradición** *(lah trah-dee-see-'ohn)*

WHAT'S YOUR NAME?
¿Cómo se llama? *('koh-moh seh 'yah-mah)*

The popular phrase **¿Cómo se llama?** *('koh-moh seh 'yah-mah)* is usually translated to mean "What's your name?" However, you may also hear **¿Cuál es su nombre?** *(kwahl ehs soo 'nohm-breh)* which literally means "Which is your name?" You should also know these:

first name	**primer nombre** (pree-'mehr 'nohm-breh)
last name	**apellido** (ah-peh-'yee-doh)

Answer this question in several ways:

I'm…	**Soy…** ('soh-ee)
I'm called…	**Me llamo…** (meh-'yah-moh)
My name is…	**Mi nombre es…** (mee 'nohm-breh ehs)

 TEMAS CULTURALES

When referring to others by name, it really helps if you are able to pronounce the names correctly, as it makes people feel much more at ease. Always remember that Spanish is pronounced the way it is written. Also, it is not uncommon for someone in Spain or Latin America to have two last names. Don't get confused. Here's the order:

First name
primer nombre (pree-'mehr 'nohm-breh) — Martín (mahr-'teen)

Father's last name
apellido paterno (ah-peh-'yee-doh pah-'tehr-noh) — Sánchez ('sahn-chehs)

Mother's last name
apellido materno (ah-peh-'yee-doh mah-'tehr-noh) — Ochoa (oh-'choh-ah)

➤ Some Hispanic people have two first names, since there is no middle name as we know it.

➤ Often, when a woman marries, she keeps her father's last name, followed by her husband's.

WINNING ONE-LINERS
Frases ganadoras *('frah-sehs gah-nah-'doh-rahs)*

Once you feel comfortable using the everyday expressions, why not give these winning one-liners a try. Whether you're chatting on the streets or over the counter, all of the following words and phases will come in handy. Most of them can be used as short, but effective, one-word responses:

Don't worry	**No se preocupe** *(noh seh preh-oh-'koo-peh)*
Good idea	**Buena idea** *('bweh-nah ee-'deh-ah)*
I agree	**De acuerdo** *(deh ah-'kwehr-doh)*
I hope so	**Ojalá** *(oh-hah-'lah)*
I see	**Ya veo** *(yah 'veh-oh)*
I think so	**Creo que sí** *('kreh-oh keh see)*
Maybe	**Quizás** *(kee-'sahs)*
Me, neither	**Yo tampoco** *(yoh tahm-'poh-koh)*
Me, too	**Yo también** *(yoh tahm-bee-'ehn)*
More or less	**Más o menos** *(mahs oh 'meh-nohs)*
Not yet	**Todavía no** *(toh-dah-'vee-ah noh)*
Really?	**¿Verdad?** *(vehr-'dahd)*
Right away!	**¡En seguida!** *(ehn seh-'gee-dah)*
Sure	**Claro** *('klah-roh)*
That depends	**Depende** *(deh-'pehn-deh)*
That's great!	**¡Qué bueno!** *(keh 'bweh-noh)*
What a shame!	**¡Qué lástima!** *(keh 'lah-stee-mah)*

I DON'T UNDERSTAND!

¡No entiendo! *(noh ehn-tee-'ehn-doh)*

Interjecting words and phrases is a nice start, but there won't be much communication if you can't understand each other. Face-to-face or on the phone, clear up the confusion with the following phrases:

Again	**Otra vez** *('oh-trah vehs)*
Another word, please	**Otra palabra, por favor** *('oh-trah pah-'lah-brah pohr fah-'vohr)*
Can you translate?	**¿Puede traducir?** *('pweh-deh trah-doo-'seer)*
Do you need an interpreter?	**¿Necesita un intérprete?** *(neh-seh-'see-tah oon een-'tehr-preh-teh)*
Do you speak English?	**¿Habla inglés?** *('ah-blah een-'glehs)*
How do you say it?	**¿Cómo se dice?** *('koh-moh seh 'dee-seh)*
I don't know	**No sé** *(noh seh)*
I don't understand!	**¡No entiendo!** *(noh ehn-tee-'ehn-doh)*
I speak a little Spanish	**Hablo poquito español** *('ah-bloh poh-'kee-toh eh-spah-'nyohl)*
I'm learning Spanish	**Estoy aprendiendo español** *(eh-'stoh-ee ah-prehdee-'ehn-doh eh-spah-'nyohl)*
Is there anyone here who speaks English?	**¿Hay alguien aquí que hable inglés?** *('ah-ee 'ahlgee-ehn ah-'kee keh 'ah-bleh een-'glehs)*
More slowly!	**¡Más despacio!** *(mahs deh-'spah-see-oh)*
Please repeat	**Repita, por favor** *(reh-'pee-tah pohr fah-'vohr)*
Thanks for your patience	**Gracias por su paciencia** *('grah-see·ahs pohr soo pah-see-'ehn-see·ah)*
What does it mean?	**¿Qué significa?** *(keh seeg-nee-'fee-kah)*

Bear in mind that hand gestures help to clarify your message. Many times, nonverbal communication is more powerful than words. Also, try to relax. It's only natural to make mistakes when you're learning a second language. Besides, the Spanish speaker is probably having as much trouble as you are!

SURVIVAL STUFF
Cosas útiles *('koh-sahs 'oo-tee-lehs)*

No matter what your responsibilities are in the field of law enforcement, not much can be communicated in Spanish without the use of basic survival vocabulary words. To talk about people and things, take extra time to practice the word lists below:

People	**La gente** *(la 'hehn-teh)*
baby	**el bebé** *(ehl beh-'beh)*
boy	**el niño** *(ehl 'nee-nyoh)*
girl	**la niña** *(lah 'nee-nyah)*
man	**el hombre** *(ehl 'ohm-breh)*
person	**la persona** *(lah pehr-'soh-nah)*
teenager (female)	**la muchacha** *(lah moo-'chah-chah)*
teenager (male)	**el muchacho** *(ehl moo-'chah-choh)*
woman	**la mujer** *(lah moo-'hehr)*
Señor (Sr.)	refers to man (Mr.) *(seh-'nyohr)*
Señora (Sra.)	refers to a married or mature woman (Mrs.) *(seh-'nyoh-rah)*
Señorita (Srta.)	refers to a young lady (Miss) *(seh-nyoh-'ree-tah)*
Everyday Things	**Las cosas diarias** *(lahs 'koh-sahs dee-'ah-ree·ahs)*
bathroom	**el baño** *(ehl 'bah-nyoh)*
bed	**la cama** *(lah 'kah-mah)*
book	**el libro** *(ehl 'lee-broh)*
car	**el carro** *(ehl 'kah-rroh)*
chair	**la silla** *(lah 'see-yah)*
door	**la puerta** *(lah 'pwehr-tah)*
floor	**el piso** *(ehl 'pee-soh)*
food	**la comida** *(lah koh-'mee-dah)*
house	**la casa** *(lah 'cah-sah)*
key	**la llave** *(lah 'yah-beh)*
light	**la luz** *(lah loos)*

paper	**el papel** *(ehl pah-'pehl)*
pen	**el lapicero** *(ehl lah-pee-'seh-roh)*
pencil	**el lápiz** *(ehl 'lah-pees)*
room	**el cuarto** *(ehl 'kwahr-toh)*
table	**la mesa** *(lah 'meh-sah)*
trash	**la basura** *(lah bah-'soo-rah)*
water	**el agua** *(ehl 'ah-gwah)*
window	**la ventana** *(lah vehn-'tah-nah)*
work	**el trabajo** *(trah-'bah-hoh)*

On the Job	**En el trabajo** *(ehn ehl trah-'bah-hoh)*
crime	**el crimen** *(ehl 'kree-mehn)*
emergency	**la emergencia** *(lah eh-mehr-'hehn-see·ah)*
help	**la ayuda** *(lah ah-'yoo-dah)*
law	**la ley** *(lah 'leh·ee)*
license	**la licencia** *(lah lee-'sehn-see·ah)*
police	**la policía** *(lah poh-lee-'see-ah)*
problem	**el problema** *(ehl proh-'bleh-mah)*
station	**la estación** *(lah eh-stah-see-'ohn)*
traffic	**el tráfico** *(ehl 'trah-fee-koh)*

INFORMACIÓN PRIVADA

➤ Notice that the names for people, places, and things have either **el** *(ehl)* or **la** *(lah)* in front. Generally, if the word ends in the letter **o** there's an **el** *(ehl)* in front (e.g., **el cuarto,** *ehl 'kwahr-toh,* **el niño,** *ehl 'nee-nyoh).* Conversely, if the word ends in an **a** there's a **la** *(lah)* in front (e.g., **la mesa,** *lah 'meh-sah,* **la persona,** *lah pehr-'soh-nah).* Some Spanish words are exceptions: **el agua** *(ehl 'ah-gwah),* **la mano** *(lah 'mah-noh).*

➤ Words not ending in either an **o** *(oh)* or **a** *(ah)* need to be memorized (i.e., **el amor,** *ehl ah-'mohr,* **la estación,** *lah ehs-tah-see-'ohn).* In the case of single objects, use **el** *(ehl)* and **la** *(lah)* much like the word "the" in English: The house is big, **La casa es grande** *(lah 'kah-sah ehs 'grahn-deh).*

➤ Remember too, that **el** and **la** are used in Spanish to indicate a person's sex. **El doctor** *(ehl dohk-'tohr)* is a male doctor, while **la doctora** *(lah dohk-'toh-rah)* is a female doctor. Here's how we change words to refer to the female gender: **la muchacha** *(lah moo-'chah-chah),* **la niña** *(lah 'nee-nyah),* **la bebé** *(lah beh-'beh).*

Once in a while, you'll come across a word that sounds like Spanish, but isn't. "Spanglish" is a universal trend to blend Spanish words with English words. All across America, millions of immigrants have come to realize that it's easier to communicate in "Spanglish" than in "Spanish." Notice the trend:

el "closet"
el "overtime"
el "show"

THE COLORS
Los colores (lohs koh-'loh-rehs)

black	**negro** ('neh-groh)
blue	**azul** (ah-'sool)
brown	**café** (kah-'feh)
gray	**gris** (grees)
green	**verde** ('vehr-deh)
orange	**anaranjado** (ah-nah-rahn-'hah-doh)
purple	**morado** (moh-'rah-doh)
red	**rojo** ('roh-hoh)
white	**blanco** ('blahn-koh)
yellow	**amarillo** (ah-mah-'ree-yoh)

THE NUMBERS
Los números *(lohs 'noo-meh-rohs)*

0	**cero** *('seh-roh)*	14	**catorce** *(kah-'tohr-seh)*
1	**uno** *('oo-noh)*	15	**quince** *('keen-seh)*
2	**dos** *(dohs)*	16	**dieciséis** *(dee-ehs-ee-'seh·ees)*
3	**tres** *(trehs)*	17	**diecisiete** *(dee-ehs-ee-see-'eh- teh)*
4	**cuatro** *('kwah-troh)*	18	**dieciocho** *(dee-ehs-ee-'oh-choh)*
5	**cinco** *('seen-koh)*	19	**diecinueve** *(dee-ehs-ee-noo-'eh-veh)*
6	**seis** *('seh·ees)*	20	**veinte** *('veh·een-teh)*
7	**siete** *(see-'eh-teh)*	30	**treinta** *('treh·een-tah)*
8	**ocho** *('oh-choh)*	40	**cuarenta** *(kwah-'rehn-tah)*
9	**nueve** *(noo-'eh-veh)*	50	**cincuenta** *(seen-'kwehn-tah)*
10	**diez** *(dee-'ehs)*	60	**sesenta** *(seh-'sehn-tah)*
11	**once** *('ohn-seh)*	70	**setenta** *(seh-'tehn-tah)*
12	**doce** *('doh-seh)*	80	**ochenta** *(oh-'chehn-tah)*
13	**trece** *('treh-seh)*	90	**noventa** *(noh-'vehn-tah)*

For all the numbers in-between, just add **y** *(ee)*, which means "and":

21	**veinte y uno** *('veh·een-teh ee 'oo-noh)*
22	**veinte y dos** *('veh·een-teh ee dohs)*
23	**veinte y tres** *('veh·een-teh ee trehs)*

Sooner or later, you'll also need to know how to say the larger numbers in Spanish. They aren't that difficult, so practice aloud:

100	**cien** *('see-ehn)*
500	**quinientos** *(kee-nee-'ehn-tohs)*
700	**setecientos** *(seh-teh-see-'ehn-tohs)*
900	**novecientos** *(noh-veh-see-'ehn-tohs)*
1000	**mil** *(meel)*
million	**millón** *(mee-'yohn)*
billion*	**billón** *(bee-'yohn)*

*Note: The English billion is a thousand million, but the Spanish billion is a million million.

➤ The cardinal numbers are valuable around the house, too! Practice:

first	**primero** *(pree-'meh-roh)*
second	**segundo** *(seh-'goon-doh)*
third	**tercero** *(tehr-'seh-roh)*
fourth	**cuarto** *('kwahr-toh)*
fifth	**quinto** *('keen-toh)*
sixth	**sexto** *('sehks-toh)*
seventh	**séptimo** *('sehp-tee-moh)*
eighth	**octavo** *(ohk-'tah-voh)*
ninth	**noveno** *(noh-'veh-noh)*
tenth	**décimo** *('deh-see-moh)*

¡Qué bueno!
¡Un carro
   sin licencia!

FORM A PHRASE
Forme una frase *('fohr-meh 'oo-nah 'frah-seh)*

By now, you should be blurting out friendly expressions, while stammering one-word responses. However, there are those times when you'll need to create a phrase or two on your own. Check over this next list of Spanish words that allow beginners to be a little more specific:

for	**por** *(pohr)* or **para** *('pah-rah)*	**por su ayuda** *(pohr soo ah-'yoo-dah)* **para dos niños** *('pah-rah dohs 'nee-nyohs)*
in, on, at	**en** *(ehn)*	**en el cuarto** *(ehn ehl 'kwahr-toh)*

of, from	**de** *(deh)*	**de la persona** *(deh lah pehr-'soh-nah)*
to	**a** *(ah)*	**a la casa** *(ah lah 'kah-sah)*
with	**con** *(kohn)*	**con rojo** *(kohn 'roh-hoh)*
without	**sin** *(seen)*	**sin la licencia** *(seen lah lee-'sehn-see·ah)*

By the way, there are only two contractions in Spanish:

of the, from the	**del** *(dehl)*	**del libro** *(dehl 'lee-broh)*
to the	**al** *(ahl)*	**al hombre** *(ahl 'ohm-breh)*

Now, use these words to link everything together:

y *(ee)* = and   **o** *(oh)* = or   **pero** *('peh-roh)* = but

black or white	**negro o blanco** *('neh-groh oh 'blahn-koh)*
lots of work, but little money	**mucho trabajo, pero poco dinero** *('moo-choh trah-'bah-hoh 'peh-roh 'poh-koh dee-'neh-roh)*
Thank you and goodbye!	**¡Gracias y adiós!** *('grah-see·ahs ee ah-dee-'ohs)*

INFORMACIÓN PRIVADA

➤ These catchy phrases will sound like you really know the language:

Above all,	**Sobre todo** *('soh-breh 'toh-doh)*
At least,	**Por lo menos** *(pohr loh 'meh-nohs)*
At the same time,	**A la vez** *(ah lah vehs)*
By the way,	**A propósito** *(ah proh-'poh-see-toh)*
Finally,	**Por fin** *(pohr feen)*
For example,	**Por ejemplo** *(pohr eh-'hehm-ploh)*
However,	**Sin embargo** *(seen ehm-'bahr-goh)*
In general,	**En general** *(ehn heh-neh-'rahl)*
In the first place,	**En primer lugar** *(ehn pree-'mehr loo-'gahr)*
Therefore,	**Por eso** *(pohr 'eh-soh)*

MOST WANTED
Las más usadas *(lahs mahs oo-'sah-dahs)*

You can never learn enough survival vocabulary. This selection provides beginners with a few opposites that fit in almost anywhere:

a lot	**mucho** *('moo-choh)*	a little	**poco** *('poh-koh)*
all	**todo** *('toh-doh)*	none	**ninguno** *(neen-'goo-noh)*
alone	**solo** *('soh-loh)*	together	**juntos** *('hoon-tohs)*
enough	**bastante** *(bah-'stahn-teh)*	too much	**demasiado** *(deh-mah-see-'ah-doh)*
few	**pocos** *('poh-kohs)*	many	**muchos** *('moo-chohs)*
more	**más** *(mahs)*	less	**menos** *('meh-nohs)*
nothing	**nada** *('nah-dah)*	something	**algo** *('ahl-goh)*
same	**mismo** *('mees-moh)*	different	**diferente** *(dee-feh-'rehn-teh)*

THE RULES
Las reglas *(lahs 'reh-glahs)*

In any language, in order to express complete messages it's important to put all the appropriate words in correct order. Broken Spanish is fine for quick exchanges, but for more elaborate speech, carefully review the following information.

First, remember that words in Spanish are often positioned in reverse order, especially when you give a description. The descriptive word usually goes after the word being described. Notice:

The black car	**El carro negro** *(ehl 'kah-rroh 'neh-groh)*
The big house	**La casa grande** *(lah 'kah-sah 'grahn-deh)*
The important law	**La ley importante** *(lah 'lee·ee eem-pohr-'tahn-teh)*

Second, when referring to more than one item in Spanish, change **el** *(ehl)* and **la** *(lah)* to **los** *(lohs)* and **las** *(lahs)*, respectively:

el carro *(ehl 'kah-rroh)*	→	**los carros** *(lohs 'kah-rrohs)*
el señor *(ehl seh-'noyhr)*	→	**los señores** *(lohs seh-'nyoh-rrehs)*
la casa *(lah 'kah-sah)*	→	**las casas** *(lahs 'kah-sahs)*
la ley *(lah 'leh·ee)*	→	**las leyes** *(lahs 'leh-yehs)*

Third, to make the sentence plural, not only do all the nouns and adjectives need to end in "s" or "es," but, when they are used together, the genders must match as well:

Many big windows   **Muchas ventanas grandes** *('moo-chahs vehn-'tah-nahs 'grahn-dehs)*

Three white doors   **Tres puertas blancas** *(trehs 'pwehr-tahs 'blahn-kahs)*

Two yellow books   **Dos libros amarillos** *(dohs 'lee-brohs ah-mah-'rree-yohs)*

INFORMACIÓN PRIVADA

➤ To say "a" in Spanish, use **un** or **una:**

A floor   **Un piso** *(oon 'pee-soh)*
    Un piso azul *(oon 'pee-soh ah-'sool)*

A bed   **Una cama** *('oo-nah 'kah-mah)*
    Una cama grande *('oo-nah 'kah-mah 'grahn-deh)*

➤ And, to say "some," use **unos** *('oo-nohs)* or **unas** *('oo-nahs)*:

Some floors   **Unos pisos** *('oo-nohs 'pee-sohs)*
    Unos pisos azules *('oo-nohs 'pee-sohs ah-'soo-lehs)*

Some beds   **Unas camas** *('oo-nahs 'kah-mahs)*
    Unas camas grandes *('oo-nahs 'kah-mahs 'grahn-dehs)*

➤ These words can help you comment about one or more things in Spanish. Notice how they follow all the rules:

that	**ese** *('eh-seh)* or **esa** *('eh-sah)*
	Ese amigo americano *('eh-seh ah-'mee-goh ah-meh-ree-'kah-noh)*
these	**estos** *('eh-stohs)* or **estas** *('eh-stahs)*
	Estos tacos grandes *('eh-stohs 'tah-kohs 'grahn-dehs)*
this	**este** *('eh-steh)* or **esta** *('eh-stah)*
	Este papel verde *('eh-steh pah-'pehl 'vehr-deh)*
those	**esos** *('eh-sohs)* or **esas** *('eh-sahs)*
	Esos hombres buenos *('eh-sohs 'ohm-brehs 'bweh-nohs)*

REPASO

A. Can you list three items under the following?

los colores *(lohs koh-'loh-rehs)*

_____   _____   _____

las cosas diarias *(lahs 'koh-sahs dee-'ah-ree·ahs)*

_____   _____   _____

los números *(lohs 'noo-meh-rohs)*

_____   _____   _____

B. Match the opposites:

nada *('nah-dah)*   diferente *(dee-feh-'rehn-teh)*
mismo *('mees-moh)*   muchos *('moo-chohs)*
pocos *('poh-kohs)*   algo *('ahl-goh)*

C. Change these from the singular to the plural:

La pluma roja *(lah 'ploo-mah 'roh-hah)*

19

20

B. nada   algo
   mismo   diferente
   pocos   muchos

C. Las leyes importantes
   Las casas grandes

D. Good morning, ma'am. How are you?
   Fine, thanks. And you?
   O.K., thanks.
   I'm Tony. What's your name?
   My name is Mary.

ANSWERS

Example:

Las plumas rojas (lahs 'ploo-mahs 'roh-hahs)

_____

La ley importante (lah 'leh-ee eem-pohr-'tahn-teh)

_____

La casa grande (lah 'kah-sah 'grahn-deh)

_____

D. Translate this conversation:

Buenos días, señora. ¿Cómo está? ('bweh-nohs 'dee-ahs seh-'nyoh-rah ¿koh-moh eh-'stah?)

Bien, gracias. ¿Y usted? ('bee-ehn 'grah-see-ahs ee oo-'stehd)

Regular, gracias. (reh-goo-'lahr 'grah-see-ahs)

Soy Antonio. ¿Cómo se llama? ('soh-ee 'toh-nee 'koh-moh seh 'yah-mah)

Mi nombre es María. (mee 'nohm-breh ehs mah-'ree-ah)

THE QUESTIONS

Las preguntas *(lahs preh-'goon-tahs)*

Perhaps the most useful Spanish words for law enforcement officials are the "questioning words." Not only are they heard frequently in daily conversations, but the following words and phrases can be used to gather much-needed information. First practice the questioning word, and then try each sample sentence:

How many?	**¿Cuántos?** *('kwahn-tohs)*	**¿Cuántos amigos?** *('kwahn-tohs ah-'mee-gohs)*
How much?	**¿Cuánto?** *('kwahn-toh)*	**¿Cuánto dinero?** *('kwahn-toh dee-'neh-roh)*
How?	**¿Cómo?** *('koh-moh)*	**¿Cómo está?** *('koh-moh eh-'stah)*
What?	**¿Qué?** *(keh)*	**¿Qué pasa?** *(keh 'pah-sah)*
When?	**¿Cuándo?** *('kwahn-doh)*	**¿Cuándo es la fiesta?** *('kwahn-doh ehs lah fee-'eh-stah)*
Where?	**¿Dónde?** *('dohn-deh)*	**¿Dónde está la casa?** *('dohn-deh eh-'stah lah 'kah-sah)*
Which?	**¿Cuál?** *(kwahl)*	**¿Cuál piso?** *(kwahl 'pee-soh)*
Who?	**¿Quién?** *(kee-'ehn)*	**¿Quién es la señora?** *(kee-'ehn ehs lah seh-'nyoh-rah)*
Whose?	**¿De quién?** *(deh kee-'ehn)*	**¿De quién es el carro?** *(deh kee-'ehn ehs ehl 'kah-rroh)*

"Why" in English is **¿Por qué?** *(pohr 'keh)* in Spanish. To respond, simply repeat the word **porque** because it means "because":

¿Por qué habla español? *(pohr-'keh 'ah-blah eh-spah-'nyohl)*
Porque es necesario. *('pohr-keh ehs neh-seh-'sah-ree·oh)*

Notice how we can combine our words to create essential question phrases:

For when?	**¿Para cuándo?** *('pah-rah 'kwahn-doh)*
From where?	**¿De dónde?** *(deh 'dohn-deh)*
To whom?	**¿A quién?** *(ah kee-'ehn)*
With what?	**¿Con qué?** *(kohn keh)*

Some question words cannot be translated literally when they become parts of common phrases:

How old are you?	**¿Cuántos años tiene?** *('kwahn-tohs 'ah-nyohs tee-'eh-neh)*

QUICK RESPONSES
Las respuestas rápidas *(lahs reh-'spweh-stahs 'rah-pee-dahs)*

Now that we've learned the fundamental question words, let's take on the most commonly heard responses.

Begin with a review of those "preguntas" that are considered friendly exchanges in daily conversations. Go ahead and translate:

¿Qué pasa? *(keh 'pah-sah)*	**Nada** *('nah-dah)*
¿Cómo está? *('koh-moh eh-'stah)*	**Muy bien** *('moo·ee bee·ehn)*
¿Cuál es su nombre? *(kwahl ehs soo 'nohm-breh)*	**Mi nombre es Bill** *(mee 'nohm-breh ehs Beel)*

Continue asking and answering with the following words and phrases. These are required throughout the world of law enforcement, and must be reviewed on a continuous basis. They are ideal for quick, yet efficient replies:

Where is it?	**¿Dónde está?** *('dohn-deh eh-'stah)*
It's...	**Está...** *(eh-'stah...)*
above	**encima** *(ehn-'see-mah)*
at the bottom	**en el fondo** *(ehn ehl 'fohn-doh)*
behind	**detrás** *(deh-'trahs)*
down	**abajo** *(ah-'bah-hoh)*

far	**lejos** *('leh-hohs)*
here	**aquí** *(ah-'kee)*
in front of	**en frente de** *(ehn 'frehn-teh deh)*
inside	**adentro** *(ah-'dehn-troh)*
near	**cerca** *('sehr-kah)*
next to	**al lado de** *(ahl 'lah-doh deh)*
outside	**afuera** *(ah-'fweh-rah)*
over there	**allá** *(ah-'yah)*
straight ahead	**adelante** *(ah-deh-'lahn-teh)*
there	**allí** *(ah-'yee)*
to the left	**a la izquierda** *(ah lah ees-kee-'ehr-dah)*
to the right	**a la derecha** *(ah lah deh-'reh-chah)*
up	**arriba** *(ah-'rree-bah)*

When?	**¿Cuándo?** *('kwahn-doh)*
a while ago	**hace un rato** *('ah-seh oon 'rah-toh)*
afterward	**después** *(deh-'spwehs)*
all day	**todo el día** *('toh-doh ehl 'dee-ah)*
always	**siempre** *(see-'ehm-preh)*
before	**antes** *('ahn-tehs)*
early	**temprano** *(tehm-'prah-noh)*
every day	**todos los días** *('toh-dohs lohs 'dee-ahs)*
in awhile	**en un rato** *(ehn oon 'rah-toh)*
late	**tarde** *('tahr-deh)*
later	**luego** *('lweh-goh)*
never	**nunca** *('noon-kah)*
nowadays	**ahora** *(ah-'oh-rah)*
often	**frecuentemente** *(freh-kwehn-teh-'mehn-teh)*
right now	**ahorita** *(ah-oh-'ree-tah)*
seldom	**casi nunca** *('kah-see 'noon-kah)*
sometimes	**a veces** *(ah-'veh-sehs)*
soon	**pronto** *('prohn-toh)*

Who?	**¿Quién?** *(kee-'ehn)*
I	**Yo** *(yoh)*
We	**Nosotros** *(noh-'soh-trohs)*
You	**Usted** *(oo-'stehd)*
You (plural)	**Ustedes** *(oo-'steh-dehs)*
She	**Ella** *('eh-yah)*
He	**El** *(ehl)*
They (feminine)	**Ellas** *('eh-yahs)*
They (masculine)	**Ellos** *('eh-yohs)*

➤ Some of you may have noticed the exclusion of the informal "tú" *(too)* form from the list of personal pronouns. Because the officer-civilian relationship is generally considered a formal one, only the "usted" *(oo-'stehd)* form is mentioned. Details about this matter will be addressed later on in this guidebook.

➤ When practicing new words in a foreign language, use animated motions with your arms, hands, or fingers to express your message.

➤ Learn where to find everything:

It's...	**Está...** *(eh-'stah...)*
everywhere	**por todas partes** *(pohr 'toh-dahs 'pahr-tehs)*
nowhere	**por ninguna parte** *(pohr neen-'goh-nah 'pahr-teh)*
somewhere	**por alguna parte** *(pohr ahl-'goo-nah 'pahr-tch)*

➤ An important group of Spanish words are used to indicate possession. This terminology tells us "whose" it is:

my	**mi** *(mee)*
your, his, her, their	**su** *(soo)*
our	**nuestra** *('nweh-strah)*

Notice what happens when you talk about more than one:

mi casa	→	**mis casas** *(mees 'kah-sahs)*
su casa	→	**sus casas** *(soos 'kah-sahs)*
nuestra casa	→	**nuestras casas** *('nweh-strahs 'kah-sahs)*

Try these other possessive words. Are you able to translate?

mine	**mío** *('mee-oh)* or **mía** *('mee-ah)*	**Es mío** *(ehs 'mee-oh)*
his, hers, theirs	**suyo** *('soo-yoh)* or **suya** *('soo-yah)*	**Es suya** *(ehs 'soo-yah)*

MAKE THE CONNECTION
Haga la conexión *('ah-gah lah koh-nehk-see-'ohn)*

Now that you can form short phrases on your own, it's time to join all of your words together. To accomplish this, you'll need to understand the difference between **está** *(eh-'stah)* and **es** *(ehs)*. Both words mean "is," but they're used differently.

The word **está** *(eh-'stah)* expresses a temporary state, condition, or location:

The girl is doing well	**La niña está bien** *(lah 'nee-nyah eh-'stah bee-'ehn)*
The girl is in the room	**La niña está en el cuarto** *(lah 'nee-nyah eh-'stah ehn ehl 'kwahr-toh)*

The word **es** *(ehs)* expresses an inherent characteristic or quality, including origin and ownership.

The girl is small	**La niña es pequeña** *(lah 'nee-nyah ehs peh-'keh-nyah)*
The girl is Maria	**La niña es María** *(lah 'nee-nyah ehs mah-'ree-ah)*
The girl is American	**La niña es americana** *(lah 'nee-nyah ehs ah-meh-ree-'kah-nah)*
The girl is my friend	**La niña es mi amiga** *(lah 'nee-nyah ehs mee ah-'mee-gah)*

Can you see how helpful these two words can be? Countless comments can be made with only a minimum of vocabulary. You'll also need to talk about more than one person, place, or thing. To do so, replace **está** *(eh-'stah)* with **están** *(eh-'stahn)*, and **es** *(ehs)* with **son** *(sohn)*. And, don't forget that words must "agree" when you change to plurals:

The book is on the table	**El libro está en la mesa** *(ehl 'lee-broh eh-'stah ehn lah 'meh-sah)*
The books are on the table	**Los libros están en la mesa** *(lohs 'lee-brohs eh-'stahn ehn lah 'meh-sah)*

It's a man	**Es un hombre** *(ehs oon 'ohm-breh)*
They are men	**Son hombres** *(sohn 'ohm-brehs)*

Check out these other examples. Read them aloud as you focus on their structure and meaning:

The chairs are black	**Las sillas son negras** *(lahs 'see-yahs sohn 'neh-grahs)*
The papers are in the house	**Los papeles están en la casa** *(lohs pah-'peh-lehs eh-'stahn ehn lah 'kah-sah)*
They're not important	**No son importantes** *(noh sohn eem-pohr-'tahn-tehs)*
Are they good?	**¿Están buenos?** *(eh-'stahn 'bweh-nohs)*

The best way to learn how to use these words correctly is to listen to Spanish-speakers in real-life conversations. They constantly use **es** *(ehs)*, **está** *(eh-'stah)*, **son** *(sohn)*, and **están** *(eh-'stahn)* to communicate simple messages.

I AM AND WE ARE

To say "I am" and "We are" in Spanish, you must also learn the different forms. As with **está** *(eh-'stah)* and **están** *(eh-'stahn)*, the words **estoy** *(eh-'stoh·ee)* and **estamos** *(eh-'stah-mohs)* refer to the location or condition of a person, place, or thing. And, just like **es** *(ehs)* and **son** *(sohn)*, the words **soy** *('soh·ee)* and **somos** *('soh-mohs)* are used with everything else:

I am fine	**Estoy bien** *(eh-'stoh·ee 'bee·ehn)*
We are in the room	**Estamos en el cuarto** *(eh-'stah-mohs ehn ehl 'kwahr-toh)*
I am Lupe	**Soy Lupe** *('soh·ee 'loo-peh)*
We are Cuban	**Somos cubanos** *('soh-mohs koo-'bah-nohs)*

Now let's group all of these forms together. Look over the present tense forms of the verbs **estar** *(eh-'stahr)* and **ser** *(sehr)*.

To Be	**Estar** *(eh-'stahr)*	**Ser** *('sehr)*
I'm	**estoy** *(eh-'stoh·ee)*	**soy** *('soh·ee)*
You're, he's, she's, it's	**está** *(eh-'stah)*	**es** *(ehs)*
They're, you're (plural)	**están** *(eh-'stahn)*	**son** *(sohn)*
We're	**estamos** *(eh-'stah-mohs)*	**somos** *('soh-mohs)*

➤ Two other words, **estás** *(eh-'stahs)* and **eres** *('eh-rehs)*, may also be used to mean "you are" among family, friends, and small children. However, since most of your beginning conversations will be between yourself and the public, try focusing primarily on the eight words mentioned above.

➤ "There is" and "There are" are very simple. In both cases, you use **hay** *('ah·ee)*:

There's one problem	**Hay un problema** *('ah·ee oon proh-'bleh-mah)*
There are many problems	**Hay muchos problemas** *('ah·ee 'moo-chohs proh-'bleh-mahs)*

➤ **No** can be used in various ways in Spanish to indicate the negative:

Don't move	**No se mueva** *(noh seh-'mweh-vah)*
It isn't important	**No es importante** *(noh ehs eem-pohr-'tahn-teh)*
No, thanks	**No, gracias** *(noh 'grah-see·ahs)*

REPASO

A. Translate these questions as briefly as possible:

¿Quién es su amigo? *(kee-'ehn ehs soo ah-'mee-goh)*

_____

¿Dónde está su familia? *('dohn-deh eh-'stah soo fah-'mee-lee·ah)*

_____

¿De quién es este libro? *(deh kee-'ehn ehs 'eh-steh 'lee-broh)*

_____

¿Cuántos niños están en su casa? *('kwahn-tohs 'nee-nyohs eh-'stahn ehn soo 'kah-sah)*

_____

ANSWERS

A. Who is your friend?
Where's your family?
Whose book is this?
How many children are in your home?
What's your favorite car?

I HAVE IT!
¡Lo tengo! *(loh 'tehn-goh)*

Tener *(teh-'nehr)* is another common linking word in Spanish and it means "to have." Its forms will become more necessary as you begin to create Spanish sentences on your own. Although these words will be discussed in more detail later, here are the basics to get you started:

I have	**tengo** *('tehn-goh)*
You have, he has, she has, it has	**tiene** *(tee-'eh-neh)*
They have, you (plural) have	**tienen** *(tee-'eh-nehn)*
We have	**tenemos** *(teh-'neh-mohs)*

Study these examples:

I have a pistol	**Tengo una pistola** *('tehn-goh 'oo-nah pee-'stoh-lah)*
She has a white car	**Tiene un carro blanco** *(tee-'eh-neh oon 'kah-rroh 'blahn-koh)*
They have four children	**Tienen cuatro niños** *(tee-'eh-nehn 'kwah-troh 'nee-nyohs)*
We have a big house	**Tenemos una casa grande** *(teh-'neh-mohs 'oo-nah 'kah-sah 'grahn-deh)*

Even though **tener** *(teh-'nehr)* literally means "to have," sometimes it is used instead of the verb **estar** *(eh-'stahr)* to express a temporary condition:

(I am) afraid	**(tengo)** *('tehn-goh)* **miedo** *(mee-'eh-doh)*
(we are) at fault	**(tenemos)** *(teh-'neh-mohs)* **la culpa** *(lah 'kool-pah)*
(they are) cold	**(tienen)** *(tee-'eh-nehn)* **frío** *('free-oh)*
(she is) 15 years old	**(tiene)** *(tee-'eh-neh)* **quince años** *('keen-seh 'ah-nyohs)*
(I am) hot	**(tengo)** *('tehn-goh)* **calor** *(kah-'lohr)*
(they are) hungry	**(tienen)** *(tee-'eh-nehn)* **hambre** *('ahm-breh)*
(he is) sleepy	**(tiene)** *(tee-'eh-neh)* **sueño** *('sweh-nyoh)*
(we are) thirsty	**(tenemos)** *(teh-'neh-mohs)* **sed** *(sehd)*

INFORMACIÓN PRIVADA

➤ Notice how **tiene** is also used to tell ages:

How old are you?	**¿Cuántos años tiene?** *('kwahn-tohs 'ah-nyohs tee-'eh-neh)*
I am twenty	**Tengo veinte** *('tehn-goh 'veh·een-teh)*

➤ To say "not" in Spanish, interject the word **no** in front of the verb:

José is my friend	**José es mi amigo** *('hoh-seh ehs mee ah-'mee-goh)*
José is not my friend	**José no es mi amigo** *('hoh-seh noh ehs mee ah-'mee-goh)*
I have the job	**Tengo el trabajo** *('tehn-goh ehl trah-'bah-hoh)*
I do not have the job	**No tengo el trabajo** *(noh 'tehn-goh ehl trah-'bah-hoh)*

ACCIÓN

Although the verb forms of **estar** *(eh-'stahr)*, **ser** *(sehr)*, and **tener** *(teh-'nehr)* are useful in police work, they do not express action. Learning how to use Spanish action verbs allows us to talk about what's going on in the world.

Take as much time as you need with this brief list of beginning verbs. Notice how they end in the letters **ar, er,** or **ir:**

to eat	**comer** *(koh-'mehr)*
to sleep	**dormir** *(dohr-'meer)*
to talk	**hablar** *(ah-'blahr)*
to work	**trabajar** *(trah-bah-'hahr)*
to read	**leer** *(leh-'ehr)*
to write	**escribir** *(eh-skree-'beer)*

You can never learn enough action words in Spanish. Over two hundred verbs are listed in the glossaries at the end of this book, so use them as a reference tool. When you come across a verb as you study and practice, look them up in Spanish or English to learn its base form and meaning.

INFORMACIÓN PRIVADA

➤ Many Spanish verb infinitives related to law enforcement are similar to English. Look at these examples:

to arrest	**arrestar** *(ah-rreh-'stahr)*
to examine	**examinar** *(ehk-sah-mee-'nahr)*
to investigate	**investigar** *(een-veh-stee-'gahr)*
to report	**reportar** *(reh-pohr-'tahr)*
to respond	**responder** *(reh-spohn-'dehr)*
to rob	**robar** *(roh-'bahr)*

➤ Be careful with a few "false cognates." These verb infinitives are *not* what they seem to be:

molestar *(moh-leh-'stahr)*	to bother
violar *(vee-oh-'lahr)*	to rape
embarazar *(ehm-bah-rah-'sahr)*	to impregnate
asistir *(ah-see-'steer)*	to attend
pretender *(preh-tehn-'dehr)*	to court

30

➤ Memorize these new Spanish verbs so that you can talk about your language learning experience:

to pronounce	**pronunciar** *(proh-noon-see-'ahr)*
to practice	**practicar** *(prahk-tee-'kahr)*
to study	**estudiar** *(eh-stoo-dee-'ahr)*

¿Quién tiene frío?
Yo tengo calor
y hambre.

GRANDES HABILIDADES

Combine your new *Action Words* with the simple phrase below. It's a great way to politely ask folks to follow your instructions. You should be able to translate these examples:

Please... **Favor de...** *(fah-'vohr deh...)*
  escribir en el papel *(eh-skree-'beer ehn ehl pah-'pehl)*
  leer el libro *(leh-'ehr ehl 'lee-broh)*
  hablar más despacio *(ah-'blahr mahs deh-'spah-see·oh)*

By adding the word **no** in front of the verb, you communicate the command "don't."

Please *don't* write **Favor de *no* escribir en el papel** *(fah-'vohr deh*
on the paper *noh eh-skree-'beer ehn ehl pah-'pehl)*

Favor de *(fah-'vohr deh)* is one of several key expressions that can be found in chapter segments entitled *Grandes Habilidades*. These phrases are combined with basic verb forms in order to raise your language skills to a whole new level!

Much of the communication between law enforcement and the public involves direct commands. Spanish command words are unique forms of "action verbs" that often times function all by themselves. Notice how they differ from the verb infinitives.

As you practice, picture a scenario where they'll be used:

	Command	**Infinitive**
Come	**Venga** *('vehn-gah)*	**venir** *(veh-'neer)*
Go	**Vaya** *('vah-yah)*	**ir** *(eer)*
Hurry up	**Apúrese** *(ah-'poo-reh-seh)*	**apurarse** *(ah-poo-'rahr-seh)*
Run	**Corra** *('koh-rrah)*	**correr** *(koh-'rrehr)*
Sit down	**Siéntese** *(see-'ehn-teh-seh)*	**sentarse** *(sehn-'tahr-seh)*
Stand up	**Levántese** *(leh-'vahn-teh-seh)*	**levantarse** *(leh-vahn-'tahr-seh)*
Stop	**Párese** *('pah-reh-seh)*	**pararse** *(pah-'rahr-seh)*
Wait	**Espere** *(eh-'speh-reh)*	**esperar** *(eh-speh-'rahr)*
Walk	**Camine** *(kah-'mee-neh)*	**caminar** *(kah-mee-'nahr)*
Watch	**Mire** *('mee-reh)*	**mirar** *(mee-'rahr)*

Let's begin with one of the easiest verb forms to use. It's the present progressive tense, and it refers to actions that are taking place at this moment. It is similar to our "–ing" form in English. Simply change the base verb ending slightly, and then combine the new form with the four forms of the verb **estar**. The **–ar** verbs become **–ando**, while the **–er** and **–ir** verbs become **–iendo.** Study these examples closely:

to talk, to speak	**hablar** *(ah-'blahr)*
speaking	**hablando** *(ah-'blahn-doh)*
We are speaking Spanish	**Estamos hablando español** *(eh-'stah-mohs ah-'blahn-doh eh-spah-'nyohl)*

to eat	**comer** *(koh-'mehr)*
eating	**comiendo** *(koh-mee-'ehn-doh)*
The man is eating	**El hombre está comiendo** *(ehl 'ohm-breh eh-'stah koh-mee-'ehn-doh)*

to write	**escribir** *(eh-skree-'beer)*
writing	**escribiendo** *(eh-skree-bee-'ehn-doh)*
I'm writing a report	**Estoy escribiendo un reporte** *(eh-'stoh·ee eh-skree-bee-'ehn-doh oon reh-'pohr-teh)*

A few Spanish verbs change in spelling when you add the **–ndo** ending. Study these two examples:

to follow	**seguir** *(see-'geer)*
following	**siguiendo** *(see-gee-'ehn-doh)*
to sleep	**dormir** *(dohr-'meer)*
sleeping	**durmiendo** *(duhr-mee-'ehn-doh)*

REPASO

A. Translate into Spanish without looking back!

I'm hungry _____

Don't write _____

Please read _____

Hurry up! _____

They're sleeping _____

B. Make sentences by following the example:

We are investigating   <u>Estamos investigando</u> *(eh-'stah-mohs een-veh-stee-'gahn-doh)*

We are practicing _____

We are working _____

C. I'll bet you can figure out the meanings of these work-related *Action Words*. Cover the English column and guess at the translation:

to abuse	abusar *(ah-boo-'sahr)*
to accept	aceptar *(ah-sehp-'tahr)*
to accuse	acusar *(ah-koo-'sahr)*

to admit	admitir *(ahd-mee-'teer)*
to affirm	afirmar *(ah-feer-'mahr)*
to analyze	analizar *(ah-nah-lee-'sahr)*
to authorize	autorizar *(ow-toh-ree-'sahr)*
to calm	calmar *(kahl-'mahr)*
to capture	capturar *(kahp-too-'rahr)*
to cause	causar *(kow-'sahr)*
to compensate	compensar *(kohm-pehn-'sahr)*
to communicate	comunicar *(koh-moo-nee-'kahr)*
to concentrate	concentrar *(kohn-sehn-'trahr)*
to confirm	confirmar *(kohn-feer-'mahr)*
to confiscate	confiscar *(kohn-fee-'skahr)*
to consult	consultar *(kohn-sool-'tahr)*
to converse	conversar *(kohn-vehr-'sahr)*
to cooperate	cooperar *(koh-oh-peh-'rahr)*
to cost	costar *(koh-'stahr)*
to defend	defender *(deh-fehn-'dehr)*
to disarm	desarmar *(dehs-ahr-'mahr)*
to determine	determinar *(deh-tehr-mee-'nahr)*
to eliminate	eliminar *(eh-lee-mee-'nahr)*
to evacuate	evacuar *(eh-vah-koo-'ahr)*
to explore	explorar *(ehk-sploh-'rahr)*
to identify	identificar *(ee-dehn-tee-fee-'kahr)*
to inform	informar *(een-fohr-'mahr)*
to insult	insultar *(een-sool-'tahr)*
to invade	invadir *(een-vah-'deer)*
to justify	justificar *(hoo-stee-fee-'kahr)*
to modify	modificar *(moh-dee-fee-'kahr)*
to note	notar *(noh-'tahr)*
to observe	observar *(ohb-sehr-'vahr)*
to obtain	obtener *(ohb-teh-'nehr)*
to participate	participar *(pahr-tee-see-'pahr)*
to permit	permitir *(pehr-mee-'teer)*
to plan	planear *(plah-neh-'ahr)*
to practice	practicar *(prahk-tee-'kahr)*
to recommend	recomendar *(reh-koh-mehn-'dahr)*
to refer	referir *(reh-feh-'reer)*
to register	registrar *(reh-hee-'strahr)*
to represent	representar *(reh-reh-sehn-'tahr)*
to restore	restaurar *(reh-stah·oo-'rahr)*
to separate	separar *(seh-pah-'rahr)*
to suffocate	sofocar *(soh-foh-'kahr)*
to transfer	transferir *(trahs-feh-'reer)*
to verify	verificar *(veh-ree-fee-'kahr)*
to visit	visitar *(vee-see-'tahr)*

WORD SEARCH 1

v	g	s	p	p	e	l	e	a	r	n
i	o	p	r	s	e	s	o	r	a	c
o	l	e	t	i	c	r	l	a	o	r
l	p	b	r	a	r	a	p	s	i	d
a	e	a	p	a	p	t	c	u	r	m
r	a	a	t	u	l	s	g	c	e	e
r	r	a	z	a	n	e	m	a	n	n
p	m	d	u	l	s	r	r	r	e	t
l	i	b	e	r	a	r	s	s	t	i
r	a	l	e	c	r	a	c	n	e	r
a	a	p	o	s	t	a	r	r	d	l

acusar
apostar
violar
perseguir
detener
escapar
pelear
arrestar
encarcelar
mentir
matar
liberar
disparar
amenazar
golpear

Answers on page 326.

35

CHAPTER TWO
Capítulo Dos
(kah-'pee-too-loh dohs)

ON DUTY
De guardia
(deh 'gwahr-dee·ah)

CITY LIFE

La vida en la ciudad *(lah 'vee-dah ehn lah see-oo-'dahd)*

One advantage to working with the public is the chance to practice Spanish in a variety of true-life settings. The easiest way to learn job-related vocabulary is to walk, ride, or drive around town—pointing to and naming things that you recognize. So, before you actually talk to anybody, fire away at these:

I'm at (the)…	**Estoy en...** *(eh-'stoh·ee ehn...)*
alley	**el callejón** *(ehl kah-yeh-'hohn)*
avenue	**la avenida** *(lah ah-veh-'nee-dah)*
bridge	**el puente** *(ehl 'pwehn-teh)*
building	**el edificio** *(ehl eh-dee-'fee-see·oh)*
bus stop	**la parada de autobús** *(lah pah-'rah-dah deh ow-toh-'boos)*
city block	**la cuadra** *(lah 'kwah-drah)*
corner	**la esquina** *(lah eh-'skee-nah)*
crosswalk	**el cruce de peatones** *(ehl 'kroo-seh deh peh-ah-'toh-nehs)*
courtyard	**el patio** *(ehl 'pah-tee-oh)*
downtown	**el centro** *(ehl 'sehn-troh)*
elevator	**el ascensor** *(ehl ah-sehn-'sohr)*
entrance	**la entrada** *(lah ehn-'trah-dah)*
escalator	**la escalera mecánica** *(lah eh-skah-'leh-rah meh-'kah-nee-kah)*
exit	**la salida** *(lah sah-'lee-dah)*
fence	**la cerca** *(lah 'sehr-kah)*
fountain	**la fuente** *(lah-'fwehn-teh)*
highway	**la carretera** *(lah kah-rreh-'teh-rah)*
mailbox	**el buzón** *(ehl boo-'sohn)*
neighborhood	**el barrio** *(ehl 'buhh-ree·oh)*
parking lot	**el estacionamiento** *(ehl eh-stah-see·oh-nah-mee-'ehn-toh)*
parking meter	**el parquímetro** *(ehl kahr-'kee-meh-troh)*
pool	**la piscina** *(lah pee-'see-nah)*
restroom	**el baño** *(ehl 'bah-nyoh)*
road	**el camino** *(ehl kah-'mee-noh)*
sidewalk	**la acera** *(lah ah-'seh-rah)*
sign	**el letrero** *(ehl leh-'treh-roh)*
skyscaper	**el rascacielos** *(ehl rah-skah-see-'eh-lohs)*
station	**la estación** *(lah eh-stah-see-'ohn)*
statue	**la estatua** *(la eh-'stah-too-ah)*

street	**la calle** *(lah 'kah-yeh)*
toll booth	**la caseta de peaje** *(lah kah-'seh-tah deh peh-'ah-heh)*
tower	**la torre** *(lah 'toh-rreh)*
traffic	**el tráfico** *(ehl 'trah-fee-koh)*
traffic signal	**el semáforo** *(ehl seh-'mah-foh-roh)*
tunnel	**el túnel** *(ehl 'too-nehl)*
wall	**la pared** *(lah pah-'rehd)*

 INFORMACIÓN PRIVADA

➤ Are any of these things in your area? You could be called to the scene:

canal	**el canal** *(ehl kah-'nahl)*
dam	**la presa** *(lah 'preh-sah)*
pier	**el muelle** *(ehl 'mweh-yeh)*
port	**el puerto** *(ehl 'pwehr-toh)*

➤ Get as detailed as you like:

toll booth	**la caseta de peaje** *(lah kah-'seh-tah deh peh-'ah-heh)*
toll bridge	**el puente de peaje** *(ehl 'pwehn-teh deh peh-'ah-heh)*
toll gate	**la puerta de peaje** *(lah 'pwehr-tah deh peh-'ah-heh)*
toll road	**la carretera de peaje** *(lah kah-rreh-'teh-rah deh peh-'ah-heh)*

PLACES AND SITES
Los lugares y los sitios *(lohs loo-'gah-rehs ee lohs 'see-tee·ohs)*

Are you still pointing? Everyone asks for directions to these:

Where's (the)...	**¿Dónde está...** *('dohn-deh eh-'stah...)*
agency	**la agencia?** *(lah ah-'hehn-see·ah)*
airport	**el aeropuerto?** *(ehl ah-eh-roh-'pwehr-toh)*
bank	**el banco?** *(ehl 'bahn-koh)*
bar	**el bar?** *(ehl bahr)*
beauty salon	**el salón de belleza?** *(ehl sah-'lohn deh beh-'yeh-sah)*
business	**el negocio?** *(ehl neh-'goh-see·oh)*

campground	**el campamento?** *(ehl kahm-pah-'mehn-toh)*
cemetery	**el cementerio?** *(ehl seh-mehn-'teh-ree·oh)*
college	**el colegio?** *(ehl koh-'leh-hee·oh)*
church	**la iglesia?** *(lah ee-'gleh-see·ah)*
city hall	**el municipio?** *(ehl moo-nee-'see-pee·oh)*
clinic	**la clínica?** *(lah 'klee-nee-kah)*
courthouse	**la corte?** *(lah 'kohr-teh)*
dry cleaners	**la tintorería?** *(lah teen-toh-reh-'ree-ah)*
dump	**el basural?** *(ehl bah-soo-'rahl)*
factory	**la fábrica?** *(lah 'fah-bree-kah)*
fire department	**el departamento de bomberos?** *(ehl deh-pahr-tah-'mehn-toh deh bohm-'beh-rohs)*
florist	**la floristería?** *(lah floh-ree-steh-'ree-ah)*
gas station	**la gasolinera?** *(lah gah-soh-lee-'neh-rah)*
grocery store	**la bodega?** *(lah boh-'deh-gah)*
hardware store	**la ferretería?** *(lah feh-rreh-teh-'ree-ah)*
hospital	**el hospital?** *(ehl oh-spee-'tahl)*
jail	**la cárcel?** *(lah 'kahr-sehl)*
library	**la biblioteca?** *(lah bee-blee·oh-'teh-kah)*
liquor store	**la licorería?** *(lah lee-koh-reh-'ree-ah)*
market	**el mercado?** *(ehl mehr-'kah-doh)*
movie theater	**el cine?** *(ehl 'see-neh)*
museum	**el museo?** *(ehl moo-'seh-oh)*
office	**la oficina?** *(lah oh-fee-'see-nah)*
open air market	**el mercado abierto?** *(ehl mehr-'kah-doh ah-bee-'ehr-toh)*
park	**el parque?** *(ehl 'pahr-keh)*
pawn shop	**la casa de empeño?** *(lah 'kah-sah deh ehm-'peh-nyoh)*
pharmacy	**la farmacia?** *(lah fahr-'mah-see·ah)*
police station	**la estación de policía?** *(lah eh-stah-see-'ohn deh poh-lee-'see-ah)*
post office	**el correo?** *(ehl koh-'rreh-oh)*
prison	**la prisión?** *(lah pree-see-'ohn)*
restaurant	**el restaurante?** *(ehl reh-stah·oo-'rahn-teh)*
school	**la escuela?** *(lah eh-'skweh-lah)*
store	**la tienda?** *(lah tee-'ehn-dah)*
studio	**el estudio?** *(ehl eh-'stoo-dee-oh)*
supermarket	**el supermercado?** *(ehl soo-pehr-mehr-'kah-doh)*
university	**la universidad?** *(lah oo-nee-vehr-see-'dahd)*
warehouse	**el almacén?** *(ehl ahl-mah-'sehn)*
workshop	**el taller?** *(ehl tah-'yehr)*

INFORMACIÓN PRIVADA

➤ Note the final letters in the words below. Do you see a pattern?

laundromat	**la lavandería** *(lah lah-vahn-deh-'ree-ah)*
book store	**la librería** *(lah lee-breh-'ree-ah)*
butcher shop	**la carnicería** *(lah kahr-nee-seh-'ree-ah)*
bakery	**la panadería** *(lah pah-nah-deh-'ree-ah)*
barber shop	**la peluquería** *(lah peh-loo-keh-'ree-ah)*
shoe store	**la zapatería** *(lah sah-pah-teh-'ree-ah)*

➤ Try to fill in these blanks with other familiar vocabulary:

The...station	**La estación de...** *(lah eh-stah-see-'ohn deh...)*
bus	**autobús** *(ow-toh-'boos)*
train	**tren** *(trehn)*
subway	**metro** *('meh-troh)*
The...center	**El centro de...** *(ehl 'sehn-troh deh)*
commerce	**comercio** *(koh-'mehr-see·oh)*
recreation	**recreo** *(reh-'kreh-oh)*
visitors	**visitantes** *(vee-see-'tahn-tehs)*

➤ And where do most people live?

They're in the...	**Están en...** *(eh-'stahn ehn...)*
apartment	**el apartamento** *(ehl ah-pahr-tah-'mehn-toh)*
condominium	**el condominio** *(ehl kohn-doh-'mee-nee·oh)*
hotel	**el hotel** *(ehl oh-'tehl)*
house	**la casa** *(lah 'kah-sah)*
mobile home	**la casa rodante** *(lah 'kah-sah roh-'dahn-teh)*
motel	**el motel** *(ehl moh-'tehl)*
shelter	**el refugio** *(ehl reh-'foo-hee-oh)*

➤ Create your own list:

circus	**el circo** *(ehl 'seer-koh)*
fair	**la feria** *(lah 'feh-ree-ah)*
zoo	**el zoológico** *(ehl soh-oh-'loh-hee-koh)*

FACE TO FACE
Cara a cara *('kah-rah ah 'kah-rah)*

Have you finished naming everything you see out there on patrol? Knowing a few words in Spanish can turn routine duties into exciting language experiences, especially if you exchange greetings or ask questions with a cheerful attitude. Try to be friendly as you approach Spanish speakers with the phrases you already know:

Hi. How are you?	**Hola. ¿Cómo está?** *('oh-lah 'koh-moh eh-'stah)*
I'm a police officer	**Soy policía** *('soh·ee poh-lee-'see-ah)*
Do you speak English?	**¿Habla usted inglés?** *('ah-blah oo-'stehd een-'glehs)*
Nice to meet you	**Mucho gusto** *('moo-choh 'goo-stoh)*
Thanks, I really appreciate it	**Gracias, muy amable** *('grah-see·ahs 'moo·ee ah-'mah-bleh)*
Have a nice day!	**¡Qué tenga un buen día!** *(keh 'tehn-gah oon 'bwehn 'dee-ah)*

Now, use a few more one-liners to assess the situation. Divide your questions into similar sets:

Do you have a question?	**¿Tiene alguna pregunta?** *(tee-'eh-neh ahl-'goo-nah preh-'goon-tah)*
May I ask you a few questions?	**¿Puedo hacerle unas preguntas?** *('pweh-doh ah-sehr-leh 'oo-nahs preh-'goon-tahs)*
What happened?	**¿Qué pasó?** *(keh pah-'soh)*
Where did it happen?	**¿Dónde pasó?** *('dohn-deh pah-'soh)*
Is there a problem?	**¿Hay un problema?** *('ah·ee oon proh-'bleh-mah)*
Do you have a problem?	**¿Tiene algún problema?** *(tee-'eh-neh ahl-'goon proh-'bleh-mah)*
Are you OK?	**¿Está bien?** *(eh-'stah 'bee·ehn)*
Are you lost?	**¿Está perdido?** *(eh-'stah pehr-'dee-doh)*
Is it an emergency?	**¿Es una emergencia?** *(ehs 'oo-nah eh-mehr-'hehn-see·ah)*
Is it important?	**¿Es importante?** *(ehs eem-pohr-'tahn-teh)*

➤ A few cordial openers may be in order. Let the folks know you care:

How can I help you?	**¿Cómo puedo ayudarle?** *('koh-moh 'pweh-doh ah-yoo-'dahr-leh)*
What do you need?	**¿Qué necesita?** *(keh neh-seh-'see-tah)*
I'm at your service	**Estoy a su servicio** *(eh-'stoh·ee ah soo sehr-'vee-see·oh)*

➤ Listen for these common responses:

I was just passing through.	**Yo sólo pasaba por aquí.** *(yoh 'soh-loh pah-'sah-bah pohr ah-'kee)*
I saw what happened.	**Yo vi lo que pasó.** *(yoh vee loh keh pah-'soh)*
I didn't see anything.	**Yo no vi nada.** *(yoh noh vee 'nah-dah)*

WHEN DID IT HAPPEN?
¿Cuándo pasó? *('kwahn-doh pah-'soh)*

Time references are crucial in law enforcement. You learned earlier how to give brief one-word retorts to the question **¿Cuándo?**:

¿Cuándo? *('kwahn-doh)*	**Mañana** *(mah-'nyah-nah)*	(Tomorrow)
¿Cuándo? *('kwahn-doh)*	**Después** *(deh-'spwehs)*	(Later)
¿Cuándo? *('kwahn-doh)*	**Nunca** *('noon-kah)*	(Never)

Clearly, anyone looking for more specific information needs to use either a clock or a calendar. To prepare for further conversation in Spanish, work diligently on these next sets of phrases and vocabulary:

AT WHAT TIME?
¿A qué hora? *(ah keh 'oh-rah)*

You can't mention police work without mentioning the clock. To read the clock in Spanish, simply give the hour, followed by the word **y** (and), and the minutes. For example, 6:15 is **seis y quince** *('seh·ees ee 'keen-seh)*. Closely examine these other examples:

It's...	**Son las...** (sohn lahs...)
At...	**A las...** (ah lahs...)
10:40	**diez y cuarenta** (dee-'ehs ee kwah-'rehn-tah)
03:25	**tres y veinte y cinco** (trehs ee 'veh·een-teh ee 'seen-koh)
02:05	**dos y cinco de la mañana** (dohs ee 'seen-koh deh lah mah-'nyah-nah)
16:00	**cuatro de la tarde** ('kwah-troh deh la 'tahr-deh)
21:30	**nueve y treinta de la noche** (noo-'eh-veh ee 'tree·een-tah deh lah 'noh-cheh)

Remember that "time" in general is **el tiempo** (ehl tee-'ehm-poh). The specific "time" is **la hora** (lah 'oh-rah). Time in reference to an occurrence is **la vez:**

the first time	**la primera vez** (lah pre-'meh-rah vehs)
the last time	**la última vez** (lah 'ool-tee-mah vehs)
the only time	**la única vez** (lah 'oo-nee-kah vehs)

DO YOU KNOW THE DATE?
¿Sabe la fecha? ('sah-beh lah 'feh-chah)

Spend a few minutes looking over the following Spanish words. Then stress each sound as you pronounce them aloud:

today	**hoy** ('oh-ee)
tomorrow	**mañana** (mah-'nyah-nah)
yesterday	**ayer** (ah-'yehr)
day	**el día** (ehl 'dee-ah)
week	**la semana** (lah seh-'mah-nah)
Monday	**lunes** ('loo-nehs)
Tuesday	**martes** ('mahr-tehs)
Wednesday	**miércoles** (mee-'ehr-koh-lehs)
Thursday	**jueves** (hoo-'eh-vehs)
Friday	**viernes** (vee-'ehr-nehs)
Saturday	**sábado** ('sah-bah-doh)
Sunday	**domingo** (doh-'meen-goh)

Read these questions and answers. See how **los días** (lohs 'dee-ahs) function as one-word responses to "when" questions:

When do I pay?	**¿Cuándo pago?** ('kwahn-doh 'pah-goh)	**Viernes** (vee-'ehr-nehs)

When is my appointment?	¿Cuándo es mi cita?	Sábado *('sah-bah-doh)*
	('kwahn-doh ehs mee 'see-tah)	
When did that happen?	¿Cuándo pasó eso?	Martes *('mahr-tehs)*
	('kwahn-doh pah-'soh 'eh-soh)	

As far as the months are concerned, just remember that most words are similar in both Spanish and English. Speak up as you practice:

month	**el mes** *(ehl mehs)*
year	**el año** *(ehl 'ah-nyoh)*
January	**enero** *(eh-'neh-roh)*
February	**febrero** *(feh-'breh-roh)*
March	**marzo** *('mahr-soh)*
April	**abril** *(ah-'breel)*
May	**mayo** *('mah-yoh)*
June	**junio** *('hoo-nee·oh)*
July	**julio** *('hoo-lee·oh)*
August	**agosto** *(ah-'goh-stoh)*
September	**septiembre** *(sehp-tee-'ehm-breh)*
October	**octubre** *(ohk-'too-breh)*
November	**noviembre** *(noh-vee-'ehm-breh)*
December	**diciembre** *(dee-see-'ehm-breh)*

To give the date in Spanish, reverse the order of your words. For example, February 2nd is **el dos de febrero** *(ehl dohs de feh-'breh-roh)*.

The year is often read as one large number:

2010	**dos mil diez** *(dohs meel dee-'ehs)*

Can you give today's date in Spanish? Use a calendar to practice all of your new vocabulary!

➤ Most students of Spanish get confused when using the words **por** *(pohr)* and **para** *('pah-rah)* for "for," because they are similar in meaning. The differences between the two are not easy to explain, so it may be best to listen to Spanish speakers as they use them, and then try them out in short, practical phrases. The worst that could happen is that you'd be wrong and might get corrected. Are you willing to take that risk? Here are a few common examples.

throughout the afternoon	**por la tarde** *(pohr lah 'tahr-deh)*
in order to drive	**para manejar** *('pah-rah mah-neh-'hahr)*
for two days	**por dos días** *(pohr dohs 'dee-ahs)*
by Friday	**para el viernes** *('pah-rah ehl vee-'ehr-nehs)*

➤ Never let up on those time-reference questions:

At what time?	**¿A qué hora?** *(ah keh 'oh-rah)*
How long ago?	**¿Hace cuánto?** *('ah-seh 'kwahn-toh)*
How much time?	**¿Cuánto tiempo?** *('kwahn-toh tee-'ehm-poh)*

➤ "The first of the month" in Spanish is **el primero del mes** *(ehl pree-'meh-roh dehl mehs)*:

January 1st	**el primero de enero** *(ehl pree-'meh-roh deh eh-'neh-roh)*

➤ For 1:00–1:59, use **Es la...** *(ehs lah...)* instead of **Son las...** *(sohn lahs...)* for example:

It's one o'clock	**Es la una** *(ehs lah 'oo-nah)*
It's one-thirty	**Es la una y treinta** *(ehs lah 'oo-nah ee 'treh·een-tah)*

➤ "On Friday" is **el viernes** *(ehl vee-'ehr-nehs)*, but "on Fridays" is **los viernes** *(lohs vee'-ehr-nehs)*.

➤ In reference to time, use the following expressions:

the next one	**el próximo** *(ehl 'prohk-see-moh)*
the past one	**el pasado** *(ehl pah-'sah-doh)*
the weekend	**el fin de semana** *(ehl feen deh seh-'mah-nah)*
noon	**mediodía** *(ehl meh-dee·oh-'dee-ah)*
midnight	**medianoche** *(meh-dee·ah-'noh-cheh)*
tomorrow morning	**mañana por la mañana** *(mah-'nyah-nah pohr lah mah-nyah-nah)*

REPASO

Look at these words:

ago	hace *('ah-seh)*
between	entre *('ehn-treh)*
following	el siguiente *(ehl see-gee-'ehn-teh)*
within	dentro *('dehn-troh)*

A. Are you able to interpret the sample phrases below?

Hace cinco meses *('ah-seh 'seen-koh 'meh-sehs)*

_____

Entre las dos y las tres *('ehn-treh lahs dohs ee lahs trehs)*

_____

El siguiente día *(ehl see-gee-'ehn-teh 'dee-ah)*

_____

Dentro de un año *('dehn-troh deh oon 'ah-nyoh)*

_____

B. Say these in Spanish:

20:00	_____
1-11-98	_____
June 1st	_____
on Mondays	_____
next week	_____
14:30	_____

ANSWERS

A. Five months ago
Between two and three
The following day
Within a year

B. las ocho de la noche
el once de enero, mil novecientos noventa y ocho
el primero de junio
los lunes
la próxima semana
las dos y media

TEMAS CULTURALES

Not all folks panic when it comes to tardiness—some cultures put less emphasis on "beating the clock" than others. Be direct, and explain the importance of punctuality in legal matters; but, be sensitive to those who believe that personal health, family, and friends are valid reasons for being a little late. If you're a stickler for punctuality, inform everyone of the concern:

You have to arrive early	**Tiene que llegar temprano** *(tee-'eh-neh keh yeh-'gahr tehm-'prah-noh)*
Don't be late	**No llegue tarde** *(noh 'yeh-geh 'tahr-deh)*
This country is different!	**¡Este país es diferente!** *('eh-steh pah-'ees ehs dee-feh-'rehn-teh)*

WHO ARE YOU?
¿Quién es usted? *(kee-'ehn ehs oo-'stehd)*

It's time to introduce yourself, so learn the name in Spanish for your particular job title. Because some words can't be translated literally from English to Spanish, resort to English when titles get really specific. Change the **el** *(ehl)* to **la** *(lah)* if you are a female and add **a** to the title (**el cajero**, **la cajera**). Note that some words do not take **a** (**el agente**, **la agente**).

I am (the)...	**Soy...** *('soh-ee...)*
administrator	**el administrador(a)** *(ehl ahd-mee-nee-strah-'dohr)*
agent	**el agente** *(ehl ah-'hehn-teh)*
animal control officer	**el oficial para el control de animales** *(ehl oh-fee-see-'ahl 'pah-rah ehl kohn-'trohl deh ah-nee-'mah-lehs)*
bodyguard	**el guardaespaldas** *(ehl gwahr-dah-eh-'spahl-dahs)*
bondsman	**el fiador(a)** *(ehl fee-ah-'dohr)*
border patrol agent	**el agente de la patrulla fronteriza** *(ehl ah-'hehn-teh deh lah pah-'troo-yah frohn-teh-'ree-sah)*
captain	**el capitán(a)** *(ehl kah-pee-'tahn)*
cashier	**el cajero(a)** *(ehl kah-'heh-roh)*
chaplain	**el capellán** *(ehl kah-peh-'yahn)*
chief	**el jefe(a)** *(ehl 'heh-feh)*
clerk	**el dependiente** *(ehl deh-pehn-dee-'ehn-teh)*
colonel	**el coronel** *(ehl koh-roh-'nehl)*
coordinator	**el director(a)** *(ehl dee-rehk-'tohr)*
coroner	**el médico legista** *(ehl 'meh-dee-koh leh-'hee-stah)*
corrections officer	**el oficial correccional** *(ehl oh-fee-see-'ahl koh-rrehk-see-oh-'nahl)*
counselor	**el consejero(a)** *(ehl kohn-seh-'heh-roh)*
customs officer	**el agente de aduana** *(ehl ah-'hehn-teh deh ah-'dwah-nah)*

deputy	**el diputado(a)** *(ehl dee-poo-'tah-doh)*
detective	**el detective** *(ehl deh-tehk-'tee-veh)*
dispatcher	**el despachador(a)** *(ehl dehs-pah-chah-'dohr)*
district attorney	**el fiscal de distrito** *(ehl fee-'skahl deh dee-'stree-toh)*
examiner	**el examinador(a)** *(ehl ehk-sah-mee-nah-'dohr)*
fire fighter	**el bombero(a)** *(ehl bohm-'beh-roh)*
first responder	**el primer(a) respondiente** *(ehl pree-'mehr rehs-pohn-dee-'ehn-teh)*
fish and game warden	**el agente de caza y pesca** *(ehl ah-'hehn-teh deh 'kah-sah ee 'pehs-kah)*
guard	**el guardia** *(ehl 'kwahr-dee·ah)*
harbor patrol officer	**el patrullero(a) de puertos** *(ehl pah-troo-'yeh-roh deh 'pwehr-tohs)*
highway patrol officer	**el oficial dc la patrulla de carreteras** *(ehl oh-fee-see-'ahl deh lah pah-'troo-yah deh kah-rreh-'teh-rahs)*
immigration officer	**el oficial de inmigración** *(ehl oh-fee-see-'ahl deh een-mee-grah-see-'ohn)*
inspector	**el inspector(a)** *(ehl een-spehk-'tohr)*
interpreter	**el intérprete** *(ehl een-'tehr-preh-teh)*
investigator	**el investigador(a)** *(ehl een-veh-stee-gah-'dohr)*
jailer	**el carcelero(a)** *(ehl kahr-seh-'leh-roh)*
judge	**el juez(a)** *(ehl hoo-'ehs)*
juror	**el miembro del jurado** *(ehl mee-'ehm-broh dehl hoo-'rah-doh)*
lawyer	**el abogado(a)** *(ehl ah-boh-'gah-doh)*
lieutenant	**el teniente** *(ehl teh-nee-'ehn-teh)*
lifeguard	**el salvavidas(a)** *(ehl sahl-vah-'vee-dahs)*
manager	**el gerente** *(ehl geh-'rehn-teh)*
mayor	**el alcalde** *(ehl ahl-'kahl-deh)*
meter reader	**el atendiente del parquímetro** *(ehl ah-tehn-dee-'ehn-teh dehl pahr-'kee-meh-troh)*
notary public	**el notario(a)** *(ehl noh-'tah-ree·oh)*
official	**cl oficial** *(ehl oh-fee-see-'ahl)*
operator	**el operador(a)** *(ehl oh-peh-rah-'dohr)*
paramedic	**el paramédico(a)** *(ehl pah-rah-'meh-dee-koh)*
patrol officer	**el patrullero(a)** *(ehl pah-troo-'yeh-roh)*
police	**el policía** *(ehl poh-lee-'see-ah)*
priest	**el sacerdote** *(ehl sah-sehr-'doh-teh)*
probation officer	**el oficial(a) a cargo de la libertad provisional** *(ehl oh-fee-see-'ahl ah 'kahr-goh deh lah lee-behr-'tahd proh-vee-see·oh-'nahl)*

public defender	**el defensor(a) público(a)** *(ehl deh-fehn-'sohr 'poo-blee-koh)*
ranger	**el guardabosques** *(ehl 'gwahr-dah-'boh-skehs)*
receptionist	**el recepcionista** *(ehl reh-sehp-see·oh-'nee-stah)*
secretary	**el secretario(a)** *(ehl seh-kreh-'tah-ree·oh)*
sergeant	**el sargento(a)** *(ehl sahr-'hehn-toh)*
sheriff	**el alguacil** *(ehl ahl-gwah-'seel)*
specialist	**el especialista** *(ehl eh-speh-see·ah-'lee-stah)*
technician	**el técnico(a)** *(ehl 'tehk-nee-koh)*
trainer	**el entrenador(a)** *(ehl ehn-treh-nah-'dohr)*
translator	**el traductor(a)** *(ehl trah-dook-'tohr)*
warden	**el guardián(a) de la prisión** *(ehl gwahr-dee-'ahn deh lah pree-see-'ohn)*
watchman	**el vigilante** *(ehl vee-hee-'lahn-teh)*

THE PUBLIC
El público *(ehl 'poo-blee-koh)*

Find out who you will be dealing with out in the community. This is just a sample. As you can see, each title below only refers to a male:

Who is the...?	**¿Quién es...** *(kee-'ehn ehs…)*
acquaintance	**el conocido?** *(ehl koh-noh-'see-doh)*
boss	**el jefe?** *(ehl 'heh-feh)*
bystander	**el espectador?** *(ehl eh-spehk-tah-'dohr)*
civilian	**el ciudadano?** *(ehl see-oo-dah-'dah-noh)*
client	**el cliente?** *(ehl klee-'ehn-teh)*
companion	**el compañero?** *(ehl kohm-pah-'nyeh-roh)*
customer	**el cliente?** *(ehl klee-'ehn-teh)*
cyclist	**el ciclista?** *(ehl see-'klee-stah)*
defendant	**el demandado?** *(ehl deh-mahn-'dah-doh)*
driver	**el chofer?** *(ehl choh-'fehr)*
employee	**el empleado?** *(ehl ehm-pleh-'ah-doh)*
employer	**el empresario?** *(ehl ehm-preh-'sah-ree·oh)*
juvenile	**el menor de edad?** *(ehl meh-'nohr deh eh-'dahd)*
landlord	**el propietario?** *(ehl proh-pee-eh-'tah-ree-oh)*
leader	**el líder?** *(ehl 'lee-dehr)*
lessee	**el arrendatario?** *(ehl ah-rrehn-dah-'tah-ree·oh)*
minor	**el menor de edad?** *(ehl meh-'nohr deh eh-'dahd)*
neighbor	**el vecino?** *(ehl veh-'see-noh)*
occupant	**el inquilino?** *(ehl een-kee-'lee-noh)*
owner	**el dueño?** *(ehl 'dweh-nyoh)*

partner	**el socio?** *(ehl 'soh-see·oh)*
passenger	**el pasajero?** *(ehl pah-sah-'heh-roh)*
patient	**el paciente?** *(ehl pah-see-'ehn-teh)*
pedestrian	**el peatón?** *(ehl peh-ah-'tohn)*
plaintiff	**el demandante?** *(ehl deh-mahn-'dahn-teh)*
stranger	**el desconocido?** *(ehl dehs-koh-noh-'see-doh)*
tenant	**el inquilino?** *(ehl een-kee-'lee-noh)*
tourist	**el turista?** *(ehl too-'rees-tah)*
victim	**la víctima?** *(lah 'veek-tee-mah)*
visitor	**el visitante?** *(ehl vee-see-'tahn-teh)*
witness	**el testigo?** *(ehl teh-'stee-goh)*

Now mention some of the folks in trouble:

accomplice	**el cómplice** *(ehl 'kohm-plee-seh)*
addict	**el adicto** *(ehl ah-'deek-toh)*
aggressor	**el agresor** *(ehl ah-greh-'sohr)*
alcoholic	**el alcohólico** *(ehl ahl-koh-'oh-lee-koh)*
arsonist	**el incendiario** *(ehl een-sehn-dee-'ah-ree-oh)*
assailant	**el asaltante** *(ehl ah-sahl-'tahn-teh)*
bank robber	**el asaltante de bancos** *(ehl ah-sahl-'tahn-teh deh 'bahn-kohs)*
beggar	**el limosnero** *(ehl lee-mohs-'neh-roh)*
bookie	**el corredor de apuestas** *(ehl koh-rreh-'dohr deh ah-'pwehs-tahs)*
convict	**el convicto** *(ehl kohn-'veek-toh)*
criminal	**el criminal** *(ehl kree-mee-'nahl)*
delinquent	**el delincuente** *(ehl deh-leen-'kwehn-teh)*
drug dealer	**el vendedor de drogas** *(ehl vehn-deh-'dohr deh 'droh-gahs)*
drunkard	**el borracho** *(ehl boh-'rrah-choh)*
escapee	**el fugitivo** *(ehl foo-hee-'tee-voh)*
felon	**el felón** *(ehl feh-'lohn)*
fence	**el perista** *(ehl peh-'rees-tah)*
forger	**el falsificador** *(ehl fahl-see-fee-kah-'dohr)*
gambler	**el jugador** *(ehl hoo-gah-'dohr)*
gang member	**el pandillero** *(ehl pahn-dee-'yeh-roh)*
homeless person	**el desamparado** *(ehl dehs-ahm-pah-'rah-doh)*
informer	**el informante** *(ehl een-fohr-'mahn-teh)*
injured person	**el herido** *(ehl eh-'ree-doh)*
inmate	**el preso** *(ehl 'preh-soh)*
kidnapper	**el secuestrador** *(ehl seh-kweh-strah-'dohr)*
killer	**el asesino** *(ehl ah-seh-'see-noh)*
panhandler	**el pordiosero** *(ehl pohr-dee·oh-'seh-roh)*

pickpocket	**el ratero** *(ehl rah-'teh-roh)*
pimp	**el alcahuete** *(ehl ahl-kah-'hweh-teh),* **el padrote** *(ehl pah-'droh-teh)*
prisoner	**el prisionero** *(ehl pree-see·oh-'neh-roh)*
prostitute	**la prostituta** *(lah proh-stee-'too-tah)*
shoplifter	**el ratero de tiendas** *(ehl rah-'teh-roh deh tee-'ehn-dahs)*
smuggler	**el contrabandista** *(ehl kohh-trah-bahn-'dees-tah)*
suspect	**el sospechoso** *(ehl soh-speh-'choh-soh)*
swindler	**el estafador** *(ehl ehs-tah-fah-'dohr)*
terrorist	**el terrorista** *(ehl teh-rroh-'ree-stah)*
thief	**el ladrón** *(ehl lah-'drohn)*
vagrant	**el vagabundo** *(ehl vah-gah-'boon-doh)*

¿Cuándo pasó este problema, a qué hora y por qué?

El jueves, el cuatro de agosto, a las seis y ocho de la mañana y porque soy un ladrón.

INFORMACIÓN PRIVADA

➤ Identify folks by their age group:

adolescent	**el adolescente** *(ehl ah-doh-leh-'sehn-teh)*
adult	**el adulto** *(ehl ah-'dool-toh)*
child	**el niño** *(ehl 'nee-nyoh)*
elderly	**el anciano** *(ehl ahn-see-'ah-noh)*
baby	**el bebé** *(ehl beh-'beh)*

➤ It's not uncommon for officials to discuss a person's citizenship:

by birth	**por nacimiento** *(pohr nah-see-mee-'ehn-toh)*
naturalized	**naturalizado** *(nah-too-rah-lee-'sah-doh)*
undocumented	**indocumentado** *(een-doh-koo-mehn-'tah-doh)*
citizen	**el ciudadano** *(ehl see-oo-dah-'dah-noh)*
resident	**el residente** *(ehl reh-see-'dehn-teh)*
immigrant	**el inmigrante** *(ehl een-mee-'grahn-teh)*
refugee	**el refugiado** *(ehl reh-foo-hee-'ah-doh)*

➤ Single words can be used at times to ellicit general responses:

Who?	**¿Quién?** *(kee-'ehn)*	**El testigo** *(ehl teh-'stee-goh)*
How many?	**¿Cuántos?** *('kwahn-tohs)*	**Tres** *(trehs)*
Where?	**¿Dónde?** *('dohn-deh)*	**En frente** *(ehn 'frehn-teh)*

➤ As we said, when referring to a female, not only must you change **el** *(ehl)* to **la** *(lah)* before each title, but the word endings change also. Notice the differences:

male sergeant	**el sargento** *(ehl sahr-'hehn-toh)*
female sergeant	**la sargenta** *(lah sahr-'hehn-tah)*
male suspect	**el sospechoso** *(ehl soh-speh-'choh-soh)*
female suspect	**la sospechosa** *(lah soh-speh-'choh-sah)*

➤ There are various ways to express "to happen" in Spanish. Learn the two important ones:

| to happen | **pasar** *(pah-'sahr)* | **¿Qué pasó?** *(keh pah-'soh)* |
| to occur | **ocurrir** *(oh-koo-'reer)* | **¿Qué ocurrió?** *(keh oh-koo-ree-'oh)* |

➤ A **ladrón** may also be translated as a prowler or burglar.

REPASO

A. Connect the English word with its Spanish translation:

witness	el ladrón *(ehl lah-'drohn)*
driver	el dependiente *(ehl deh-pehn-dee-'ehn-teh)*
officer	el bombero *(ehl bohm-'beh-roh)*
clerk	el extranjero *(ehl ehs-trahn-'heh-roh)*
foreigner	el vecino *(ehl veh-'see-noh)*
firefighter	el chofer *(ehl choh-'fehr)*
neighbor	el oficio *(ehl oh-'fee-see·oh)*
thief	el testigo *(ehl teh-'stee-goh)*

ANSWERS

A. witness — el testigo
driver — el chofer
officer — el oficio
clerk — el dependiente
foreigner — el extranjero
firefighter — el bombero
neighbor — el vecino
thief — el ladrón

THE INTERVIEW
La entrevista *(lah ehn-treh-'vee-stah)*

Once you have figured out what's going on and who everybody is, pull out the proper forms and begin the documentation process. To fill out a personal information form on someone who speaks only Spanish, utilize this next series of vocabulary. Observe the language patterns:

What's your...?	**¿Cuál es su...** *('kwahl ehs soo...)*
address	**dirección?** *(dee-rehk-see-'ohn)*
age	**edad?** *(eh-'dahd)*
alias (a.k.a.)	**el alias?** *(ehl 'ah-lee-ahs)*
date of birth	**fecha de nacimiento?** *('feh-chah deh nah-see-mee-'ehn-toh)*
e-mail	**el correo electrónico?** *(ehl koh-'rreh-oh eh-lehk-'troh-nee-koh)*
first language	**primer idioma?** *(pree-'mehr ee-dee-'oh-mah)*
first name	**primer nombre?** *(pree-'mehr 'nohm-breh)*
full name	**nombre completo?** *('nohm-breh kohm-'pleh-toh)*
grade level	**último año de estudios?** *('ool-tee-moh 'ah-nyoh deh eh-'stoo-dee·ohs)*
height	**estatura?** *(eh-stah-'too-rah)*
last name	**apellido paterno?** *(ah-peh-'yee-doh pah-'tehr-noh)*
maiden name	**nombre de soltera?** *('nohm-breh deh sohl-'teh-rah)*
marital status	**estado civil?** *(eh-'stah-doh see-'veel)*
medical history	**historia médica?** *(ee-'stoh-ree·ah 'meh-dee-kah)*
middle initial	**segunda inicial?** *(seh-'goon-dah ee-nee-see-'ahl)*
name	**nombre?** *('nohm-breh)*
nationality	**nacionalidad?** *(nah-see·oh-nah-lee-'dahd)*
nickname	**apodo?** *(ah-'poh-doh)*
occupation	**ocupación?** *(oh-koo-pah-see'ohn)*
place of birth	**lugar de nacimiento?** *(loo-'gahr deh nah-see-mee-'ehn-toh)*
place of employment	**lugar de empleo?** *(loo-'gahr deh ehm-'pleh-oh)*
previous residence	**residencia anterior?** *(reh-see-'dehn-see·ah ahn-teh-ree-'ohr)*
race	**raza?** *('rah-sah)*
relationship	**parentezco?** *(pah-rehn-'teh-skoh)*
religion	**religión?** *(reh-lee-hee-'ohn)*
sex	**sexo?** *('sehk-soh)*
weight	**peso?** *('peh-soh)*
zip code	**código postal?** *('koh-dee-goh poh-'stahl)*

INFORMACIÓN PRIVADA

➤ The city is not everything. These words refer to other living places:

country	**el país** *(ehl pah-'ees)*
county	**el condado** *(ehl kohn-'dah-doh)*
district	**el distrito** *(ehl dee-'stree-toh)*
region	**la región** *(lah reh-hee-'ohn)*
state	**el estado** *(ehl eh-'stah-doh)*
town	**el pueblo** *(ehl 'pweh-bloh)*
village	**la aldea** *(lah ahl-'deh-ah)*

➤ The more you practice in public, the more confidence you will gain. In addition, you'll probably pick up on two or more ways to express the same message. Here are a few examples:

What's your height?	**¿Cuál es su estatura?** *(kwahl ehs soo eh-stah-'too-rah)*
How tall are you?	**¿Cuánto mide?** *('kwahn-toh 'mee-deh)*
What's your weight?	**¿Cuál es su peso?** *(kwahl ehs soo 'peh-soh)*
How much do you weigh?	**¿Cuánto pesa?** *('kwahn-toh 'peh-sah)*
What's your date of birth?	**¿Cuál es su fecha de nacimiento?** *(kwahl ehs soo 'feh-chah deh nah-see-mee-'ehn-toh)*
When were you born?	**¿Cuándo nació?** *('kwahn-doh nah-see-'oh)*

➤ When responses are hard to understand, ask them to write down what they are trying to say:

How do you write it?	**¿Cómo se escribe?** *('koh-moh seh eh-'skree-beh)*

➤ "Female" is **femenino** *(feh-meh-'nee-noh),* while "male" is **masculino** *(mah-skoo-'lee-noh).*

THE NUMBER, PLEASE

El número, por favor *(ehl 'noo-meh-roh pohr fah-'vohr)*

What's your... number?	**¿Cuál es su número de...** *(kwahl ehs soo 'noo-meh roh deh...)*
apartment	**apartamento?** *(ah-pahr-tah-'mehn-toh)*
area code	**área?** *('ah-reh-ah)*
business	**negocios?** *(neh-'goh-see·ohs)*
card	**tarjeta?** *(tahr-'heh-tah)*
case	**caso?** *('kah-soh)*
cell phone	**teléfono celular?** *(teh-'leh-foh-noh seh-loo-'lahr)*
check	**cheque?** *('cheh-keh)*
citation	**citación?** *(see-tah-see-'ohn)*
classification	**clasificación?** *(klah-see-fee-kah-see-'ohn)*
code	**código?** *('koh-dee-goh)*
credit card	**tarjeta de crédito?** *(tahr-'heh-tah deh 'kreh-dee-toh)*
extension	**extensión?** *(ehks-tehn-see-'ohn)*
fax	**facsímile?** *(fahk-'see-mee-leh)*
home	**hogar?** *(oh-'gahr)*
identification	**identificación?** *(ee-dehn-tee-fee-kah-see-'ohn)*
immigration	**inmigración?** *(een-mee-grah-see-'ohn)*
insurance	**seguro?** *(seh-'goo-roh)*
license	**licencia?** *(lee-'sehn-see·ah)*
page	**página?** *('pah-hee-nah)*
passport	**pasaporte?** *(pah-sah-'pohr-teh)*
plate	**placa?** *('plah-kah)*
policy	**póliza?** *('poh-lee-sah)*
registration	**registro?** *(reh-'hee-stroh)*
residence	**residencia?** *(reh-see-'dehn-see·ah)*
school	**escuela?** *(eh-'skweh-lah)*
section	**sección?** *(sehk-see-'ohn)*
serial	**serie?** *('seh-ree-eh)*
social security	**seguro social?** *(seh-'goo-roh soh-see-'ahl)*
telephone	**teléfono?** *(teh-'leh-foh-noh)*
vehicle	**vehículo?** *(veh-'ee-koo-loh)*
visa	**visa?** *('vee-sah)*
work	**trabajo?** *(trah-'bah-hoh)*

WHERE DO YOU WORK?

¿**Dónde trabaja?** *('dohn-deh trah-'bah-hah)*

Here's a list that will help you understand job titles. These items identify various occupations and professions. Again, add an **a** for female subjects. Note that some jobs—those without an **a**—are spelled the same way for both genders.

I'm (the)... **Soy...** *('soh-ee...)*

accountant	**el/la contador(a)** *(ehl/lah kohn-tah-'dohr/ah)*
artist	**el/la artista** *(ehl/lah ahr-'tee-stah)*
assistant	**el/la asistente(a)** *(ehl/lah ah-sees-'tehn-teh/tah)*
babysitter	**el/la niñero(a)** *(ehl/lah nee-'nyeh-roh/rah)*
baker	**el/la panadero(a)** *(ehl/lah pah-nah-'deh-roh/rah)*
bartender	**el/la cantinero(a)** *(ehl/lah kahn-tee-'neh-roh/rah)*
beautician	**el/la cosmetólogo(a)** *(ehl/lah kohs-meh-'toh-loh-goh/gah)*
bellhop	**el/la botones** *(ehl/lah boh-'toh-nehs)*
busboy	**el/la ayudante de camarero** *(ehl/lah ah-yoo-'dahn-teh deh kah-mah-'reh-roh)*
butcher	**el/la carnicero(a)** *(ehl/lah kahr-nee-'seh-roh/rah)*
car wash attendant	**el/la lavacarros** *(ehl/lah lah-vah-'kah-rrohs)*
carpenter	**el/la carpintero(a)** *(ehl/lah kahr-peen-'teh-roh/rah)*
cashier	**el/la cajero(a)** *(ehl/lah kah-'heh-roh/rah)*
clerk	**el/la dependiente** *(ehl/lah deh-pehn-dee-'ehn-teh)*
construction worker	**el/la trabajador(a) en construcción** *(ehl/lah trah-bah-hah-'dohr/rah ehn kohns-trook-see-'ohn)*
cook	**el/la cocinero(a)** *(ehl/lah koh-see-'neh-roh/rah)*
dentist	**el/la dentista** *(ehl/lah dehn-'tee-stah)*
dish washer	**el/la lavaplatos** *(ehl/lah lah-vah-'plah-tohs)*
doctor	**el/la doctor(a)** *(ehl/lah dohk-'tohr/rah)*
dress maker	**la modista(a)** *(lah moh-'dee-stah)*
electician	**el/la electricista** *(ehl/lah eh-lehk-tree-'see-stah)*
engineer	**el/la ingeniero(a)** *(ehl/lah een-heh-nee-'eh-roh/rah)*
factory worker	**el/la obrero(a)** *(ehl/lah oh-'breh-roh/rah)*
farm worker	**el/la granjero(a)** *(ehl/lah grahn-'heh-roh/rah)*
fisherman	**el/la pescador(a)** *(ehl/lah peh-skah-'dohr/ah)*
foreman	**el/la patrón(a)** *(ehl/lah pah-'trohn/ah)*
gardener	**el/la jardinero(a)** *(ehl/lah hahr-dee-'neh-roh/rah)*
hairdresser	**el/la peluquero(a)** *(ehl/lah peh-loo-'keh-roh/rah)*
helper	**el/la ayudante(a)** *(ehl/lah ah-yoo-'dahn-teh/tah)*
house cleaner	**el/la empleado(a) doméstico(a)** *(ehl/lah ehm-pleh-'ah-doh/dah doh-'mehs-tee-koh/kah)*
janitor	**el/la conserje** *(ehl/lah kohn-'sehr-heh)*
laborer	**el/la obrero(a)** *(ehl/lah oh-'breh-roh/rah)*

lawyer	**el/la abogado(a)** *(ehl/lah ah-boh-'gah-doh/dah)*
machinist	**el/la maquinista** *(ehl/lah mah-kee-'nee-stah)*
mail carrier	**el/la cartero(a)** *(ehl/lah kahr-'teh-roh/rah)*
manager	**el/la gerente(a)** *(ehl/lah heh-'rehn-teh/tah)*
mechanic	**el/la mecánico** *(ehl/lah meh-'kah-nee-koh)*
merchant	**el/la comerciante** *(ehl/lah koh-mehr-see-'ahn-teh)*
minister	**el pastor** *(ehl pah-'stohr)*
musician	**el/la músico** *(ehl/lah 'moo-see-koh)*
nurse	**el/la enfermero(a)** *(ehl/lah ehn-fehr-'meh-roh/ah)*
painter	**el/la pintor(a)** *(ehl/lah peen-'tohr/ah)*
plumber	**el/la plomero(a)** *(ehl/lah ploh-'meh-roh/rah)*
priest	**el cura** *(ehl 'koo-ra)*
salesman	**el/la vendedor(a)** *(ehl/lah vehn-deh-'dohr/ah)*
secretary	**el/la secretario(a)** *(ehl/lah seh-kreh-'tah-ree-oh/ah)*
shopkeeper	**el/la tendero(a)** *(ehl/lah tehn-'deh-roh/rah)*
soldier	**el/la soldado** *(ehl/lah sohl-'dah-doh)*
student	**el/la estudiante** *(ehl/lah eh-stoo-dee-'ahn-teh)*
tailor	**el/la sastre** *(ehl/lah 'sah-streh)*
teacher	**el/la maestro(a)** *(ehl/lah mah-'eh-stroh/ah)*
truck driver	**el/la camionero(a)** *(ehl/lah kah-mee·oh-'neh-roh/rah)*
waiter	**el/la mesonero(a)** *(ehl/lah meh-'soh-neh-roh/rah)*
worker	**el/la trabajador(a)** *(ehl/lah trah-bah-hah-'dohr/ah)*

Are you aware of these official titles?

Congressman	**el congresista** *(ehl kohn-greh-'see-stah)*
Governor	**el gobernador(a)** *(ehl goh-behr-nah-'dohr)*
President	**el presidente(a)** *(ehl preh-see-'dehn-teh)*
Representative	**el delegado(a)** *(ehl deh-leh-'gah-doh)*
Senator	**el senador(a)** *(ehl seh-nah-'dohr)*

57

A. Fill out this questionnaire:

Nombre completo *('nohm-breh kohm-'pleh-toh)* _____

Dirección *(dee-rehk-see-'ohn)* _____

Número de teléfono *('noo-meh-roh deh teh-'leh-foh-noh)* _____

Fecha de nacimiento *('feh-chah deh nah-see-mee-'ehn-toh)* _____

Número de seguro social *('noo-meh-roh deh seh-'goo-roh soh-see-'ahl)* _____

B. Answer in Spanish. Follow the example.

¿Dónde trabaja la maestra? *('dohn-deh trah-'bah-hah lah mah-'eh-strah)*   <u>En la escuela.</u> *(ehn lah eh-'skweh-lah)*

¿Dónde trabaja el cocinero? *('dohn-deh trah-'bah-hah ehl koh-see-'neh-roh)* _____

¿Dónde trabaja el secretario? *('dohn-deh trah-'bah-hah ehl seh-kreh-'tah-ree·oh)* _____

¿Dónde trabaja la enfermera? *('dohn-deh trah-'bah-hah ehl ehn-fehr-'meh-rah)* _____

¿Dónde trabaja el sacerdote? *('dohn-deh trah-'bah-hah ehl sah-sehr-'doh-teh)* _____

¿Dónde trabaja el Presidente? *('dohn-deh trah-'bah-hah ehl preh-see-'dehn-teh)* _____

ANSWERS

A. Complete name	B. En el restaurante
Address	En la oficina
Phone number	En el hospital
Date of birth	En la iglesia
Social Security Number	En Washington D.C.

AND YOUR FAMILY?

¿Y su familia? *(ee soo fah-'mee-lee·ah)*

As long as we're talking about people, why not spend time with the family? Plug in the word where it belongs:

Is he/she (the)...?   **¿Es...** *(ehs...)*

adopted child	**el niño adoptado?** *(ehl 'nee-nyoh ah-dohp-'tah-doh)*
aunt	**la tía?** *(lah 'tee-ah)*
brother	**el hermano?** *(ehl ehr-'mah-noh)*
brother-in-law	**el cuñado?** *(ehl koo-'nyah-doh)*
cousin	**el primo?** *(ehl 'pree-moh)*
daughter	**la hija?** *(lah 'ee-hah)*
daughter-in-law	**la nuera?** *(lah 'nweh-rah)*
father	**el padre?** *(ehl 'pah-dreh)*
father-in-law	**el suegro?** *(ehl 'sweh-groh)*
fiancée	**el prometido?** *(ehl proh-meh-'tee-doh)*
granddaughter	**la nieta?** *(lah nee-'eh-tah)*
grandfather	**el abuelo?** *(chl ah-'bweh-loh)*
grandmother	**la abuela?** *(lah ah-'bweh-lah)*
grandson	**el nieto?** *(ehl nee-'eh-toh)*
husband	**el esposo?** *(ehl eh-'spoh-soh)*
legal guardian	**el tutor?** *(ehl too-'tohr)*
mother	**la madre?** *(lah 'mah-dreh)*
mother-in-law	**la suegra?** *(lah 'sweh-grah)*
nephew	**el sobrino?** *(ehl soh-'bree-noh)*
next of kin	**el pariente más cercano?** *(ehl pah-ree-'ehn-teh mahs sehr-'kah-noh)*
niece	**la sobrina?** *(lah soh-'bree-nah)*
sister	**la hermana?** *(lah ehr-'mah-nah)*
sister-in-law	**la cuñada?** *(lah koo-'nyah-dah)*
son	**el hijo?** *(ehl 'ee-hoh)*
son-in-law	**el yerno?** *(ehl 'yehr-noh)*
stepdaughter	**la hijastra?** *(lah ee-'hah-strah)*
stepfather	**el padrastro?** *(ehl pah-'drah-stroh)*
stepmother	**la madrastra?** *(lah mah-'drah-strah)*
stepson	**el hijastro?** *(ehl ee-'hah-stroh)*
uncle	**el tío?** *(ehl 'tee-oh)*
wife	**la esposa?** *(lah eh-'spoh-sah)*

➤ A few family words are a little confusing, so be careful:

parents   **los padres** (*lohs 'pah-drehs*)
relatives   **los parientes** (*lohs 'pah-ree-'ehn-tehs*)

WORD SEARCH 2

h	i	j	o	i	e	o	o	u
h	e	r	m	a	n	o	t	n
i	o	t	e	i	n	n	n	r
j	l	m	o	u	g	r	n	e
a	e	e	i	s	a	e	b	p
s	u	e	g	r	o	y	j	a
t	b	a	e	i	p	p	r	d
r	a	u	i	h	e	u	s	r
a	n	i	r	b	o	s	j	e

hermano
primo
nuera
padre
suegro
abuelo
esposo
sobrina
yerno
hijo
hijastra
nieto

In-laws and godparents, **padrinos** (*pah-'dree-nohs*), are considered important family members, and often assist in decisions over legal matters. The extended family may also include friends or neighbors who have lent their support to family members in the past.

Latino families respect the elderly. Older children, too, are given more responsibilities and are treated differently. When dealing with a large family, it is usually a good idea to find out who is in charge.

JUST A FEW MORE QUESTIONS
Solamente unas pocas preguntas más
(soh-lah-'mehn-teh 'oo-nahs 'poh-kahs preh-'goon-tahs mahs)

How's that field interview coming along? Look at all the comments you can make with **es** *(ehs)*:

Are you...?	**¿Es usted...?** *(ehs oo-'stehd)*
a legal resident	**un residente legal?** *(oon reh-see-'dehn-teh leh-'gahl)*
a U.S. citizen	**un ciudadano de los Estados Unidos?** *(oon see-oo-dah-'dah-noh deh lohs eh-'stah-dohs oo-'nee-dohs)*
a veteran	**un veterano?** *(oon veh-teh-'rah-noh)*
American	**americano?** *(ah-meh-ree-'kah-noh)*
Cuban	**cubano?** *(koo-'bah-noh)*
divorced	**divorciado?** *(dee-vohr-see-'ah-doh)*
married	**casado?** *(kah-'sah-doh)*
Mexican	**mejicano?** *(meh-hee-'kah-noh)*
Puerto Rican	**puertorriqueño?** *(pwehr-toh-rree-'keh-nyoh)*
separated	**separado?** *(seh-pah-'rah-doh)*
single	**soltero?** *(sohl-'teh-roh)*
Spanish	**español?** *(eh-spah-'nyohl)*
widowed	**viudo?** *(vee-'oo-doh)*

Watch closely as we continue with this simple pattern. Remember that **es** *(ehs)* can also mean **he is** or **she is.** In all of these cases, when you refer to women, the **o** ending must change to an **a:**

Are you...?	¿Es... *(ehs...)*
Buddhist	**budista?** *(boo-'dee-stah)*
Catholic	**católico?** *(kah-'toh-lee-koh)*
Christian	**cristiano?** *(kree-stee-'ah-noh)*
Jewish	**judío?** *(hoo-'dee-oh)*
Muslim	**musulmán?** *(moo-sool-'mahn)*
Protestant	**protestante?** *(proh-teh-'stahn-teh)*

Are you a member of...	¿Es miembro de... *(ehs mee-'ehm-broh deh...)*
a club	**un club?** *(oon kloob)*
a gang	**una pandilla?** *('oo-nah pahn-'dee-yah)*
an organization	**una organización?** *('oo-nah ohr-gah-nee-sah-see-'ohn)*

Keep going, but this time, check on their "current condition." Remember to use the word **está:**

You are...	Used está...
He, She is...	**El, Ella está...** *(oo-'stehd, ehl 'eh-yah eh-'stah)*
approved	**aprobado** *(ah-proh-'bah-doh)*
available	**disponible** *(dees-poh-'nee-bleh)*
busy	**ocupado** *(oh-koo-'pah-doh)*
free to go	**libre para irse** *('lee-breh 'pah-rah 'eer-seh)*
in line	**en la fila** *(ehn lah 'fee-lah)*
in our data	**en nuestros datos** *(ehn noo-'eh-strohs 'dah-tohs)*
in our files	**en nuestros archivos** *(ehn noo-'eh-strohs ahr-'chee-vohs)*
on the calendar	**en el calendario** *(ehn ehl kah-lehn-'dah-ree·oh)*
on the waiting list	**en la lista de espera** *(ehn lah 'lee-stah deh eh-'speh-rah)*
punctual	**puntual** *(poon-too-'ahl)*

INFORMACIÓN PRIVADA

➤ Combine all of your question words to collect the data you need. Write down a few of these phrases so that you won't forget. Good news! The answers to these questions are often brief and to the point:

Whose is it?	**¿De quién es?** *(deh kee-'ehn ehs)*
How many times?	**¿Cuántas veces?** *('kwahn-tahs 'veh-sehs)*
What's that?	**¿Qué es eso?** *(keh ehs 'eh-soh)*
Where are you from?	**¿De dónde es?** *(deh 'dohn-deh ehs)*
Where do you live?	**¿Dónde vive?** *('dohn-deh 'vee-veh)*
For what reason?	**¿Por qué razón?** *(pohr keh rah-'sohn)*
What kind?	**¿Qué clase?** *(keh 'klah-seh)*

➤ This next Spanish action form is helpful in any conversation, and we'll be talking more about it later. For the time being, simply do the best you can with these sample questions:

Have you been in jail?	**¿Ha estado en la cárcel?** *(ah eh-'stah-doh ehn lah 'kahr-sehl)*
Have you been drinking?	**¿Ha estado tomando alcohol?** *(ah eh-'stah-doh toh-'mahn-doh ahl-koh-'ohl)*
Have you been taking drugs?	**¿Ha estado tomando drogas?** *(ah eh-'stah-doh toh-'mahn-doh 'droh-gahs)*
Have you ever been arrested?	**¿Ha sido arrestado alguna vez?** *(ah 'see-doh ah-rreh-'stah-doh ahl-'goo-nah vehs)*

COUNTRIES AND NATIONALITIES
Países y nacionalidades *(pah-'ee-sehs ee nah-see-oh-nah-lee-'dah-dehs)*

la Argentina — argentino *(lah ahr-hehn-'tee-nah — ahr-hehn-'tee-noh)*
el Brasil — brasileño *(ehl brah-'seel—brah-see-'leh-nyoh)*
Bolivia — boliviano *(boh-'lee-vee-ah — boh-lee-vee-'ah-noh)*
Chile — chileno *('chee-leh — chee-'leh-noh)*
Colombia — colombiano *(koh-'lohm-bee-ah — koh-lohm-bee-'ah-noh)*
Costa Rica — costarriqueño, costarricense *('kohs-tah 'rree-kah — kohs-tah-rree-'keh-nyoh / kohs-tah-rree-'sehn-seh)*
Cuba — cubano *('koo-bah — koo-'bah-noh)*
el Ecuador — ecuatoriano *(ehl eh-kwah-'dohr — eh-kwah-toh-ree-'ah-noh)*
El Salvador — salvadoreño *(ehl sahl-vah-'dohr — sahl-vah-doh-'reh-nyoh)*
España — español *(ehs-'pah-nyah — ehs-pah-'nyohl)*
los Estados Unidos — estadounidense, norteamericano *(lohs ehs-'tah-dohs oo-'nee-dohs — ehs-tah-doh-oo-nee-'dehn-seh / nohr-teh-ah-meh-ree-'kah-noh)*
Guatemala — guatemalteco *(gwah-teh-'mah-lah — gwah-teh-mahl-'teh-koh)*
Honduras — hondureño *(ohn-'doo-rahs — ohn-doo-'reh-nyoh)*
México — mejicano *('meh-hee-koh — meh-hee-'kah-noh)*
Nicaragua — nicaragüense *(nee-kah-'rah-gwah — nee-kah-rah-'gwehn-seh)*
el Panamá — panameño *(ehl pah-nah-'mah — pah-nah-'meh-nyoh)*

el Paraguay — **paraguayo** *(ehl pah-rah-'gwah-ee — pah-rah-'gwah-yoh)*

el Perú — **peruano** *(ehl peh-'roo — peh-roo-'ah-noh)*

Puerto Rico — **puertorriqueño** *('pwehr-toh 'rree-koh — pwehr-toh-rree-'keh-nyoh)*

la República Dominicana — **dominicano** *(lah reh-'poo-blee-kah doh-mee-nee-'kah-nah — doh-mee-nee-'kah-noh)*

el Uruguay — **uruguayo** *(ehl oo-roo-'gwah-ee — oo-roo-'gwah-yoh)*

Venezuela — **venezolano** *(veh-neh-'sweh-lah — veh-neh-soh-'lah-noh)*

➤ Can you guess who these people are?

filipino *(fee-lee-'pee-noh)*

afroamericano *(ah-froh-ah-meh-ree-'kah-noh)*

italiano *(ee-tah-lee-'ah-noh)*

japonés *(hah-poh-'nehs)*

vietnamita *(vee-eht-nah-'mee-tah)*

WHAT DO YOU HAVE?

¿Qué tiene usted? *(keh tee-'eh-neh oo-'stehd)*

Here's a key word we learned earlier. You'll need it day to day in situations everywhere:

Do you have (the)...?	**¿Tiene...** *(tee-'eh-neh...)*
affidavit	**la declaración jurada?** *(lah deh-klah-rah-see-'ohn hoo-'rah-dah)*
appointment	**la cita?** *(lah 'see-tah)*
authorization	**la autorización?** *(lah ow-toh-ree-sah-see-'ohn)*
certificate	**el certificado?** *(ehl sehr-tee-fee-'kah-doh)*
complaint	**la queja?** *(lah 'keh-hah)*
copy	**la copia?** *(lah 'koh-pee·ah)*
criminal record	**los antecedentes penales?** *(lohs ahn-teh-seh-'dehn-tehs peh-'nah-lehs)*
diploma	**el diploma?** *(ehl dee-'ploh-mah)*
disability	**la incapacidad?** *(lah een-kah-pah-see-'dahd)*
document	**el documento?** *(ehl doh-koo-'mehn-toh)*
employment	**el empleo?** *(ehl ehm-'pleh-oh)*
form	**el formulario?** *(ehl fohr-moo-'lah-ree·oh)*
identification	**la identificación?** *(lah ee-dehn-tee-fee-kah-see-'ohn)*
identifying characteristic	**la seña identificadora?** *(lah 'seh-nyah ee-dehn-tee-fee-kah-'doh-rah)*
information	**la información?** *(lah een-fohr-mah-see-'ohn)*

64

insurance	**el seguro?** *(ehl seh-'goo-roh)*
medical problem	**el problema médico?** *(ehl proh-'bleh-mah 'meh-dee-koh)*
meeting	**la reunión?** *(lah reh-oo-nee-'ohn)*
military service	**el servicio militar?** *(ehl sehr-'vee-see·oh mee-lee-'tahr)*
original	**el original?** *(ehl oh-ree-hee-'nahl)*
passport	**el pasaporte?** *(ehl pah-sah-'pohr-teh)*
proof	**la prueba?** *(lah proo-'eh-bah)*
question	**la pregunta?** *(lah preh-'goon-tah)*
relative	**el familiar?** *(ehl fah-mee-lee-'ahr)*
scar	**la cicatriz?** *(lah see-kah-'trees)*
subpoena	**el comparendo?** *(ehl kohm-pah-'rehn-doh)*
tattoo	**el tatuaje?** *(ehl tah-too-'ah-heh)*
transportation	**el transporte?** *(ehl trahs-'pohr-teh)*
warrant	**la orden?** *(lah 'ohr-dehn)*

Sí. Mi nombre es Otto von Weimar, soy mejicano y budista. ¿Tiene algún problema?

INFORMACIÓN PRIVADA

➤ Not everyone is responsible, so get ready to respond to these excuses:

I lost it.	**Se me perdió.** *(seh meh pehr-dee-'oh)*
I forgot it.	**Se me olvidó.** *(seh meh ohl-vee-'doh)*
I don't know.	**No sé.** *(noh seh)*
I don't remember.	**No recuerdo.** *(noh reh-'kwehr-doh)*
I left it at home.	**Lo dejé en casa.** *(loh deh-'heh ehn 'kah-sah)*
I don't have it with me.	**No lo tengo conmigo.** *(noh loh 'tehn-goh kohn-'mee-goh)*
No one told me.	**Nadie me dijo.** *('nah-dee-eh meh 'dee-hoh)*

REPASO

A. Translate and then respond:

¿Es usted casado? *(ehs oo-'stehd kah-'sah-doh)*

_____

¿Es usted puntual? *(ehs oo-'stehd poon-too-'ahl)*

_____

¿Es usted americano? *(ehs oo-'stehd ah-meh-ree-'kah-noh)*

_____

¿Tiene empleo? *(tee-'eh-neh ehm-'pleh-oh)*

_____

¿Tiene anteojos? *(tee-'eh-neh ahn-teh-'oh-hohs)*

_____

¿Tiene tatuajes? *(tee-'eh-neh tah-too-'ah-hehs)*

_____

B. Write in the opposites:

hermano *(ehr-'mah-noh)*   hermana *(ehr-'mah-nah)*

madre *('mah-dreh)*   _____

abuelo *(ah-'bweh-loh)*   _____

yerno *('yehr-noh)*   _____

hija *('ee-hoh)*   _____

ANSWERS

A. Are you married?
Are you punctual?
Are you American?
Do you have employment?
Do you have glasses?
Do you have tattoos?

B. madre   padre
abuelo   abuela
yerno   nuera
hija   hijo

WHAT IS THE PROBLEM?

¿Cuál es el problema? *('kwahl ehs ehl proh-'bleh-mah)*

Let's be honest. It would be impossible to list every possible question and answer related to routine activities in law enforcement. Unique situations arise all the time. However, take a look at this next set of comments and concerns. They refer to cases where Spanish is needed in unusual circumstances.

I hear a strange noise	**Escucho un ruido raro** *(eh-'skoo-choh oon roo-'ee-doh 'rah-roh)*
There is a suspicious-looking person	**Hay una persona que se ve sospechosa** *('ah·ee 'oo-nah pehr-'soh-nah keh seh veh soh-speh-'choh-sah)*
A car hit our cat	**Un carro atropelló nuestro gato** *(oon 'kah-rroh 'ah-troh-peh-'yoh 'nweh-stroh 'gah-toh)*
The lights went out	**Se apagaron las luces** *(seh ah-pah-'gah-rohn lahs 'loo-sehs)*
We can't find our dog	**No podemos encontrar nuestro perro** *(noh poh-'deh-mohs ehn-kohn-'trahr 'nweh-stroh 'peh-rroh)*
It was a hit and run	**Un carro chocó y escapó** *(oon 'kah-rroh choh-'koh ee ehs-kah-'poh)*
I have no place to sleep	**No tengo ningún sitio para dormir** *(noh 'tehn-goh neen-'goon 'see-tee·oh 'pah-rah dohr-'meer)*
There's a loud party	**Hay una fiesta muy ruidosa** *('ah·ee 'oo-nah fee-'eh-stah 'moo·ee roo-ee-'doh-sah)*
My bike was stolen	**Me robaron la bicicleta** *(meh roh-'bah-rohn lah bee-see-'kleh-tah)*
I can't turn off the alarm	**No puedo apagar la alarma** *(noh 'pweh-doh ah-pah-'gahr lah ah-'lahr-mah)*
I left the keys in my car	**Dejé las llaves dentro del carro** *(deh-'heh lahs 'yah-vehs 'dehn-troh dehl 'kah-rroh)*

I saw (the)...	**Yo vi...** *(yoh vee)*
accident	**el accidente** *(ehl ahk-see-'dehn-teh)*
attack	**el ataque** *(ehl ah-'tah-keh)*
fight	**la pelea** *(lah peh-'leh-ah)*
incident	**el incidente** *(ehl een-see-'dehn-teh)*
robbery	**el robo** *(ehl 'roh-boh)*
shooting	**el disparo** *(ehl dees-'pah-roh)*

➤ When you feel that enough questions have been answered, inform the person that the interview is finished, and then let them know what you plan to do next:

I don't have any more questions	**No tengo más preguntas** *(noh 'tehn-goh mahs preh-'goon-tahs)*
We finished	**Terminamos** *(tehr-mee-'nah-mohs)*
Is there anything else?	**¿Hay algo más?** *('ah·ee 'ahl-goh mahs)*

I'm going to...	**Voy a...**
give you a warning	**darle una advertencia** *('dahr-leh 'oo-nah ahd-vehr-'tehn-see·ah)*
arrest you	**arrestarle** *(ah-rreh-'stahr-leh)*
make a call	**hacer una llamada** *(ah-'sehr 'oo-nah yah-'mah-dah)*
give you a ticket	**darle una boleta** *('dahr-leh 'oo-nah boh-'leh-tah)*
take care of it	**resolverlo** *(reh-sohl-'vehr-loh)*
notify the authorities	**notificar a las autoridades** *(noh-tee-fee-'kahr ah lahs ow-toh-ree-'dah-dehs)*
give you a ride	**llevarle en mi carro** *(yeh-'vahr-leh ehn mee 'kah-rroh)*
take you home	**llevarle a casa** *(yeh-'vahr-leh ah 'kah-sah)*
fingerprint you	**tomar sus huellas digitales** *(toh-'mahr soos 'weh-yahs dee-hee-'tah-lehs)*
take your picture	**tomar su foto** *(toh-'mahr soo 'foh-toh)*
check it out	**averiguarlo** *(ah-veh-ree-'gwahr-loh)*

➤ Use these whenever there are questions about a report:

Case Report	**El Reporte del Caso** *(ehl reh-'pohr-teh dehl 'kah-soh)*
What kind of report is it?	**¿Qué tipo de reporte es?** *(keh 'tee-poh deh reh-'pohr-teh ehs)*
Do you have the case number?	**¿Tiene usted el número de su caso?** *(tee-'eh-neh oos-'tehd ehl 'noo-meh-roh deh soo 'kah-soh)*
Would you like a copy of the report?	**¿Quisiera una copia del reporte?** *(kee-see-'eh-rah 'oo-nah 'koh-pee-ah dehl reh-'pohr-teh)*
We cannot release the report.	**No podemos darle el reporte.** *(noh poh-'deh-mohs 'dahr-leh ehl reh-'pohr-teh)*
You need to complete a request.	**Necesita llenar una solicitud.** *(neh-seh-'see-tah yeh-'nahr 'oo-nah soh-lee-see-'tood)*

There will be a $_____ charge.	**Le costará** _____ **dólares.** *(leh kohs-tah-'rah* _____ *'doh-lah-rehs)*
We will mail it to you.	**Se lo mandaremos por correo.** *(seh loh mahn-dah-'reh-mohs pohr koh-'rreh-oh)*
We must send it to _____ for approval.	**Tenemos que mandarlo a** _____ **para que lo aprueben.** *(teh-'neh-mohs keh mahn-'dahr-loh ah* _____ *'pah-rah keh loh ah-proo-'eh-behn)*
It takes at least three days.	**Tomará tres días por lo menos.** *(toh-mah-'rah trehs 'dee-ahs pohr loh 'meh-nohs)*
Include the case number, your name, date of birth, and the location and date of occurrence.	**Incluya el número del caso, su nombre, fecha de nacimiento, y el lugar y fecha del incidente.** *(een-'kloo-yah ehl 'noo-meh-roh dehl 'kah-soh, soo 'nohm-breh, 'feh-chah deh nah-see-mee-'ehn-toh ee ehl loo-'gahr ee 'feh-chah dehl een-see-'dehn-teh)*

ON THE PHONE
En el teléfono *(ehn ehl teh-'leh-foh-noh)*

Working at the station, office, or department headquarters isn't quite the same as handling calls out in the field. There are specialized commands, questions, and expressions that typically apply to over-the-counter personnel. To begin with, set aside the phrases you'll need to handle phone calls or **las llamadas** *(lahs yah-'mah-dahs)* in Spanish. These are tough, since you can't use hand-signals or look at their face:

Hello!	**¡Hola!** *('oh-lah)* or **¡Bueno!** *('bweh-noh)*
Can I help you?	**¿Puedo ayudarle?** *('pweh-doh ah-yoo-'dahr-leh)*
What's your name and number?	**¿Cuál es su nombre y número de teléfono?** *(kwahl ehs soo 'nohm-breh ee 'noo-meh-roh deh teh-'leh-foh-noh)*
Why are you calling?	**¿Por qué está llamando?** *(pohr keh eh-'stah yah-'mahn-doh)*
What's the problem?	**¿Cuál es el problema?** *('kwahl ehs ehl proh-'bleh-mah)*
From what phone are you calling?	**¿De qué teléfono está llamando?** *(deh keh teh-'leh-foh-noh eh-'stah yah-'mahn-doh)*
Do you want the police to contact you?	**¿Quiere que la policía se comunique con usted?** *(kee-'eh-reh keh lah poh-lee-'see-ah seh koh-moo-'nee-keh kohn oo-'stehd)*

Is there someone there who speaks English?	**¿Hay alguien allí que habla inglés?** *('ah·ee 'ahl-gee·ehn ah-'yee keh 'ah-blah een-'glehs)*
I'll call back later	**Llamaré más tarde** *(yah-mah-'reh mahs 'tahr-deh)*
Please don't hang up	**No cuelgue, por favor** *(noh 'kwehl-geh pohr fah-'vohr)*
Wait a moment, please	**Espere un momento, por favor** *(eh-'speh-reh oon moh-'mehn-toh pohr fah-'vohr)*
I am going to transfer you	**Le voy a transferir** *(leh 'voh·ee ah trahns-feh-'reer)*
This is _____ from the City of _____	**Este es _____ de la cuidad de _____** *('eh-steh ehs _____ deh lah see-oo-'dahd deh _____)*
More slowly, please	**Más despacio, por favor** *(mahs deh-'spah-see·oh pohr fah-'vohr)*
Am I speaking clearly?	**¿Estoy hablando claramente?** *(eh-'stoh-ee ah-'blahn-doh klah-rah-'mehn-teh)*
Answer as briefly as possible	**Conteste lo más breve posible** *(kohn-'teh-steh loh mahs 'breh-veh poh-'see-bleh)*
You need to speak with _____	**Necesita hablar con _____** *(neh-seh-'see-tah ah-'blahr kohn _____)*
I need to speak with _____	**Necesito hablar con _____** *(neh-seh-'see-toh ah-'blahr kohn _____)*
May I leave a message?	**¿Puedo dejar un mensaje?** *('pweh-doh deh-'hahr oon mehn-'sah-heh)*
When will they return?	**¿Cuándo regresan?** *('kwahn-doh reh-'greh-sahn)*
I am calling about the _____	**Estoy llamando acerca de _____** *(eh-'stoh-ee yah-'mahn-doh ah-'sehr-kah deh _____)*
Keep calm	**Mantega la calma** *(mahn-'tehn-gah lah 'kahl-mah)*
Tell me what happened—slowly	**Dígame qué pasó—despacio** *('dee-gah-meh keh pah-'soh deh-'spah-se·oh)*
Please call me at _____	**Favor de llamarme al número _____** *(fah-'vohr deh yah-'mahr-meh ahl 'noo-meh-roh _____)*
Do they have a cell phone?	**¿Tienen un teléfono celular?** *(tee-'eh-nehn oon teh-'leh-foh-noh seh-loo-'lahr)*

Now tell the person who they should be calling:

Call...	Llame... *('yah-meh...)*
911	**al nueve-uno-uno** *(ahl noo-'eh-veh 'oo-noh 'oo-noh)*
the fire department	**a los bomberos** *(ah lohs bohm-'beh-rohs)*
the ambulance	**a la ambulancia** *(ah lah ahm-boo-'lahn-see·ah)*
a neighbor	**a un vecino** *(ah oon veh-'see-noh)*
a family member	**a un familiar** *(ah oon fah-mee-lee-'ahr)*
your family doctor	**a su doctor familiar** *(ah soo dohk-'tohr fah-mee-lee-'ahr)*
your work	**a su trabajo** *(ah soo trah-'bah-hoh)*
long distance	**a larga distancia** *(ah 'lahr-gah dee-'stahn-see·ah)*
the phone company	**a la compañía de teléfonos** *(ah lah kohm-pah-'nyee-ah deh teh-'leh-foh-nohs)*
the operator	**a la operadora** *(ah lah oh-peh-rah-'doh-rah)*
the main line	**a la línea principal** *(ah lah 'lee-neh-ah preen-see-'pahl)*
for information	**para la información** *('pah-rah lah een-fohr-mah-see-'ohn)*
the other number	**al otro número** *(ahl 'oh-troh 'noo-meh-roh)*
the voice mail	**a la grabadora** *(ah lah grah-bah-'doh-rah)*
the extension	**a la extensión** *(ah lah ehks-tehn-see-'ohn)*

INFORMACIÓN PRIVADA

➤ Keep going! The telephone one-liners never end:

Press the number again!	**¡Oprima el número otra vez!** *(oh-'pree-mah ehl 'noo-meh-roh 'oh-trah vehs)*
Don't play with the telephone!	**¡No juegue con el teléfono!** *(noh hoo-'eh-geh kohn ehl teh-'leh-foh-noh)*
Use the phone book!	**¡Use la guía telefónica!** *('oo-seh lah 'gee-ah teh-leh-'foh-nee-kah)*
We are recording this phone call!	**¡Estamos grabando esta llamada!** *(eh-'stah-mohs grah-'bahn-doh 'eh-stah yah-'mah-dah)*

Phone courtesy is important. It's easy to cut people off, hang up, or release your frustrations on those who don't speak English fluently on the phone. Try to be patient, and avoid raising your voice. Sometimes all it takes are a few key expressions to get your message across. Consider writing a "cheat-sheet" of Spanish phrases that can be posted near your telephone. They'll never know that you are reading!

COMPUTER VOCABULARY
El vocabulario de computación
(ehl voh-kah-boo-'lah-ree-oh deh kohm-poo-tah-see-'ohn)

Computer vocabulary is often the same as in English (**el CD-ROM**, **el DVD**, **la internet**, etc.). However, these other words may also be useful:

application	**la aplicación** *(lah ah-plee-kah-see-'ohn)*
attachment	**el adjunto** *(ehl ahd-'hoon-toh)*
browser	**el navegador** *(ehl nah-veh-gah-'dohr)*
cable	**el cable** *(ehl 'kah-bleh)*
computer file	**el fichero** *(ehl fee-'cheh-roh)*
connection	**la conexión** *(lah koh-nehk-see-'ohn)*
database	**la base de datos** *(lah 'bah-seh deh 'dah-tohs)*
disc	**el disco** *(ehl 'dees-koh)*
drive	**la disquetera** *(lah dees-keh-'teh-rah)*
e-mail	**el correo electrónico** *(ehl koh-'rreh-oh eh-lehk-'troh-nee-koh)*
hard drive	**el disco duro** *(ehl 'dees-koh 'doo-roh)*
home page	**la página inicial** *(lah 'pah-hee-nah ee-nee-see-'ahl)*
keyboard	**el teclado** *(ehl teh-'klah-doh)*
mailbox	**el buzón** *(ehl boo-'sohn)*
menu	**el menú** *(ehl meh-'noo)*
message	**el mensaje** *(ehl mehn-'sah-heh)*
monitor	**el monitor** *(ehl moh-nee-'tohr)*
mouse	**el ratón** *(ehl rah-'tohn)*
password	**la contraseña** *(lah kohn-trah-'seh-nyah)*
program	**el programa** *(ehl proh-'grah-mah)*
screen	**la pantalla** *(lah pahn-'tah-yah)*
search engine	**el buscador** *(ehl boos-kah-'dohr)*
server	**el servidor** *(ehl sehr-vee-'dohr)*
trash	**la basura** *(lah bah-'soo-rah)*
web site	**el sitio web** *(ehl 'see-tee-oh web)*

MORE CALLS FOR HELP!

¡Más llamadas para ayuda! *(mahs yah-'mah-dahs 'pah-rah ah-'yoo-dah)*

How many times have you heard about these concerns? Share this list of common occurrences with anyone who receives emergency calls:

There is...	**Hay...** *('ah·ee...)*
a baby in a pool	**un bebé en la piscina** *(oon beh-'beh ehn lah pee-'see-nah)*
a bomb threat	**una amenaza de una bomba** *('oo-nah ah-meh-'nah-sah deh 'oo-nah 'bohm-bah)*
a stuck elevator	**un ascensor detenido** *(oon ah-sehn-'sohr deh-teh-'nee-doh)*
a broken fire hydrant	**una llave de incendios rota** *('oo-nah 'yah-veh deh een-'sehn-dee-ohs 'roh-tah)*
a broken street light	**una luz de calle rota** *('oo-nah loos deh 'kah-yeh 'roh-tah)*
a car race	**una carrera de carros** *('oo-nah kah-'rreh-rah deh 'kah-rrohs)*
a crowd	**una muchedumbre** *('oo-nah moo-cheh-'doom-breh)*
a dead body	**un cadáver** *(oon kah-'dah-vehr)*
a family dispute	**una disputa de familia** *('oo-nah des-'spoo-tah deh fah-'mee-lee-ah)*
a fire	**un incendio** *(oon een-'sehn-dee-oh)*
a gas leak	**una fuga de gas** *('oo-nah 'foo-gah deh gahs)*
a jumper	**alguien que va a saltar del edificio** *('ahl-gee·ehn keh vah ah sahl-'tahr dehl eh-dee-'fee-see·oh)*
a lost child	**un niño perdido** *(oon 'nee-nyoh pehr-'dee-doh)*
a parked car	**un carro estacionado** *(oon 'kah-rroh eh-stah-see·oh-'nah-doh)*
a suspicious person in the park	**un sospechoso en el parque** *(oon soh-speh-'choh-soh ehn ehl 'pahr-keh)*
a poisonous chemical	**un producto químico venenoso** *(oon proh-'dook-toh 'kee-mee-koh veh-neh-'noh-soh)*
a strange package	**un paquete extraño** *(oon pah-'keh-teh eh-'strah-nyoh)*
a wild animal	**un animal salvaje** *(oon ah-nee-'mahl sahl-'vah-heh)*
an abandoned building	**un edificio abandonado** *(oon eh-dee-'fee-see-oh ah-bahn-doh-'nah-doh)*
an explosion	**una explosión** *('oo-nah ehks-ploh-see-'ohn)*

| an obscene phone call | **una llamada obscena** *('oo-nah yah-'mah-dah ohb-'seh-nah)* |
| someone selling drugs | **alguien vendiendo drogas** *('ahl-gee·ehn vehn-dee-'ehn-doh 'droh-gahs)* |

YOU HAVE TO PAY
Tiene que pagar *(tee-'eh-neh keh pah-'gahr)*

Business matters also require your special attention. Place this list near the cash register:

Bring (the)...	**Traiga...** *('trah·ee-gah...)*
You need (the)...	**Necesita...** *(neh-seh-'see-tah...)*
bank account	**la cuenta del banco** *(lah 'kwehn-tah dehl 'bahn-koh)*
bill	**la cuenta** *(lah 'kwehn-tah)*
cash	**dinero al contado** *(dee-'neh-roh ahl kohn-'tah-doh)*
change	**el cambio** *(ehl 'kahm-bee·oh)*
check	**el cheque** *(ehl 'cheh-keh)*
coin	**la moneda** *(lah moh-'neh-dah)*
coupon	**el cupón** *(ehl koo-'pohn)*
credit card	**la tarjeta de crédito** *(lah tahr-'heh-tah deh 'kreh-dee-toh)*
currency bill	**el billete** *(ehl bee-'yeh-teh)*
invoice	**la factura** *(lah fahk-'too-rah)*
money	**el dinero** *(ehl dee-'neh-roh)*
order	**el orden** *(ehl 'ohr-dehn)*
payment	**el pago** *(ehl 'pah-goh)*
receipt	**el recibo** *(ehl reh-'see-boh)*
ticket	**el boleto** *(ehl boh-'leh-toh)*
It's (the)...	**Es...** *(ehs...)*
bargain	**la ganga** *(lah 'gahn-gah)*
cost	**el costo** *(ehl 'koh-stoh)*
discount	**el descuento** *(ehl dehs-'kwehn-toh)*
fee	**el honorario** *(ehl oh-noh-'rah-ree·oh)*
fine	**la multa** *(lah 'mool-tah)*
offer	**la oferta** *(lah oh-'fehr-tah)*
price	**el precio** *(ehl 'preh-see·oh)*
sale	**la venta** *(lah 'vehn-tah)*

INFORMACIÓN PRIVADA

➤ Mutter the phrases that you use all the time:

Is that all?	**¿Es todo?** *(ehs 'toh-doh)*
Is that free?	**¿Es gratis?** *(ehs 'grah-tees)*
Is that included?	**¿Está incluído?** *(eh-'stah een-kloo-'ee-doh)*
Is that enough?	**¿Es bastante?** *(ehs bah-'stahn-teh)*

I'm sorry for the...	**Lo siento por...** *(loh see-'ehn-toh pohr...)*
delay	**la tardanza** *(lah tahr-'dahn-sah)*
misunderstanding	**el malentendido** *(ehl mahl-ehn-tehn-'dee-doh)*
error	**el error** *(ehl eh-'rrohr)*
inconvenience	**la inconveniencia** *(lah een-kohn-veh-nee-'ehn-see·ah)*

➤ Specify your requests by adding words to the phrases below. See the sample sentences. These also work well as parts of written notes or messages:

Make sure that...	**Asegúrese que...** *(ah-seh-'goo-reh-seh keh...)*	**Asegúrese que su nombre está en el papel** *(ah-seh-'goo-reh-seh keh soo 'nohm-breh eh-'stah ehn ehl pah-'pehl)*
I told you that...	**Le dije que...** *(leh 'dee-heh keh...)*	**Le dije que no puede pagar aquí** *(leh 'dee-heh keh noh 'pweh-dehpah-'gahr ah-'kee)*

75

| Remember that... | **Recuerde que...** *(reh'kwehr-deh keh...)* | **Recuerde que mañana es el último día.** *(reh-'kwehr-deh keh mah-'nyah-nay ehs ehl 'ool-tee-moh 'dee-ah)* |

TEMAS CULTURALES

Does everyone understand U.S. currency? New immigrants could get confused about our bills and coins:

cent	**el centavo** *(ehl sehn-'tah-voh)*
dime	**diez centavos** *(dee-'ehs sehn-'tah-vohs)*
dollar	**el dólar** *(ehl 'doh-lahr)*
nickel	**cinco centavos** *('seen-koh sehn-'tah-vohs)*
penny	**un centavo** *(oon sehn-'tah-voh)*
quarter	**veinticinco centavos** *(veh·een-tee-'seen-koh sehn-'tah-vohs)*

WHAT DO YOU NEED?
¿Qué necesita? *(keh neh-seh-'see-tah)*

Serving people involves finding out the needs of others. To do so in Spanish, use the following expression of courtesy. It works great in any customer service situation:

Would you like...?	**¿Quisiera...** *(kee-see-'eh-rah...)*
the address	**la dirección?** *(lah dee-rehk-see-'ohn)*
help	**ayuda?** *(ah-'yoo-dah)*
the number	**el número?** *(ehl 'noo-meh-roh)*
to come back tomorrow	**regresar mañana?** *(reh-greh-'sahr mah-'nyah-nah)*
to fill out the form	**llenar el formulario?** *(yeh-'nahr ehl fohr-moo-'lah-ree·oh)*
to pay the fine now	**pagar la multa ahora?** *(pah-'gahr lah 'mool-tah ah-'oh-rah)*
to read the instructions	**leer las instrucciones?** *(leh-'ehr lahs een-strook-see-'oh-nehs)*
to sign the document	**firmar el documento?** *(feer-'mahr ehl doh-koo-'mehn-toh)*

76

to speak with an interpreter	**hablar con un intérprete?** *(ah-'blahr kohn oon een-'tehr-preh-teh)*
to use the bathroom	**usar el baño?** *(oo-'sahr ehl 'bah-nyoh)*
to write the address	**escribir la dirección?** *(eh-skree-'beer lah dee-rehk-see-'ohn)*
I need (the)...	**Necesito...** *(neh-seh-'see-toh...)*
You need (the)...	**Necesita...** *(neh-seh-'see-tah...)*
approval	**la aprobación** *(lah ah-proh-bah-see-'ohn)*
assistance	**la ayuda** *(lah ah-'yoo-dah)*
birth certificate	**el certificado de nacimiento** *(ehl sehr-tee-fee-'kah-doh deh nah-see-mee-'ehn-toh)*
claim	**la petición** *(lah peh-tee-see-'ohn)*
copy	**la copia** *(lah 'koh-pee·ah)*
death certificate	**la partida de defunción** *(lah pahr-tee-dah deh deh-foon-see-'ohn)*
education	**la educación** *(lah eh-doo-kah-see-'ohn)*
example	**el ejemplo** *(ehl eh-'hehm-ploh)*
explanation	**la explicación** *(lah ehk-splee-kah-see-'ohn)*
form	**el formulario** *(ehl fohr-moo-'lah-ree·oh)*
inquiry	**la interrogación** *(lah een-teh-rroh-gah-see-'ohn)*
instruction	**la instrucción** *(lah een-strook-see-'ohn)*
interview	**la entrevista** *(lah ehn-treh-'vee-stah)*
investigation	**la investigación** *(lah een-veh-stee-gah-see-'ohn)*
legal service	**el servicio legal** *(ehl sehr-'vee-see·oh leh-'gahl)*
marriage certificate	**el certificado de matrimonio** *(ehl sehr-tee-fee-'kah-doh deh mah-tree-'moh-nee·oh)*
procedure	**el procedimiento** *(ehl proh-seh-dee-mee-'ehn-toh)*
permit	**el permiso** *(ehl pehr-'mee-soh)*
request	**la petición** *(lah peh-tee-see-'ohn)*
resource	**el recurso** *(ehl reh-'koor-soh)*
schedule	**el horario** *(ehl oh-'rah-ree·oh)*
training	**el entrenamiento** *(ehl ehn-treh-nah-mee-'ehn-toh)*

➤ How much do you really know about your job?

It's my...	Es mi... *(ehs mee...)*
assignment	**tarea** *(tah-'reh-ah)*
batallion	**batallón** *(bah-tah-'yohn)*
department	**departamento** *(deh-pahr-tah-'mehn-toh)*
division	**división** *(dee-vee-see-'ohn)*
duty	**obligación** *(oh-blee-gah-see-'ohn)*
job	**trabajo** *(trah-'bah-hoh)*
mission	**misión** *(mee-see-'ohn)*
post	**puesto** *('pweh-stoh)*
precinct	**distrito** *(dee-'stree-toh)*
sector	**sector** *(sehk-'tohr)*
responsibility	**responsabilidad** *(reh-spohn-sah-bee-lee-'dahd)*
route	**recorrido** *(reh-koh-'rree-doh)*

DO YOU KNOW?
¿Sabe? *('sah-beh)*

When you don't understand the language, it can be quite difficult to figure out what a person is trying to say. Sometimes, it's necessary to go on the offensive and find out exactly how much a Spanish-speaker may already know. Stick with the pattern below:

Do you know...	¿Sabe... *('sah-beh...)*
how to spell it	**cómo se deletrea?** *('koh-moh seh deh-leh-'treh-ah)*
how to read and write	**leer y escribir?** *(leh-'ehr ee eh-skree-'beer)*
how to speak English	**hablar inglés?** *(ah-'blahr eeng-'lehs)*
This paper explains...	**Este papel explica...** *('eh-steh pah-'pehl ehk-'splee-kah...)*
what this is about	**de qué se trata esto** *(deh keh seh 'trah-tah 'eh-stoh)*
how to do it	**cómo hacerlo** *('koh-moh ah-'sehr-loh)*
what to do	**qué hacer** *(keh ah-'sehr)*

who it is	**quién es** (kee-'ehn ehs)
when it is	**cuándo es** ('kwahn-doh ehs)
where it is	**dónde está** ('dohn-deh eh-'stah)
which one it is	**cuál es** (kwahl ehs)
whose it is	**de quién es** (deh kee-'ehn ehs)
how much it is	**cuánto es** ('kwahn-toh ehs)
why	**por qué** (pohr keh)
how many	**cuántos** ('kwahn-tohs)

INFORMACIÓN PRIVADA

➤ In Spanish, there are two primary ways to say "to know."

"To know something" requires the verb **saber** (sah-'behr), while "to know someone" requires the verb **conocer** (koh-noh-'sehr). Instead of working on all the conjugated forms of these new verbs, why not put them to practical use. Next time you need "to know," pull a line from the sentences below:

I don't know	**No sé** (noh seh)
I don't know him	**No lo conozco** (noh loh koh-'noh-koh)
Do you know English?	**¿Sabe usted inglés?** ('sah-beh oo-'stehd een-'glehs)
Do you know her?	**¿La conoce a ella?** (lah koh-'noh-seh ah 'eh-yah)
I didn't know it	**No lo sabía** (noh loh sah-'bee-ah)
I didn't know him	**No lo conocía a él** (noh loh koh-noh-'see-ah ah 'ehl)

AT THE STATION

En la estación *(ehn lah eh-stah-see-'ohn)*

Does everyone know their way around the building? Agencies worldwide need to learn the following words:

Where is (the)...	**¿Dónde está...** *('dohn-deh eh-'stah...)*
agency	**la agencia?** *(lah ah-'hehn-see·ah)*
bathroom	**el baño?** *(ehl 'bah-nyoh)*
cafeteria	**la cafetería?** *(lah kah-feh-teh-'ree-ah)*
counter	**el mostrador?** *(ehl moh-strah-'dohr)*
clerk's window	**la ventanilla?** *(lah vehn-tah-'nee-yah)*
department	**el departamento?** *(ehl deh-pahr-tah-'mehn-toh)*
double door	**la puerta doble?** *(lah 'pwehr-tah 'doh-bleh)*
entrance	**la entrada?** *(lah ehn-'trah-dah)*
elevator	**el ascensor?** *(ehl ah-sehn-'sohr)*
exit	**la salida?** *(lah sah-'lee-dah)*
floor	**el piso?** *(ehl 'pee-soh)*
hallway	**el pasillo?** *(ehl pah-'see-yoh)*
lobby	**el salón?** *(ehl sah-'lohn)*
office	**la oficina?** *(lah oh-fee-'see-nah)*
parking lot	**el estacionamiento?** *(ehl eh-stah-see·oh-nah-mee-'ehn-toh)*
public telephone	**el teléfono público?** *(ehl teh-'leh-foh-noh 'poo-blee-koh)*
room	**el cuarto?** *(ehl 'kwahr-toh)*
stairway	**la escalera?** *(lah eh-skah-'leh-rah)*
wall	**la pared?** *(lah pah-'rehd)*
water fountain	**la fuente de agua?** *(lah 'fwehn-teh deh 'ah-gwah)*

INFORMACIÓN PRIVADA

➤ Become familiar with each part of the agency:

interrogating room	**el cuarto para interrogatorios** *(ehl 'kwahr-toh 'pah-rah een-teh-rroh-gah-'toh-ree·ohs)*
headquarters	**el cuartel general** *(ehl kwahr-'tehl heh-neh-'rahl)*
crime laboratory	**el laboratorio criminológico** *(ehl lah-boh-rah-'toh-ree·oh kree-mee-noh-'loh-hee-koh)*

80

➤ Are you using your location words from Chapter One?

in front of	**en frente de** *(ehn 'frehn-teh deh)*	<u>**Está en frente de la oficina**</u> *(eh-'stah ehn 'frehn-teh deh lah oh-fee-'see-nah)*
behind	**detrás de** *(deh-'trahs deh)*	<u>**Está detrás de la cafetería**</u> *(eh-'stah deh-'trahs deh lah kah-feh-teh-'ree-ah)*
to the left	**a la izquierda** *(ah lah ees-kee-'ehr-dah)*	_____
to the right	**a la derecha** *(ah lah deh-'reh-chah)*	_____
next to	**al lado de** *(ahl 'lah-doh deh)*	_____
upstairs	**arriba** *(ah-'rree-bah)*	_____
downstairs	**abajo** *(ah-'bah-hoh)*	_____

THE COMPLAINTS
Las quejas *(lahs 'keh-huhs)*

No doubt you'll get a few complaints from civilians about legal procedures, or perhaps the behavior of fellow law enforcement officials. Respond professionally and with tact:

It's our responsibility	**Es nuestra responsabilidad** *(ehs 'nweh-strah reh-spohn-sah-bee-lee-'dahd)*
We are very sorry	**Lo sentimos mucho** *(loh sehn-'tee-mohs 'moo-choh)*
We will do everything possible	**Haremos todo lo posible** *(ah-'reh-mohs 'toh-doh loh poh-'see-bleh)*
We're going to check it out	**Vamos a averiguarlo** *('vah-mohs ah ah-veh-ree-'gwahr-loh)*
It's going to be corrected	**Va a ser corregido** *(vah ah sehr koh-rreh-'hee-doh)*
It won't happen again	**No volverá a pasar** *(noh vohl-veh-'rah ah pah-'sahr)*
It's our obligation	**Es nuestra obligación** *(ehs 'nweh-strah oh-blee-gah-see-'ohn)*
The supervisors will be notified	**Se notificará a los supervisores** *(seh noh-tee-fee-kah-'rah ah lohs soo-pehr-vee-'soh-rehs)*
Write down everything that happened	**Escriba todo lo que pasó** *(eh-'skree-bah 'toh-doh loh keh pah-'soh)*
We want to resolve it	**Queremos resolverlo** *(keh-'reh-mohs reh-sohl-'vehr-loh)*
We will notify you soon	**Le notificaremos pronto** *(leh noh-tee-fee-kah-'reh-mohs 'prohn-toh)*

What are they complaining about?	¿De qué se quejan? *(deh keh seh 'keh-hahn)*
The officer...	El oficial... *(ehl oh-fee-see-'ahl...)*
arrived late	llegó tarde *('yeh-goh 'tahr-deh)*
was not polite	no fue cortés *(noh fweh kohr-'tehs)*
was violent	era violento *('eh-rah vee·oh-'lehn-toh)*
damaged my property	hizo daño a mi propiedad *('ee-soh 'dah-nyoh ah mee proh-pee-eh-'dahd)*

REPASO

A. Use all your key question words inside the office or out. These words aren't new, so go ahead and translate:

¿Quisiera un formulario? *(kee-see-'eh-rah oon fohr-moo-'lah-ree·oh)*

_____

¿Tiene usted carro? *(tee-'eh-neh oo-'stehd 'kah-rroh)*

_____

¿Necesita usar el teléfono? *(neh-seh-'see-tah oo-'sahr ehl teh-'leh-foh-noh)*

_____

B. Match these translations:

change	el dinero *(ehl dee-'neh-roh)*
money	el cambio *(ehl 'kahm-bee·oh)*
account	al contado *(ahl kohn-'tah-doh)*
fine	la cuenta *(lah 'kwehn-tah)*
cash	la multa *(lah 'mool-tah)*

C. In Spanish,

...name three common problems that the public reports to the police.

_____ _____ _____

...name four things most people ask for when they visit a police station.

_____ _____ _____

...name three one-liners that you need for answering phone calls.

_____ _____ _____

...name four parts of a typical government building.

_____ _____ _____ _____

...name three standard comments in response to a citizen's complaint.

_____ _____ _____ _____

ANSWERS

THE DEPARTMENTS, UNITS, TEAMS, AND DETAILS
Los departamentos, las unidades, los equipos, los destacamentos
(lohs deh-pahr-tah-'mehn tohs, lahs oo-nee-'dah-dehs, lohs eh-'kee-pohs, lohs deh-stah-kah-'mehn-tohs)

These are only a few of the countless assignments linked to law enforcement in our cities. Go ahead and direct folks to the appropriate authorities:

bombs	**las bombas** _(lahs 'bohm-bahs)_
canine	**los perros de la policía** _(lohs 'peh-rrohs deh lah poh-lee-'see-ah)_
community relations	**las relaciones con la comunidad** _(lahs reh-lah-see-'oh-nehs kohn lah koh-moo-nee-'dahd)_
coroner	**el médico legista** _(ehl 'meh-dee-koh leh-'hee-stah)_
crime prevention	**la prevención del crimen** _(lah pre-vehn-see-'ohn dehl 'kree-mehn)_
data processing	**el procesamiento de datos** _(ehl proh-seh-sah-mee-'ehn-toh deh 'dah-tohs)_
drugs	**las drogas** _(lahs 'droh-gahs)_
forensic medicine	**la medicina forense** _(lah meh-dee-'see-nah foh-'rehn-seh)_
gangs	**las pandillas** _(lahs pahn-'dee-yahs)_
harbor patrol	**la patrulla de los puertos** _(lah pah-'troo-yah deh lohs 'pwehr-tohs)_
homeland security	**la seguridad de la patria** _(lah seh-goo-ree-'dahd deh lah 'pah-tree-ah)_
homicide	**los homicidios** _(lohs oh-mee-'see-dee·ohs)_

hostage negotiations	**las negociaciones sobre rehenes** *(lahs neh-goh-see-ah-see-'oh-nehs 'soh-breh reh-'eh-nehs)*
intelligence	**la pesquisa** *(lah 'pehs-kee-sah)*
internal affairs	**las investigaciones internas** *(lahs een-veh-stee-gah-see-'oh-nehs een-'tehr-nahs)*
investigations	**las investigaciones** *(lahs een-veh-stee-gah-see-'oh-nehs)*
juveniles	**los menores de edad** *(lohs meh-'noh-rehs deh eh-'dahd)*
mounted police	**la policía montada** *(lah poh-lee-'see-ah mohn-'tah-dah)*
patrol	**la patrulla** *(lah pah-'troo-yah)*
police pilots	**los pilotos policiales** *(lohs pee-'loh-tohs poh-lee-see-'ah-lehs)*
sex crimes	**los crímenes sexuales** *(lohs 'kree-meh-nehs sehk-soo-'ah-lehs)*
traffic	**el tráfico** *(ehl 'trah-fee-koh)*
vice police	**la policía contra el vicio** *(lah poh-lee-'see-ah 'kohn-trah ehl 'vee-see·oh)*

COUNTY, STATE, AND FEDERAL AGENCIES, AND THEIR PEOPLE
Las agencias del condado, del estado, del gobierno federal y su gente
(lahs ah-'hehn-see·ahs dehl kohn-'dah-doh, dehl eh-'stah-doh, dehl goh-bee-'ehr-noh feh-deh-'rahl ee suh 'hehn-teh)

New titles appear regularly, so this is only a partial list:

| Highway patrol | **La patrulla de carreteras** *(lah pah-'troo-yah deh kah-rreh-'teh-rahs)* |

Fish and Game	**La pesca y la caza** *(lah 'pehs-kah ee lah 'kah-sah)*
Deputy sheriff	**El alguacil diputado** *(ehl ahl-gwah-'seel dee-poo-'tah-doh)*
State police officer	**El oficial de la policía estatal** *(ehl oh-fee-see-'ahl deh lah poh-lee-'see-ah eh-stah-'tahl)*
Federal protective officer	**El oficial de la policía federal estatal** *(ehl oh-fee-see-'ahl deh lah poh-lee-'see-ah feh-deh-'rahl eh-stah-'tahl)*
Border patrol	**La patrulla fronteriza** *(lah pah-'troo-yah frohn-teh-'ree-sah)*
Special agent	**El agente especial** *(ehl ah-'hehn-teh eh-speh-see-'ahl)*
Customs agent	**El agente de aduana** *(ehl ah-'hehn-teh deh ah-'dwah-nah)*
Secret Service agent	**El agente del Servicio Secreto** *(ehl ah-'hehn-teh dehl sehr-'vee-see·oh seh-'kreh-toh)*
ATF	**El Departamento de Alcohol, Tabaco y Armas de Fuego** *(ehl deh-pahr-tah-'mehn-toh deh ahl-koh-'ohl, tah-'bah-koh ee 'ahr-mahs deh 'fweh-goh)*
FBI	**El Departmento Federal de Investigación** *(ehl deh-pahr-tah-'mehn-toh feh-deh-'rahl deh een-veh-stee-gah-see-'ohn)*
CIA	**La Agencia Central de Inteligencia** *(lah ah-'hehn-see·ah cehn-'trahl deh een-teh-lee-'hehn-see·ah)*
Park and Ranger Service	**El Servicio Nacional de Parques** *(ehl sehr-'vee-see·oh nah-see·oh-'nah deh 'pahr-kehs)*
State troopers	**La policía estatal motorizada** *(lah poh-lee-'see-ah eh-stah-'tahl moh-toh-ree-'sah-dah)*
U.S. marshal	**El alguacil de los EEUU** *(ehl ahl-gwah-'seel deh lohs eh-'stah-dohs oo-'nee-dohs)*
DEA	**El Departamento Federal Antidrogas** *(ehl deh-pahr-tah-'mehn-toh feh-deh-'rahl ahn-tee-'droh-gahs)*
IRS	**El Departamento de Recaudación de Impuestos** *(ehl deh-pahr-tah-'mehn-toh deh reh-kow-dah-see-'ohn deh eem-'pweh-stohs)*
Immigration Department	**El Departamento de Inmigración** *(ehl deh-pohr-tah-'mehn-toh deh een-mee-grah-see-'ohn)*

➤ There's always room for more vocabulary. Make comments about your duties at the desk:

It's...	**Es...** *(ehs...)*
accurate	**correcto** *(koh-'rrehk-toh)*
beneficial	**beneficioso** *(beh-neh-fee-see-'oh-soh)*
civic matter	**asunto cívico** *(ah-'soon-toh 'see-vee-koh)*
complete	**completo** *(kohm-'pleh-toh)*
evidence	**evidencia** *(eh-vee-'dehn-see·ah)*
important	**importante** *(eem-pohr-'tahn-teh)*
legal	**legal** *(leh-'gahl)*
necessary	**necesario** *(neh-seh-'sah-ree·oh)*
overdue	**sobrevencido** *(soh-breh-vehn-'see-doh)*
paperwork	**papeleo** *(pah-peh-'leh-oh)*
routine	**rutina** *(roo-'tee-nah)*
urgent	**urgente** *(oor-'hehn-teh)*

➤ Pick up on all city agencies and offices:

Code Enforcement	**El Departamento de Códigos** *(ehl deh-pahr-tah-'mehn-toh deh 'koh-dee-gohs)*
Fire Department	**El Departamento de Bomberos** *(ehl deh-pahr-tah-'mehn-toh deh bohm-'beh-rohs)*
Health Services	**El Departamento de Servicios de Salud** *(ehl deh-pahr-tah-'mehn-toh deh sehr-'vee-see·ohs deh sah-'lood)*
Housing Authority	**El Departamento de Vivienda** *(ehl deh-pahr-tah-'mehn-toh deh vee-vee-'ehn-dah)*
Postal Service	**El Departamento de Correos** *(ehl deh-pahr-tah-'mehn-toh deh koh-rreh-ohs)*
Transit Authority	**El Departamento del Tránsito** *(ehl deh-pahr-tah-'mehn-toh dehl 'trahn-see-toh)*

➤ Tell folks about office procedures:

It opens/closes at _____ on _____
Se abre/se cierra a las _____ los _____ *(seh 'ah-breh / seh see-'eh-rrah a las _____ lohs _____*

Normal business hours are from _____ to _____
Las horas de atención son desde las _____ hasta las _____ *(lahs 'oh-rahs deh ah-tehn-see-'ohn sohn 'dehs-deh lahs _____ 'ah-stah lahs _____)*

It is done in person, by mail, or by phone

Debe hacerse en persona, por correo, o por teléfono *('deh-beh ah-'sehr-seh ehn pehr-'soh-nah, pohr koh-'rreh-oh, oh pohr teh-'leh-foh-noh)*

For more information, please call _____

Para más información, llame al número _____ *('pah-rah mahs een-fohr-mah-see-'ohn, 'yah-meh ahl 'noo-meh-roh)*

➤ You need a license for...   **Necesita una licencia para...** *(neh-seh-'see-tah 'oo-nah lee-'sehn-see·ah 'pah-rah...)*

bicycles	**bicicletas** *(bee-see-'kleh-tahs)*
boating	**navegar** *(nah-veh-'gahr)*
business	**negocios** *(neh-'goh-see·ohs)*
dogs	**perros** *('peh-rrohs)*
driving	**manejar** *(mah-neh-'hahr)*
firearms	**armas de fuego** *('ahr-mahs deh 'fweh-goh)*
fishing	**pescar** *(peh-'skahr)*
hunting	**cazar** *(kah-'sahr)*
marriage	**matrimonio** *(mah-tree-'moh-nee·oh)*

¡A MIS ÓRDENES!

While making contact with Spanish speakers in the field, many of the "command words" will surface from time to time. Remember these commands we learned earlier:

Come!	**¡Venga!** *('vehn-gah)*
Go!	**¡Vaya!** *('vah-yah)*
Hurry up!	**¡Apúrese!** *(ah-'poo-reh-seh)*

Commands are essential no matter where you are assigned, so try to acquire as many as possible. Study each new word command, and take time to translate the sample sentences:

Answer	**Conteste**	**Conteste la pregunta** *(kohn-'teh-steh lah preh-'goon-tah)*	_____ _____
Bring	**Traiga**	**Traiga la licencia** *('trah·ee-gah lah lee-'sehn-see·ah)*	_____ _____

Call	**Llame**	**Llame a su familia** *('yah-meh ah soo fah-'mee-lee·ah)*	_____
Close	**Cierre**	**Cierre la puerta** *(see-'eh-rreh lah 'pwehr-tah)*	_____
Empty	**Vacíe**	**Vacíe el carro** *(vah-'see-eh ehl 'kah-rroh)*	_____
Fill out	**Llene**	**Llene el formulario** *('yeh-neh ehl fohr-moo-'lah-ree·oh)*	_____
Give	**Dé**	**Déle dinero al señor** *('deh-leh ehl dee-'neh-roh ahl seh-'nyohr)*	_____
Listen	**Escuche**	**Escuche bien** *(eh-'skoo-cheh 'bee·ehn)*	_____
Open	**Abra**	**Abra la ventana** *('ah-brah lah vehn-'tah-nah)*	_____
Put	**Ponga**	**Ponga el papel aquí** *('pohn-gah ehl pah-'pehl ah-'kee)*	_____
Read	**Lea**	**Lea el español** *('leh-ah ehl eh-spah-'nyohl)*	_____
Send	**Mande**	**Mande todo a la oficina** *('mahn-deh 'toh-doh ah lah oh-fee-'see-nah)*	_____
Sign	**Firme**	**Firme su nombre** *('feer-meh soo 'nohm-breh)*	_____
Take	**Tome**	**Tome agua** *('toh-meh 'ah-gwah)*	_____
Write	**Escriba**	**Escriba el número** *(eh-'skree-bah ehl 'noo-meh-roh)*	_____

Here are a few more. Notice how some commands end in the letters **se:**

Get going	**Váyase** *('vah-yah-seh)*
Stay put	**Quédese** *('keh-deh-seh)*
Turn around	**Dése vuelta** *('deh-seh 'vwehl-tah)*

Can you figure out the pattern in this series?

Follow me	**Sígame** *('see-gah-meh)*
Give me	**Deme** *('deh-meh)*
Listen to me	**Escúcheme** *(ehs-'koo-cheh-meh)*

Look at me	**Míreme** (*'mee-reh-meh*)
Show me	**Enséñeme** (*ehn-'seh-nyeh-meh*)
Take me	**Lléveme** (*'yeh-veh-meh*)
Tell me	**Dígame** (*'dee-gah-meh*)

Practice!

Turn around and put your hands on top of the car!	**¡Dése vuelta y ponga las manos encima del carro!** (*'deh-seh 'vwehl tah ee 'pohn-gah lahs 'mah-nohs ehn 'see-mah dehl 'kah-rroh*)
Take a seat	**Tome asiento** (*'toh-meh ah-see-'ehn toh*)
Read and sign	**Lea y firme** (*'leh-ah ee 'feer-meh*)
Tell me everything	**Dígame todo** (*'dee-gah-meh 'toh doh*)

INFORMACIÓN PRIVADA

➤ No other profession requires "commands" like law enforcement, so jot down as many as you can handle. Notice below how some word phrases may also be used to send command messages:

Against the wall!	**¡Contra la pared!** (*'kohn-trah lah pah-'rehd*)
Hands up!	**¡Manos arriba!** (*'mah-nohs ah-'rree-bah*)
Let's go!	**¡Vamos!** (*'vah-mohs*)

Let's see!	**¡A ver!** *(ah vehr)*
One at a time!	**¡Una persona a la vez!** *('oo-nah pehr-'soh-nah ah lah vehs)*
Quiet!	**¡Silencio!** *(see-'lehn-see·oh)*

➤ In Spanish, single words are often complete command expressions. Are you pronouncing everything correctly? These words can be tricky:

Give it to me!	**¡Démelo!** *('deh-meh-loh)*
Put it in!	**¡Métalo!** *('meh-tah-loh)*
Put it on!	**¡Póngaselo!** *('pohn-gah-seh-loh)*
Take it off!	**¡Quíteselo!** *('kee-teh-seh-loh)*
Take it out!	**¡Sáquelo!** *('sah-keh-loh)*
Turn it off!	**¡Apáguelo!** *(ah-'pah-geh-loh)*
Turn it on!	**¡Préndalo!** *('prehn-dah-loh)*

GRANDES HABILIDADES

You were shown earlier how the basic *Action Words* in Spanish are often parts of complete "command" expressions. Review these patterns:

to read	**leer** *(leh-'ehr)*	Please read	**Favor de leer** *(fah-'vohr deh leh-'ehr)*
to talk	**hablar** *(ah-'blahr)*	Don't talk	**No hablar** *(noh ah-'blahr)*

Care to learn a few more Spanish verbs for daily use? Again, notice the **–ar, –er,** and **–ir** endings:

to answer	**contestar** *(kohn-teh-'stahr)*
to arrive	**llegar** *(yeh-'gahr)*
to ask	**preguntar** *(preh-goon-'tahr)*
to call	**llamar** *(yah-'mahr)*
to carry	**llevar** *(yeh-'vahr)*
to choose	**elegir** *(eh-leh-'heer)*
to do	**hacer** *(ah-'sehr)*
to drive	**manejar** *(mah-neh-'hahr)*
to give	**dar** *('dahr)*
to greet	**saludar** *(sah-loo-'dahr)*
to leave	**salir** *(sah-'leer)*
to listen	**escuchar** *(eh-skoo-'chahr)*

to live	**vivir** *(vee-'veer)*
to pay	**pagar** *(pah-'gahr)*
to run	**correr** *(koh-'rrehr)*
to sign	**firmar** *(feer-'mahr)*
to return	**regresar** *(reh-greh-'sahr)*
to send	**mandar** *(mahn-'dahr)*
to take	**tomar** *(toh-'mahr)*
to turn in	**entregar** *(ehn-treh-'gahr)*
to use	**usar** *(oo-'sahr)*
to walk	**caminar** *(kah-mee-'nahr)*

This time, combine the *Action Words* with more key phrases. Study each one carefully:

You have to...	**Tiene que...** *(tee-'eh-neh keh)*
You have to pay	**Tiene que pagar** *(tee-'eh-neh keh pah-'gahr)*
You need to...	**Necesita...** *(neh-seh-'see-tah)*
You need to call	**Necesita llamar** *(neh-seh-'see-tah yah-'mahr)*
I'm going to...	**Voy a...** *('voh·ee ah)*
I'm going to leave	**Voy a salir** *('voh·ee ah sah-'leer)*

Practice!

Using the list of verbs above, come up with new one-liners on your own:

Voy a _____ *('voh·ee ah* _____)
¿Necesita _____**?** *(neh-seh-'see-tah* _____)
Tiene que _____ *(tee-'eh-neh keh* _____)

INFORMACIÓN PRIVADA

➤ Statements in Spanish can become questions, simply by changing your tone:

You need to drive.	**Necesita manejar** *(neh-seh-'see-tah mah-neh-'hahr)*
Do you need to drive?	**¿Necesita manejar?** *(neh-seh-'see-tah mah-neh-'hahr)*

➤ Many Spanish *Action Words* have more than one meaning. For example, **llevar** *(yeh-'vahr)* also means "to wear" and **hacer** *(ah-'sehr)* also means "to make."

➤ Here are other ways to tell folks they ought to do something:

You should…	**Debe…** *('deh-beh…)*
You should sleep	**Debe dormir** *('deh-beh dohr-'meer)*
One must…	**Hay que…** *('ah·ee keh…)*
One must eat	**Hay que comer** *('ah·ee keh koh-'mehr)*

➤ Learn all the forms of your new key phrases!

I need…	**Necesito…** *(neh-seh-'see-toh…)*
You need, He/She needs…	**Necesita…** *(neh-seh-'see-tah…)*
They need, You need (pl.)…	**Necesitan…** *(neh-seh-'see-tahn…)*
We need…	**Necesitamos…** *(neh-seh-see-'tah-mohs…)*
I'm going to…	**Voy a…** *(voh·ee ah…)*
You're going to, He's/ She's going to…	**Va a…** *(vah ah…)*
They're going to, You're going to (pl.)…	**Van a…** *(vahn ah…)*
We're going to…	**Vamos a…** *('vah-mohs ah…)*
I have to…	**Tengo que…** *('tehn-goh keh…)*
You have to, He/ She has to…	**Tiene que…** *(tee-'eh-neh keh…)*
They have to, You have to (pl.)…	**Tienen que…** *(tee-'eh-nehn keh…)*
We have to…	**Tenemos que…** *(teh-'meh-mohs keh…)*

➤ Read these practice sentences aloud:

I need the papers	**Necesito los papeles** *(neh-seh-'see-toh lohs pah-'peh-lehs)*
We're going to the office	**Vamos a la oficina** *('vah-mohs ah lah oh-fee-'see-nah)*
They don't have to return	**No tienen que regresar** *(noh tee-'eh-nehn keh reh-greh-'sahr)*

Tengo que salir. Voy a regresar más tarde.

92

In Chapter One, you saw how we added the **–ndo** endings to our *Action Words* in order to talk about current actions in progress. Remember?

speak	I'm speaking	**habl<u>ar</u>** *('ah-'blahr)*	**Estoy hablando** *(eh-'stoh-ee ah-'blahn-doh)*
eat	We're eating	**com<u>er</u>** *(koh-'mehr)*	**Estamos comiendo** *(eh-'stah-mohs koh-mee-'ehn-doh)*
write	He's writing	**escrib<u>ir</u>** *(eh-skree-'beer)*	**Está escribiendo** *(eh-'stoh-ee eh-skree-bee-'ehn-doh)*

Now, use this simple form to develop practical questions and comments for daily application in the field:

Are you...?	**¿Está...?** *(eh-'stah...)*
They are...	**Están...** *(eh-'stahn...)*
driving fast	**manejando rápido** *(mah-neh-'hahn-doh 'rah-pee-doh)*
drinking a lot	**tomando mucho** *(toh-'mahn-doh 'moo-choh)*
sending the form	**mandando el formulario** *(mahn-'dahn-doh ehl fohr-moo-'lah-ree·oh)*

The same thing happens consistently when we refer to "everyday" activities. But this time the verbs shift according to **who** completes the action. Look closely! This next pattern is the same for most action words:

To Speak	**Hablar** *(ah-'blahr)*
I speak	**hablo** *('ah-bloh)*
You speak, He/She speaks	**habla** *('ah-blah)*
You (pl.) speak, They speak	**hablan** *('ah-blahn)*
We speak	**hablamos** *(ah-'blah-mohs)*

To Eat	**Comer** *(koh-'mehr)*
I eat	**como** *('koh-moh)*
You eat, He/She eats	**come** *('koh-meh)*
You (pl.) eat, They eat	**comen** *('koh-mehn)*
We eat	**comemos** *(koh-'meh-mohs)*

To Write	**Escriber** (eh-skree-'beer)
I write	**escribo** (eh-'skree-boh)
You write, He/She writes	**escribe** (eh-'skree-beh)
You (pl.) write, They write	**escriben** (eh-'skree-behn)
We write	**escribimos** (eh-skree-'bee-mohs)

Notice how the **–ar** verb changes are different from the **–er** and **–ir** verbs! This will be helpful as you pick up more action forms later on.

As with all languages, not every Spanish verb is considered "regular." Here's a classic example of an exception.

To Go	**Ir** (eer)
I go	**voy** ('voh-ee)
You go, He/She goes	**va** (vah)
You (pl.) go, They go	**van** (vahn)
We go	**vamos** ('vah-mohs)

While on patrol, go ahead and practice this helpful expression:

What are you doing here?	**¿Qué está haciendo aquí?** (keh eh-'stah ah-see-'ehn-doh ah-'kee)

Notice what's happening here! Say each word slowly as you practice:

approximately	**aproximadamente** (ah-prohk-see-mah-dah-'mehn-teh)
automatically	**automáticamente** (ow-tow-mah-tee-kah-'mehn-teh)
electronically	**electrónicamente** (eh-lehk-troh-nee-kah-'mehn-teh)
legally	**legalmente** (leh-gahl-'mehn-teh)
exactly	**exactamente** (ehk-sahk-tah-'mehn-teh)
completely	**completamente** (kohm-pleh-tah-'mehn-teh)
rapidly	**rápidamente** (rah-pee-dah-'mehn-teh)

 REPASO

A. Name five local, state, or federal government agencies in Spanish.

_____ _____ _____

_____ _____

B. Match these opposites:

Dé	Préndalo *('prehn-dah-loh)*
Abra	Cierre *(see-'eh-reh)*
Váyase	Quédese *('keh-deh-seh)*
Vacíe	Tome *('toh-meh)*
Apáguelo	Llene *('yeh-neh)*

C. Make sentences using the words provided. They're all directed at you:

¿Tiene que usar usted mucho español en su trabajo? *(tee-'eh-neh keh oo-'sahr oo-'stehd 'moo-choh eh-spah-'nyohl ehn soo trah-'bah-hoh)*

_____

¿Maneja usted un carro grande? *(mah-'neh-hah oo-'stehd oon 'kah-rroh 'grahn-deh)*

_____

¿Necesita pagar mucho dinero en las tiendas? *(neh-seh-'see-tah pah-'gahr 'moo-choh dee-'neh-roh ehn lahs tee-'ehn-dahs)*

_____

¿Llama por teléfono a sus amigos? *('yah-mah pohr teh-'leh-foh-noh ah soos ah-'mee-gohs*

_____

¿Llega temprano o tarde a su trabajo? *('yeh-gah tehm-'prah-noh oh 'tahr-deh ah soo trah-'bah-hoh)*

_____

ANSWERS

B. Dé Tome
Abra Cierre
Váyase Quédese
Vacíe Llene
Apáguelo Préndalo

CHAPTER THREE
Capítulo Tres
(kah-'pee-too-loh trehs)

TRAFFIC CONTROL
El control del tráfico
(ehl kohn-'trohl dehl 'trah-fee-koh)

ON THE STREET
En la calle *(ehn lah 'kah-yeh)*

Everybody in the field needs some "street language." Familiarize yourself with those items that repeatedly surface while you're out and about. Point to each one as you cruise along:

Where's the...?	¿**Dónde está...** *('dohn-deh eh-'stah...)*
arrow	**la flecha?** *(lah 'fleh-chah)*
barrier	**la barrera?** *(lah bah-'rreh-rah)*
bicycle lane	**la pista para ciclistas?** *(lah 'pee-stah 'pah-rah see-'klee-stahs)*
billboard	**el letrero?** *(ehl leh-'treh-roh)*
broken line	**la línea quebrada?** *(lah 'lee-neh-ah keh-'brah-dah)*
car pool lane	**la pista de transporte en grupo?** *(lah 'pee-stah deh trahs-'pohr-teh ehn 'groo-poh)*
center divider	**el divisor central?** *(ehl dee-vee-'sohr sehn-'trahl)*
channel	**el canal?** *(ehl kah-'nahl)*
crosswalk	**el cruce de peatones?** *(ehl 'kroo-seh deh peh-ah-'toh-nehs*
cul-de-sac	**la calle sin salida?** *(lah 'kah-yeh seen sah-'lee-dah)*
curb	**la orilla?** *(lah oh-'ree-yah)*
curve	**la curva?** *(lah 'koor-vah)*
ditch	**la zanja?** *(lah 'sahn-hah)*
divided highway	**la carretera dividida?** *(lah kah-rreh-'teh-rah dee-vee-'dee-dah)*
double line	**la línea doble?** *(lah 'lee-neh-ah 'doh-bleh)*
drainage	**el drenaje?** *(ehl dreh-'nah-heh)*
embankment	**la presa?** *(lah 'preh-sah)*
flashing light	**la luz relampagueante?** *(lah loos reh-lahm-pah-geh-'ahn-teh)*
freeway	**la autopista?** *(lah ow-toh-'pee-stah)*
intersection	**la bocacalle?** *(lah boh-kah-'kah-yeh)*
irrigation	**la irrigación?** *(lah ee-rree-gah-see-'ohn)*
island	**la isla?** *(lah 'ees-lah)*
lane	**la pista?** *(lah 'pee-stah)*
left turn lane	**la pista de viraje a la izquierda?** *(lah 'pee-stah deh vee-'rah-heh ah lah ees-kee-'ehr-dah)*
main street	**la calle principal?** *(lah 'kah-yeh preen-see-'pahl)*
manhole cover	**la tapa del drenaje?** *(lah 'tah-pah dehl dreh-'nah-heh)*

off ramp	**la rampa de salida?** *(lah 'rahm-pah deh sah-'lee-dah)*
on ramp	**la rampa de entrada?** *(lah 'rahm-pah deh ehn-'trah-dah)*
one way street	**la calle de dirección única?** *(lah dee-rehk-see-'ohn 'oo-nee-kah)*
overpass	**el pasaje sobre carretera?** *(ehl pah-'sah-heh 'soh-breh kah-rreh-'teh-rah)*
parking meter	**el parquímetro?** *(ehl pahr-'kee-meh-troh)*
post	**el poste?** *(ehl 'poh-steh)*
power line	**el cable eléctrico?** *(ehl 'kah-bleh eh-'lehk-tree-koh)*
private property	**el terreno privado?** *(ehl teh-'rreh-noh pree-'vah-doh)*
public highway	**la carretera pública?** *(lah kah-rreh-'teh-rah 'poo-blee-kah)*
railroad track	**la vía del ferrocarril?** *(lah 'vee-ah dehl feh-rroh-kah-'rreel)*
red light	**la luz roja?** *(lah loos 'roh-hah)*
reflector	**el reflector?** *(ehl reh-flehk-'tohr)*
sewage	**el desagüe?** *(ehl dehs-'ah-gweh)*
shoulder	**el borde?** *(ehl 'bohr-deh)*
sidewalk	**la acera?** *(lah ah-'seh-rah)*
slope	**el declive?** *(ehl deh-'klee-veh)*
solid line	**la línea sólida?** *(lah 'lee-neh-ah 'soh-lee-dah)*
speed bump	**el tope?** *(ehl 'toh-peh)*
speed limit	**el límite de velocidad?** *(ehl 'lee-mee-teh deh veh-loh-see-'dahd)*
sprinkler	**la rociadora?** *(lah roh-see·ah-'doh-rah)*
stop sign	**la señal de alto?** *(lah seh-'nyahl deh 'ahl-toh)*
street light	**la luz de la calle?** *(lah loos deh lah 'kah-yeh)*
street sign	**la señal de la calle?** *(lah seh-'nyahl deh lah 'kah-yeh)*
telephone pole	**el poste de teléfono?** *(ehl 'poh-steh deh teh-'leh-foh-noh)*
traffic light	**el semáforo?** *(ehl seh-'mah-foh-roh)*
traffic sign	**la señal de tráfico?** *(lah seh-'nyahl deh 'trah-fee-koh)*
trash bin	**el bote de basura?** *(ehl 'boh-teh deh bah-'soo-rah)*
two way street	**la calle de dirección doble?** *(lah 'kah-yeh deh dee-rehk-see-'ohn 'doh-bleh)*
white line	**la línea blanca?** *(lah 'lee-neh-ah 'blahn-kah)*

¡Criminal!
¡Esta es una acera,
no una autopista!

INFORMACIÓN PRIVADA

➤ There are plenty of names for streets, also. Practice:

alley	**el callejón** *(ehl kah-yeh-'hohn)*
avenue	**la avenida** *(lah ah-veh-'nee-dah)*
boulevard	**el bulevar** *(ehl boo-leh-'vahr)*
circle	**el círculo** *(ehl 'seer-koo-loh)*
lane	**la pista** *(lah 'pee-stah)*
path	**la senda** *(lah 'sehn-dah)*
road	**el camino** *(ehl kah-'mee-noh)*
route	**la ruta** *(lah 'roo-tah)*
street	**la calle** *(lah 'kah-yeh)*
way	**el paseo** *(ehl pah-'seh-oh)*

CRUCIGRAMA 1

Across

3 la carretera
4 la calle
6 la esquina
7 el edificio
8 la entrada
10 el centro
11 el camino
12 la avenida
13 la cerca
17 el patio
19 la torre
20 la pared

Down

1 la acera
2 el barrio
5 la fuente
9 el ascensor
14 la salida
15 la estatua
16 el puente
18 la piscina

VEHICLE STOP
La detención de vehículos
(lah deh-tehn-see-'ohn deh veh-'ee-koo-lohs)

Up and down the streets of America, English-speaking officers are doing their best to communicate with drivers who speak only Spanish. It's imperative that vehicle regulations are explained and problems are avoided. If you're assigned duties related to traffic safety and control, study these next few pages very carefully. They can save you lots of valuable time and energy.

As usual, when it comes to initial contact with anyone, start things off with a greeting or two:

Hi. Good morning. How are you?	**Hola. Buenos días. ¿Cómo está?** *('oh-lah 'bweh-nohs 'dee-ahs 'koh-moh eh-'stah)*

Now, depending upon the situation, let them know who you are, and briefly explain your concern. Don't worry about some of these action-word forms. They'll be discussed in detail a little later on:

I'm _____ from _____ (Fill in the lines with your job title and place of employment.)	**Soy _____ de _____** *('soh-ee _____ deh _____)*
You have broken the law	**Ha violado la ley** *(ah vee-oh-'lah-doh lah 'leh·ee)*
I need to talk with you	**Necesito hablar con usted** *(neh-seh-'see-toh ah-'blahr kohn oo-'stehd)*
Do you know why I stopped you?	**¿Sabe por qué lo paré?** *('sah-beh pohr keh loh pah-'reh)*
Do you know the speed limit?	**¿Sabe el límite de velocidad?** *('sah-beh ehl 'lee-mee-teh deh veh-loh-see-'dahd)*
Do you know how fast you were driving?	**¿Sabe cuán rapido estaba manejando?** *('sah-beh kwahn 'rah-pee-doh eh-'stah-bah mah-neh-'hahn-doh)*

DO YOU KNOW WHAT YOU DID?

¿Sabe lo que hizo? *('sah-beh loh keh 'ee-soh)*

You didn't have the right of way
No tenía el derecho de vía *(noh teh-'nee-ah ehl deh-'reh-choh deh 'vee-ah)*

You didn't yield
No cedió el paso *(noh seh-dee-'oh ehl 'pah-soh)*

You didn't obey the sign
No obedeció la señal *(noh oh-beh-deh-see-'oh lah seh-'nyahl)*

You didn't signal
No hizo las señales *(noh 'ee-soh lahs seh-'nyah-lehs)*

You stopped suddenly
Paró de repente *('pah-roh deh reh-'pehn-teh)*

You made an illegal turn
Hizo una vuelta ilegal *('ee-soh 'oo-nah 'vwehl-tah ee-leh-'gahl)*

You almost crashed
Casi chocó *('kah-see choh-'koh)*

You almost hit it
Casi le pegó *('kah-see leh peh-'goh)*

You crossed the line
Cruzó la línea *(kroo-'soh lah 'lee-neh-ah)*

You went through a red light
Pasó por la luz roja *(pah-'soh pohr lah loos 'roh-hah)*

Your visibility is obstructed
Su visibilidad está obstruida *(soo vee-see-bee-lee-'dahd eh-'stah ohb-stroo-'ee-dah)*

You were driving very fast
Estaba manejando muy rápido *(eh-'stah-bah mah-neh-'hahn-doh 'moo·ee 'rah-pee-doh)*

You were driving too slow
Estaba manejando muy lento *(eh-'stah-bah mah-neh-'hahn-doh 'moo·ee 'lehn-toh)*

You were following too close
Estaba siguiendo muy cerca *(eh-'stah-bah see-gee-'ehn-doh 'moo·ee 'sehr-kah)*

You were swerving
Estaba zigzagueando *(eh-'stah-bah seeg-sahg-eh-'ahn-doh)*

You were going against the traffic
Estaba manejando contra el tráfico *(eh-'stah-bah mah-neh-'hahn-doh 'kohn-trah ehl 'trah-fee-koh)*

You were in the car pool lane
Estaba en la pista de transporte en grupo *(eh-'stah-bah ehn lah 'pees-tah deh trahns-'pohr-teh ehn 'groo-poh)*

You were cutting the corner
Estaba recortando la esquina *(eh-'stah-bah reh-kohr-'tahn-doh lah eh-'skee-nah)*

You were backing up
Estaba retrocediendo *(eh-'stah-bah reh-troh-seh-dee-'ehn-doh)*

You have to slow down
Tiene que disminuir la velocidad *(tee-'eh-neh keh dees-mee-noo-'eer lah veh-loh-see-'dahd)*

You have too many passengers
Tiene demasiados pasajeros *(tee-'eh-neh deh-mah-see-'ah-dohs pah-sah-'heh-rohs)*

Your load is too big	**Su carga es muy grande** (soo 'kahr-gah ehs 'moo·ee 'grahn-deh)
You are littering	**Está tirando basura** (eh-'stah tee-'rahn-doh bah-'soo-rah)
Your load is not secure	**Su carga no está segura** (soo 'kahr-gah noh eh-'stah seh-'goo-rah)
You were racing	**Estaba haciendo carreras** (eh-'stah-bah ah-see-'ehn-doh kah-'rreh-rahs)
You drove at ___ m.p.h.	**Manejó a ___ millas por hora** (mah-neh-'hoh ah ___ 'mee-yahs pohr 'oh-rah)

IT'S THE LAW

Es la ley (ehs lah 'leh·ee)

You might have a discussion, so follow up with a brief explanation:

It's blocked off	**Está obstruida** (eh-'stah ohb-stroo-'ee-dah)
It's a school zone	**Es zona escolar** (ehs 'soh-nah eh-skoh-'lahr)
It's in the other direction	**Está en la otra dirección** (eh-'stah ehn lah 'oh-trah dee-rehk-see-'ohn)
It's not a safe distance	**No es una distancia segura** (noh ehs 'oo-nah dee-'stahn-see·ah seh-'goo-rah)
It goes in both directions	**Va en ambas direcciones** (vah ehn 'ahm-bahs dee-rehk-see-'oh-nehs)
It's congested	**Está congestionada** (eh-'stah kohn-heh-stee-oh-'nah-dah)
It's a residential district	**Es un distrito residencial** (ehs oon dee-'stree-toh reh-see-dehn-see-'ahl)
You didn't stop for (the)...	**No paró para...** (noh pah-'roh 'pah-rah...)
ambulance	**la ambulancia** (lah ahm-boo-'lahn-see·ah)
fire engine	**el camión de bomberos** (ehl kah-mee-'ohn deh bohm-'beh-rohs)
pedestrian	**el peatón** (ehl peh-ah-'tohn)
police car	**el carro de policía** (ehl 'kah-rroh deh poh-lee-'see-ah)
red light	**la luz roja** (lah loos 'roh-hah)
school bus	**el autobús escolar** (ehl ow-tow-'boos eh-skoh-'lahr)
siren	**la sirena** (lah see-'reh-nah)
train	**el tren** (ehl trehn)

You cannot...	**No puede...** *(noh 'pweh-deh...)*
drive without a license	**manejar sin licencia** *(mah-neh-'hahr seen lee-'sehn-see·ah)*
change lanes that way	**cambiar pistas así** *(kahm-bee-'ahr 'pee-stahs ah-'see)*
stop there	**pararse ahí** *(pah-'rahr-seh ah-'ee)*
turn here	**dar vuelta aquí** *(dahr 'vwewhl-tah ah-'kee)*
pass on the right	**pasar por el lado derecho** *(pah-'sahr pohr ehl 'lah-doh deh-'reh-choh)*
tow another car	**remolcar otro carro** *(reh-mohl-'kahr 'oh-troh 'kah-rroh)*
carry this	**cargar esto** *(kahr-'gahr eh-'stoh)*
drive without an adult	**manejar sin un adulto** *(mah-neh-'hahr seen oon ah-'dool-toh)*
block traffic	**obstruir el tráfico** *(ohb-stroo-'eer ehl 'trah-fee-koh)*
make a "U" turn	**darse vuelta en "U"** *('dahr-seh 'vwehl-tah ehn oo)*
back up	**retroceder** *(reh-troh-seh-'dehr)*
drive in reverse	**manejar en reverso** *(mah-neh-'hahr ehn reh-'vehr-soh)*
hitch-hike here	**pedir ser llevado en carro aquí** *(peh-'deer sehr yeh-'vah-doh ehn 'kah-rroh ah-'kee)*

Once everyone understands what's going on, ask for the necessary documents, and then run a check on everything:

Do you have...?	**¿Tiene...** *(tee-'eh-neh...)*
driver's license	**la licencia de conducir?** *(lah lee-'sehn-see·ah deh kohn-doo-'seer)*
proof of insurance	**la prueba de aseguramiento?** *(lah proo-'eh-bah deh ah-seh-goo-rah-mee-'ehn-toh)*
proof of ownership	**la prueba de propiedad?** *(lah proo-'eh-bah deh proh-pee·eh-'dahd)*
registration	**el registro?** *(ehl reh-'hee-stroh)*
smog certificate	**la prueba del examen de emisiones?** *(lah proo-'eh-bah dehl ehk-'sah-mehn deh eh-mee-see-'oh-nehs)*

Remember to ask more questions if you feel it's necessary:

Are you the owner?	**¿Es usted el dueño?** *(ehs oo-'stehd ehl 'dweh-nyoh)*
Is this information correct?	**¿Es correcta esta información?** *(ehs koh-'rrehk-tah 'eh-stah een-fohr-mah-see-'ohn)*

Do you have any more I.D.?	**¿Tiene más pruebas de identificación?** *(tee-'eh-neh oo-'stehd mahs proo-'eh-bahs deh ee-dehn-tee-fee-kah-see-'ohn)*
What's the...?	**¿Cuál es...** *(kwahl ehs...)*
date of purchase	**la fecha de compra?** *(lah 'feh-chah deh 'kohm-prah)*
design	**el diseño?** *(ehl dee-'seh-nyoh)*
make	**la marca?** *(lah 'mahr-kah)*
model	**el modelo?** *(ehl moh-'deh-loh)*
original color	**el color original?** *(ehl koh-'lohr oh-ree-hee-'nahl)*
shape	**la forma?** *(lah 'fohr-mah)*
size	**el tamaño?** *(ehl tah-'mah-nyoh)*
style	**el estilo?** *(ehl eh-'stee-loh)*
type	**el tipo?** *(ehl 'tee-poh)*
value	**el valor?** *(ehl vah-'lohr)*
VIN number	**el número del motor?** *(ehl 'noo-meh-roh dehl moh-'tohr)*
year	**el año?** *(ehl 'ah-nyoh)*

INFORMACIÓN PRIVADA

➤ If there's something unusual about the situation, probe a little deeper:

Where are you headed?	**¿Adónde va?** *(ah-'dohn-deh vah)*
How long have you been driving?	**¿Por cuánto tiempo ha estado manejando?** *(pohr 'kwahn-toh tee-'ehm-poh ah eh-'stah-doh mah-neh-'hahn-doh)*
Where did you get this?	**¿Dónde lo consiguió?** *('dohn-deh loh kohn-see-gee-'oh)*
Do you know how to drive manual stick shift?	**¿Sabe manejar un carro de cambio manual?** *('sah-beh mah-neh-'hahr oon 'kah-rroh deh 'kahm-bee·oh mah-noo-'ahl)*

➤ Now let them know what the trouble is:

There seems to be a problem	**Parece que hay un problema** *(pah-'reh-seh keh 'ah·ee oon proh-'bleh-mah)*
Your license has expired	**Ha vencido su licencia** *(ah vehn-'see-doh soo lee-'sehn-see·ah)*
You are too young to drive	**Es demasiado joven para manejar** *(ehs deh-mah-see-'ah-doh 'hoh-vehn 'pah-rah mah-neh-'hahr)*

Your plates have expired	**Han vencido sus placas** *(ahn vehn-'see-doh soos 'plah-kahs)*
Your license has been revoked	**Su licencia ha sido cancelada** *(soo lee-'sehn-see·ahah 'see-doh kahn-seh-'lah-dah)*
This isn't your picture	**Este no es su retrato** *('eh-steh noh ehs soo reh-'trah-toh)*
You are not classified to drive this vehicle	**No está clasificado para manejar este vehículo** *(noh eh-'stah klah-see-fee-'kah-doh 'pah-rah mah-neh-'hahr 'eh-steh veh-'ee-koo-loh)*
It's incorrect	**Está incorrecto** *(ehs-'tah een-koh-'rrehk-toh)*
It's invalid	**Está inválido** *(ehs-'tah een-'vah-lee-doh)*
It's stolen	**Es robado** *(ehs roh-'bah-doh)*

 REPASO

A. List three things in Spanish that you might see on a typical city street:

_____ _____ _____

_____ _____ _____

_____ _____ _____

B. **Good morning**

I'm an official from the city of Denver

Do you know why I stopped you?

You made an illegal turn

You cannot make a turn here

Do you have a driver's license?

Is this information correct?

Your license has expired

ANSWERS

Ha expirado su licencia (*ah ehk-spee-'rah-doh soo lee-'sehn-see-ah*)

¿Es correcta esta información? (*ehs koh-'rrehk-tah 'eh-stah een-fohr-mah-see-'ohn*)

¿Tiene licencia de manejar? (*tee-'eh-neh lee-'sehn-see-ah deh mah-neh-'hahr*)

No puede dar vuelta aquí (*noh 'pweh-deh dahr 'vwehl-tah ah-'kee*)

Usted hizo una vuelta ilegal (*oo-'stehd 'ee-soh 'oo-nah 'vwehl-tah ee-leh-'gahl*)

¿Sabe por qué lo paré? (*'sah-beh pohr keh loh pah-'reh*)

Soy un oficial de la ciudad de Denver (*'soh-ee oon oh-fee-see-'ahl deh lah see-oo-'dahd deh 'dehn-vehr*)

B. **Translate into English:**

Buenos días (*'bweh-nohs 'dee-ahs*)

EXPLAIN, DESCRIBE, AND MAKE SUGGESTIONS

Explique, describa y haga sugerencias
(ehk-'splee-keh, deh-'skree-bah, ee 'ah-gah soo-heh-'rehn-see·ahs)

It's (the)...	**Es...** *(ehs...)*
crime	**el crimen** *(ehl 'kree-mehn)*
felony	**el delito mayor** *(ehl deh-'lee-toh mah-'yohr)*
fine	**la multa** *(lah 'mool-tah)*
hazard	**el peligro** *(ehl peh-'lee-groh)*
infraction	**la infracción** *(lah een-frahk-see-'ohn)*
misdemeaner	**el delito menor** *(ehl deh-'lee-toh meh-'nohr)*
notice	**la noticia** *(lah noh-'tee-see·ah)*
regulation	**la regla** *(lah 'reh-glah)*
requirement	**el requisito** *(ehl reh-kee-'see-toh)*
restriction	**la restricción** *(lah reh-streek-see-'ohn)*
speed	**la velocidad** *(lah veh-loh-see-'dahd)*
ticket	**la boleta** *(lah boh-'leh-tah)*
truth	**la verdad** *(lah vehr-'dahd)*
violation	**la violación** *(lah vee-oh-lah-see-'ohn)*
warning	**el aviso** *(ehl ah-'vee-soh)*

It's...	**Es...** *(ehs...)*
against the law	**contra la ley** *('kohn-trah lah 'leh·ee)*
altered	**alterado** *(ahl-teh-'rah-doh)*
canceled	**cancelado** *(kahn-seh-'lah-doh)*
defective	**defectuoso** *(deh-fehk-too-'oh-soh)*
denied	**negado** *(neh-'gah-doh)*
drivable	**manejable** *(mah-neh-'hah-bleh)*
fake	**falso** *('fahl-soh)*
illegal	**ilegal** *(ee-leh-'gahl)*
improper	**incorrecto** *(een-koh-'rrehk-toh)*
irresponsible	**irresponsable** *(ee-reh-spohn-'sah-bleh)*
provisional	**provisional** *(proh-vee-see·oh-'nahl)*
reckless	**temerario** *(teh-meh-'rah-ree·oh)*
registered	**registrado** *(reh-hee-'strah-doh)*
reported	**reportado** *(reh-pohr-'tah-doh)*
suspended	**suspendido** *(soos-pehn-'dee-doh)*
unmarked	**sin marcas** *(seen 'mahr-kahs)*
valid	**válido** *('vah-lee-doh)*

You have to...	**Tiene que...** *(tee-'eh-neh keh)*
You need to...	**Necesita...** *(neh-seh-'see-tah)*
approve it	**aprobarlo** *(ah-proh-'bahr-loh)*
arrange it	**arreglarlo** *(ah-rreh-'glahr-loh)*
change it	**cambiarlo** *(kahm-bee-'ahr-loh)*
clean it	**limpiarlo** *(leem-pee-'ahr-loh)*
complete it	**completarlo** *(kohm-pleh-'tahr-loh)*
empty it	**vaciarlo** *(vah-see-'ahr-loh)*
fix it	**repararlo** *(reh-pah-'rahr-loh)*
move it	**moverlo** *(moh-'vehr-loh)*
park it	**estacionarlo** *(eh-stah-see-oh-'nahr-loh)*
pay it	**pagarlo** *(pah-'gahr-loh)*
read it	**leerlo** *(leh-'ehr-loh)*
renew it	**renovarlo** *(reh-noh-'vahr-loh)*
replace it	**reemplazarlo** *(reh-ehm-plah-'sahr-loh)*
return it	**devolverlo** *(deh-vohl-'vehr-loh)*
send it	**mandarlo** *(mahn-'dahr-loh)*
sign it	**firmarlo** *(feer-'mahr-loh)*
tow it	**remolcarlo** *(reh-mohl-'kahr-loh)*

Next, inform them of your decision:

I'm going to...	**Voy a...** *('voh-ee ah...)*
check it out	**investigarlo** *(een-veh-stee-'gahr-loh)*
cite you	**darle una boleta** *('dahr-leh 'oo-nah boh-'leh-tah)*
give you a warning	**darle una advertencia** *('dahr-leh 'oo-nah ahd-vehr-'tehn-see·ah)*
impound it	**embargarlo** *(ehm-bahr-'gahr-loh)*
return in a minute	**regresar en un minuto** *(reh-greh-'sahr ehn oon mee-'noo-toh)*
verify it	**verificarlo** *(veh-ree-fee-'kahr-loh)*

Review these locations, as you send folks on their way:

Go to (the)...	**Vaya** *('vah-yah)*
car lot	**al lote de carros** *(ahl 'loh-teh deh 'kah-rrohs)*
counter	**al mostrador** *(ahl moh-strah-'dohr)*
gas station	**a la gasolinera** *(ah lah gah-soh-lee-'neh-rah)*
police station	**a la estación de policía** *(ah lah eh-stah-see-'ohn deh poh-lee-'see-ah)*
towing company	**a la compañía de remolque** *(ah lah kohm-pah-'nyee-ah deh reh-'mohl-keh)*
window	**a la ventana** *(ah lah vehn-'tah-nah)*

Go to this...	**Vaya a esta...** *('vah-yah ah 'eh-stah ...)*
city	**ciudad** *(see-oo-'dahd)*
court	**corte** *('kohr-teh)*
address	**dirección** *(dee-rehk-see-'ohn)*

INFORMACIÓN PRIVADA

➤ Throw in all your words and phrases:

in this building	**en este edificio** *(ehn 'eh-steh eh-deh-'fee-see-oh)*
on this date	**en esta fecha** *(ehn 'eh-stah 'feh-chah)*
at this time	**a esta hora** *(ah 'eh-stah 'oh-rah)*

FINAL DECISION
La decisión final *(lah deh-see-see-'ohn fee-'nahl)*

If there are questions about your decision, go ahead and lay down the law. Speak clearly as you read:

I measured you	**Lo medí** *(loh meh-'dee)*
I recorded you	**Lo grabé** *(loh grah-beh)*
I've been watching	**He estado mirando** *(eh eh-'stah-doh mee-'rahn-doh)*
I followed you	**Lo seguí** *(loh seh-'gee)*
I saw you	**Lo ví** *(loh vee)*
I used this equipment	**Usé este equipo** *(oo-'seh 'eh-steh eh-'kee-poh)*

I have (the)...	**Tengo...** *('tehn-goh...)*
camera	**la cámara** *(lah 'kah-mah-rah)*
computer	**la computadora** *(lah kohm-poo-tah-'doh-rah)*
machine	**la máquina** *(lah 'mah-kee-nah)*
monitor	**el monitor** *(ehl moh-nee-'tohr)*
radar	**el radar** *(ehl rah-'dahr)*
radio	**el radio** *(ehl 'rah-dee·oh)*

Do you know...	**¿Sabe...?** *('sah-beh...)*
You should read (the)...	**Debe leer...** *('deh-beh leh-'ehr...)*
code	**el código** *(ehl 'koh-dee-goh)*
law	**la ley** *(lah 'leh·ee)*
regulation	**el reglamento** *(ehl reh-glah-'mehn-toh)*
rule	**la regla** *(lah 'reh-glah)*
section	**la sección** *(lah sehk-see-'ohn)*

AUTO PARTS
Las partes del auto *(lahs 'pahr-tehs dehl 'ow-toh)*

How can you drive around without knowledge of these? To practice, walk over to any vehicle, touch, and talk:

This is (the)...	**Esto es...** *('eh-stoh ehs...)*
accelerator	**el acelerador** *(ehl ah-seh-leh-rah-'dohr)*
air conditioning	**el aire acondicionado** *(ehl 'ah·ee-reh ah-kohn-dee-see-oh-'nah-doh)*
antenna	**la antena** *(lah ahn-'teh-nah)*
axle	**el eje** *(ehl 'eh-heh)*
back seat	**el asiento trasero** *(ehl ah-see-'ehn-toh trah-'seh-roh)*
battery	**la batería** *(lah bah-teh-'ree-ah)*
brake	**el freno** *(ehl 'freh-noh)*
brake light	**la luz de frenada** *(lah loos deh freh-'nah-dah)*
bumper	**el parachoques** *(ehl pah-rah-'choh-kehs)*
CD player	**el tocadiscos** *(ehl toh-kah-'dees-kohs)*
cable	**el cable** *(ehl 'kah-bleh)*
carburetor	**el carburador** *(ehl kahr-boo-rah-'dohr)*
clutch	**el embrague** *(ehl ehm-'brah-geh)*

computer	**la computadora** (*lah kohm-poo-tah-'doh-rah*)
dashboard	**el tablero de instrumentos** (*ehl tah-'bleh-roh deh een-stroo-'mehn-tohs*)
distributor	**el distribuidor** (*ehl dee-stree-boo·ee-'dohr*)
door	**la puerta** (*lah 'pwehr-tah*)
emergency light	**la señal de emergencia** (*lah seh-'nyahl deh eh-mehr-'hehn-see·ah*)
engine	**el motor** (*ehl moh-'tohr*)
equipment	**el equipo** (*ehl eh-'kee-poh*)
exterior	**el exterior** (*ehl ehks-teh-ree-'ohr*)
fan belt	**la correa del ventilador** (*lah koh-'rreh-ah dehl vehn-tee-lah-'dohr*)
fan	**el ventilador** (*ehl vehn-tee-lah-'dohr*)
fender	**el guardabarro** (*ehl gwahr-dah-'bah-rroh*)
fog lights	**la luz de niebla** (*lah loos deh nee-'eh-blah*)
fuse	**el fusible** (*ehl foo-'see-bleh*)
gas cap	**el tapón del tanque** (*ehl tah-'pohn dehl 'tahn-keh*)
gas tank	**el tanque de gasolina** (*ehl 'tahn-keh deh gah-soh-'lee-nah*)
gauge	**el indicador** (*ehl een-dee-kah-'dohr*)
gear	**el engranaje** (*ehl ehn-grah-'nah-heh*)
glove compartment	**la guantera** (*lah gwahn-'teh-rah*)
handle	**el tirador** (*ehl tee-rah-'dohr*)
hatch	**el portillo** (*ehl pohr-'tee-yoh*)
headlight	**el faro delantero** (*ehl 'fah-roh deh-lahn-'teh-roh*)
heater	**el calentador** (*ehl kah-lehn-tah-'dohr*)
high beam	**la iluminación alta** (*lah ee-loo-mee-nah-see-'ohn 'ahl-tah*)
hood	**el capot** (*ehl kah-'poht*)
horn	**la bocina** (*lah boh-'see-nah*)
hubcap	**el tapacubo** (*ehl tah-pah-'koo-boh*)
ignition	**el encendido** (*ehl ehn-sehn-'dee-doh*)
instrument	**el instrumento** (*ehl een-stroo-'mehn-toh*)
interior	**el interior** (*ehl een-teh-ree-'ohr*)
lever	**la palanca** (*lah pah-'lahn-kah*)
light	**la luz** (*lah loos*)
lock	**el pestillo** (*ehl peh-'stee-yoh*)
low beam	**la baja iluminación** (*lah 'bah-hah ee-loo-mee-nah-see-'ohn*)

muffler	**el silenciador** (ehl see-lehn-see·ah-'dohr)
navigation system	**el sistema de guía** (ehl sees-'teh-mah deh 'gee-ah)
odometer	**el odómetro** (ehl oh-'doh-meh-troh)
paint	**la pintura** (lah peen-'too-rah)
pedal	**el pedal** (ehl peh-'dahl)
pump	**la bomba** (lah 'bohm-bah)
radiator	**el radiador** (ehl rah-dee·ah-'dohr)
radio	**el radio** (ehl 'rah-dee·oh)
rearview mirror	**el espejo retrovisor** (ehl eh-'speh-hoh reh-troh-vee-'sohr)
roof	**el techo** (ehl 'teh-choh)
safety belt	**el cinturón de seguridad** (ehl seen-too-'rohn deh seh-goo-ree-'dahd)
seat	**el asiento** (ehl ah-see-'ehn-toh)
shock absorber	**el amortiguador** (ehl ah-mohr-tee-gwah-'dohr)
smog device	**el aparato antismog** (ehl ah-pah-'rah-toh ahn-tee-'smohg)
spare tire	**el neumático de repuesto** (ehl neh-oo-'mah-tee-koh deh reh-'pweh-stoh)
spark plug	**la bujía** (lah boo-'hee-ah)
speedometer	**el indicador de velocidad** (ehl een-dee-kah-'dohr deh veh-loh-see-'dahd)
starter	**el arrancador** (ehl ah-rrahn-kah-'dohr)
steering wheel	**el volante** (ehl voh-'lahn-teh)
stick shift	**el cambio manual** (ehl 'kahm-bee-oh mah-noo-'ahl)
tail light	**el faro trasero** (ehl 'fah-roh trah-'seh-roh)
timing belt	**la correa de distribución** (lah koh-'rreh-ah deh dees-tree-boo-see-'ohn)
tire	**el neumático** (ehl neh-oo-'mah-tee-koh)
transmission	**la transmisión** (lah trahns-mee-see-'ohn)
trunk	**la maletera** (lah mah-leh-'teh-rah)
turn signal	**la señal de dirección** (lah seh-'nyahl deh dee-rehk-see-'ohn)
upholstery	**la tapicería** (lah tah-pee-seh-'ree-ah)
valve	**la válvula** (lah 'vahl-voo-lah)
visor	**la visera** (lah vee-'seh-rah)
window	**la luna, la ventana** (lah 'loo-nah, lah vehn-'tah-nah)
wheel	**la rueda** (lah roo-'eh-dah)

windshield	**el parabrisas** *(ehl pah-rah-'bree-sahs)*
windshield wiper	**el limpiaparabrisas** *(ehl leem-pee-ah-pah-rah-'bree-sahs)*
wire	**el alambre** *(ehl ah-'lahm-breh)*

INFORMACIÓN PRIVADA

➤ Get specific!

front seat	**el asiento delantero** *(ehl ah-see-'ehn-toh deh-lahn-'teh-roh)*
passenger side	**el lado del pasajero** *(ehl 'lah-doh dehl pah-sah-'heh-roh)*
rear seat	**el asiento trasero** *(ehl ah-see-'ehn-toh trah-'seh-roh)*

➤ Here's a set of open-ended comments. Complete them any way you want:

Your vehicle is unsafe because...	**Su vehículo no está seguro porque...** *(soo veh-'ee-koo-loh noh eh-'stah seh-'goo-roh 'pohr-keh...)*
Something's wrong with your...	**Hay algo mal con su...** *('ah·ee 'ahl-goh mahl kohn soo...)*
Your... doesn't work	**Su...no funciona** *(soo...noh foonk-see-'oh-nah)*
You are missing...	**Le falta...** *(leh 'fahl-tah...)*
Your... has fallen off	**Se ha caído su...** *(seh ah kah-'ee-doh soo...)*
You need a new...	**Necesita un nuevo...** *(neh-seh-'see-tah oon noo-'eh-voh...)*

➤ Talk about fuel:

It takes...	**Toma...** *('toh-mah...)*
diesel	**diésel** *(dee-eh-'sehl)*
regular	**regular** *(reh-goo-'lahr)*
unleaded	**sin plomo** *(seen 'ploh-moh)*
premium	**súper** *('soo-pehr)*

A. These words are easy. Keep reading aloud as you translate:

infracción *(een-frahk-see-'ohn)* _____

irresponsable *(ee-reh-spohn-'sah-bleh)* _____

registrado *(reh-hee-'strah-doh)* _____

reglamento *(reh-glah-'mehn-toh)* _____

válido *('vah-lee-doh)* _____

violación *(vee-oh-lah-see-'ohn)* _____

B. Some terms are even spelled the same. Make a sentence for each:

el monitor *(ehl moh-nee-'tohr)*

_____

el radar *(ehl rah-'dahr)*

_____

el radio *(ehl 'rah-dee·oh)*

_____

C. Can you name at least five parts of an automobile in Spanish?

_____   _____   _____

_____   _____

ANSWERS

A. infraction
irresponsible
registered
regulation
valid
violation

115

Le falta la puerta, necesita un nuevo silenciador, y no funciona la bomba.

Eso no es importante. ¿Cómo está el radio?

IT NEEDS REPAIR!
¡Necesita reparación! *(neh-seh-'see-tah reh-pah-rah-see-'ohn)*

Write down any three of these one-liners on a piece of paper, and come back for more later on.

Practice:

Can you drive it?	**¿Puede manejarlo?** *('pweh-deh mah-neh-'hahr-loh)*
Is anything wrong?	**¿Hay algo mal?** *('ah·ee 'ahl-goh mahl)*
Can you start the engine?	**¿Puede arrancar el motor?** *('pweh-deh ah-rrahn-'kahr ehl moh-'tohr)*
Do you need to charge the battery?	**¿Necesita cargar la batería?** *(neh-seh-'see-tah kahr-'gahr lah bah-teh-'ree-ah)*
Are you able to steer?	**¿Puede dirigir el vehículo?** *('pweh-deh dee-ree-'heer ehl veh-'ee-koo-loh)*
Do you want a push?	**¿Quiere un empujón?** *(kee-'eh-reh oon ehm-poo-'hohn)*
Should I call a mechanic?	**¿Debo llamarle al mecánico?** *('deh-boh yah-'mahr-leh ahl meh-'kah-nee-koh)*
You're losing water	**Está perdiendo agua** *(eh-'stah pehr-dee-'ehn-doh 'ah-gwah)*
You need a new filter	**Necesita un nuevo filtro** *(neh-seh-'see-tah oon noo-'eh-voh 'feel-troh)*
You should check the oil	**Debe verificar el aceite** *('deh-beh veh-ree-fee-'kahr ehl ah-'seh·ee-teh)*
Your tires are worn out	**Sus neumáticos están gastados** *(soos neh-oo-'mah-tee-kohs eh-'stahn gah-'stah-dohs)*

You don't have any fluid	**No tiene líquido** (*noh tee-'eh-neh 'lee-kee-doh*)
You're out of gas	**Le falta gasolina** (*leh 'fahl-tah gah-soh-'lee-nah*)
Your tires are flat	**Sus neumáticos están desinflados** (*soos neh-oo-'mah-tee-kohs eh-'stahn dehs-een-'flah-dohs*)
There's...	**Hay...** (*'ah·ee...*)
something loose	**algo que está flojo** (*'ahl-goh keh eh-'stah 'floh-hoh*)
a loud noise	**un sonido ruidoso** (*oon soh-'nee-doh roo-ee-'doh-soh*)
a major problem	**un problema muy grave** (*oon proh-'bleh-mah 'moo·ee 'grah-veh*)
fire and smoke	**fuego y humo** (*'fweh-goh ee 'oo-moh*)
lots of exhaust	**mucho escape de humo** (*'moo-choh eh-'skah-peh deh 'oo-moh*)
a leak	**una gotera** (*'oo-nah goh-'teh-rah*)
It's cut	**Está cortado** (*eh-'stah kohr-'tah-doh*)
It's broken	**Está roto** (*eh-'stah 'roh-toh*)
It's dirty	**Está sucio** (*eh-'stah 'soo-see·oh*)
It's old	**Está viejo** (*eh-'stah vee-'eh-hoh*)
It's not working	**No está funcionando** (*noh eh-'stah foonk-see·oh-'nahn-doh*)
It's stuck	**Está pegado** (*eh-'stah peh-'gah-doh*)
It fell off	**Se cayó** (*seh kah-'yoh*)
It's damaged	**Está dañado** (*eh-'stah dah-'nyah-doh*)
It's locked	**Está cerrado con llave** (*eh-'stah seh-'rrah-doh kohn 'yah-veh*)

ROAD ASSISTANCE
Ayuda en el camino (*ah-'yoo-dah ehn ehl kah-'mee-noh*)

You need (the)...	**Necesita...** (*neh-seh-'see-tah...*)
Where's (the)...	**¿Dónde está...** (*'dohn-deh eh-'stah...*)
alarm	**la alarma?** (*lah ah-'lahr-mah*)
flare	**la antorcha?** (*lah ahn-'tohr-chah*)
jack	**la gata?** (*lah 'gah-tah*)
key	**la llave?** (*lah 'yah-veh*)
latch	**el pestillo?** (*ehl pehs-'tee-yoh*)
lever	**la palanca?** (*lah pah-'lahn-kah*)
locksmith	**el cerrajero?** (*ehl seh-rrah-'heh-roh*)

manual	**el manual?** *(ehl mah-noo-'ahl)*
map	**el mapa?** *(ehl 'mah-pah)*
mechanic	**el mecánico?** *(ehl meh-'kah-nee-koh)*
seat belt	**el cinturón de seguridad?** *(ehl seen-too-'rohn deh seh-goo-ree-'dahd)*
spare tire	**el neumático de repuesto?** *(ehl neh-oo-'mah-tee-koh deh reh-'pweh-stoh)*
tire iron	**el desarmador?** *(ehl dehs-ahr-mah-'dohr)*
tool	**la herramienta?** *(lah eh-rah-mee-'ehn-tah)*
tow truck	**la grúa?** *(lah 'groo-ah)*

Open your trunk, and offer some assistance:

I have (the)...	**Tengo...** *('tehn-goh...)*
board	**la tabla** *(lah 'tah-blah)*
chain	**la cadena** *(lah kah-'deh-nah)*
cone	**el cono** *(ehl 'koh-noh)*
flag	**la bandera** *(lah bahn-'deh-rah)*
flashlight	**la linterna** *(lah leen-'tehr-nah)*
hook	**el gancho** *(ehl 'gahn-choh)*
pipe	**el tubo** *(ehl 'too-boh)*
rope	**la soga** *(lah 'soh-gah)*
siren	**la sirena** *(lah see-'reh-nah)*
string	**el hilo** *(ehl 'ee-loh)*
tape	**la cinta** *(lah 'seen-tah)*
tow bar	**la barra** *(lah 'bah-rrah)*
wire	**el alambre** *(ehl ah-'lahm-breh)*

You never know when you'll have to put these words to work!

Give me (the)...	**Deme...** *('deh-meh...)*
bolt	**el perno** *(ehl 'pehr-noh)*
chisel	**el cincel** *(ehl seen-'sehl)*
clamp	**la prensa de sujetar** *(lah 'prehn-sah deh soo-heh-'tahr)*
compressor	**el compresor de aire** *(ehl kohm-preh-'sohr deh 'ah·ee-reh)*
drill	**el taladro** *(ehl tah-'lah-droh)*
electric cord	**el cordón eléctrico** *(ehl kohr-'dohn eh-'lehk-tree-koh)*
first aid kit	**el botiquín** *(ehl boh-tee-'keen)*
glue	**el pegamento** *(ehl peh-gah-'mehn-toh)*

hacksaw	**la sierra para metales** *(lah see-'eh-rÚah-'pah-rah meh-'tah-lehs)*
hammer	**el martillo** *(ehl mahr-'tee-yoh)*
measuring tape	**la cinta para medir** *(lah 'seen-tah 'pah-rah meh-'deer)*
nail	**el clavo** *(ehl 'klah-voh)*
nut	**la tuerca** *(lah too-'ehr-kah)*
pliers	**las pinzas** *(lahs 'peen-sahs)*
ramp	**la rampa** *(lah 'rahm-pah)*
safety glasses	**los lentes de seguridad** *(lohs 'lehn-tehs deh seh-goo-ree-'dahd)*
sandpaper	**el papel de lija** *(ehl pah-'pehl deh 'lee-hah)*
saw	**el serrucho** *(ehl seh-'rroo-choh)*
scraper	**el raspador** *(ehl rah-spah-'dohr)*
screw	**el tornillo** *(ehl tohr-'nee-yoh)*
screwdriver	**el atornillador** *(ehl ah-tohr-nee-yah-'dohr)*
shovel	**la pala** *(lah 'pah-lah)*
staple	**la grapa** *(lah 'grah-pah)*
tape	**la cinta** *(lah 'seen-tah)*
toolbox	**la caja de herramientas** *(lah 'kah-hah deh eh-rrah-mee-'ehn-tahs)*
wire	**el alambre** *(ehl ah-'lahm-breh)*
wrench	**la llave inglesa** *(lah 'yah-veh een-'gleh-sah)*

Close out your traffic talk with some of these standard statements:

I don't make the laws, I only enforce them	**Yo no hago las leyes, sólo las hago cumplir** *(yoh noh 'ah-goh lahs 'leh-yehs, 'soh-loh lahs 'ah-goh koom-'pleer)*
By signing this ticket, you are not admitting guilt	**Al firmar esta citación no se admite culpabilidad** *(ahl feer-'mahr 'eh-stah see-tah-see-'ohn noh seh ahd-'mee-teh kool-pah-bee-lee-'dahd)*
You can fight it in court	**Puede pelearlo en la corte** *('pweh-deh peh-leh-'ahr-loh ehn lah 'kohr-teh)*
Do you understand everything?	**¿Entiende todo?** *(ehn-tee-'ehn-deh 'toh-doh)*
You may go now	**Puede irse ahora** *('pweh-deh 'eer-seh ah-'oh-rah)*

Whenever you depart, always send folks away with a friendly expression:

Drive with care!	**¡Maneje con cuidado!** *(mah-'neh-heh kohn kwee-'dah-doh)*

| Have a nice day! | ¡Que tenga un buen día! *(keh 'tehn-gah oon bwehn 'dee-ah)* |
| See you later! | ¡Hasta luego! *('ah-stah loo-'eh-goh)* |

TEMAS CULTURALES

Motorists worldwide are accustomed to negotiating traffic fines at the scene with law enforcement officials. In some parts of Latin America, **sobornos** *(soh-'bohr-nohs)* (bribes) and **mordidas** *(mohr-'dee-dahs)* (extra fees) are used to settle matters on the spot. Let them know that such activity is very illegal in this country:

| It is not legal in the United States | No es legal en los Estados Unidos *(noh ehs leh-'gahl ehn lohs eh-'sta dohs oo-'nee-dohs)* |

REPASO

A. What's wrong with your vehicle? Complete these statements using words that you know:

Hay _____ en el motor *('ah·ee ___ ehn ehl moh-'tohr)*

El vehículo necesita _____ y _____ *(ehl veh-'ee-koo-loh neh-seh-'see-tah _____ ee _____)*

Está muy _____ y _____ *(eh-'stah 'moo·ee _____ ee _____)*

B. Name three tools that are usually needed for roadside assistance.

_____   _____   _____

C. List five other tools that are always handy around the house:

_____   _____   _____

_____   _____

CRUCIGRAMA 2

Across

1 el engranaje
3 el fusible
6 el embrague
9 el tirador
12 el ventilador
13 el acelerador
14 el parachoques
15 el radiador
16 el faro delantero
19 la puerta
20 el guardabarro

Down

2 el equipo
4 el indicador de velocidad
5 el tablero de instrumentos
7 la bocina
8 el calentador
10 el freno
11 el carburador
17 el motor
18 la maletera

Está sucio, está viejo y no está funcionando.

¿Su carro o su marido?

PARKING

El estacionamiento *(ehl eh-stah-see·oh-nah-mee-'ehn-toh)*

Moving vehicles aren't the only cause of traffic troubles. These deal with parking problems:

You need (the)…	**Necesita…** *(neh-seh-'see-tah…)*
permit	**el permiso** *(ehl pehr-'mee-soh)*
sticker	**la etiqueta** *(lah eh-tee-'keh-tah)*
ticket	**el boleto** *(ehl boh-'leh-toh)*
You have to put more money in the meter	**Tiene que poner más dinero en el parquímetro** *(tee-'eh-neh keh poh-'nehr mahs dee-'neh-roh ehn ehl pahr-'kee-meh-troh)*
You are double parked	**Está estacionado en doble hilera** *(eh-'stah eh-stah-see·oh-'nah-doh ehn 'doh-bleh ee-'leh-rah)*
It's parked poorly	**Está mal estacionado** *(eh-'stah mahl eh-stahsee·oh-'nah-doh)*
This is handicapped parking	**Este es estacionamiento para gente incapacitada** *('eh-steh ehs eh-stah-see·oh-nah-mee-'ehn-toh 'pah-rah 'hehn-teh een-kah-pah-see-'tah-dah)*

Can you read the sign?	**¿Puede leer la señal?** *('pweh-deh leh-'ehr lah seh-'nyahl)*
Your time has expired	**La hora ya ha expirado** *(lah 'oh-rah yah ah ehks pee-'rah-doh)*
You cannot park in the red zone	**No puede estacionar en la zona roja** *(noh 'pweh-deh eh-stah-see·oh-'nahr ehn lah 'soh-nah 'roh-hah)*
This zone is for loading and unloading	**Esta zona es para cargar y descargar** *('eh-stah 'soh -nah ehs 'pah-rah kahr-'gahr ee dehs-kahr-'gahr)*
This is for emergency parking	**Este es estacionamiento para emergencias** *('eh-steh ehs eh-stah-see·oh-nah-mee-'ehn-toh 'pah-rah eh-mehr-'hehn-see·ahs)*
You are too close to the hydrant	**Está muy cerca de la llave de incedios** *(eh-'stah 'moo·ee 'sehr-kah deh lah 'yah-veh deh een-'sehn-dee-ohs)*
This zone is clearly marked	**Esta zona está marcada claramente** *('eh-stah 'soh-nah eh-'stah mahr-'kah-dah klah-rah-'mehn-teh)*
There's a space over there	**Hay un espacio allí** *('ah·ee oon eh-'spah-see·oh ah-'yee)*
This section is reserved	**Esta parte está reservada** *('eh-stah 'pahr-teh eh-'stah reh-sehr-'vah-dah)*
If you have a complaint, call this number	**Si tiene una queja, llame a este número** *(see tee-'eh-neh 'oo-nah 'keh-hah, 'yah-meh ah 'eh-steh 'noo-meh-roh)*
Look at the...	**Mire...** *('mee-reh...)*
arrow	**la flecha** *(lah 'fleh-chah)*
color	**el color** *(ehl koh-'lohr)*
cone	**el cono** *('koh-noh)*
hydrant	**la llave de incendios** *(lah 'yah-veh deh een-'sehn-dee-ohs)*
line	**la línea** *(lah 'lee-neh-ah)*
meter	**el parquímetro** *(ehl pahr-'kee-meh-troh)*
sign	**la señal** *(lah seh-'nyahl)*
space	**el espacio** *(ehl eh-'spah-see·oh)*

➤ Put the vehicle in...

Ponga el vehículo en... *('pohn-gah ehl veh-'ee-koo loh ehn...)*

parking structure

el edificio para estacionamiento *(ehl eh-dee-'fee see·oh 'pah-rah eh-stah-see·oh-nah-mee-'ehn-toh)*

parking lot

el lote de estacionamiento *(ehl 'loh-teh deh eh-stah-see·oh-nah-mee-'ehn-toh)*

enclosed garage

el garage encerrado *(ehl gah-'rah-heh ehn-seh-'rrah-doh)*

➤ Mutter one of these phrases when you don't have all the answers!

It depends	**Depende** *(deh-'pehn-deh)*
It's possible	**Es posible** *(ehs poh-'see-bleh)*
Maybe	**Quizás** *(kee-'sahs)*

➤ Remember your simple commands.

Get in the car	**Suba al carro** *('soo-bah ahl 'kah-rroh)*
Stay in the car	**Quédese en el carro** *('keh-deh-seh ehn ehl 'kah-rroh)*
Get out of the car	**Salga del carro** *('sahl-gah dehl 'kah-rroh)*

TRANSPORTATION

El transporte *(ehl trahns-'pohr-teh)*

Have you ever noticed how many different kinds of vehicles there are? Take this opportunity to practice several common modes of transportation. Add words to this list if you like:

It was (the)...

Fue... *(fweh...)*

ambulance	**la ambulancia** *(lah ahm-boo-'lahn-see·ah)*
armored car	**el carro blindado** *(ehl 'kah-rroh bleen-'dah-doh)*
bicycle	**la bicicleta** *(lah bee-see-'kleh-tah)*
boat	**el bote** *(ehl 'boh-teh)*
bulldozer	**la niveladora** *(lah nee-veh-lah-'doh-rah)*
bus	**el autobús** *(ehl ow-toh-'boos)*
camper	**el cámper** *(ehl 'kahm-pehr)*
car	**el carro** *(ehl 'kah-rroh)*

cement truck	**la mezcladora de cemento** *(lah meh-sklah-'doh-rah deh seh-'mehn-toh)*
commercial vehicle	**el vehículo comercial** *(ehl veh-'ee-koo-loh koh-mehr-see-'ahl)*
convertible	**el descapotable** *(ehl dehs-kah-poh-'tah-bleh)*
delivery truck	**el camión de reparto** *(ehl kah-mee-'ohn deh reh-'pahr-toh)*
dump truck	**el volquete** *(ehl vohl-'keh-teh)*
firetruck	**el camión de bomberos** *(ehl kah-mee-'ohn deh bohm-'beh-rohs)*
flatbed truck	**el camión de plataforma** *(ehl kah-mee-'ohn deh plah-tah-'fohr-mah)*
helicopter	**el helicóptero** *(ehl eh-lee-'kohp-teh-roh)*
house trailer	**el coche habitación** *(ehl 'koh-cheh ah-bee-tah-see-'ohn)*
jeep	**el jip** *(ehl yeep)*
moped	**la bicicleta motorizada** *(lah bee-see-'kleh-tah moh-toh-ree-'sah-dah)*
motorcycle	**la motocicleta** *(lah moh-toh-see-'kleh-tah)*
pickup	**la camioneta** *(lah kah-mee·oh-'neh-tah)*
plane	**el avión** *(ehl ah-vee-'ohn)*
recreation vehicle	**el vehículo de recreo** *(ehl veh-'ee-koo-loh deh reh-'kreh-oh)*
school bus	**el autobús escolar** *(ehl ow-toh-'boos eh-skoh-'lahr)*
sedan	**el sedán** *(ehl seh-'dahn)*
semi-trailer	**el semi-remolque** *(ehl seh-mee-reh-'mohl-keh)*
sportscar	**el carro deportivo** *(ehl 'kah-rroh deh-pohr-'tee-voh)*
station wagon	**el coche vagón** *(ehl 'koh-cheh vah-'gohn)*
streetcar	**el tranvía** *(ehl trahn-'vee-ah)*
subway	**el metro** *(ehl 'meh-troh)*
tank truck	**el camión cisterna** *(ehl kah-mee-'ohn sees-'tehr-nah)*
taxi	**el taxi** *(ehl 'tahk-see)*
tour bus	**el autobús de turismo** *(ehl ow-toh-'boos deh too-'rees-moh)*
tow truck	**la grúa** *(lah 'groo-ah)*
tractor	**el tractor** *(ehl trahk-'tohr)*
tractor trailer	**el camión tractor** *(ehl kah-mee-'ohn trahk-'tohr)*
train	**el tren** *(ehl trehn)*
truck	**el camión** *(ehl kah-mee-'ohn)*
van	**la vagoneta, la furgoneta** *(lah vah-goh-'neh-tah, lah fuhr-goh-'neh-tah)*

➤ There's always something going on at the airport. Learn how to talk about air travel:

airstrip	**la pista de aterrizaje** *(lah 'pee-stah deh ah-teh-rree-'sah-heh)*
flight	**el vuelo** *(ehl 'vweh-loh)*
terminal	**el terminal** *(ehl tehr-mee-'nahl)*

➤ You'll need these phrases as well:

by foot	**a pie** *(ah 'pee-eh)*
by horse	**a caballo** *(ah kah-'bah-yoh)*
by skateboard	**a patineta** *(ah pah-tee-'neh-tah)*

➤ Speak more "Spanglish"!

el jet	**el minivan**
el rollerblading	**el SUV**
el trailer	**el 4-wheel drive**
el 4 by 4	**el sixteen-wheeler**
el hatchback	

¿Sabe por qué la paré?
¿Sabe el límite de velocidad?
¿Sabe cuán rápido estaba manejando?

No sé.
Es posible.
Quizás.

Occasionally, law enforcement officials on patrol run across lost travelers in need of more than just directions. Not only will these words help you relate to Spanish-speaking visitors, but they can be used whenever *you* vacation in Spain or Latin America.

airport	**el aeropuerto** *(ehl ah-eh-roh-'pwehr-toh)*
busboy	**el botones** *(ehl boh-'toh-nehs)*
camera	**la cámara** *(lah 'kah-mah-rah)*
concierge	**el conserje** *(ehl kohn-'sehr-heh)*
customs	**la aduana** *(lah ah-'dwah-nah)*
drinking water	**el agua potable** *(ehl 'ah-gwah poh-'tah-bleh)*
exchange	**el cambio** *(ehl 'kahm-bee·oh)*
hotel	**el hotel** *(ehl oh-'tehl)*
passport	**el pasaporte** *(ehl pah-sah-'pohr-teh)*
point of interest	**el lugar de interés** *(ehl loo-'gahr deh een-teh-'rehs)*
reservation	**la reservación** *(lah reh-sehr-vah-see-'ohn)*
round trip ticket	**el boleto de ida y vuelta** *(ehl boh-'leh-toh deh 'ee-dah ee 'vwehl-tah)*
shuttle	**el transbordador** *(ehl trahns-bohr-dah-'dohr)*
suitcase	**la maleta** *(lah mah-'leh-tah)*
travel agency	**la agencia de viajes** *(lah ah-'hehn-see·ah deh vee-'ah-hehs)*
visa	**la visa** *(lah 'vee-sah)*

THE PEDESTRIAN
El peatón *(ehl peh-ah-'tohn)*

Many people travel by foot or bicycle, which creates a unique set of problems for law enforcement. This is especially true in larger cities, where things may get a little hectic. Are you able to use any of these words and phrases?

You crossed when the light was red	**Cruzó cuando la luz estaba en rojo** *(kroo-'soh 'kwahn-doh lah loos eh-'stah-bah ehn 'roh-hoh)*
You crossed when the "Don't walk" sign was on	**Cruzó cuando la señal decía "No caminar"** *(kroo-'soh 'kwahn-doh lah seh-'nyahl deh-'see-ah noh kah-mee-'nahr)*
You didn't use the crosswalk	**No usó el cruce de peatones** *(noh oo-'soh ehl 'kroo-seh deh peh-ah-'toh-nehs)*
You were walking in the street	**Caminaba en la calle** *(kah-mee-'nah-bah ehn lah 'kah-yeh)*

| You crossed when there was a lot of traffic | **Cruzó con mucho tráfico** *(kroo'-soh kohn 'moo-choh 'trah-fee-koh)* |
| You didn't wait for the green light | **No esperó para la luz verde** *(noh eh-speh-'roh 'pah-rah lah loos 'vehr-deh* |

Make everyone aware of our special civilians:

He/She has (the)...	**Tiene...** *(tee-'eh-neh...)*
wheelchair	**la silla de ruedas** *(lah 'see-yah deh roo-'eh-dahs)*
seeing eye dog	**el perro guía** *(ehl 'peh-rroh 'gee-ah)*
white cane	**el bastón blanco** *(ehl bah-'stohn 'blahn-koh)*
crutches	**las muletas** *(lahs moo-'leh-tahs)*

BICYCLES!

¡Las bicicletas! *(lahs bee-see-'kleh-tahs)*

You must follow the same rules as automobile drivers	**Tiene que seguir las mismas reglas que los choferes de autos** *(tee-'eh-neh keh seh-'geer lahs 'mees-mahs 'reh-glahs keh lohs choh-'feh-rehs deh 'ow-tohs)*
The bicycle should be registered	**La bicicleta debe estar registrada** *(lah bee-see-'kleh-tah 'deh-beh eh-'stahr reh-hee-'strah-dah)*
You cannot carry passengers on that bicycle	**No puede llevar pasajeros en esa bicicleta** *(noh 'pweh-deh yeh-'vahr pah-sah-'heh-roh sehn 'eh-sah bee-see-'kleh-tah)*
You need a helmet	**Necesita un casco** *(neh-seh-'see-tah oon 'kah-skoh)*
Lock your bike to the bike rack	**Asegure su bicicleta en el sujetador de bicicletas** *(ah-seh-'goo-reh soo bee-see-'kleh-tah ehn ehl soo'heh-tah-'dohr deh bee-see-'kleh-tahs)*

INFORMACIÓN PRIVADA

➤ People all over the world seem to find pleasure in walking their dog or **perro** *('peh-rroh)*. This establishes a very unique set of problems for law enforcement:

| It needs a leash | **Necesita una correa** *(neh-seh-'see-tah 'oo-nah koh-'rreh-ah)* |

You have to clean up its mess	**Tiene que limpiar el excremento** *(tee-'eh-neh keh leem-pee-'ahr ehl ehks-kreh-'mehn-toh)*
It's lost	**Está perdido** *(eh-'stah pehr-'dee-doh)*
It is ferocious and dangerous	**Es feroz y peligroso** *(ehs feh-'rohs ee peh-lee-'groh-soh)*
Dogs are not allowed	**Los perros están prohibidos** *(lohs 'peh-rrohs eh-'stahn proh·ee-'bee-dohs)*
It barks a lot	**Ladra mucho** *('lah-drah 'moo-choh)*

PLEASE READ THE SIGN
Favor de leer el letrero *(fah-'vohr deh leh-'ehr ehl leh-'treh-roh)*

Adjusting to a foreign country involves learning about the different city signs and signals. Help out the Spanish speaker who seems confused:

Curve	**Curva** *('koor-vah)*
Detour	**Desviación** *(dehs-vee-ah-see-'ohn)*
Do Not Enter	**Prohibido Entrar** *(proh-ee-'bee-doh ehn-'trahr)*
Do Not Litter	**No Tire Basura** *(noh 'tee-reh bah-'soo-rah)*
Do Not Pass	**Prohibido Pasar** *(proh-ee-'bee-doh pah-'sahr)*
Don't Walk	**No Camine** *(noh kah-'mee-neh)*
Entrance	**Entrada** *(ehn-'trah-dah)*
Exit	**Salida** *(sah-'lee-dah)*
Narrow Road	**Camino Estrecho** *(kah-'mee-noh eh-'streh-choh)*
No Left Turn	**No Doblar a la Izquierda** *(noh doh-'blahr ah lah ees-kee-'ehr-dah)*
No Parking	**Estacionamiento Prohibido** *(eh-stah-see·oh-nah-mee-'ehn-toh proh·ee-'bee-doh)*

No U Turn	**Prohibida la Vuelta en "U"** *(proh·ee-'bee-dah lah 'vwehl-tah ehn oo)*
One Way	**Dirección Unica** *(dee-rehk-see-'ohn 'oo-nee-kah)*
Passing Lane	**Pista para Pasar** *('pee-stah 'pah-rah pah-'sahr)*
Railroad Crossing	**Cruce de Ferrocarril** *('kroo-seh deh feh-rroh-kah-'rreel)*
Road Closed	**Camino Cerrado** *(kah-'mee-noh seh-'rrah-doh)*
Road Crossing	**Cruce de Caminos** *('kroo-seh deh kah-'mee-nohs)*
School Zone	**Zona Escolar** *('soh-nah eh-skoh-'lahr)*
Slow	**Despacio** *(dehs-'pah-see·oh)*
Speed Limit	**Velocidad Máxima** *(veh-loh-see-'dahd 'mahk-see-mah)*
Stop	**Parada** (or **Alto**) *(pah-'rah-dah, 'ahl-toh)*
Stop Ahead	**Parada Más Adelante** *(pah-'rah-dah mahs ah-deh-'lahn-teh)*
Traffic Circle	**Glorieta** *(gloh-ree-'eh-tah)*
Wait	**Espere** *(eh-'speh-reh)*
Walk	**Camine** *(kah-'mee-neh)*
Wrong Way	**Vía Equivocada** *('vee-ah eh-kee-voh-'kah-dah)*
Yield	**Ceder** *(seh-'dehr)*

INFORMACIÓN PRIVADA

➤ Learn the translations of all the signs you can:

Closed	**Cerrado** *(seh-'rrah-doh)*
Emergency	**Emergencia** *(eh-mehr-'hehn-see·ah)*
For Rent	**Se Alquila** *(seh ahl-'kee-lah)*
For Sale	**Se Vende** *(seh 'vehn-deh)*
Handicapped	**Minusválidos** *(mee-noos-'vah-lee-dohs)*
No Smoking	**No Fumar** *(noh foo-'mahr)*
Open	**Abierto** *(ah-bee-'ehr-toh)*
Out of Order	**Descompuesto** *(dehs-kohm-'pweh-stoh)*
Pull	**Jale** *('hah-leh)*
Push	**Empuje** *(ehm-'poo-heh)*
Restrooms	**Servicios sanitarios** *(sehr-'vee-see·ohs sah-nee-'tah-ree·ohs)*

A. Translate and connect:

sign	la zona *(lah 'soh-nah)*
line	el lote *(ehl 'loh-teh)*
space	la máquina *(lah 'mah-kee-nah)*
machine	la señal *(lah seh-'nyahl)*
lot	la fecha *(lah 'feh-chah)*
arrow	el espacio *(ehl eh-'spah-see·oh)*
zone	la línea *(lah 'lee-neh-ah)*

B. List five popular modes of public transportation:

_____   _____   _____

_____   _____

C. Can you name three different kinds of automobiles?

_____   _____   _____

D. Make a comment to the public about each of the following concerns:

el peatón *(ehl peh-ah-'tohn)* _____

la bicicleta *(lah bee-see-'kleh-tah)* _____

el perro *(ehl 'peh-rroh)* _____

E. Explain to a Spanish speaker what these signs mean:

Detour_____

Out of order_____

One way_____

ANSWERS

A.			
sign	la señal	lot	el lote
line	la línea	arrow	la flecha
space	el espacio	zone	la zona
machine	la máquina		

131

ROAD HAZARDS

Los obstáculos de la calle *(lohs ohb-'stah-koo-lohs deh lah 'kah-yeh)*

One common sign that nonEnglish speakers must be made aware of is Danger Ahead! Inform the Spanish-speaking public that there are hazards down the road. Using these words correctly could prevent death or serious injury:

It's (the)...	**Es...** *(ehs...)*
accident	**el accidente** *(ehl ahk-see-'dehn-teh)*
asphalt work	**el asfaltado** *(ehl ahs-fahl-'tah-doh)*
bump	**el rompemuelle** *(ehl rohm-peh-'mweh-yeh)*
chemical danger	**el peligro químico** *(ehl peh-'lee-groh 'kee-mee-koh)*
construction	**la construcción** *(lah kohn-strook-see-'ohn)*
detour	**el desvío** *(ehl dehs-'vee-oh)*
dirt	**la tierra** *(lah tee-'eh-rrah)*
glass	**el vidrio** *(ehl 'vee-dree-oh)*
gravel	**el cascajo** *(ehl kahs-'kah-hoh)*
hole	**el hoyo** *(ehl 'oh-yoh)*
mud	**el lodo** *(ehl 'loh-doh)*
oil	**el aceite** *(ehl ah-'seh·ee-teh)*
pavement	**el pavimento** *(ehl pah-vee-mee-'ehn-toh)*
pothole	**el bache** *(ehl 'bah-cheh)*
puddle	**la charca** *(lah 'chahr-kah)*
roadblock	**la barricada** *(lah bah-rree-'kah-dah)*
rock	**la piedra** *(lah pee-'eh-drah)*
sand	**la arena** *(lah ah-'reh-nah)*
spill	**el derramamiento** *(ehl deh-rrah-mee-'ehn-toh)*
tar	**la brea** *(lah 'breh-ah)*
trash	**la basura** *(lah bah-'soo-rah)*

What else is wrong? Use **está:** *('eh-stah)*

The street is...	**La calle está...** *(lah 'kah-yeh eh-'stah...)*
blocked off	**obstruida** *(ohb-stroo-'ee-dah)*
defective	**defectuosa** *(deh-fehk-too-'oh-sah)*
dangerous	**peligrosa** *(peh-lee-'groh-sah)*
flooded	**inundada** *(een-oon-'dah-dah)*
narrow	**estrecha** *(eh-'streh-chah)*
not marked	**sin marcadores** *(seen mahr-kah-'doh-rehs)*
not complete	**incompleta** *(een-kohm-'pleh-tah)*
slippery	**resbaladiza** *(rehs-bah-lah-'dee-sah)*

twisted	**torcida** *(tohr-'see-dah)*
uneven	**desigual** *(dehs-ee-'gwahl)*
without lights	**sin luces** *(seen 'loo-sehs)*

HOW'S THE WEATHER?
¿Cómo está el tiempo? *('koh-moh eh-'stah ehl tee-'ehm-poh)*

A primary cause of traffic trouble involves the weather. Take extra time to practice these words daily. Look outside right now and make a statement:

It's...	**Está...** *(eh-'stah...)*
clear	**despejado** *(dehs-peh-'hah-doh)*
cloudy	**nublado** *(noo-'blah-doh)*
cool	**fresco** *('frehs-koh)*
drizzling	**lloviznando** *(yoh-vees-'nahn-doh)*
freezing	**helado** *(eh-'lah-doh)*
humid	**húmedo** *('oo-meh-doh)*
raining	**lloviendo** *(yoh-vee-'ehn-doh)*
snowing	**nevando** *(neh-'vahn-doh)*
stormy	**tempestuoso** *(tehm-peh-stoo-'oh-soh)*
warm	**tibio** *('tee-bee·oh)*

Here are some other ways to talk about Mother Nature:

It's...	Hace... *('ah-seh...)*
cold	**frío** *('free-oh)*
good weather	**buen tiempo** *('bwehn tee-'ehm-poh)*
hot	**calor** *(kah-'lohr)*
windy	**viento** *(vee-'ehn-toh)*

I don't like (the)...	No me gusta(n)... *(noh meh 'goo-stah[n]...)*
climate	**el clima** *(ehl 'klee-mah)*
clouds	**las nubes** *(lahs 'noo-behs)*
fog	**la neblina** *(lah neh-'blee-nah)*
frost	**la escarcha** *(lah eh-'skahr-chah)*
hail	**el granizo** *(ehl grah-'nee-soh)*
humidity	**la humedad** *(lah oo-meh-'dahd)*
lightning	**el relámpago** *(ehl reh-'lahm-pah-goh)*
rain	**la lluvia** *(lah 'yoo-vee·ah)*
snow	**la nieve** *(lah nee-'eh-veh)*
storm	**la tormenta** *(lah tohr-'mehn-tah)*
sun	**el sol** *(ehl sohl)*
thunder	**el trueno** *(ehl troo-'eh-noh)*
wind	**el viento** *(ehl vee-'ehn-toh)*

INFORMACIÓN PRIVADA

➤ Learn the names of the seasons in Spanish:

It's...	Es... *(ehs...)*
spring	**la primavera** *(lah pree-mah-'veh-rah)*
summer	**el verano** *(ehl veh-'rah-noh)*
fall	**el otoño** *(ehl oh-'toh-nyoh)*
winter	**el invierno** *(ehl een-vee-'ehr-noh)*

The process of questioning civilians is often accompanied by clear and concise commands. This is particularly true in the world of vehicle patrol. Add these command words and phrases to those you have already learned.

Lower	**Baje**	**Baje la ventana** *('bah-heh lah vehn-'tah-nah)*
Move	**Mueva**	**Mueva el camión** *(moo-'eh-vah ehl kah-mee-'ohn)*
Park	**Estacione**	**Estacione su carro** *(eh-stah-see-'oh-neh soo 'kah-rroh)*
Pay	**Pague**	**Pague el dinero** *('pah-geh ehl dee-'neh-roh)*
Put inside	**Meta**	**Meta el papel aquí** *('meh-tah ehl pah-'pehl ah-'kee)*
Raise	**Levante**	**Levante el capot** *(leh-'vahn-teh ehl kah-'poht)*
Take out	**Saque**	**Saque la licencia** *('sah-keh lah lee-'sehn-see·ah)*
Turn off	**Apague**	**Apague el motor** *(ah-'pah-geh ehl moh-'tohr)*
Turn on	**Prenda**	**Prenda la luz** *('prehn-dah lah loos)*
Use	**Use**	**Use la pluma** *('oo-seh lah 'ploo-mah)*

Study these word phrases!

Keep the hands up	**Mantenga las manos en alto** *(mahn-'tehn-gah lahs 'mah-nohs ehn 'ahl-toh)*
Lie down	**Acuéstese** *(ah-'kweh-steh-seh)*
Listen to me	**Escúcheme** *(eh-'skoo-cheh-meh)*
Pull over	**Hágase a un lado** *('ah-gah-seh ah oon 'lah-doh)*

We've been using command words all along. Care to review? All of this vocabulary has been presented:

Give it to me, now!	**¡Démelo ya!** *('deh-meh-loh yah)*
Give me the keys	**Deme las llaves** *('deh-meh lahs 'yah-vehs)*
Go with the flow of traffic	**Vaya con la corriente de tráfico** *('vah-yah kohn lah koh-rree-'ehn-teh deh 'trah-fee-koh)*
Open the trunk	**Abra la maletera** *('ah-brah lah mah-leh-'teh-rah)*
Show me your registration	**Muéstreme su registro** *('mweh-streh-meh soo reh-'hee-stroh)*
Sign here on the ticket	**Firme aquí en la boleta** *('feer-meh ah-'kee ehn lah boh-'leh-tah)*
Stop at the corner	**Párese en la esquina** *('pah-reh-seh ehn lah eh-'skee-nah)*
Take it out of the glove box!	**¡Sáquelo de la guantera!** *('sah-keh-loh deh lah gwahn-'teh-rah)*
Turn it off, please!	**¡Apáguelo, por favor!** *(ah-'pah-geh-loh, pohr fah-'vohr)*
Wait a moment	**Espere un momento** *(eh-'speh-reh oon moh-'mehn-toh)*

And here are a few new ones:

Take two steps to the left	**Camine dos pasos a la izquierda** *(kah-'mee-neh dohs 'pah-sohs ah la ees-kee-'ehr-dah)*
Turn your back towards me	**Voltéese de espaldas a mí** *(vohl-'teh-eh-seh deh ehs-'pahl-dahs ah mee)*
Get down on your knees	**Póngase de rodillas** *('pohn-gah-seh deh roh-'dee-yahs)*
Sit back on your feet	**Siéntese sobre los talones** *(see-'ehn-teh-seh 'soh-breh lohs tah-'loh-nehs)*
Interlock your fingers	**Cruce los dedos de las manos** *('kroo-seh lohs 'deh-dohs deh lahs 'mah-nohs)*
Put your knees together	**Junte las rodillas** *('hoon-teh lahs roh-'dee-yahs)*
Cross your ankles	**Cruce los tobillos** *('kroo-seh lohs toh-'bee-yohs)*
Turn your head to the right	**Gire la cabeza a la derecha** *('hee-reh lah kah-'beh-sah ah lah deh-'reh-chah)*

INFORMACIÓN PRIVADA

➤ What do you think of "that"? Practice:

Don't do that	**No haga eso** *(noh 'ah-gah 'eh-soh)*
Give me that	**Deme eso** *('deh-meh 'eh-soh)*
Keep that	**Guarde eso** *('gwahr-deh'eh-soh)*

➤ Some of your auto stops involve unfriendly encounters. Suspects are pulled over for alleged crimes, and must be apprehended—with as little confrontation as possible. Do you have enough Spanish to get it handled?

I represent the law	**Represento la ley** *(reh-preh-'sehn-toh lah 'leh·ee)*
You are under arrest	**Usted está arrestado** *(oo-'stehd eh-'stah ah-rreh-'stah-doh)*
Listen carefully	**Escuche con cuidado** *(eh-'skoo-cheh kohn kwee-'dah-doh)*
Keep your hands...	**Mantenga las manos...** *(mahn-'tehn-gah lahs 'mah-nohs...)*
where I can see them	**dónde las pueda ver** *('dohn-deh lahs 'pweh-dah vehr)*
over your head	**sobre la cabeza** *('soh-breh lah kah-'beh-sah)*
on the dashboard	**en el tablero** *(ehn ehl tah-'bleh-roh)*
on the steering wheel	**en el volante** *(ehn ehl voh-'lahn-teh)*
on top of the car	**encima del carro** *(ehn-'see-mah dehl 'kah-rroh)*
on the windshield	**en el parabrisas** *(ehn ehl pah-rah-'bree-sahs)*

136

Pull over and stop	**Hágase a un lado y párese** *('ah-gah-seh ah oon 'lah-doh ee 'pah-reh-seh)*
Turn off the engine	**Apague el motor** *(ah-'pah-geh ehl moh-'tohr)*
Take the keys out of the ignition	**Saque las llaves del encendido** *('sah-keh lahs 'yah-vehs dehl ehn-sehn-'dee-doh)*
Throw the keys out of the car	**Tire las llaves fuera del carro** *('tee-reh lahs 'yah-vehs 'fweh-rah dehl 'kah-rroh)*
Get out of the car	**Salga del carro** *('sahl-gah dehl 'kah-rroh)*
Walk backwards toward me	**Camine hacia mí de espalda** *('kah-mee-neh 'ah-see·ah mee deh eh-'spahl-dah)*
Lie on the ground face down	**Acuéstese boca abajo** *(ah-'kweh-steh-seh 'boh-kah ah-'bah-hoh)*

Hoy hace buen tiempo y está tibio y despejado.

 GRANDES HABILIDADES

Literally hundreds of *Action Words* relate in some way to the world of traffic control. And they all work well with the *Super Skill* phrases you studied earlier. Here's a quick review:

Please…	**Favor de…** *(fah-'vohr deh…)*
Don't…	**No…** *(noh…)*
You have to…	**Tiene que…** *(tee-'eh-neh keh…)*
You need…	**Necesita…** *(neh-seh-'see-tah…)*
I'm going to…	**Voy a…** *('voh-ee ah…)*
You should…	**Debe…** *('deh-beh…)*
One must…	**Hay que…** *('ah·ee keh…)*

Now take these super phrases and pull words from the list below to make useful comments for traffic control. This is enough to get you started:

Please fasten your belts	**Favor de *amarrar* sus cinturones** *(fah-'vohr deh ah-mah-'rrahr soos seen-too-'roh-nehs)*
You have to continue forward	**Tiene que *seguir* adelante** *(tee-'eh-neh keh seh-'geer ah-deh-'lahn-teh)*

I'm going to push your vehicle	Voy a *empujar* su vehículo *('voh-ee ah ehm-poo-'hahr soo veh-'ee-koo-loh)*
to approve	**aprobar** *(ah-proh-'bahr)*
to arrange	**arreglar** *(ah-rreh-'glahr)*
to back up	**retroceder** *(reh-troh-seh-'dehr)*
to begin	**empezar** *(ehm-peh-'sahr)*
to break	**quebrar** *(keh-'brahr)*
to change	**cambiar** *(kahm-bee-'ahr)*
to charge	**cargar** *(kahr-'gahr)*
to check out	**averiguar** *(ah-veh-ree-'gwahr)*
to clean	**limpiar** *(leem-pee-'ahr)*
to continue	**seguir** *(seh-'geer)*
to crash	**chocar** *(choh-'kahr)*
to cross	**cruzar** *(croo-'sahr)*
to deny	**negar** *(neh-'gahr)*
to fasten	**amarrar** *(ah-mah-'rrahr)*
to find	**encontrar** *(ehn-kohn-'trahr)*
to finish	**terminar** *(tehr-mee-'nahr)*
to go	**ir** *(eer)*
to impound	**embargar** *(ehm-bahr-'gahr)*
to look	**mirar** *(mee-'rahr)*
to lose	**perder** *(pehr-'dehr)*
to measure	**medir** *(meh-'deer)*
to obey	**obedecer** *(oh-beh-deh-'sehr)*
to obstruct	**obstruir** *(ohb-stroo-'eer)*
to park	**estacionar** *(eh-stah-see·oh-'nahr)*
to pass	**pasar** *(pah-'sahr)*
to pull	**jalar** *(hah-'lahr)*
to push	**empujar** *(ehm-poo-'hahr)*
to renew	**renovar** *(reh-noh-'vahr)*
to replace	**reemplazar** *(reh-ehm-plah-'sahr)*
to search	**buscar** *(boo-'skahr)*
to see	**ver** *(vehr)*
to signal	**señalar** *(seh-nyah-'lahr)*
to start up	**arrancar** *(ah-rrahn-'kahr)*
to steer	**dirigir** *(dee-ree-'heer)*
to stop	**parar** *(pah-'rahr)*
to swerve	**zigzaguear** *(seeg-sah-geh-'ahr)*
to tow	**remolcar** *(reh-mohl-'kahr)*
to travel	**viajar** *(vee-ah-'hahr)*
to trust	**confiar** *(kohn-fee-'ahr)*
to turn	**virar** *(vee-'rahr)*
to warn	**advertir** *(ahd-vehr-'teer)*
to yield	**ceder el paso** *(seh-'dehr ehl 'pah-soh)*

Bear in mind that all *Action Words* can be altered to communicate time-referenced messages. For example, you know that the **–ndo** ending can indicate actions that are taking place *right now*:

> **manejar** (to drive)   I am driving   **Estoy manejando** *(eh-'stoh-ee mah-neh-'hahn-doh)*

And you know that there are at least four consistent changes that occur when *Action Words* refer to *everyday activities*:

I drive	**Manejo** *(mah-'neh-hoh)*
You drive, **He/She** drives	**Maneja** *(mah-'neh-hah)*
You (pl.) drive, **They** drive	**Manejan** *(mah-'neh-hahn)*
We drive	**Manejamos** *(mah-neh-'hah-mohs)*

You've also probably realized that not all *Action Words* like to follow the rules. Look at these very important three irregular verbs:

	Ir (to go) *(eer)*	**Tener** (to have) *(teh-'nehr)*	**Ser** (to be) *('sehr)*
(I)	**voy** *('voh-ee)*	**tengo** *('tehn-goh)*	**soy** *('soh-ee)*
(you, he, she)	**va** *(vah)*	**tiene** *(tee-'eh-neh)*	**es** *(ehs)*
(you [pl.], they)	**van** *(vahn)*	**tienen** *(tee-'eh-nehn)*	**son** *(sohn)*
(we)	**vamos** *('vah-mohs)*	**tenemos** *(teh-'neh-mohs)*	**somos** *('soh-mohs)*

See how they don't follow the regular pattern? Notice the other unusual patterns below. These two verbs are used daily by law enforcement officials everywhere, so spend as much time as you need to review:

Poder (to be able) *(poh-'dehr)*

(I)	**puedo** *('pweh-doh)*	I can drive	**Puedo manejar** *('pweh-doh mah-neh-'hahr)*
(you, he, she)	**puede** *('pweh-deh)*	He can go	**Puede ir** *('pweh-deh eer)*
(you [pl.], they)	**pueden** *('pweh-dehn)*	They can move	**Pueden mover** *('pweh-dehn moh-'vehr)*
(we)	**podemos** *(poh-'deh-mohs)*	We can back up	**Podemos retroceder** *(poh-'deh-mohs reh-troh-seh-'dehr)*

Querer (to want) *(keh-'rehr)*

(I)	**quiero** *(kee-'eh-roh)*	I want to park	**Quiero estacionar** *(kee-'eh-roh eh-stah-see·oh-'nahr)*
(you, he, she)	**quiere** *(kee-'eh-reh)*	She wants to stop	**Quiere parar** *(kee-'eh-reh pah-'rahr)*
(you [pl.], they)	**quieren** *(kee-'eh-rehn)*	They want to pass	**Quieren pasar** *(kee-'eh-rehn pah-'sahr)*
(we)	**queremos** *(keh-'reh-mohs)*	We want to turn	**Queremos virar** *(keh-'reh-mohs vee-'rahr)*

Many irregular verbs follow a **–ue** or **–ie** pattern that becomes familiar with practice:

	Dormir (to sleep) *(dohr-'meer)*	**Entender** (to understand) *(ehn-tehn-'dehr)*
(I)	**duermo** *('dwehr-moh)*	**entiendo** *(ehn-tee-'ehn-doh)*
(you, he, she)	**duerme** *('dwehr-meh)*	**entiende** *(ehn-tee-'ehn-deh)*
(you [pl.], they)	**duermen** *('dwehr-mehn)*	**entienden** *(ehn-tee-'ehn-dehn)*
(we)	**dormimos** *(dohr-'mee-mohs)*	**entendemos** *(ehn-tehn-'deh-mohs)*

	Encontrar (to find) *(ehn-kohn-'trahr)*	**Preferir** (to prefer) *(preh-feh-'reer)*
(I)	**encuentro** *(ehn-'kwehn-troh)*	**prefiero** *(preh-fee-'eh-roh)*
(you, he, she)	**encuentra** *(ehn-'kwehn-trah)*	**prefiere** *(preh-fee-'eh-reh)*
(you [pl.], they)	**encuentran** *(ehn-'kwehn-trahn)*	**prefieren** *(preh-fee-'eh-rehn)*
(we)	**encontramos** *(ehn-kohn-'trah-mohs)*	**preferimos** *(preh-feh-'ree-mohs)*

Here are three other ways to discuss one's likes and dislikes. Note how unique each form is:

Do you like...?	**¿Le gusta...?** *(leh 'goo-stah...)*
Yes, I like...	**Sí, me gusta...** *(see, meh-'goo-stah...)*
Would you like...?	**¿Quisiera...?** *(kee-see-'eh-rah...)*
Yes, I'd like...	**Sí, quisiera...** *(see, kee-see-'eh-rah...)*
Do you desire...?	**¿Desea...?** *(deh-'seh-ah...)*
Yes, I desire...	**Sí, deseo...** *(see, deh-'seh-oh...)*

Everyday talk about traffic will include comments concerning the driver's strengths and weaknesses. Study this vocabulary when you find the time:

blind spot	**el punto ciego** *(ehl 'poon-toh see-'eh-goh)*
coordination	**la coordinación** *(lah koh-ohr-dee-nah-see-'ohn)*
corrective lens	**el lente correctivo** *(ehl 'lehn-teh koh-rrehk-'tee-voh)*
DMV	**el Departamento de Vehículos Motorizados** *(ehl deh-pahr-tah-'mehn-toh deh veh-'ee-koo-lohs moh-toh-ree-'sah-dohs)*
driving school	**la escuela de manejar** *(lah eh-'skweh-lah deh mah-neh-'hahr)*
driving test	**el examen de manejar** *(ehl ehk-'sah-mehn deh mah-neh-'hahr)*
experience	**la experiencia** *(lah ehk-speh-ree-'ehn-see·ah)*
practice	**la práctica** *(lah 'prahk-tee-kah)*
reaction time	**el tiempo para reaccionar** *(ehl tee-'ehm-poh 'pah-rah reh-ahk-see·oh-'nahr)*
skill	**la habilidad** *(lah ah-bee-lee-'dahd)*
vision	**la visión** *(lah vee-see-'ohn)*

In every language, there are always two or more ways to express the same idea. These are just a few examples:

car	**el carro, el coche, el auto** *(ehl 'kah-rroh, ehl 'koh-cheh, ehl 'ow-toh)*
citation	**la citación, el citatorio, el tíquet** *(lah see-tah-see-'ohn, ehl see-tah-'toh-ree·oh, ehl 'tee-keht)*
sidewalk	**la banqueta, la acera, la vereda** *(lah bahn-'keh-tah, lah ah-'seh-rah, lah veh-'reh-dah)*
sign	**el letrero, el cartel, la señal** *(ehl leh-'treh-roh, ehl kahr-'tehl, lah seh-'nyahl)*
speeding	**manejar rápido, el exceso de velocidad** *(mah-neh-'hahr 'rah-pee-doh, ehl ehk-'seh-soh deh veh-loh-see-'dahd)*
traffic	**el tráfico, el tránsito** *(ehl 'trah-fee-koh, ehl 'trahn-see-toh)*

Remember that **no** in Spanish may also be used to express the concept of "not":

Does he speak English?	**¿Habla inglés?** *('ah-blah een-'glehs)*
No, he does not speak English	**No, no habla inglés** *(noh, noh 'ah-blah een-'glehs)*

Don't get hung up on all the differences between Spanish verb forms. Simply look over a pattern and insert another *Action Word* in its place. Make the changes as best as you can. Being off a little won't do much harm since the basic form is still intact:

to walk	**caminar** *(kah-mee-'nahr)*
Walk!	**¡Camine!** *(kah-'mee-neh)*
I'm walking	**Estoy caminando** *(eh-'stoh-ee kah-mee-'nahn-doh)*
She walks	**Ella camina** *('eh-yah kah-'mee-nah)*
Can you walk?	**¿Puede caminar?** *('pweh-deh kah-mee-'nahr)*

Many verbs in English have more than one meaning. Other languages, such as Spanish, are more precise:

Know	**saber** *(sah-'behr)* (to <u>know</u> something), **conocer** *(koh-noh-'sehr)* (to <u>know</u> someone)
Leave	**salir** *(sah-'leer)* (to take <u>leave</u>), **dejar** *(deh-'hahr)* (to <u>leave</u> behind)
Return	**volver** *(vohl-'vehr)* (to <u>return</u> to a location), **devolver** *(deh-vohl-'vehr)* (to <u>return</u> something)

Are you still searching for Spanish verbs that look a lot like English? Many of them relate to traffic control:

to cancel	**cancelar** *(kahn-seh-'lahr)*
to expire	**expirar** *(ehk-spee-'rahr)*
to move	**mover** *(moh-'vehr)*
to repair	**reparar** *(reh-pah-'rahr)*
to suspend	**suspender** *(soos-pehn-'dehr)*

A. Answer in Spanish:

¿Cómo está el clima hoy? *('koh-moh eh-'stah ehl 'klee-mah 'oh-ee)*

_____

¿Hace mucho frío en el verano? *('ah-seh 'moo-choh 'free-oh ehn ehl veh-'rah-noh)*

_____

¿Cuáles son tres obstáculos de la calle? *('kwah-lehs sohn lohs ohb-'stah-koo-lohs deh lah 'kah-yeh)*

_____

B. Fill in the Spanish translations:

dirt   _____

glass   _____

mud   _____

oil   _____

rock   _____

sand   _____

trash   _____

hole   _____

C. Finish the sentences:

¡Mantenga las manos _____! *(mahn-'tehn-gah lahs 'mah-nohs_____)*

¿Quiere usted _____? *(kee-'eh-reh oo-'stehd_____)*

Muchas personas estacionan _____. *('moo-chahs pehr-'soh-nahs eh-stah-see·'oh-nahn_____)*

D. Answer these questions with sí or no:

¿Puede usted manejar un carro? *('pweh-deh oo-'stehd mah-neh-'hahr oon 'kah-rroh)*___

¿Puede usted correr rápido? *('pweh-deh oo-'stehd koh-'rrehr 'rah-pee-doh)*___

¿Puede usted leer este libro? *('pweh-deh oo-'stehd leh-'ehr 'eh-steh 'lee-broh)*___

ANSWERS

hole	el agujero
trash	la basura
sand	la arena
rock	la piedra
oil	el aceite
mud	el lodo
glass	el vidrio
B. dirt	la tierra

JUMBLE PUZZLE 1

amtlu	
lorpeig	
tinaoic	
iriuotseq	
olceddaiv	
leobat	
arddve	
aoivs	
srteargiod	
ndpssueodi	

144

CHAPTER FOUR
Capítulo Cuatro
(kah-'pee-too-loh 'kwah-troh)

EMERGENCY
La emergencia
(lah eh-mehr-'hehn-see·ah)

ARE YOU OK?
¿Está bien? *(eh-'stah 'bee·ehn)*

When it comes to communication in a foreign language, dealing with routine responsibilities on the job isn't that difficult. Practice steadily and you will realize that most conversations are predictable. That's not the case in emergency situations. Quick thinking and automatic reflex mix with personal experience and professional skill. Usually, there isn't enough time to think in English, let alone in another language.

Let's begin with those questions you'll need right from the start. Whether it's a traffic accident, an assault, a fire, or a family dispute, the key is to find out what happened and who needs your immediate attention. Start off with the standard greetings and then ask questions to figure out what the real problem is:

Hi. I'm with the _____ Department	**Hola. Estoy con el Departamento de _____** *('oh-lah, eh-'stoh-ee kohn ehl deh-pahr-tah-'mehn-toh deh _____)*
What happened?	**¿Qué pasó?** *(keh pah-'soh)*
Where are the victims?	**¿Dónde están las víctimas?** *('dohn-deh eh-'stahn lahs 'veek-tee-mahs)*
Do you need help?	**¿Necesita ayuda?** *(neh-seh-'see-tah ah-'yoo-dah)*
Where are you hurt?	**¿Dónde está lastimado?** *('dohn-deh eh-'stah lah-stee-'mah-doh)*

WHAT IS THE TROUBLE?
¿Cuál es el problema? *(kwahl ehs soo proh-'bleh-mah)*

While everyone around you is trying to explain what happened, listen carefully for the words below. Repeat what you hear to make sure that there's absolutely no misunderstanding:

There was (a/an)...	**Había (un/una)...** *(ah-'bee-ah oon) ('oo-nah...)*
accident	**accidente** *(ahk-see-'dehn-teh)*
assault	**asalto** *(ah-'sahl-toh)*
fight	**pelea** *(peh-'leh-ah)*
rape	**violación** *(vee-oh-lah-see-'ohn)*
robbery	**robo** *('roh-boh)*
shooting	**disparo** *(dees-'pah-roh)*

It's...	**Es...** *(ehs...)*
a bad fall	**una mala caída** *('oo-nah 'mah-lah kah-'ee-dah)*
a coma	**una coma** *('oo-nah 'koh-mah)*
a convulsion	**una convulsión** *('oo-nah kohn-vool-see-'ohn)*
dehydration	**deshidratación** *(dehs-ee-drah-tah-see-'ohn)*
fatigue	**fatiga** *(fah-'tee-gah)*
frostbite	**congelamiento** *(kohn-heh-lah-mee-'ehn-toh)*
a gunshot wound	**una herida de bala** *('oo-nah eh-'ree-dah deh 'bah-lah)*
a heart attack	**un ataque cardíaco** *(oon ah-'tah-keh kahr-'dee-ah-koh)*
heat stroke	**postración** *(pohs-trah-see-'ohn)*
intoxication	**intoxicación** *(een-tohk-see-kah-see-'ohn)*
an overdose	**una sobredosis** *('oo-nah soh-breh-'doh-sees)*
a seizure	**un ataque** *(oon ah-'tah-keh)*
shock	**postración nerviosa** *(poh-strah-see-'ohn nehr-vee-'oh-sah)*
a snake bite	**una mordedura de culebra** *('oo-nah mohr-deh-'doo-rah deh koo-'leh-brah)*
a spasm	**un espasmo** *(oon eh-'spahs-moh)*
a stabbing	**una puñalada** *('oo-nah poo-nyah-'lah-dah)*
strangulation	**estrangulamiento** *(eh-strahn-goo-lah-mee-'ehn-toh)*
a stroke	**un ataque fulminante** *(oon ah-'tah-keh fool-mee-'nahn-teh)*
sun stroke	**insolación** *(een-soh-lah-see-'ohn)*
suffocation	**sofocación** *(soh-foh-kah-see-'ohn)*
trauma	**traumatismo** *(trah-oo-mah-'tees-moh)*

Now move right in and calm the victim's fears:

Don't be afraid	**No tenga miedo** *(noh 'tehn-gah mee-'eh-doh)*
I will help you	**Le ayudaré** *(leh ah-yoo-dah-'reh)*
You will be OK	**Estará bien** *(eh-stah-'rah 'bee·ehn)*

INFORMACIÓN PRIVADA

➤ When drug overdose is the cause for emergency assistance, interject some of these useful terms to communicate your messages:

It's (the)...   **Es...** *(ehs...)*
   capsule   **la cápsula** *(lah 'kahp-soo-lah)*
   injection   **la inyección** *(lah een-yehk-see-'ohn)*
   overdose   **la sobredosis** *(lah soh-breh-'doh-sees)*
   pill   **la píldora** *(lah 'peel-doh-rah)*
   prescription   **la receta** *(lah reh-'seh-tah)*
   reaction   **la reacción** *(lah reh-ahk-see-'ohn)*
   suicide   **el suicidio** *(ehl soo-ee-'see-dee·oh)*
   tablet   **la tableta** *(lah tah-'bleh-tah)*

He wants...   **Quiere...** *(kee-'eh-reh...)*
   to confess   **confesar** *(kohn-feh-'sahr)*
   to die   **morir** *(moh-'reer)*
   to drink   **beber** *(beh-'behr)*
   to eat   **comer** *(koh-'mehr)*
   to smoke   **fumar** *(foo-'mahr)*
   to vomit   **vomitar** *(voh-mee-'tahr)*

He's...   **Está...** *(eh-'stah...)*
   acting crazy   **enloquecido** *(ehn-loh-keh-'see-doh)*
   asleep   **dormido** *(dohr-'mee-doh)*
   awake   **despierto** *(dehs-pee-'ehr-toh)*
   dizzy   **mareado** *(mah-reh-'ah-doh)*
   drugged   **drogado** *(droh-'gah-doh)*
   passed out   **desmayado** *(dehs-mah-'yah-doh)*
   unconscious   **inconsciente** *(een-kohn-see-'ehn-teh)*

➤ If the victim consumed something he shouldn't have, ask around:

What did he swallow?	**¿Qué tragó?**	*(keh-trah-'goh)*
What did he eat?	**¿Qué comió?**	*(keh koh-mee-'oh)*
What did he drink?	**¿Qué bebió?**	*(keh beh-bee-'oh*

WHAT DO YOU HAVE?

¿Qué tiene? *(keh tee-'eh-neh)*

If illness is the concern, spend a few moments with these:

He/She has...	**Tiene...** *(tee-'eh-neh...)*
AIDS	**SIDA** *('see-dah)*
bird flu	**la gripe aviar** *(lah 'gree-peh ah-vee-'ahr)*
cancer	**cáncer** *('kahn-sehr)*
chicken pox	**varicela** *(vah-ree-'seh-lah)*
diabetes	**diabetes** *(dee-ah-'beh-tehs)*
diptheria	**difteria** *(deef-'teh-ree-ah)*
epilepsy	**epilepsia** *(eh-pee-'lehp-see-ah)*
heart disease	**enfermedad del corazón** *(ehn-fehr-meh-'dahd dehl koh-rah-'sohn)*
hepatitis	**hepatitis** *(ehp-ah-'tee-tees)*
leukemia	**leucemia** *(leh-oo-'seh-mee-ah)*
measles	**sarampión** *(sah-rahm-pee-'ohn)*
meningitis	**meningitis** *(meh-neen-'hee-tees)*
mumps	**paperas** *(pah-'peh-rahs)*
pneumonia	**pulmonía** *(pool-moh-'nee-ah)*
polio	**polio** *('poh-lee·oh)*
rheumatic fever	**fiebre reumática** *(fee-'eh-breh reh-oo-'mah-tee-kah)*
scarlet fever	**escarlatina** *(eh-skahr-lah-'tee-nah)*
tetanus	**tétano** *('teh-tah-noh)*
tuberculosis	**tuberculosis** *(too-behr-koo-'loh-sees)*
typhoid	**fiebre tifoidea** *(fee-'eh-breh tee-foh-ee-'deh-ah)*
West Nile virus	**el virus West Nile** *(ehl 'vee-roos west 'nah-eel)*

Before you go on, check up on their medical background:

Does this happen a lot?	**¿Le pasa mucho esto?**	*(leh 'pah-sah 'moo-choh 'eh-stoh)*
Are you under a doctor's care?	**¿Está bajo el cuidado de un doctor?**	*(eh-'stah 'bah-hoh ehl kwee-'dah-doh deh oon dohk-'tohr)*

Did you lose consciousness?	**¿Perdió el conocimiento?** *(pehr-dee-'oh ehl koh-noh-see-mee-'ehn-toh)*
Do you have heart trouble?	**¿Tiene problemas del corazón?** *(tee-'eh-neh proh-'bleh-mahs dehl koh-rah-'sohn)*
Are you allergic?	**¿Es alérgico?** *(ehs ah-'lehr-hee-koh)*
Are you taking medication?	**¿Toma usted medicina?** *('toh-mah oo-'stehd meh-deh-'see-nah)*
How much do you drink?	**¿Cuánto bebe usted?** *('kwahn-toh 'beh-beh oo-'stehd)*
How many?	**¿Cuántos?** *('kwahn-tohs)*
What color?	**¿De qué color?** *(deh keh koh-'lohr)*
How long ago?	**¿Desde cuándo?** *('dehs-deh 'kwahn-doh)*

Being familiar with a few medications will be of some help. Notice how many Spanish words in medicine look like their English equivalents:

antibiotic	**el antibiótico** *(ehl ahn-tee-bee-'oh-tee-koh)*
aspirin	**la aspirina** *(lah ah-spee-'ree-nah)*
codeine	**la codeína** *(lah koh-deh-'ee-nah)*
insulin	**la insulina** *(lah een-soo-'lee-nah)*
penicilin	**la penicilina** *(lah peh-nee-see-'lee-nah)*

INFORMACIÓN PRIVADA

➤ There are countless groups of words related to health care. Make comments with those expressions you like best.

Everyone suffers from these ailments:

I have...	**Tengo...** *('tehn-goh...)*
backache	**dolor de espalda** *(doh-'lohr deh eh-'spahl-dah)*
cold	**resfrío** *(rehs-'free-oh)*

cough	**tos** *(tohs)*
fever	**fiebre** *(fee-'eh-breh)*
flu	**influenza** *(een-floo-'ehn-sah)*
headache	**dolor de cabeza** *(doh-'lohr deh kah-'beh-sah)*
pain	**dolor** *(doh-'lohr)*
sore throat	**dolor de garganta** *(doh-'lohr deh gahr-'gahn-tah)*
stomachache	**dolor de estómago** *(doh-'lohr deh eh-'stoh-mah-goh)*
toothache	**dolor de muelas** *(doh-'lohr deh 'mweh-lahs)*

You should be aware of any special problems:

He's...	**Es...** *(ehs...)*
blind	**ciego** *(see-'eh-goh)*
deaf	**sordo** *('sohr-doh)*
disabled	**incapacitado** *(een-kah-pah-see-'tah-doh)*
far-sighted	**présbita** *('prehs-bee-tah)*
handicapped	**minusválido** *(mee-noos-'vah-lee-doh)*
mute	**mudo** *('moo-doh)*
near-sighted	**miope** *(mee-'oh-peh)*

It's...	**Está...** *(eh-'stah...)*
contagious	**contagioso** *(kohn-tah-hee-'oh-soh)*
infectious	**infeccioso** *(een-fehk-see-'oh-soh)*

HOW DO YOU FEEL?
¿Cómo se siente? *('koh-moh seh see-'ehn-teh)*

Inquire about the victim's emotional status, and wait for a response:

I am...	**Estoy...** *(eh-'stoh-ee...)*
alert	**alerta** *(ah-'lehr-tah)*
angry	**enojado** *(eh-noh-'hah-doh)*
anxious	**ansioso** *(ahn-see-'oh-soh)*
awake	**despierto** *(dehs-pee-'ehr-toh)*
bad	**mal** *(mahl)*
better	**mejor** *(meh-'hohr)*
calm	**calmado** *(kahl-'mah-doh)*
comfortable	**cómodo** *('koh-moh-doh)*
confused	**confundido** *(kohn-foo-'dee-doh)*
dehydrated	**deshidratado** *(dehs-ee-drah-'tah-doh)*
dizzy	**mareado** *(mah-reh-'ah-doh)*
drunk	**borracho** *(boh-'rrah-choh)*

exhausted	**agotado** *(ah-goh-'tah-doh)*
fine	**bien** *('bee·ehn)*
furious	**furioso** *(foo-ree-'oh-soh)*
happy	**feliz** *(feh-'lees)*
hurt	**lastimado** *(lah-stee-'mah-doh)*
injured	**herido** *(eh-'ree-doh)*
irritated	**irritado** *(ee-rree-'tah-doh)*
lost	**perdido** *(pehr-'dee-doh)*
nervous	**nervioso** *(nehr-vee-'oh-soh)*
numb	**adormecido** *(ah-dohr-meh-'see-doh)*
pregnant	**embarazada** *(ehm-bah-rah-'sah-dah)*
relaxed	**relajado** *(reh-lah-'hah-doh)*
restless	**inquieto** *(een-kee-'eh-toh)*
sad	**triste** *('tree-steh)*
sick	**enfermo** *(ehn-'fehr-moh)*
sore	**dolorido** *(doh-loh-'ree-doh)*
strong	**fuerte** *('fwehr-teh)*
sweaty	**sudoroso** *(soo-doh-'roh-soh)*
tired	**cansado** *(kahn-'sah-doh)*
uncomfortable	**incómodo** *(een-'koh-moh-doh)*
upset	**molesto** *(moh-'leh-stoh)*
weak	**débil** *('deh-beel)*
worried	**preocupado** *(preh-oh-koo-'pah-doh)*
worse	**peor** *(peh-'ohr)*

INFORMACIÓN PRIVADA

➤ Don't forget to change the word endings when you refer to females:

He's sick	**Está enfermo** *(eh-'stah ehn-'fehr-moh)*
She's sick	**Está enferma** *(reh-'stah ehn-'fehr-mah)*

➤ Use little words to emphasize your descriptions:

They're strong	**Están fuertes** *(eh-'stahn 'fwehr-tehs)*
They're stronger	**Están *más* fuertes** *(eh-'stahn mahs 'fwehr-tehs)*
They're as strong as...	**Están *tan* fuertes *como*...** *(eh-'stahn tahn 'fwehr-tehs 'koh-moh)*
They're very strong	**Están *muy* fuertes** *(eh-'stahn 'moo·ee 'fwehr-tehs)*

➤ We mentioned these words about health in Chapter One:

I'm...	**Tengo...** *('tehn-goh...)*
afraid	**miedo** *(mee-'eh-doh)*
cold	**frío** *('free-oh)*
hot	**calor** *(kah-'lohr)*
hungry	**hambre** *('ahm-breh)*
sleepy	**sueño** *('sweh-nyoh)*
thirsty	**sed** *(sehd)*

➤ Don't begin emergency treatment until all your questions get answered. The answer is usually **sí** or **no**:

Do you have...?	**¿Tiene...** *(tee-'eh-neh...)*
chills	**escalofríos?** *(eh-skah-loh-'free-ohs)*
constipation	**estreñimiento?** *(eh-streh-nyee-mee-'ehn-toh)*
diarrhea	**diarrea?** *(dee-ah-'rreh-ah)*
nausea	**náusea?** *('nah-oo-seh-'ah)*
palpitations	**palpitaciones?** *(pahl-pee-tah-see-'oh-nehs)*

Está borracho, sudoroso, tiene náuseas y diarrea. ¡Y yo estoy muy molesto!

REPASO

A. What are these two people talking about? Translate while you practice:

¿Qué pasó? *(keh pah-'soh)*   Hubo un accidente *('oo-boh oon ahk-see-'dehn-teh)*

¿Dónde está la víctima? *('dohn-deh eh-'stah lah 'veek-tee-mah)*   Está en el apartamento *(eh-'stah ehn ehl ah-pahr-tah-'mehn-toh)*

¿Qué tiene? *(keh tee-'eh-neh)*   Tiene dolor de cabeza *(tee-'eh-neh doh-'lohr deh kah-'beh-sah)*

¿Cómo se siente ahora? Está mejor *(eh-'stah meh-'hohr)*
('koh-moh seh see-'ehn-teh ah-'oh-rah)

Yo le ayudaré *(yoh leh ah-yoo-dah-'reh)*   Muchas gracias *('moo-chahs 'grah-see·ahs)*

B. Name three common illnesses in Spanish:

_____   _____   _____

ANSWERS

I'll help him/her.	Thanks a lot.
How's he/she feeling now?	He/she's better.
What's wrong?	He/she has a headache.
Where's the victim?	He/she's in the apartment.
A. What happened?	There was an accident.

HOMELAND SECURITY

La seguridad de la patria *(lah seh-goo-ree-'dahd deh lah 'pah-tree-ah)*

If a major disaster were to strike, Homeland Security experts would use some of the following words and expressions:

There was a strange _____.	**Había un _____ raro.** *(ah-'bee-ah oon _____ 'rah-roh)*
smell	**olor** *(oh-'lohr)*
sound	**sonido** *(soh-'nee-doh)*
package	**paquete** *(pah-'keh-teh)*
object	**objeto** *(ohb-'heh-toh)*
vehicle	**vehículo** *(veh-'ee-koo-loh)*

There is/are...	**Hay...** *('ah-ee)*
panic	**pánico** *('pah-nee-koh)*
looting	**saqueo** *(sah-'keh-oh)*
survivors	**sobrevivientes** *(soh-breh-vee-vee-'ehn-tehs)*
trapped people	**personas atrapadas** *(pehr-'soh-nahs at-trah-'pah-dahs)*
bodies	**cadáveres** *(kah-'dah-veh-rehs)*

You need...	**Necesita...** (*neh-seh-'see-tah*)
to call public services	**llamar los servicios públicos** (*yah-'mahr lohs sehr-'vee-see-ohs 'poo-blee-kohs*)
to take out the disaster kit	**sacar el estuche de sumistros para desastres** (*sah-'kahr ehl ehs-'too-cheh deh soo-mee-'nees-trohs 'pah-rah deh-'sahs-trehs*)
to extinguish the fire	**extinguir el incendio** (*ehks-teen-'geer ehl een-'sehn-dee-oh*)
to treat the wounds	**atender las heridas** (*ah-tehn-'dehr lahs eh-'ree-dahs*)
to search and rescue	**hacer búsqueda y rescate** (*ah-'sehr 'boos-keh-dah ee rehs-'kah-teh*)
to use first aid	**usar los primeros auxilios** (*oo-'sahr lohs pree-'meh-rohs ah-ook-'see-lee-ohs*)
to safeguard the community	**salvaguardar la comunidad** (*sahl-vah-'gwahr-dahr lah koh-moo-nee-'dahd*)
to protect the children	**proteger a los niños** (*proh-teh-'hehr ah lohs 'nee-nyohs*)
to find shelter	**encontrar albergues** (*ehn-kohn-'trahr ahl-'behr-gehs*)
to apply CPR techniques	**aplicar resucitación cardiopulmonar** (*ah-plee-'kahr reh-soo-see-tah-see-'ohn kahr-dee-oh-pool-moh-'nahr*)
to come up with a plan	**hacer un plan** (*ah-'sehr oon plahn*)

When it's time to use commands, try practicing them in sets of three:

Carry him/her	**Llévelo(a)** (*'yeh-veh-loh[ah]*)
Cover him/her	**Cúbralo(a)** (*'koo-brah-loh[ah]*)
Help him/her	**Ayúdelo(a)** (*ah-'yoo-deh-loh[ah]*)

Don't touch it	**No lo toque** (*noh loh 'toh-keh*)
Don't move it	**No lo mueva** (*noh loh 'mweh-vah*)
Report it	**Repórtelo** (*reh-'pohr-teh-loh*)

Follow the procedures	**Siga los procedimientos** (*'see-gah lohs proh-seh-dee-mee-'ehn-tohs*)
Stay alert	**Permanezca alerta** (*pehr-mah-'nehs-kah ah-'lehr-tah*)
Wait for the rescuers	**Espere a los socorristas** (*ehs-'peh-reh ah lohs soh-koh-'rrees-tahs*)

MEDICAL ATTENTION

La atención médica *(lah ah-tehn-see-'ohn 'meh-dee-kah)*

There's no time to lose! Get the information fast...

What's happening to you?	**¿Qué le pasa?** *(keh leh 'pah-sah)*
What are your symptoms?	**¿Cuáles son sus síntomas?** *('kwah-lehs sohn soos 'seen-toh-mahs)*
Where does it hurt?	**¿Dónde le duele?** *('dohn-deh leh 'dweh-leh)*
Do you have lots of pain?	**¿Tiene mucho dolor?** *(tree-'eh-neh 'moo-choh doh-'lohr)*
Are you bleeding?	**¿Está sangrando?** *(eh-'stah sahn-'grahn-doh)*

Were you...	**¿Fue...** *(fweh...)*
beaten?	**golpeado?** *(gohl-peh-'ah-doh)*
raped?	**violada?** *(vee-oh-'lah-dah)*
shot?	**balcado?** *(bah-leh-'ah-doh)*

Is it...	**¿Está...** *(eh-'stah...)*
broken?	**roto?** *('roh-toh)*
burned?	**quemado?** *(keh-'mah-doh)*
twisted?	**torcido?** *(tohr-'see-doh)*
swollen?	**hinchado?** *(een-'chah-doh)*

I see (the)...	**Veo...** *('veh-oh...)*
bruise	**la contusión** *(lah kohn-too-see-'ohn)*
burn	**la quemadura** *(lah keh-mah-'doo-rah)*
cut	**la cortada** *(lah kohr-'tah-dah)*
dislocation	**la dislocación** *(lah dees-loh-kah-see-'ohn)*
fracture	**la fractura** *(lah frahk-'too-rah)*
laceration	**la laceración** *(lah lah-seh-rah-see-'ohn)*
puncture	**la perforación** *(lah pehr-foh-rah-see-'ohn)*
scrape	**el rasguño** *(ehl rahs-'goo-nyoh)*
sprain	**la torcedura** *(lah tohr-seh-'doo-rah)*

While emergency treatment is being applied, more invaluable medical information can be collected:

Is your pain...?	**¿Tiene un dolor...** *(tee-'eh-neh oon doh-'lohr...)*
constant	**constante?** *(kohn-'stahn-teh)*
deep	**profundo?** *(proh-'foon-doh)*
dull	**sordo?** *('sohr-doh)*
burning	**quemante?** *(keh-'mahn-teh)*
throbbing	**intermitente?** *(een-tehr-mee-'tehn-teh)*
mild	**moderado?** *(moh-deh-'rah-doh)*

| severe | **muy fuerte?** *('moo·ee 'fwehr-teh)* |
| sharp | **agudo?** *(ah-'goo-doh)* |

Do you want...?	**¿Quiere...** *(kee-'eh-reh...)*
to see a doctor	**ver a un doctor?** *(vehr ah oon dohk-'tohr)*
to take something for the pain	**tomar algo para el dolor?** *(toh-'mahr 'ahl-goh 'pah-rah ehl doh-'lohr)*
to go to the hospital	**ir al hospital?** *(eer ahl ohs-pee-'tahl)*
to lie down	**acostarse?** *(ah-koh-'stahr-seh)*

 INFORMACIÓN PRIVADA

➤ Be on the alert for one of these expressions. They're usually screamed:

Danger!	**¡Peligro!** *(peh-'lee-groh)*
Fire!	**¡Fuego!** *('fweh-goh)*
Help!	**¡Socorro!** *(soh-'koh-rroh)*

➤ Acquire these phrases related to pain as soon as you can:

Does it hurt?	**¿Le duele?** *(leh 'dweh-leh)*
It hurts!	**¡Me duele!** *(meh 'dweh-leh)*
Do they hurt?	**¿Le duelen?** *(leh 'dweh-lehn)*
They hurt!	**¡Me duelen!** *(meh 'dweh-lehn)*

➤ Have you taken all the names of everyone at the scene?

Who saw what happened?	**¿Quién vio lo que pasó?** *('kee-ehn vee-'oh loh keh pah-'soh)*
Who is the victim?	**¿Quién es la víctima?** *('kee-ehn ehs lah 'veek-tee-mah)*
Who else needs help?	**¿Quién más necesita ayuda?** *('kee-ehn mahs neh-seh-'see-tah ah-'yoo-dah)*
Who is your doctor?	**¿Quién es su doctor?** *('kee-ehn ehs soo dohk-'tohr)*
Who can we call?	**¿A quién podemos llamar?** *(ah 'kee-ehn poh-'deh-mohs yah-'mahr)*
Who are the witnesses?	**¿Quiénes son los testigos?** *(kee-'eh-nehs sohn lohs teh-'stee-gohs)*

➤ Once you have taken care of their emergency medical needs, let the victims know that everything is under control:

| The ambulance is on its way | **La ambulancia está en camino** *(lah ahm-boo-'lahn-see·ah eh-'stah ehn kah-'mee-noh)* |

We're taking you to the hospital	**Vamas a llevarle al hospital** ('vah-mohs ah yeh-'vahr-leh ahl ohs-pee-'tahl)
I will notify your family	**Notificaré a su familia** (noh-tee-fee-kah-'reh ah soo fah-'mee-lee·ah)
I have done all that I can	**He hecho todo lo que pude** (eh 'eh-choh 'toh-doh loh keh 'poo-deh)

TEMAS CULTURALES

The word **tú** is the informal way of saying "you" in Spanish. This informal form is usually exchanged among children, family, and friends. When kids are involved in an emergency situation, use this form to communicate:

How are you?	**¿Cómo estás tú?** ('koh-moh eh-'stahs too)
Where's your house?	**¿Dónde está tu casa?** ('dohn-deh eh-'stah too 'kah-sah)
It's yours	**Es tuyo** (ehs 'too-yoh)
We're going with you	**Vamos contigo** ('vah-mohs kohn-'tee-goh)
Does it hurt you?	**¿Te duele?** (teh 'dweh-leh)

When it comes to the **tú** form, the *Action Words* change, also. Many changes are awkward, so memorize only the lines that you need:

Come here	**Ven aquí** (vehn ah-'kee)
Don't move	**No te muevas** (noh teh 'mweh-vahs)
What do you need?	**¿Qué necesitas?** (keh neh-seh-'see-tahs)
Are you OK?	**¿Estás bien?** (eh-'stahs 'bee·ehn)
Lie down!	**¡Acuéstate!** (ah-'kweh-stah-teh)

THE BODY
El cuerpo (ehl 'kwehr-poh)

To discuss in Spanish any form of emergency medical treatment, you must be able to identify the parts of the human body. The best practice technique is to touch, point to, or move these body parts as you say them aloud:

Move (the)...	**Mueva** ('mweh-vah...)
Point to (the)...	**Señale** (seh-'nyah-leh...)
Touch (the)...	**Toque** ('toh-keh...)
arm	**el brazo** (ehl 'brah-soh)
back	**la espalda** (lah eh-'spahl-dah)
blood	**la sangre** (lah 'sahn-greh)

bone	**el hueso** (ehl 'weh-soh)
chest	**el pecho** (ehl 'peh-choh)
ear	**la oreja** (lah oh-'reh-hah)
eye	**el ojo** (ehl 'oh-hoh)
elbow	**el codo** (ehl 'koh-doh)
face	**la cara** (lah 'kah-rah)
finger	**el dedo** (ehl 'deh-doh)
foot	**el pie** (ehl pee-'eh)
hair	**el cabello** (ehl kah-'beh-yoh)
hand	**la mano** (lah 'mah-noh)
head	**la cabeza** (lah kah-'beh-sah)
knee	**la rodilla** (lah roh-'dee-yah)
leg	**la pierna** (lah pee-'ehr-nah)
mouth	**la boca** (lah 'boh-kah)
muscle	**el músculo** (ehl 'moo-skoo-loh)
neck	**el cuello** (ehl 'kweh-yoh)
nerve	**el nervio** (ehl 'nehr-vee-oh)
nose	**la nariz** (lah nah-'rees)
shoulder	**el hombro** (ehl 'ohm-broh)
skin	**la piel** (lah pee-'ehl)
stomach	**el estómago** (ehl eh-'stoh-mah-goh)
toe	**el dedo del pie** (ehl 'deh-doh dehl pee-'eh)
tooth	**el diente** (ehl dee-'ehn-teh)

A la derecha es un dolor agudo y a la izquierda es un dolor quemante.

INFORMACIÓN PRIVADA

➤ Make general statements with this phrase:

He's/She's got problems with his/her...	**Tiene problemas con su...** (tee-'eh-neh proh-'bleh-mahs kohn soo...)
balance	**equilibrio** (eh-kee-'lee-bree·oh)
hearing	**oído** (oh-'ee-doh)

mind	**mente** *(mehn-teh)*
sight	**vista** *(vee-stah)*
system	**organismo** *(ohr-gah-'nees-moh)*

MORE BODY PARTS
Más partes del cuerpo *(mahs 'pahr-tehs dehl 'kwehr-poh)*

Point to a body part and ask "Does it hurt?," **¿Le duele?** *(leh 'dweh-leh)*. You could also instruct the person to "Point to where it hurts" (**Señale dónde le duele,** *seh-'nyah-leh 'dohn-deh leh 'dweh-leh*), and let the victim point at the painful area. Although you have already learned several parts of the body, there are others you may need to know:

It's (the)...	**Es...** *(ehs...)*
ankle	**el tobillo** *(ehl toh-'bee-yoh)*
breast	**el seno** *(ehl 'seh-noh)*
buttock	**la nalga** *(lah 'nahl-gah)*
calf	**la pantorrilla** *(lah pahn-toh-'rree-yah)*
forearm	**el antebrazo** *(ehl ahn-teh-'brah-soh)*
groin	**la ingle** *(lah 'een-gleh)*
hip	**la cadera** *(lah kah-'deh-rah)*
rib	**la costilla** *(lah koh-'stee-yah)*
spine	**la columna** *(lah koh-'loom-nah)*
thigh	**el muslo** *(ehl 'moos-loh)*
throat	**la garganta** *(lah gahr-'gahn-tah)*
tongue	**la lengua** *(lah 'lehn-gwah)*
wrist	**la muñeca** *(lah moo-'nyeh-kah)*

INFORMACIÓN PRIVADA

➤ Can you see how learning body parts will also help out when it's time to describe the suspect?

long legs	**piernas largas** *(pee-'ehr-nahs 'lahr-gahs)*
small hands	**manos chicas** *('mah-nohs 'chee-kahs)*
big feet	**pies grandes** *('pee-ehs 'grahn-dehs)*

➤ Here are two one-liners you have to know in law enforcement:

He's/she's alive   **Está vivo/a** *(eh-'stah 'vee-voh / vah)*
He's/she's dead   **Está muerto/a** *(eh-'stah 'mwehr-toh / tah)*

➤ Have you explained to the family members what the trouble is?

The injury is...	**La herida es...** *(lah eh-'ree-dah ehs...)*
critical	**crítica** *('kree-tee-kah)*
fatal	**fatal** *(fah-'tahl)*
minor	**menor** *(meh-'nohr)*
serious	**grave** *('grah-veh)*
He/She needs (the)...	**Necesita...** *(neh-seh-'see-tah...)*
blood tranfusion	**la transfusión de sangre** *(lah trahns-foo-see-'ohn deh 'sahn-greh)*
cast	**la armadura de yeso** *(lah ahr-mah-'doo-rah deh 'yeh-soh)*
first aid	**los primeros auxilios** *(lohs pree-'meh-rohs owk-'see-lee·ohs)*
intensive care	**el cuidado intensivo** *(ehl kwee-'dah-doh een-tehn-'see-voh)*
intravenous fluid	**el líquido intravenoso** *(ehl 'lee-kee-doh een-trah-veh-'noh-sohs)*
operation	**la operación** *(lah oh-peh-rah-see-'ohn)*
oxygen	**el oxígeno** *(ehl ohk-'see-heh-noh)*
physical therapy	**la terapia física** *(lah teh-'rah-pee·ah 'fee-see-kah)*
serum	**el suero** *(ehl 'sweh-roh)*
shot	**la inyección** *(lah een-yehk-see-'ohn)*
CPR	**la respiración artificial** *(lah reh-spee-rah-see-'ohn ahr-tee-fee-see-'ahl)*
stitches	**las puntadas** *(lahs poon-'tah-dahs)*
X-rays	**los rayos equis** *(lohs 'rah-yohs 'eh-kees)*

➤ If there's a crowd gathering, cry out the standard command expressions:

Everyone get back!	**¡Todos hacia atrás!** *('toh-dohs 'ah-see·ah ah-'trahs)*
I'm coming through!	**¡Déjenme pasar!** *('deh-hehn-meh pah-'sahr)*
Get out of this area!	**¡Váyanse de esta área!** *('vah-yahn-seh deh 'eh-stah 'ah-reh·ah)*

A. Use body parts to complete these sentences:

Me duele *(meh 'dweh-leh)* _____.

¡Señale *(seh-'nyah-leh)* _____!

¿Le duelen *(leh 'dweh-lehn)* _____?

B. Match the English with the Spanish:

bruise   la quemadura *(lah keh-mah-'doo-rah)*

sprain   la torcedura *(lah tohr-seh-'doo-rah)*

burn   la contusión *(lah kohn-too-see-'ohn)*

C. Translate!

la respiración artificial *(lah reh-spee-rah-see-'ohn ahr-tee-fee-see-'ahl)*

_____

el oxígeno *(ehl ohk-'see-heh-noh)*

_____

los rayos equis *(lohs 'rah-yohs 'eh-kees)*

_____

ANSWERS

x-rays   sprain – la torcedura

oxygen   burn – la quemadura

C. CPR   B. bruise – la contusión

MEDICAL HISTORY

La historia médica *(lah ee-'stoh-ree·ah 'meh-dee-kah)*

Team up with a medical staff member, and get started on that initial report:

What's your...?	**¿Cuál es su...** *(kwahl ehs soo…)*
blood pressure	**presión de sangre?** *(preh-see-'ohn deh 'sahn-greh)*
blood type	**tipo de sangre?** *('tee-poh deh 'sahn-greh)*
height	**estatura?** *(eh-stah-'too-rah)*
insurance company	**compañía de seguros?** *(kohm-pah-'nyee-ah deh seh-'goo-rohs)*
policy number	**número de póliza?** *('noo-meh-roh deh 'poh-lee-sah)*
weight	**peso?** *('peh-soh)*
Do you have... ?	**¿Tiene...** *(tee-'eh-neh…)*
allergies	**alergias?** *(ah-'lehr-hee·ahs)*
any illness	**alguna enfermedad?** *(ahl 'goo-nah ehn-fehr-meh-'dahd)*
emotional problems	**problemas emocionales?** *(proh-'bleh-mahs eh-moh-see·oh-'nah-lehs)*
good health	**buena salud?** *('bweh-nah sah-'lood)*
heart problems	**problemas del corazón?** *(proh-'bleh-mahs dehl koh-rah-'sohn)*

medical problems	**problemas médicos?** *(proh-'bleh-mahs 'meh-dee-kohs)*
reactions to drugs	**reacciones a las drogas?** *(reh-ahk-see-'oh-nehs ah lahs 'droh-gahs)*

¡A MIS ÓRDENES!

When emergency situations arise, resort to your command expressions to get control of everything. Several commands that were previously presented can do wonders for safety and emergency personnel. Take a moment to review:

Call an ambulance!	**¡Llame la ambulancia!** *('yah-meh lah ahm-boo-'lahn-see·ah)*
Hurry up!	**¡Apúrese!** *(ah-'poo-reh-seh)*
Raise the head!	**¡Levante la cabeza!** *(leh-'vahn-teh lah kah-'beh-sah)*
Show me!	**¡Muéstreme!** *('mweh-streh-meh)*
Be careful!	**¡Tenga cuidado!** *('tehn-gah kwee-'dah-doh)*

Let's add to our list of commands as we search, rescue, and assist where we are needed most:

Ask for	**Pida**	**Pida un doctor** *('pee-dah oon dohk-'tohr)*
Breathe	**Respire**	**Respire normalmente** *(reh-'spee-reh nohr-mahl-'mehn-teh)*
Clean	**Limpie**	**Limpie el área** *('leem-pee·eh ehl 'ah-reh-ah)*
Cover	**Cubra**	**Cubra el niño** *('koo-brah ahl 'nee-nyoh)*
Explain	**Explique**	**Explique el problema** *(ehk-'splee-keh ehl proh-'bleh-mah)*
Grab	**Agarre**	**Agarre la pierna** *(ah-'gah-rreh lah pee-'ehr-nah)*
Help	**Ayude**	**Ayude al paramédico** *(ah-'yoo-deh ahl pah-rah-'meh-dee-koh)*
Lift	**Levante**	**Levante los brazos** *(leh-'vahn-teh lohs 'brah-sohs)*
Look for	**Busque**	**Busque al niño** *('boos-keh ahl 'nee-nyoh)*
Pick up	**Recoja**	**Recoja la medicina** *(reh-'koh-hah lah meh-dee-'see-nah)*
Relax	**Relaje**	**Relaje la cabeza** *(reh-'lah-heh lah kah-'beh-sah)*
Remove	**Quite**	**Quite la basura** *('kee-teh lah bah-'soo-rah)*
Rest	**Descanse**	**Descanse un minuto** *(dehs-'kahn-seh oon mee-'noo-toh)*
Speak	**Hable**	**Hable más despacio** *('ah-bleh mahs deh-'spah-see·oh)*
Squeeze	**Apriete**	**Apriete mi mano** *(ah-pree-'eh-teh mee 'mah-noh)*

164

➤ Utilize a one-word command phrase to get what you need:

Calm down!	**¡Cálmese!** *('kahl-meh-seh)*
Answer me!	**¡Contésteme!** *(kohn-'tehs-teh-meh)*
Help me!	**¡Ayúdeme!** *(ah-'yoo-deh-meh)*
Lie down!	**¡Acuéstese!** *(ah-'kweh-steh-seh)*
Sit down!	**¡Siéntese!** *(see-'ehn-teh-seh)*
Tell me!	**¡Dígame!** *('dee-gah-meh)*

➤ Just say "no" when you don't want something done:

Don't come in	**No entre** *(noh 'ehn-treh)*
Don't move	**No se mueva** *(noh seh 'mweh-vah)*
Don't touch it	**No lo toque** *(noh loh 'toh-keh)*
Don't be afraid	**No tenga miedo** *(noh 'tehn-gah mee-'eh-doh)*
Don't worry	**No se preocupe** *(noh seh preh-oh-'koo-peh)*
Don't be nervous	**No se ponga nervioso** *(noh seh 'pohn-gah nehr-vee-'oh-soh)*

➤ Fortunately, there are several ways to get people to hurry up!

Hurry up!	**¡Apúrese!** *(ah-'poo-reh-seh)*
Quickly!	**¡Rápido!** *('rah-pee-doh)*
Right now!	**¡Ahora mismo!** *(ah-'oh-rah 'mees-moh)*

➤ Make sure parents know what to do the moment things suddenly go wrong. Your instructions should include:

Cover the children with a blanket!	**¡Cubra a los niños con una frazada!** *('koo-brah ah lohs 'nee-nyohs kohn 'oo-nah frah-'sah-dah)*
Go to the neighbors and ask for help!	**¡Vaya donde los vecinos y pida ayuda!** *('vah-yah 'dohn-deh lohs veh-'see-nohs ee 'pee-dah ah-'yoo-dah)*
Grab the children and run outside!	**¡Agarre a los niños y corra hacia afuera!** *(ah-'gah-rreh ah lohs 'nee-nyohs ee 'koh-rrah 'ah-see·ah ah-'fweh-rah)*
Keep the children away from windows!	**¡Mantenga a los niños lejos de las ventanas!** *(mahn-'tehn-gah ah lohs 'nee-nyohs 'leh-hohs deh lahs vehn-'tah-nahs)*
Put the children under the table!	**¡Ponga a los niños debajo de la mesa!** *('pohn-gah ah lohs 'nee-nyohs deh-'bah-hoh deh lah 'meh-sah)*

THE PROFESSIONALS

Los profesionales *(lohs proh-feh-see·oh-'nah-lehs)*

Choose what you need from the following list. Step aside and let the experts do their job:

Here comes (the)...	**Aquí viene...** *(ah-'kee vee-'eh-neh)*
doctor	**el médico** *(ehl 'meh-dee-koh)*
fire fighter	**el bombero** *(ehl bohm-'beh-roh)*
interpreter	**el intérprete** *(ehl een-'tehr-preh-teh)*
medical assistant	**el ayudante médico** *(ehl ah-yoo-'dahn-teh 'meh-dee-koh)*
nurse	**la enfermera** *(lah ehn-fehr-'meh-rah)*
paramedic	**el paramédico** *(ehl pah-rah-'meh-dee-koh)*
Red Cross	**la Cruz Roja** *(lah kroos 'roh-hah)*
specialist	**el especialista** *(ehl eh-speh-see·ah-'leeh-stah)*
surgeon	**el cirujano** *(ehl see-roo-'hah-noh)*
technician	**el técnico** *(ehl 'tehk-nee-koh)*
therapist	**el terapeuta** *(ehl teh-rah-peh-'oo-tah)*

Get familiar with who you're treating, also!

Help the...	**Ayude a...** *(ah-'yoo-deh ah...)*
survivor	**el sobreviviente** *(ehl soh-breh-vee-vee-'ehn-teh)*
victim	**el víctima** *(ehl 'veek-tee-mah)*
patient	**el paciente** *(ehl pah-see-'ehn-teh)*
injured	**el herido** *(ehl eh-'ree-doh)*
sick	**el enfermo** *(ehl ehn-'fehr-moh)*

166

➤ Notice how many medical terms look like their English equivalents:

anesthetist	**el anestesista** *(ehl ah-neh-steh-'sees-tah)*
cardiologist	**el cardiólogo** *(ehl kahr-dee-'oh-loh-goh)*
obstetrician	**el obstetra** *(ehl ohb-'steh-trah)*
optometrist	**el optometrista** *(ehl ohp-toh-meh-'tree-stah)*
orthopedist	**el ortopedista** *(ehl ohr-toh-peh-'dee-stah)*
pediatrician	**el pediatra** *(ehl peh-dee-'ah-trah)*
pharmacist	**el farmacéutico** *(ehl fahr-mah-'seh-oo-tee-koh)*
radiologist	**el radiólogo** *(ehl rah-dee-'oh-loh-goh)*

➤ Where are they taking them? You should know a little about the hospital:

Emergency Room	**la sala de emergencia** *(lah 'sah-lah deh eh-mehr-'hehn-see·ah)*
Intensive Care	**la sala de cuidados intensivos** *(lah 'sah-lah deh kwee-'dah-dohs een-tehn-'see-vohs)*
Maternity Ward	**la sala de maternidad** *(lah 'sah-lah deh mah-tehr-nee-'dahd)*
Operating Room	**la sala de operaciones** *(lah 'sah-lah deh oh-peh-rah-see-'oh-nehs)*
Recovery Room	**la sala de recuperación** *(lah 'sah-lah deh reh-koo-peh-rah-see-'ohn)*
Waiting Room	**la sala de espera** *(lah 'sah-lah deh eh-'speh-rah)*

DELIVERY IS COMING!
¡Viene el parto! *(vee-'eh-neh ehl 'pahr-toh)*

It's a classic case. A woman cries out to a law enforcement officer because the contractions are coming. Are you prepared? Scribble down those Spanish words that apply to such a scenario, and carry them wherever you go:

Do you have...?	**¿Tiene...** *(tee-'eh-neh...)*
any discharge	**alguna pérdida?** *(ahl-'goo-nah 'pehr-dee-dah)*
bleeding	**sangramiento?** *(sahn-grah-mee-'ehn-toh)*
contractions	**contracciones?** *(kohn-trahk-see-'oh-nehs)*
cramps	**calambres?** *(kah-'lahm-brehs)*

| labor pains | **dolores de parto?** (doh-'loh-rehs deh 'pahr-toh) |
| trouble breathing | **problemas para respirar?** (proh-'bleh-mahs 'pah-rah reh-spee-'rahr) |

How many...?	**¿Cuántos...** ('kwahn-tohs...)
days	**días?** ('dee-ahs)
hours	**horas?** ('oh-rahs)
minutes	**minutos?** (mee-'noo-tohs)
months	**meses?** ('meh-sehs)
seconds	**segundos?** (seh-'goon-dohs)
weeks	**semanas?** (seh-'mah-nahs)

If you are forced to help with the delivery, communicate with all the commands you just learned:

Bend your knee	**Doble la rodilla** ('doh-bleh lah roh-'dee-yah)
Breathe deeply	**Respire profundamente** (reh-'spee-rreh proh-foon-dah-'mehn-teh)
Calm down	**Cálmese** ('kahl-meh-seh)
Close your mouth	**Cierre la boca** (see-'eh-reh lah 'boh-kah)
Grab my hand	**Agarre mi mano** (ah-'gah-rreh mee 'mah-noh)
Lie down	**Acuéstese** (ah-'kweh-steh-seh)
Open your eyes	**Abra los ojos** ('ah-brah lohs 'oh-hohs)
Pull	**Jale** ('hah-leh)
Push	**Empuje** (ehm-'poo-heh)
Raise your head	**Levante la cabeza** (leh-'vahn-teh lah kah-'beh-sah)
Rest	**Descanse** (deh-'skahn-seh)

168

TEMAS CULTURALES

Babies are sacred creatures in most cultures. In many Hispanic homes, the traditions and rituals of childbearing are not easily changed. Some family customs are centuries old, even though they may contradict modern science. Keep these things in mind as you give advice to expectant mothers.

REPASO

A. Answer these questions in Spanish:

¿Cuál es el peso? *(kwahl ehs ehl 'peh-soh)*

_____

¿Tiene alguna enfermedad? *(tee-'eh-neh ahl-'goo-nah ehn-fehr-meh-'dahd)*

_____

¿Cuál es su tipo de sangre? *(kwahl ehs soo 'tee-poh deh 'sahn-greh)*

_____

B. List three professionals trained to handle medical emergencies:

_____   _____   _____

C. The following sentences should be memorized. Translate:

¿Tiene dolores de parto? *(tee-'eh-neh doh-'loh-rehs deh 'pahr-toh)*

_____

Cálmese y respire profundamente *('kahl-meh-seh ee reh-'spee-reh proh-foon-dah-'mehn-teh)*

_____

Vamos a la sala de maternidad *('vah-mohs ah lah 'sah-lah deh mah-tehr-nee-'dahd)*

MORE EMERGENCIES
Más emergencias *('mahs eh-mehr-'hehn-see·ahs)*

Here are lists of vocabulary for more emergencies, including burns and poisonings:

BURNS
Las quemaduras *(lahs keh-mah-'doo-rahs)*

The burns were caused by the...	**Las quemaduras fueron causadas por...** *(lahs keh-mah-'doo-rahs 'fweh-rohn kow-'sah-dahs pohr...)*
acid	**el ácido** *(ehl 'ah-see-doh)*
bomb	**la bomba** *(lah 'bohm-bah)*
chemicals	**los productos químicos** *(lohs proh-'dook-tohs 'kee-mee-kohs)*
explosive	**el explosivo** *(ehl ehk-sploh-'see-voh)*
electricity	**la electricidad** *(lah eh-lehk-tree-see-'dahd)*
fire	**el fuego** *(ehl 'fweh-goh)*
fireworks	**los fuegos artificiales** *(lohs 'fweh-gohs ahr-tee-fee-see-'ah-lehs)*
flames	**las llamas** *(lahs 'yah-mahs)*
gas	**el gas** *(ehl gahs)*
grease	**la grasa** *(lah 'grah-sah)*
hot water	**el agua caliente** *(ehl 'ah-gwah kah-lee-'ehn-teh)*
oil	**el aceite** *(ehl ah-'seh·ee-teh)*

POISONINGS

Los envenenamientos *(lohs ehn-veh-neh-nah-mee-'ehn-tohs)*

Much like the drug overdose, be certain about what was actually consumed:

He/she ate...	**Comió...** *(koh-mee-'oh...)*
He/she drank...	**Bebió...** *(beh-bee-'oh...)*
alcohol	**el alcohol** *(ehl ahl-koh-'ohl)*
bleach	**el cloro** *(ehl 'kloh-roh)*
cyanide	**el cianuro** *(ehl see-ah-'noo-roh)*
detergent	**el detergente** *(ehl deh-tehr-'hehn-teh)*
bad food	**la comida mala** *(lah koh-'mee-dah 'mah-lah)*
insecticide	**el insecticida** *(ehl een-sehk-tee-'see-dah)*
liquor	**el licor** *(ehl lee-'kohr)*
lye	**la lejía** *(lah leh-'hee-ah)*
mushroom	**el hongo** *(ehl 'ohn-goh)*
paint	**la pintura** *(lah peen-'too-rah)*
poison	**el veneno** *(ehl veh-'neh-noh)*
sleeping pill	**el tranquilizante** *(ehl trahn-kee-lee-'sahn-teh)*

INFORMACIÓN PRIVADA

➤ If fire is involved, ask witnesses if they know anything:

Where did the fire start?	**¿Dónde comenzó el fuego?** *('dohn-deh koh-mehn-'sohn ehl 'fweh-goh)*
How did it start?	**¿Cómo comenzó?** *('koh-moh koh-mehn-'soh)*
Who started it?	**¿Quién lo prendió?** *(kee-'ehn loh prehn-dee-'oh)*
When did it start?	**¿Cuándo empezó?** *('kwahn-doh ehm-peh-'soh)*
Did you see anything unusual?	**¿Vio algo raro?** *(vee·'oh ahl-goh 'rah-roh)*
Who called the fire department?	**¿Quién llamó a los bomberos?** *('kee-'ehn yah-'moh ah lohs bohm-'beh-rohs)*
Have you been breathing smoke?	**¿Ha estado respirando humo?** *(ah eh-'stah-doh reh-spee-'rahn-doh 'oo-moh)*
Did you get burned?	**¿Se quemó?** *(seh keh-'moh)*
How many people are inside?	**¿Cuántas personas están adentro?** *('kwahn-tahs pehr-'soh-nahs eh-'stahn ah-'dehn-troh)*
Was there an explosion?	**¿Hubo explosión?** *('oo-boh ehk-sploh-see-'ohn)*

➤ How's that first aid kit? Tell the victim that...

You need (the)...	**Necesita...** *(neh-seh-'see-tah...)*
aspirin	**la aspirina** *(lah ah-spee-'ree-nah)*
bandage	**el vendaje** *(ehl vehn-'dah-heh)*
capsules	**las cápsulas** *(lahs 'kahp-soo-lahs)*
cough syrup	**el jarabe para la tos** *(ehl hah-'rah-beh 'pah-rah lah tohs)*
cream	**la crema** *(lah 'kreh-mah)*
disinfectant	**el desinfectante** *(ehl dehs-een-fehk-'tahn-teh)*
drops	**las gotas** *(lahs 'goh-tahs)*
iodine	**el yodo** *(ehl 'yoh-doh)*
liniment	**el linimento** *(ehl lee-nee-'mehn-toh)*
lotion	**la loción** *(lah loh-see-'ohn)*
lozenges	**las pastillas** *(lahs pah-'stee-yahs)*
penicillin	**la penicilina** *(lah peh-nee-see-'lee-nah)*
pills	**las píldoras** *(lahs 'peel-doh-rahs)*
tablets	**las tabletas** *(lahs tah-'bleh-tahs)*
bandaid	**la curita** *(lah koo-'ree-tah)*
vaseline	**la vaselina** *(lah vah-seh-'lee-nah)*

➤ Be very careful with it comes to medication! These phrases work wonders around kids:

Don't take it	**No la tome** *(noh lah 'toh-meh)*
Don't give it to him/her	**No se la dé** *(noh seh lah deh)*
It isn't for children	**No es para niños** *(noh ehs 'pah-rah 'nee-nyohs)*

172

TRAFFIC ACCIDENT

El accidente de tráfico *(ehl ahk-see-'dehn-teh deh 'trah-fee-koh)*

The most common emergency call in cities worldwide involves automobile accidents. Know what to say if you are the first to arrive:

Everybody get back!	**¡Todos hacia atrás!** *(toh-dohs 'ah-see·ah ah-'trahs)*
I'm a police officer	**Soy oficial de policía** *('soh-ee oh-fee-see-'ahl deh poh-lee-'see-ah)*
Where are you hurt?	**¿Dónde le duele?** *('dohn-deh leh 'dweh-leh)*
How do you feel?	**¿Cómo se siente?** *('koh-moh seh see-'ehn-teh)*
I will help you	**Yo lo ayudaré** *(yoh loh ah-yoo-dah-'reh)*

Now add a few commands:

Calm down	**Cálmese** *('kahl-meh-seh)*
Don't move	**No se mueva** *(noh seh 'mweh-vah)*
Lie down	**Acuéstese** *(ah-'kweh-steh-seh)*

If things look serious, do what you can until more help arrives:

Are you bleeding?	**¿Está sangrando?** *(eh-'stah sahn-'grahn-doh)*
Do you have heart trouble?	**¿Tiene problemas del corazón?** *(tee-'eh-neh proh-'bleh-mahs dehl koh-rah-'sohn)*
Are you taking medication?	**¿Está tomando medicinas?** *(eh-'stah toh-'mahn-doh meh-dee-'see-nahs)*
Have you been drinking?	**¿Ha estado tomando?** *(ah eh-'stah-doh toh-'mahn-doh)*
Were you unconscious?	**¿Estaba inconsciente?** *(eh-'stah-bah een-kohn-see-'ehn-teh)*
Do you want...	**¿Quiere...** *(kee-'eh-reh...)*
a blanket	**una frazada?** *('oo-nah frah-'sah-dah)*
more air	**más aire?** *(mahs 'ah·ee-reh)*
water	**agua?** *('ah-gwah)*
This is (the)...	**Este es...** *('eh-steh ehs...)*
cast	**la armadura de yeso** *(lah ahr-mah-'doo-rah deh 'yeh-soh)*
sling	**el soporte para el brazo** *(ehl soh-'pohr-teh 'pah-rah ehl 'brah-soh)*
splint	**el cabestrillo** *(ehl kah-beh-'stree-yoh)*
tourniquet	**el torniquete** *(ehl tohr-nee-'keh-teh)*
You will be OK	**Estará bien** *(eh-stah-'rah 'bee·ehn)*
The ambulance is coming	**La ambulancia viene** *(lah ahm-boo-'lahn-see·ah vee-'eh-neh)*

➤ In the midst of turmoil, the key is to stay calm and make sure all communication is clear. If your Spanish is limited, clarify everything with one of the lines below. Most of these words were introduced in earlier chapters:

Do you understand?	**¿Entiende?** *(ehn-tee-'ehn-deh)*
Please speak more slowly	**Favor de hablar más despacio** *(fah-'vohr deh ah-'blahr mahs deh-'spah-see·oh)*
Tell me precisely	**Dígamelo exactamente** *('dee-gah-meh-loh ehk-sahk-tah-'mehn-teh)*
Word for word, please	**Palabra por palabra, por favor** *(pah-'lah-brah pohr pah-'lah-brah, pohr fah-'vohr)*
Only one person speak at a time	**Solo una persona hable a la vez** *('soh-loh 'oo-nah pehr-'soh-nah 'ah-bleh ah lah vehs)*
I'm calling for an interpreter	**Estoy llamando a un intérprete** *(eh-'stoh-ee yah-'mahn-doh ah oon een-'tehr-preh-teh)*

If everyone involved is well enough to communicate, use these questions to figure out what really happened:

How did this happen?	**¿Cómo pasó esto?** *('koh-moh pah-'soh 'eh-stoh)*
Did you see what happened?	**¿Vio lo que pasó?** *('vee·oh loh keh pah-'soh)*
Who is a witness?	**¿Quién es testigo?** *(kee-'ehn ehs teh-'stee-goh)*
Was it a hit and run?	**¿Chocó y se dio a la fuga?** *(choh-'koh ee see 'dee·oh ah lah 'foo-gah)*
Was it a blowout?	**¿Fue un reventón?** *(fweh oon reh-vehn-'tohn)*
Who was at fault?	**¿Quién tenía la culpa?** *(kee-'ehn teh-'nee-ah lah 'kool-pah)*
How many vehicles?	**¿Cuántos vehículos?** *('kwahn-tohs veh-'ee-koo-lohs)*
Who hit you?	**¿Quién lo chocó?** *(kee-'ehn loh choh-'koh)*
Did you have mechanical problems?	**¿Tenía problemas mecánicos?** *(teh-'nee-ah proh-'bleh-mahs meh-'kah-nee-kohs)*
Are you the driver or passenger?	**¿Es el chofer o el pasajero?** *(ehs ehl choh-'fehr oh ehl pah-sah-'heh-roh)*
Did you lose control?	**¿Perdió el control?** *(pehr-dee-'oh ehl kohn-'trohl)*
Was it parked?	**¿Estaba estacionado?** *(eh-'stah-bah eh-stah-see·oh-'nahn-doh)*
Can you prove it?	**¿Puede probarlo?** *('pweh-deh proh-'bahr-loh)*

Do you want...?	¿**Quiere...** *(kee-'eh-reh...)*
to exchange information	**cambiar información?** *(kahm-bee-'ahr een-fohr-mah-see-'ohn)*
to use the telephone	**usar el teléfono?** *(oo-'sahr ehl teh-'leh-foh-noh)*
to file a report	**hacer un reporte?** *(ah-'sehr oon reh-'pohr-teh)*

Do you have...?	¿**Tiene...** *(tee-'eh-neh...)*
license and registration	**la licencia y el registro?** *(lah lee-'sehn-see·ah ee ehl reh-'hee-stroh)*
automobile insurance	**el seguro para el carro?** *(ehl seh-'goo-roh 'pah-rah ehl 'kah-rroh)*
identification	**la identificación?** *(lah ee-dehn-tee-fee-kah-see-'ohn)*

Get on with the process of sorting out all the details:

| Where were you going? | ¿**Adónde iba?** *(ah-'dohn-deh 'ee-bah)* |
| In which direction? | ¿**En qué dirección?** *(ehn keh dee-rehk-see-'ohn)* |

Was it headed...?	¿**Iba al...** *('ee-bah ahl...)*
north	**norte?** *('nohr-teh)*
west	**oeste?** *(oh-'eh-steh)*
south	**sur?** *(soor)*
east	**este?** *('eh-steh)*
northwest	**noroeste?** *(nohr-oh-'eh-steh)*
northeast	**noreste?** *(nohr-'eh-steh)*
southwest	**suroeste?** *(soor-oh-'eh-steh)*
southeast	**sureste?** *(soor-'eh-steh)*
north-bound	**hacia** <u>el norte</u> *('ah-see·ah ehl 'nohr-teh)*
south-bound	**hacia** _____ *('ah-see·ah)*
east-bound	_____
west-bound	_____

Were you ejected?	¿**Fue arrojado?** *(fweh ah-rroh-'hah-doh)*
Did you faint?	¿**Se desmayó?** *(seh dehs-mah-'yoh)*
Were you wearing a safety belt?	¿**Estaba usando cinturón de seguridad?** *(eh-'stah-bah oo-'sahn-doh seen-too-'rohn deh seh-goo-ree-'dahd)*
Did you fall asleep?	¿**Se durmió?** *(seh duhr-mee-'oh)*
Did you signal?	¿**Señalizó?** *(seh-'nyah-lee-'soh)*
Did you brake on time?	¿**Frenó a tiempo?** *(freh-'noh ah tee-'ehm-poh)*
Were your lights on?	¿**Estaban prendidas las luces?** *(eh-'stah-bahn prehn-'dee-dahs lahs 'loo-sehs)*

What part was damaged?	¿Cuál parte estaba dañada? *(kwahl 'pahr-teh eh-'stah-bah dah-'nyah-dah)*
Did it run off the road?	¿Saltó del camino? *(sahl-'toh dehl kah-'mee-noh)*

What's the...?	¿Cuál es... *(kwahl ehs...)*
exact location	el sitio exacto? *(ehl 'see-tee·oh ehk-'sahk-toh)*
name of the registered owner	el nombre del dueño registrado? *(ehl 'nohm-breh dehl 'dweh-nyoh reh-hee-'strah-doh)*
name of the insurance company	el nombre de la compañía de seguros? *(ehl 'nohm-breh deh lah kohm-pah-'nyee-ah deh seh-'goo-rohs)*
number of passengers	el número de pasajeros? *(ehl 'noo-meh-roh deh pah-sah-'heh-rohs)*
home phone number	el número del teléfono de la casa? *(ehl 'noo-meh-roh dehl teh-'leh-foh-noh deh lah 'kah-sah)*
work phone number	el número del teléfono del trabajo? *(ehl 'noo-meh-roh dehl teh-'leh-foh-noh dehl trah-'bah-hoh)*
estimated loss	el alcance del daño? *(ehl ahl-'kahn-seh dehl 'dah-nyoh)*
license plate number	el número de la placa? *(ehl 'noo-meh-roh deh lah 'plah-kah)*
make	la marca? *(lah 'mahr-kah)*
model	el modelo? *(ehl moh-'deh-loh)*
year	el año? *(ehl 'ah-nyoh)*
state	el estado? *(ehl eh-'stah-doh)*
color	el color? *(ehl koh-'lohr)*

WHAT KIND OF DAMAGE?
¿Qué clase de daño? *(keh 'klah-seh deh 'dah-nyoh)*

It's...	Está... *(eh-'stah...)*
broken	roto *('roh-toh)*
bent	doblado *(doh-'blah-doh)*
dented	abollado *(ah-boh-'yah-doh)*
twisted	torcido *(tohr-'see-doh)*
overturned	volteado *(vohl-teh-'ah-doh)*
scratched	rayado *(rah-'yah-doh)*
wrecked	arruinado *(ah-rroo·ee-'nah-doh)*

It's...	Es daño... *(ehs 'dah-nyoh...)*
major	**mayor** *(mah-'yohr)*
minor	**menor** *(meh-'nohr)*
moderate	**moderado** *(moh-deh-'rah-doh)*
total	**total** *(toh-'tahl)*

INFORMACIÓN PRIVADA

➤ When you're caught up in a conversation about collisions, this will be handy:

condition	**la condición** *(lah kohn-dee-see-'ohn)*
cyclists	**los ciclistas** *(lohs see-'klee-stahs)*
description	**la descripción** *(lah deh-skreep-see-'ohn)*
drivers	**los choferes** *(lohs choh-'feh-rehs)*
front	**el frente** *(ehl 'frehn-teh)*
injured	**los heridos** *(lohs eh-'ree-dohs)*
insured	**asegurado** *(ah-seh-goo-'rah-doh)*
investigation	**la investigación** *(lah een-veh-stee-gah-see-'ohn)*
left side	**el lado izquierdo** *(ehl 'lah-doh ees-kee-'ehr-doh)*
liable	**expuesto** *(ehk-'spweh-stoh)*
passengers	**los pasajeros** *(lohs pah-sah-'heh-rohs)*
pedestrians	**los peatones** *(lohs peh-ah-'toh-nehs)*
position	**la posición** *(lah poh-see-see-'ohn)*
rear	**la parte de atrás** *(lah 'pahr-teh deh ah-'trahs)*
right side	**el lado derecho** *(ehl 'lah-doh deh-'reh-choh)*
suspects	**los sospechosos** *(lohs soh-speh-'choh-sohs)*
uninsured	**sin seguro** *(seen seh-'goo-roh)*
victims	**las víctimas** *(lahs 'veek-tee-mahs)*
witnesses	**los testigos** *(lohs teh-'stee-gohs)*
to broadside	**chocar de lado** *(choh-'kahr deh 'lah-doh)*
to hit and run	**chocar y escapar** *(choh-'kahr ee ehs-kah-'pahr)*
to hit head on	**chocar de frente** *(choh-'kahr deh 'frehn-teh)*
to run over	**atropellar** *(ah-troh-peh-'yahr)*
to sideswipe	**raspar al lado** *(rah-'spahr ahl 'lah-doh)*

WHAT WAS THE CAUSE?

¿Cuál fue la causa? *(kwahl fweh lah 'kow-sah)*

It was caused by the...	**Fue causado por...** *(fweh kow-'sah-doh pohr...)*
animal	**el animal** *(ehl ah-nee-'mahl)*
broken street light	**el semáforo roto** *(ehl seh-'mah-foh-roh 'roh-toh)*
construction	**la construcción** *(lah kohn-strook-see-'ohn)*
other car	**el otro carro** *(ehl 'oh-troh 'kah-rroh)*
road condition	**la condición del camino** *(lah kohn-dee-see-'ohn dehl kah-'mee-noh)*
weather	**el clima** *(ehl 'klee-mah)*

To explain, in Spanish, why most accidents happen, you'll probably need words that refer to the weather.

It was caused by the...	**Fue causado por...** *(fweh kow-'sah-doh pohr...)*
debris	**los escombros** *(lohs eh-'skohm-brohs)*
ice	**el hielo** *(ehl 'yeh-loh)*
rain	**la lluvia** *(lah 'yoo-vee·ah)*
snow	**la nieve** *(lah nee-'eh-veh)*
storm	**la tormenta** *(lah tohr-'mehn-tah)*
wind	**el viento** *(ehl vee-'ehn-toh)*

You'll also have to comment on the road conditions:

It's...	**Está...** *(eh-'stah...)*
dry	**seco** *('seh-koh)*
flooded	**inundado** *(een-oon-'dah-doh)*
icy	**helado** *(eh-'lah-doh)*

muddy	**lodoso** (loh-'doh-soh)
slippery	**resbaloso** (rehs-bah-'loh-soh)
torn up	**roto** ('roh-toh)
wet	**mojado** (moh-'hah-doh)

TEMAS CULTURALES

When discussing the weather, the thermometer, or body temperatures, remember that people from Spanish-speaking countries may be more familiar with **centígrados** (sehn-'tee-grah-dohs) (C°) instead of Fahrenheit (F°).

To Convert Fahrenheit Temperatures into Celsius
- Begin by subtracting 32 from the Fahrenheit number.
- Divide the answer by 9.
- Then multiply that answer by 5.

REPASO

A. List three key words under each category:

Las quemaduras
(lahs keh-mah-'doo-rahs)

Los envenenamientos
(lohs ehn-veh-neh-nah-mee-'ehn-tohs)

_____   _____

_____   _____

_____   _____

B. Name three items you'd find in a first-aid kit:

_____   _____   _____

C. Name three primary causes for traffic accidents in Spanish:

_____

_____

_____

D. Traffic accidents happen all the time. Translate:

Was it a hit and run?

_____

Who was at fault?

_____

Do you have auto insurance?

_____

Were you wearing a safety belt?

_____

What's the work phone number?

_____

E. Match the opposites:

vida *('vee-dah)*   **mojado** *(moh-'hah-doh)*

norte *('nohr-teh)*   **este** *('eh-steh)*

oeste *(oh-'eh-steh)*   **sur** *(soor)*

menor *(meh-'nohr)*   **mayor** *(mah-'yohr)*

seco *('seh-koh)*   **muerte** *('mwehr-teh)*

ANSWERS

E. vida – muerte
norte – sur
oeste – este
menor – mayor
seco – mojado

D. ¿Chocó y se dio a la fuga? (choh-'koh ee seh 'dee-oh ah lah 'foo-gah)
¿Quién tenía la culpa? (kee-'ehn teh-'nee-ah lah 'kool-pah)
¿Tiene el seguro para el carro? (tee-'eh-neh ehl seh-'goo-roh 'pah-rah ehl 'kah-rroh)
¿Estaba usando un cinturón de seguridad? (eh-'stah-bah oo-'sahn-doh oon seen-too-'rohn deh seh-goo-ree-'dahd)
¿Cuál es el número de teléfono del trabajo? (kwahl ehs ehl 'noo-meh-roh deh teh-'leh-foh-noh dehl trah-'bah-hoh)

THE OUTDOORS
Las afueras *(lahs ah-'fweh-rahs)*

It is not uncommon for emergencies to take place outside an urban setting. Here are the blocks needed to build sentences:

Where's the...?	¿Dónde está... *('dohn-deh eh-'stah...)*
barn	**la granja?** *(lah 'grahn-hah)*
barnyard	**el corral?** *(ehl koh-'rrahl)*
beach	**la playa?** *(lah 'plah-yah)*
dairy	**la lechería?** *(lah leh-cheh-'ree-ah)*
farm	**la finca?** *(lah 'feen-kah)*
field	**el campo?** *(ehl 'kahm-poh)*
forest	**el bosque?** *(ehl 'boh-skeh)*
gulch	**la barranca?** *(lah bah-'rrahn-kah)*
hill	**el cerro?** *(ehl 'seh-rroh)*
lake	**el lago?** *(ehl 'lah-goh)*
mountain	**la montaña?** *(lah mohn-'tah-nyah)*
pasture	**el pastizal?** *(ehl pahs-tee-'sahl)*
ranch	**el rancho?** *(ehl 'rahn-choh)*
river	**el río?** *(ehl 'ree-oh)*
sea	**el mar?** *(ehl mahr)*
stable	**el establo?** *(ehl eh-'stah-bloh)*
stream	**el arroyo?** *(ehl ah-'rroh-yoh)*
swamp	**el pantano?** *(ehl pahn-'tah-noh)*
valley	**el valle?** *(ehl 'vah-yeh)*

Now point to these things along the road. You might need to search them for evidence:

Look at (the)...	Mire... *('mee-reh...)*
bush	**el arbusto** *(ehl ahr-'boo-stoh)*
crop	**la cosecha** *(lah koh-'seh-chah)*
dirt	**la tierra** *(lah tee-'eh-rrah)*
dust	**el polvo** *(ehl 'pohl-voh)*
flower	**la flor** *(lah flohr)*
foliage	**el follaje** *(ehl foh-'yah-heh)*
garden	**el jardín** *(ehl hahr-'deen)*
ground	**el suelo** *(ehl 'sweh-loh)*
grass	**el césped** *(ehl 'sehs-pehd)*
gravel	**la grava** *(lah 'grah-vah)*
grove	**la arboleda** *(lah ahr-boh-'leh-dah)*
land	**el terreno** *(ehl teh-'rreh-noh)*

mud	**el lodo** *(ehl 'loh-doh)*
orchard	**la huerta** *(lah 'wehr-tah)*
rock	**la piedra** *(lah pee-'eh-drah)*
sand	**la arena** *(lah ah-'reh-nah)*
tree	**el árbol** *(ehl 'ahr-bohl)*
weed	**la hierba** *(lah 'yehr-bah)*

No se preocupe, ¡todo está asegurado!

PET PROBLEMS
Los problemas con animales domésticos
(lohs proh-'bleh-mahs kohn ah-nee-'mah-lehs doh-'meh-stee-kohs)

Wherever people reside, domestic pets can be found. The trouble is, animals aren't always that easy to manage. Look over this next group of phrases, and insert any vocabulary word that seems to fit.

The...bit me	**...me mordió** *(...meh mohr-dee-'oh)*
I ran into the...	**Choqué con** ...*(choh-'keh kohn...)*
The... ran away	**... se escapó** *(...seh eh-skah-'poh)*
canary	**el canario** *(ehl kah-'nah-ree·oh)*
cat	**el gato** *(ehl 'gah-toh)*
chicken	**el pollo** *(ehl 'poh-yoh)*
cow	**la vaca** *(lah 'vah-kah)*
dog	**el perro** *(ehl 'peh-rroh)*
duck	**el pato** *(ehl 'pah-toh)*
fish	**el pez** *(ehl pehs)*

hamster	**el hámster** (ehl 'hahm-stehr)
horse	**el caballo** (ehl kah-'bah-yoh)
mouse	**el ratón** (ehl rah-'tohn)
parakeet	**el perico** (ehl peh-'ree-koh)
pig	**el cerdo** (ehl 'sehr-doh)
rabbit	**el conejo** (ehl koh-'neh-hoh)
sheep	**la oveja** (lah oh-'veh-hah)
turtle	**la tortuga** (lah tohr-'too-gah)

INFORMACIÓN PRIVADA

➤ Put it in (the)... **Póngalo en...** ('pohn-gah-loh ehn...)
  cage **la jaula** (lah 'hah·oo-lah)
  doghouse **la perrera** (lah peh-'rreh-rah)
  pen **el corral** (ehl koh-'rahl)

➤ If you do any work around household pets, share your thoughts using the new words and phrases below:

It bit me	**Me mordió** (meh mohr-dee-'oh)
It's a scratch	**Es un rasguño** (ehs oon rahs-'goo-nyoh)
It needs shots	**Necesita las vacunas** (neh-seh-'see-tah lahs vah-'koo-nahs)
It has a license	**Tiene licencia** (tee-'eh-neh lee-'sehn-see·ah)
It destroys property	**Destruye la propiedad** (deh-'stroo-yeh lah proh-pee-eh-'dahd)
It's castrated	**Está castrado** (eh-'stah kah-'strah-doh)
It's not neutered	**No está castrado** (noh eh-'stah kah-'strah-doh)
That is cruelty	**Eso es cruel** ('eh-soh ehs kroo-'ehl)
It has rabies	**Está rabioso** (eh-'stah rah-bee-'oh-soh)
It's trapped	**Está atrapado** (eh-'stah ah-trah-'pah-doh)
I'll put it to sleep	**Voy a matarlo** ('voh·ee ah mah-'tahr-loh)
We'll capture it	**Lo capturaremos** (loh kahp-too-rah-'reh-mohs)
Where's the tag?	**¿Dónde está la medalla de identificación?** ('dohn-'deh eh-'stah lah meh-'dah-yah deh ee-dehn-tee-fee-kah-see-'ohn)
It's in the animal shelter	**Está en el refugio de animales** (eh-'stah ehn ehl reh-'foo-hee·oh deh ah-nee-'mah-lehs)
It needs a veterinarian	**Necesita un veterinario** (neh-seh-'see-tah oon veh-teh-ree-'nah-ree·oh)

| It's harmless | **Es inofensivo** *(ehs een-oh-fehn-'see-voh)* |
| Call the Animal Control Service! | **¡Llame al servicio del control de animales!** *('yah-meh ahl sehr-'vee-see·oh dehl kohn-'trohl deh ah-nee-'mah-lehs)* |

Provide the Spanish words:

The dog attacked me	_____ **me atacó** (_____ *meh ah-tah-'koh)*
The cat is in my yard	_____ **está en mi jardín** (_____ *eh-'stah ehn mee hahr-'deen)*
I killed the mouse	**Maté** _____ *(mah-'teh)*

Do you work at a state or national park? Check these:

bear	**el oso** *(ehl 'oh-soh)*
beaver	**el castor** *(ehl kah-'stohr)*
coyote	**el coyote** *(ehl koh-'yoh-teh)*
deer	**el venado** *ehl veh-'nah-doh)*
eagle	**el águila** *(ehl 'ah-gee-lah)*
fox	**el zorro** *(ehl 'soh-rroh)*
frog	**el sapo** *(ehl 'sah-poh)*
hawk	**el halcón** *(ehl ahl-'kohn)*
lizard	**el lagarto** *(ehl lah-'gahr-toh)*
mole	**el topo** *(ehl 'toh-poh)*
mountain lion	**el puma** *(ehl 'poo-mah)*
opossum	**la zarigüeya** *(lah sah-ree-'gweh-yah)*
porcupine	**el puercoespín** *(ehl pwehr-koh-eh-'speen)*
raccoon	**el mapache** *(ehl mah-'pah-cheh)*
rat	**la rata** *(lah 'rah-tah)*
skunk	**el zorrillo** *(ehl soh-'rree-yoh)*
snake	**la culebra** *(lah koo-'leh-brah)*
squirrel	**la ardilla** *(lah ahr-'dee-yah)*
wolf	**el lobo** *(ehl 'loh-boh)*

REPASO

A. Match these words with their translations:

bush	la montaña *(lah mohn-'tah-nyah)*
mountain	el bosque *(ehl 'boh-skeh)*
sea	el árbol *(ehl 'ahr-bohl)*
tree	el arbusto *(ehl ahr-'boo-stoh)*
forest	la flor *(lah flohr)*
flower	el mar *(ehl mahr)*

B. Name three common house pets in Spanish:

_____ _____ _____

C. Name three animals that might be considered dangerous:

_____ _____ _____

ANSWERS

A. bush – el arbusto
mountain – la montaña
sea – el mar
tree – el árbol
forest – el bosque
flower – la flor

185

Observe what we've already learned about Spanish *Action Words*. All of the verb forms below were explained earlier, and are always welcome in case of emergency:

to look for (**buscar**) *(boos-'kahr)*

I'm looking for the children — **Estoy buscando a los niños** *(eh-'stoh-ee boo-'skahn-doh ah lohs 'nee-nyohs)*

to use (**usar**) *(oo-'sahr)*

He uses a tow truck — **El usa una grúa** *(ehl 'oo-sah 'oo-nah 'groo-ah)*

to go (**ir**) *(eehr)*

Let's go to the hospital — **Vamos al hospital** *('vah-mohs ahl oh-spee-'tahl)*

To this point, we are capable of handling activities that take place in the present. Notice what happens to some familiar verbs when we refer to the future:

to return (**regresar**) *(reh-greh-'sahr)*

I will return with the medicine — **Regresaré con la medicina** *(reh-greh-sah-'reh kohn lah meh-dee-'see-nah)*

to park (**estacionar**) *(eh-stah-see·oh-'nahr)*

He will park his car — **Estacionará su carro** *(eh-stah-see·oh-nah-'rah soo 'kah-rroh)*

to speak (**hablar**) *(ah-'blahr)*

They will speak to the victims — **Hablarán con las víctimas** *(ah-blah-'rahn kohn lahs 'veek-tee-mahs)*

to take (**tomar**) *(toh-'mahr)*

We will take the airplane — **Tomaremos el avión** *(toh-mah-'reh-mohs ehl ah-vee-'ohn)*

INFORMACIÓN PRIVADA

➤ As usual, a few irregular verbs interfere with the simple pattern of adding a few letters to the end of base *Action Word* forms. Here are the most important ones.

	to leave (**salir**) (sah-'leer)
(I)	**saldré** (sahl-'dreh)
(you, he, she)	**saldrá** (sahl-'drah)
(you [pl.], they)	**saldrán** (sahl-'drahn)
(we)	**saldremos** (sahl-'dreh-mohs)

	to put (**poner**) (poh-'nehr)	to do (**hacer**) (ah-'sehr)
(I)	**pondré** (pohn-'dreh)	**haré** (ah-'reh)
(you, he, she)	**pondrá** (pohn-'drah)	**hará** (ah-'rah)
(you [pl.], they)	**pondrán** (pohn-'drahn)	**harán** (ah-'rahn)
(we)	**pondremos** (pohn-'dreh-mohs)	**haremos** (ah-'reh-mohs)

➤ Here's a shortcut to telling others what you're going to do. In Spanish, the verb **ir** means "to go," so use the same four forms to refer to future actions:

I'm going to drive	**voy** ('voh-ee)	**Voy a manejar** ('voh-ee ah mah-neh-'hahr
He's going to back up	**va**	**Va a retroceder** (vah ahreh-troh-seh-'dehr)
They're going to stop	**van** (vahn)	**Van a parar** (vahn ahpah-'rahr)
We're going to park	**vamos** ('vah-mohs)	**Vamos a estacionar** ('vah-mohs ah eh-stah-see·oh-'nahr)

GRANDES HABILIDADES

To converse in Spanish at the scene of an emergency you're going to need all the appropriate *Action Words*. Whether it's in reference to present or future, manage the situation with the verbs below, and create sentences as shown.

to bend	**doblar** (doh-'blahr)	_____
to bleed	**sangrar** (sahn-'grahr)	_____
to breathe	**respirar** (reh-spee-'rahr)	<u>**Está respirando**</u> (eh-'stah reh-spee-'rahn-doh)
to die	**morir** (moh-'reer)	<u>**No va a morir**</u> (noh vah ah moh 'reer)
to hear	**oír** (oh-'eer)	_____
to help	**ayudar** (ah-yoo-'dahr)	_____

to injure	**herir** *(eh-'reer)*	_____
to kill	**matar** *(mah-'tahr)*	_____
to maintain	**mantener** *(mah-teh-'nehr)*	_____
to rest	**descansar** *(deh-skahn-'sahr)*	_____
to save	**salvar** *(sahl-'vahr)*	_____
to suffer	**sufrir** *(soo-'freer)*	_____
to survive	**sobrevivir** *(soh-breh-vee-'veer)*	<u>**Ella sobrevivirá**</u> *('eh-yah soh-breh-vee-vee-'rah)*
to swallow	**tragar** *(trah-'gahr)*	_____
to sweat	**sudar** *(soo-'dahr)*	_____
to touch	**tocar** *(toh-'kahr)*	_____

A fast, effective way to tell someone in Spanish that an activity was just completed is to add any base verb infinitive to the verb **acabar** which, together with **de,** means "to just finish." Here's how it functions in normal speech:

I just finished...
Acabo de... *(ah-'kah-boh deh...)*

I just finished driving
Acabo de manejar *(ah-'kah-boh deh mah-neh-'hahr)*

You, He, She just finished...
Acaba de... *(ah-'kah-bah deh...)*

He just finished sleeping
Acaba de dormir *(ah-'kah-bah deh dohr-'meer)*

They, You (plural) just finished...
Acaban de... *(ah-'kah-bahn deh...)*

They just finished talking
Acaban de hablar *(ah-kah-bahn deh ah-'blahr)*

We just finished...
Acabamos de... *(ah-kah-'bah-mohs deh...)*

We just finished eating
Acabamos de comer *(ah-kah-'bah-mohs deh koh-'mehr)*

INFORMACIÓN PRIVADA

➤ By the way, the verb **acabar** *(ah-kah-'bahr)* can be used as a regular *Action Word*:

I'm finishing now
Estoy acabando ahora *(eh-'stoh-ee ah-kah-'bahn-doh ah-'oh-rah)*

I finish at five o'clock	**Acabo a las cinco** *(ah-'kah-boh ah lahs 'seen-koh)*
I will finish tomorrow	**Acabaré mañana** *(ah-kah-bah-'reh mah-'nyah-nah)*
I want to finish here	**Quiero acabar aquí** *(kee-'eh-roh ah-kah-'bahr ah-'kee)*

REPASO

A. Practice your skills by adding these verb infinitives to the phrases below:

descansar *(deh-skahn-'sahr)*
tocar *(toh-'kahr)*
ayudar *(ah-yoo-'dahr)*

vivir *(vee-'veer)*
respirar *(reh-spee-'rahr)*

Favor de... *(fah-'vohr deh)*
Favor de descansar *(fah-'vohr deh deh-skahn-'sahr)*

Tiene que... *(tee-'eh-neh keh)*
Tiene que respirar más despacio *(tee-'eh-neh keh reh-spee-'rahr mahs deh-'spah-see·oh)*

Necesita... *(neh-seh-'see-tah)* _____

¿Quiere...? *(kee-'eh-reh)* _____

¿Puede...? *('pweh-deh)* _____

Acabo de... *(ah-'kah-boh deh...)* _____

CHAPTER FIVE
Capítulo Cinco
(kah-'pee-too-loh 'seen-koh)

CRIME SCENE
(Part 1)
La escena del crimen
(Primera parte)
(lah eh-'seh-nah dehl 'kree-mehn)
(pree-'meh-rah 'pahr-teh)

CRIME

El crimen *(ehl 'kree-mehn)*

Until now, handling everyday mishaps, routine traffic incidents, and minor medical emergencies has been the focus of our Spanish language experience. Obviously, we also need to communicate in Spanish at the crime scene.

D.U.I.

Manejó bajo la influencia del alcohol

(mah-'neh-hoh 'bah-hoh lah een-floo-'ehn-see·ah dehl ahl-koh-'ohl)

In recent years, one common street crime has drawn national public attention. It is driving under the influence, and since we've already covered the topic of motor vehicles in Spanish, this selection should not be that difficult for you:

Good evening	**Buenas noches** *('bweh-nahs 'noh-chehs)*
How are you?	**¿Cómo está?** *('koh-moh eh-'stah)*
Do you have a license?	**¿Tiene licencia?** *(tee-'eh-neh lee-'sehn-see·ah)*
Are you injured or ill?	**¿Está lastimado o enfermo?** *(eh-'stah lah-stee-'mah-doh oh ehn-'fehr-moh)*
Do you know what you did?	**¿Sabe lo que hizo?** *('sah-beh loh keh 'ee-soh)*
Why were you swerving?	**¿Por qué estaba zigzagueando?** *(pohr keh eh-'stah-bah seeg-sah-geh-'ahn-doh)*

Continue with your questions, and check for signs of trouble:

Have you been drinking?	**¿Ha estado tomando licor?** *(ah eh-'stahn-doh toh-'mahn-doh lee-'kohr)*
What did you drink?	**¿Qué tomó?** *(keh toh-'moh)*
How long ago?	**¿Cuánto tiempo hace?** *('kwahn-toh tee-'ehm-poh 'ah-seh)*
For how long did you drink?	**¿Por cuánto tiempo tomó?** *(pohr 'kwahn-toh tee-'ehm-poh toh-'moh)*
How many?	**¿Cuántas?** *('kwahn-tahs)*
How much?	**¿Cuánto?** *('kwahn-toh)*
At what time?	**¿A qué hora?** *(ah keh 'oh-rah)*
With whom?	**¿Con quién?** *(kohn kee-'ehn)*

Continue:

Where are you coming from?	**¿De dónde viene?** *(deh 'dohn-deh vee-'eh-neh)*
When did you start to drink?	**¿Cuándo empezó a tomar?** *('kwahn-doh ehm-peh-'soh ah toh-'mahr)*
When did you stop?	**¿Cuándo terminó?** *('kwahn-doh tehr-mee-'noh)*
What type of alcohol?	**¿Qué tipo de alcohol?** *(keh 'tee-poh deh ahl-koh-'ohl)*
What brand?	**¿Qué marca?** *(keh 'mahr-kah)*
Do you know where you are?	**¿Sabe dónde está?** *('sah-beh 'dohn-deh eh-'stah)*
Where are you going?	**¿Adónde va?** *(ah-'dohn-deh vah)*
When did you eat?	**¿Cuándo comió?** *('kwahn-doh koh-mee-'oh)*
What have you eaten?	**¿Qué ha comido?** *(keh ah koh-'mee-doh)*
How much have you slept?	**¿Cuánto ha dormido?** *('kwahn-toh ah dohr-'mee-doh)*
Did you take medication?	**¿Tomó medicina?** *(toh-'moh meh-dee-'see-nah)*
Do you have diabetes?	**¿Tiene diabetes?** *(tee-'eh-neh dee-ah-'beh-tehs)*
Did you take drugs?	**¿Tomó drogas?** *(toh-'moh 'droh-gahs)*
Do you have physical problems?	**¿Tiene problemas físicos?** *(tee-'eh-neh proh-'bleh-mahs 'fee-see-kohs)*
Do you feel the effects?	**¿Siente los efectos?** *(see-'ehn-teh lohs eh-'fehk-tohs)*
Is something wrong with your car?	**¿Hay algo mal con su carro?** *('ah·ee 'ahl-goh mahl kohn soo 'kah-rroh)*

If you suspect a problem, get a little more personal, and then inform the driver of what's coming next:

Are you drunk?	**¿Está borracho?** *(eh-'stah boh-'rrah-choh)*
What do you have...?	**¿Qué tiene...** *(keh tee-'eh-neh...)*
under the seat	**debajo del asiento?** *(deh-'bah-hoh dehl ah-see-'ehn-toh)*
in the trunk	**en la maletera?** *(ehn lah mah-leh-'teh-rah)*
in the bag	**en la bolsa?** *(ehn lah 'bohl-sah)*
in the bottle	**en la botella?** *(ehn lah boh-'teh-yah)*
in the can	**en la lata?** *(ehl lah 'lah-tah)*
in the glove box	**en la guantera?** *(ehl lah gwahn-'teh-rah)*
in the cup	**en la copa?** *(ehn lah 'koh-pah)*

I'm going to give you...	**Voy a darle...** *('voh-ee ah 'dahr-leh...)*
a warning	**un aviso** *(oon ah-'vee-soh)*
a ticket	**una citación** *('oo-nah see-tah-see-'ohn)*
a...test	**un examen de ...** *(oon ehk-'sah-mehn deh...)*
balance	**equilibrio** *(eh-kee-'lee-bree·oh)*
coordination	**coordinación** *(koh-ohr-dee-nah-see-'ohn)*
urine	**orina** *(oh-'ree-nah)*
blood	**sangre** *('sahn-greh)*
breath	**aliento** *(ah-lee-'ehn-toh)*
sobriety	**sobriedad** *(soh-bree-eh-'dahd)*

You may choose	**Puede elegir** *('pweh-deh eh-leh-'heer)*
If you refuse the test, you may lose your license	**Si rehusa tomar el examen, podría perder su licencia** *(see reh-'oo-sah toh-'mahr ehl ehk-'sah-mehn, poh-'dree-ah pehr-'dehr soo lee-'sehn-see·ah)*
It's the law	**Es la ley** *(ehs lah 'leh·ee)*
You have to obey	**Tiene que obedecer** *(tee-'eh-neh keh oh'beh-deh-'sehr)*
Please follow my instructions	**Favor de seguir mis instrucciones** *(fah-'vohr deh seh-'geer mees een-strook-see-'oh-nehs)*
Wait for the results	**Espere para ver los resultados** *(eh-'speh-reh 'pah-rah vehr lohs reh-sool-'tah-dohs)*

INFORMACIÓN PRIVADA

➤ Give legal terminology when the occasion calls for it:

| The law requires a test to determine how much alcohol is in the blood | **La ley require una prueba para saber cuanto alcohol hay en su sangre** *(lah 'leh·ee reh-kee-'eh-reh 'oo-nah 'proo·eh-bah 'pah-rah sah-'behr 'kwahn -toh ahl-koh-'ohl 'ah·ee ehn soo 'sahn-greh)* |

➤ If you're dealing with a minor, lay down the law:

| You are under the legal age to consume alcohol | **No tiene la edad legal para consumir alcohol** *(noh tee-'eh-neh lah eh-'dahd leh-'gahl 'pah-rah kohn-soo-'meer ahl-koh-'ohl)* |

Where did you get the alcohol?	**¿Dónde consiguió el alcohol?** *('dohn-deh kohn-see-gee-'oh ehl ahl-koh-'ohl)*
Who sold it to you?	**¿Quién se lo vendió?** *(kee-'ehn seh loh vehn-dee-'oh)*
I'm going to call your home	**Voy a llamar a su casa** *('voh·ee ah yah-'mahr ah soo 'kah-sah)*
We are going to the detention center	**Vamos al centro de detención** *('vah-mohs ahl 'sehn-troh deh deh-tehn-see-'ohn)*
Where is the party?	**¿Dónde está la fiesta?** *('dohn-deh eh-'stah lah fee-'eh-stah)*

THE TEST

El examen *(ehl ehk-'sah-mehn)*

Test procedures are made up of several commands and a few body parts. This is how they go together. Do you recognize any of these Spanish words?

Keep your arms to the side	**Mantenga los brazos al lado** *(mahn-'tehn-gah lohs 'brah-sohs ahl 'lah-doh)*
Put your feet together	**Ponga los pies juntos** *('pohn-gah lohs 'pee-ehs 'hoon-tohs)*
Move your head back	**Mueva la cabeza hacia atrás** *('mweh-vah lah kah-'beh-sah 'ah-see·ah ah-'trahs)*
Touch your nose	**Tóquese la nariz** *('toh-keh-seh lah nah-'rees)*
Look at my eyes	**Mire mis ojos** *('mee-reh mees 'oh-hohs)*
Follow my hand	**Siga mi mano** *('see-gah mee 'mah-noh)*
Raise your leg	**Levante la pierna** *(leh-'vahn-teh lah pee-'ehr-nah)*
Come here	**Venga aquí** *('vehn-gah ah-'kee)*
Turn around	**Dése vuelta** *('deh-seh 'vwehl-tah)*
Go back	**Regrese** *(reh-'greh-seh)*
Walk a straight line	**Camine en línea recta** *(kah-'mee-neh ehn 'lee-neh-ah 'rehk-tah)*
Get out of the car	**Salga del carro** *('sahl-gah dehl 'kah-rroh)*
Go over there	**Vaya allí** *('vah-yah ah-'yee)*
Calm down	**Cálmese** *('kahl-meh-seh)*

Use short phrases to simplify the process:

Like this	**Así** *(ah-'see)*
Extended	**Extendidos** *(ehk-stehn-'dee-dohs)*
You do it	**Hágalo usted** *('ah-gah-loh oo-'stehd)*
Nine steps	**Nueve pasos** *('nweh-veh 'pah-sohs)*
Eyes closed	**Ojos cerrados** *('oh-hohs seh-'rrah-dohs)*
Silence	**Silencio** *(see-'lehn-see·oh)*
I'll show you	**Le mostraré** *(leh moh-strah-'reh)*
Straight	**Recto** *('rehk-toh)*
The forefinger	**El dedo índice** *(ehl 'deh-doh 'een-dee-seh)*
Do not move	**No se mueva** *(noh seh 'mweh-vah)*
The same way	**De la misma forma** *(deh lah 'mees-mah 'fohr-mah)*
Behind	**Detrás** *(deh-'trahs)*
The right one	**El derecho** *(ehl deh-'reh-choh)*
The left one	**El izquierdo** *(ehl ees-kee-'ehr-doh)*
Watch me	**Míreme** *('mee-reh-meh)*
Like me	**Como yo** *('koh-moh yoh)*

Try saying several one-liners in a row:

This won't hurt	**Esto no le dolerá** *('eh-stoh noh leh doh-leh-'rah)*
I'm taking a sample	**Estoy tomando una muestra** *(eh-'stoh-ee toh-'mahn-doh 'oo-nah 'mweh-strah)*
You need to use this	**Necesita usar esto** *(neh-seh-'see-tah oo-'sahr 'eh-stoh)*
You have to breathe deep	**Tiene que respirar profundo** *(tee-'eh-neh keh reh-spee-'rahr proh-'foon-doh)*
The urine goes in this cup	**La orina va en este vaso** *(lah oh-'ree-nah vah ehn 'eh-steh 'vah-soh)*

Now make your final comments:

Put your hands behind your back	**Ponga las manos detrás suyo** *('pohn-gah lahs 'mah-nohs deh-'trahs 'soo-yoh)*
You are under arrest for drunk driving	**Está arrestado por manejar bajo la influencia del alcohol** *(eh-'stah ah-rreh-'stah-doh pohr mah-neh-'hahr 'bah-hoh lah een-floo-'ehn-see·ah dehl ahl-koh-'ohl)*
Give me the keys	**Déme las llaves** *('deh-meh lahs 'yah-vehs)*

But sometimes there's good news!

You did all right	**Salió bien** *(sah-lee-'oh 'bee·ehn)*
You are free to go	**Puede irse** *('pweh-deh 'eer-seh)*
I will follow you	**Lo voy a seguir** *(loh 'voh-ee ah seh-'geer)*

¡No! Tóquese **su** nariz!
¡Tóquese **su** nariz!

INFORMACIÓN PRIVADA

➤ If a person is drunk in public, yet not behind the wheel, use these key phrases:

You cannot drink in public	**No puede tomar alcohol en público** *(noh 'pweh-deh toh-'mahr ahl-koh-'ohl ehn 'poo-blee-koh)*
You cannot have an open container	**No puede tener un envase abierto** *(noh 'pweh-deh teh-'nehr oon ehn-'vah-seh ah-bee-'ehr-toh)*
You have had too much to drink	**Ha tomado demasiado alcohol** *(ah toh-'mah-doh deh-mah-see-'ah-doh ahl-koh-'ohl)*
I need some identification	**Necesito algún tipo de identificación** *(neh-seh-'see-toh ahl-'goon 'tee-poh deh ee-dehn-tee-fee-kah-see-'ohn)*
I'm taking you to jail	**Lo estoy llevando a la cárcel** *(loh eh-'stoh-ee yeh-'vahn-doh ah lah 'kahr-sehl)*
I'm taking you home	**Lo estoy llevando a su casa** *(loh eh-'stoh-ee yeh-'vahn-doh ah soo 'kah-sah)*
Do you have somebody to drive you?	**¿Tiene alguien que le puede llevar?** *(tee-'eh-neh 'ahl-gee·ehn keh leh 'pweh-deh yeh-'vahr)*
Do not drink and drive!	**¡No tome alcohol y maneje!** *(noh 'toh-meh ahl-koh-'ohl ee mah-'neh-heh)*

196

THE ALCOHOLIC BEVERAGE

La bebida alcohólica *(lah beh-'bee-dah ahl-koh-'oh-lee-kah)*

Consider all items containing alcohol. This is just a sample:

It was (the…)	**Fue...** *(fweh…)*
alcohol	**el alcohol** *(ehl ahl-koh-'ohl)*
beer	**la cerveza** *(lah sehr-'veh-sah)*
brandy	**el brandy** *(ehl 'brahn-dee)*
champagne	**la champaña** *(lah chahm-'pah-nyah)*
cocktail	**el cóctel** *(ehl 'kohk-tehl)*
drink	**el trago** *(ehl 'trah-goh)*
gin	**la ginebra** *(lah hee-'neh-brah)*
glass	**el vaso** *(ehl 'vah-soh)*
liquor	**el licor** *(ehl lee-'kohr)*
pitcher	**la jarra** *(lah 'hah-rrah)*
rum	**el ron** *(ehl rohn)*
shot	**el vasito** *(ehl vah-'see-toh)*
six-pack	**el paquete de seis** *(ehl pah-'keh-teh deh 'seh·ees)*
tequila	**la tequila** *(lah teh-'kee-lah)*
vodka	**el vodka** *(ehl 'vohd-kah)*
whiskey	**el whisky** *(ehl 'wees-kee)*
wine	**el vino** *(ehl 'vee-noh)*

FOOD AND DRINK

La comida y la bebida *(lah koh-'mee-dah ee lah beh-'bee-dah)*

The topic of food and drink also surfaces during discussions about alcohol consumption. Therefore, it would be wise to scan these next few series of Spanish vocabulary words:

Have you had (the)...?	**¿Ha tenido...** *(ah teh-'nee-doh…)*
breakfast	**el desayuno?** *(ehl deh-sah-'yoo-noh)*
dessert	**el postre?** *(ehl 'poh-streh)*
dinner	**la cena?** *(lah 'seh-nah)*
lunch	**el almuerzo?** *(ehl ahl-moo-'ehr-soh)*
meal	**la comida?** *(lah koh-'mee-dah)*
snack	**la merienda?** *(lah meh-ree-'ehn-dah)*

He/She ate (the)...	**Comió...** *(koh-mee-'oh…)*
bacon	**el tocino** *(ehl toh-'see-noh)*
bread	**el pan** *(ehl pahn)*
cake	**la torta** *(lah 'tohr-tah)*

cereal	**el cereal** *(ehl seh-reh-'ahl)*
cheese	**el queso** *(ehl 'keh-soh)*
chicken	**el pollo** *(ehl 'poh-yoh)*
cookie	**la galleta** *(lah gah-'yeh-tah)*
cracker	**la galleta salada** *(lah gah-'yeh-tah sah-'lah-dah)*
egg	**el huevo** *(ehl 'weh-voh)*
fish	**el pescado** *(ehl peh-'skah-doh)*
ham	**el jamón** *(ehl hah-'mohn)*
hamburger	**la hamburguesa** *(lah ahm-boor-'geh-sah)*
ice cream	**el helado** *(ehl eh-'lah-doh)*
meat	**la carne** *(lah 'kahr-neh)*
noodle	**el fideo** *(ehl fee-'deh-oh)*
pie	**el pastel** *(ehl pah-'stehl)*
pork	**el cerdo** *(ehl 'sehr-doh)*
rice	**el arroz** *(ehl ah-'rrohs)*
salad	**la ensalada** *(lah ehn-sah-'lah-dah)*
sausage	**la salchicha** *(lah sahl-'chee-chah)*
seafood	**el marisco** *(ehl mah-'ree-skoh)*
soup	**la sopa** *(lah 'soh-pah)*
steak	**el bistec** *(ehl bee-'stehk)*
turkey	**el pavo** *(ehl 'pah-voh)*

FRUITS AND VEGETABLES
Las frutas y los vegetales *(lahs 'froo-tahs ee lohs veh-heh-'tah-lehs)*

Practice around your house by touching each fruit or vegetable, and then saying its name in Spanish:

Give me...	**Déme...** *('deh-meh...)*
apple	**la manzana** *(lah mahn-'sah-nah)*
apricot	**el albaricoque** *(ehl ahl-bah-ree-'koh-keh)*
artichoke	**la alcachofa** *(lah ahl-kah-'choh-fah)*
banana	**el plátano** *(ehl 'plah-tah-noh)*
beans	**los frijoles** *(lohs free-'hoh-lehs)*
blackberry	**la mora** *(lah 'moh-rah)*
blueberry	**el mirtilo** *(ehl meer-'tee-loh)*
broccoli	**el brócoli** *(ehl 'broh-koh-lee)*
cabbage	**el repollo** *(ehl reh-'poh-yoh)*
carrot	**la zanahoria** *(lah sah-nah-'oh-ree·ah)*
cauliflower	**la coliflor** *(lah koh-lee-'flohr)*

celery	**el apio** *(ehl 'ah-pee·oh)*
cherry	**la cereza** *(lah seh-'reh-sah)*
coconut	**el coco** *(ehl 'koh-koh)*
corn	**el elote** *(ehl eh-'loh-teh)*
cucumber	**el pepino** *(ehl peh-'pee-noh)*
eggplant	**la berenjena** *(lah beh-rehn-'heh-nah)*
lettuce	**la lechuga** *(lah leh-'choo-gah)*
grape	**la uva** *(lah 'oo-vah)*
grapefruit	**la toronja** *(lah toh-'rohn-hah)*
lemon	**el limón** *(ehl lee-'mohn)*
mushroom	**el champiñón** *(ehl chahm-pee-'nyohn)*
onion	**la cebolla** *(lah seh-'boh-yah)*
orange	**la naranja** *(lah nah-'rahn-hah)*
pea	**la arvejita** *(lah ahr-veh-'hee-tah)*
peach	**el melocotón** *(ehl meh-loh-koh-'tohn)*
pear	**la pera** *(lah 'peh-rah)*
pineapple	**la piña** *(lah 'pee-nyah)*
plum	**la ciruela** *(lah see-roo-'eh-lah)*
potato	**la papa** *(lah 'pah-pah)*
pumpkin	**la calabaza** *(lah kah-lah-'bah-sah)*
radish	**el rábano** *(ehl 'rah-bah-noh)*
spinach	**la espinaca** *(lah eh-spee-'nah-kah)*
strawberry	**la fresa** *(lah 'freh-sah)*
sweet potato	**el camote** *(ehl kah-'moh-teh)*
tomato	**el tomate** *(ehl toh-'mah-teh)*
zucchini	**la calabacita verde** *(lah kah-lah-bah-'see-tah 'vehr-deh)*.

INFORMACIÓN PRIVADA

➤ Be specific! Refer to your favorite foods with the words below:

Mexican food	**la comida mejicana** *(lah koh-'mee-dah meh-hee-'kah-nah)*
Italian food	**la comida italiana** *(lah koh-'mee-dah ee-tah-lee-'ah-nah)*
Chinese food	**la comida china** *(lah koh-'mee-dah 'chee-nah)*
fried chicken	**el pollo frito** *(ehl 'poh-yoh 'free-toh)*
fried fish	**el pescado frito** *(ehl peh-'skah-doh 'free-toh)*

fried potato	la papa frita *(lah 'pah-pah 'free-tah)*
hard boiled egg	el huevo duro *(ehl 'weh-voh 'doo-roh)*
fried egg	el huevo frito *(ehl 'weh-voh 'free-toh)*
scrambled egg	el huevo revuelto *(ehl 'weh-voh reh-'vwehl-toh)*

➤ Have you noticed? Several foods are pronounced almost the same in both Spanish and English:

broccoli	el brócoli *(ehl 'broh-koh-lee)*
macaroni	los macarrones *(lohs mah-kah-'rroh-nehs)*
pancake	el panqueque *(ehl pahn-'keh-keh)*
pizza	la pizza *(lah 'peet-sah)*
pudding	el pudín *(ehl poo-'deen)*
spaghetti	el espagueti *(ehl eh-spah-'geh-tee)*

HAVE A DRINK!

¡Tome una bebida! *('toh-meh 'oo-nah beh-'bee-dah)*

For drinking in Spanish you may use either **tomar** ("to take") or **beber** ("to drink"). Both are equally valid.

| Is she drinking tea? | ¿Está bebiendo té? *(eh-'stah beh-bee-'ehn-doh teh)* |
| No, she takes coffee | No, toma café *(noh, 'toh-mah kah-'feh)* |

I drink...	Tomo... *('toh-moh...)*
coffee	el café *(ehl kah-'feh)*
decaffeinated coffee	el café descafeinado *(ehl kah-'feh dehs-kah-feh·ee-'nah-doh)*
juice	el jugo *(ehl 'hoo-goh)*
lemonade	la limonada *(lah lee-moh-'nah-dah)*
milk	la leche *(lah 'leh-cheh)*
shake	el batido *(ehl bah-'tee-doh)*
soda	la soda *(lah 'soh-dah)*
soft drink	el refresco *(ehl reh-'freh-skoh)*
tea	el té *(ehl teh)*
water	el agua *(ehl 'ah-gwah)*

These terms refer to the various containers:

bag	la bolsa *(lah 'bohl-sah)*
bottle	la botella *(lah boh-'teh-yah)*
box	la caja *(lah 'kah-hah)*

can	la lata *(lah 'lah-tah)*
jar	el frasco *(ehl 'frah-skoh)*
package	el paquete *(ehl pah-'keh-teh)*

DRUG ABUSE

El abuso de las drogas *(ehl ah-'boo-soh deh lahs 'droh-gahs)*

In society today, law enforcement officials must be able to identify the major types of drugs out there—both legal and illegal. Once in a while, you'll have to talk about them in Spanish. Fortunately in the drug world, most of the Spanish and English words are spelled about the same.

Glance over these examples:

Stimulants	**Los estimulantes** *(lohs eh-stee-moo-'lahn-tehs)*
amphetamine	**la anfetamina** *(lah ahn-feh-tah-'mee-nah)*
benzedrine	**la bencedrina** *(lah behn-seh-'dree-nah)*
caffeine	**la cafeína** *(lah kah-feh-'ee-nah)*
cocaine	**la cocaína** *(lah koh-kah-'ee-nah)*
dexedrine	**la dextroanfetamina** *(lah dehks-troh-ahn-feh-tah-'mee-nah)*
methedrine	**la metanfetamina** *(lah meh-tahn-feh-tah-'mee-nah)*
	la cristalina *(lah kree-stah-'lee-nah)*
nicotine	**la nicotina** *(lah nee-koh-'tee-nah)*

Depressants	**Los sedantes** *(lohs seh-'dahn-tehs)*
alcohol	**el alcohol** *(ehl ahl-koh-'ohl)*
barbiturate	**el barbitúrico** *(ehl bahr-bee-'too-ree-koh)*
seconal	**el seconal** *(ehl seh-koh-'nahl)*
sedative	**el sedante** *(ehl seh-'dahn-teh)*
sleeping pill	**la píldora para dormir** *(lah 'peel-doh-rah 'pah-rah dohr-'meer)*
tranquilizer	**el tranquilizante** *(ehl trahn-kee-lee-'sahn-teh)*
tuinal	**el tuinal** *(ehl too-ee-'nahl)*
Hallucinogens	**Los alucinógenos** *(lohs ah-loo-see-'noh-heh-nohs)*
LSD (acid)	**LDS (el ácido)** *(ehl 'ah-see-doh)*
mescaline	**la mescalina** *(lah meh-skah-'lee-nah)*
peyote	**el peyote** *(ehl peh-'yoh-teh)*
psilocybin	**la silocibina** *(lah see-loh-see-'bee-nah)*
STP	**el STP** *(ehl 'eh-seh teh peh)*
Narcotics	**Los narcóticos** *(lohs nahr-'koh-tee-kohs)*
cocaine	**la cocaína** *(lah koh-kah-'ee-nah)*
crack	**el crack** *(ehl krahk)*
heroin	**la heroína** *(lah eh-roh-'ee-nah)*
morphine	**la morfina** *(lah mohr-'fee-nah)*
opium	**el opio** *(ehl 'oh-pee·oh)*
Cannabis	**Canabis** *(kah-'nah-bees)*
hashish	**el hashish** *(ehl hah-'sheesh)*
marijuana	**la marijuana** *(lah mah-ree-'wah-nah)*
Inhalants	**Inhaladores** *(een-ah-lah-'doh-rehs)*
cleaning fluid	**el líquido para limpiar** *(ehl 'lee-kee-doh 'pah-rah leem-pee-'ahr)*
ether	**el éter** *(ehl 'eh-tehr)*
freon	**el freón** *(ehl freh-'ohn)*
gasoline	**la gasolina** *(lah gah-soh-'lee-nah)*
hydrocarbons	**hidrocarbonos** *(ee-droh-kahr-'boh-nohs)*
lighter fluid	**el líquido de encendedor** *(ehl 'lee-kee-doh deh ehn-sehn-deh-'dohr)*
model glue	**el pegamento de modelos** *(ehl peh-gah-'mehn-toh deh moh-'deh-lohs)*

➤ "Slang" also plays a part in drug-related activities. Although these words may vary from one region to the next, most Spanish speakers in the drug subculture will know exactly what you are talking about:

blue heavens	**los cielos** *(lohs see-'eh-lohs)*
coke	**la coca** *(lah 'koh-kah)*
dime bag	**el diez** *(ehl dee-'ehs)*
grass	**la hierba** *(lah 'yehr-bah)*
hearts	**los corazones** *(lohs koh-rah-'soh-nehs)*
joint	**el pitillo** *(ehl pee-'tee-yoh)*
lid	**el bote** *(ehl 'boh-teh)*
MDMA	**el cristal** *(ehl kree-'stahl)*
nickel bag	**el cinco** *(ehl 'seen-koh)*
rainbows	**los iris** *(lohs 'ee-rees)*
red devils	**las rojas** *(lahs 'roh-hahs)*
rock	**la roca** *(lah 'roh-kah)*
speed	**la pep** *(lah pehp)*
steroids	**los esteroides** *(lohs ehs-teh-'roh-ee-dehs)*
stuff	**la chiva** *(lah 'chee-vah)*
trip	**el viaje** *(ehl vee-'ah-heh)*
whites	**las blancas** *(lahs 'blahn-kahs)*
yellow jackets	**las amarillas** *(lahs ah-mah-'rree-yahs)*

➤ Use English!

el "crack"
el "crank"
el "ecstasy"
el "special K"
la "PCP"
los "bennies"
los "dexies"
los "goof balls"

A. Translate this set of questions:

¿Ha estado tomando licor? *(ah eh-'stah-doh toh-'mahn-doh lee-'kohr)*

_____

¿Qué tomó? *(keh toh-'moh)*

_____

¿Qué tiene en la botella? *(keh tee-'eh-neh ehn lah boh-'teh-yah)*

_____

B. Complete these sentences:

Voy a darle un examen de _____ *('voh-ee ah 'dahr-leh oon ehk-'sah-mehn deh*
  _____ *)*

Está arrestado por _____ *eh-'stah ah-rreh-'stah-doh pohr _____)*

No puede _____ *(noh pweh-deh _____)*

C. In Spanish, name three different kinds of:

narcotics	_____	_____	_____
beverages	_____	_____	_____
fruits	_____	_____	_____
vegetables	_____	_____	_____

ANSWERS

What do you have in the bottle?
What did you drink?
A. Have you been drinking alcohol?

NARCOTICS BUST

Un arresto de narcóticos *(oon ah-'rreh-stoh deh nahr-'koh-tee-kohs)*

There's no need to elaborate on this topic of international concern. Stop the suspect, and get a few questions answered. Remember that **está** can refer to "he" or "she," as well as "you":

What is he/she...? or
What are you...?   **¿Qué está...** *(keh eh-'stah...)*
   buying   **comprando?** *(kohm-'prahn-doh)*
   carrying   **llevando?** *(yeh-'vahn-doh)*
   doing   **haciendo?** *(ah-see-'ehn-doh)*
   selling   **vendiendo?** *(vehn-dee-'ehn-doh)*
   taking   **tomando?** *(toh-'mahn-doh)*
   using   **usando?** *(oo-'sahn-doh)*

Is he/she...? or
Are you...?   **¿Está...** *(eh-'stah...)*
   chewing   **masticando?** *(mah-stee-'kahn-doh)*
   shooting   **inyectando?** *(een-yehk-'tahn-doh)*
   smoking   **fumando?** *(foo-'mahn-doh)*
   sniffing   **inhalando?** *(een-ah-'lahn-doh)*
   swallowing   **tragando?** *(trah-'gahn-doh)*

Formulate more questions using the language you know:

What are you doing in this area?	**¿Qué está haciendo en esta área?** *(keh eh-'stah ah-see-'ehn-doh ehn 'eh-stah 'ah-reh-ah)*
Where did you get that?	**¿Dónde consiguió eso?** *('dohn-deh kohn-see-gee-'oh 'eh-soh)*
Do you have a prescription?	**¿Tiene una receta?** *(tee-'eh-neh 'oo-nah reh-'seh-tah)*
Have you been arrested before?	**¿Ha estado arrestado antes?** *(ah eh-'stah-doh ah-rreh-'stah-doh 'ahn-tehs)*
How long have you been using?	**¿Por cuánto tiempo ha estado usando?** *(pohr 'kwahn-toh tee-'ehm-poh ah eh-'stah-doh oo-'sahn-doh)*
Do you have any scars or tattoos?	**¿Tiene cicatrices o tatuajes?** *(tee-'eh-neh see-kah-'tree-sehs oh tah-too-'ah-hehs)*
What's the name of your contact?	**¿Cuál es el nombre de su conexión?** *(kwahl ehs ehl 'nohm-breh deh soo koh-nehk-see-'ohn)*
What is that for?	**¿Para qué es eso?** *('pah-rah keh ehs 'eh-soh)*
How much did it cost you?	**¿Cuánto le costó?** *('kwahn-toh leh koh-'stoh)*
When did you stop using drugs?	**¿Cuándo paró de usar drogas?** *('kwahn-doh pah-'roh deh oo-'sahr 'droh-gahs)*
When did you buy it?	**¿Cuándo lo compró?** *('kwahn-doh loh kohm-'proh)*
Where did you buy it?	**¿Dónde lo compró?** *('dohn-deh loh kohm-'proh)*
When did you start using drugs?	**¿Cuándo comenzó a tomar drogas?** *('kwahn-doh koh-mehn-'soh ah toh-'mahr 'droh-gahs)*
How much money do you have?	**¿Cuánto dinero tiene?** *('kwahn-toh dee-'neh-roh tee-'eh-neh)*
What kind have you taken?	**¿Qué clase ha tomado?** *(keh 'klah-'seh ah toh-'mah-doh)*
What color and shape?	**¿De qué color y forma?** *(deh keh koh-'lohr ee 'fohr-mah)*
How many times?	**¿Cuántas veces?** *('kwahn-tahs 'veh-sehs)*
At what time?	**¿A qué hora?** *(ah keh 'oh-rah)*

TEMAS CULTURALES

Careful! Don't rush to any conclusions. What may appear to be a bizarre herb or chemical could be a medicinal home remedy. Certain **especias** *(eh-'speh-see·ahs)* (spices), for example, are taken to cure everything from a headache to heart disease. To avoid misunderstandings, you may want to read up on such methods and practices.

DO YOU FEEL O.K.?

¿Se siente bien? *(seh see-'ehn-teh 'bee·ehn)*

Play it safe. Make sure you know what mood they're in.

Is he...? or
Are you...?   **¿Está...** *(eh-'stah...)*

  agitated   **agitado?** *(ah-hee-'tah-doh)*

  alert   **alerto?** *(ah-'lehr-toh)*

  angry   **enojado?** *(eh-noh-'hah-doh)*

  confused   **confundido?** *(kohn-foon-'dee-doh)*

  dehydrated   **deshidratado?** *(dehs-ee-drah-'tah-doh)*

  depressed   **deprimido?** *(deh-pree-'mee-doh)*

  drunk   **borracho?** *(boh-'rrah-choh)*

  excited   **excitado?** *(ehk-see-'tah-doh)*

  hallucinating   **alucinando?** *(ah-loo-see-'nahn-doh)*

  high   **drogado?** *(droh-'gah-doh)*

  lethargic   **letárgico?** *(leh-'tahr-hee-koh)*

  lost   **perdido?** *(pehr-'dee-doh)*

  nervous   **nervioso?** *(nehr-vee-'oh-soh)*

  relaxed   **relajado?** *(reh-lah-'hah-doh)*

  sick   **enfermo?** *(ehn-'fehr-moh)*

  unattentive   **desatento?** *(dehs-ah-'tehn-toh)*

  upset   **molesto?** *(moh-'leh-stoh)*

  worried   **preocupado?** *(preh-oh-koo-'pah-doh)*

Is he/she...? or
Are you...?   **¿Tiene...** *(tee-'eh-neh...)*

  afraid   **miedo?** *(mee-'eh-doh)*

  cold   **frío?** *('free-oh)*

  hot   **calor?** *(kah-'lohr)*

  hungry   **hambre?** *('ahm-breh)*

  thirsty   **sed?** *(sehd)*

➤ Are you changing the word endings when you refer to females?

He's depressed	She's depressed
Está deprimido	**Está deprimida**
(eh-'stah deh-pree-'mee-doh)	*(eh-'stah deh-pree-'mee-dah)*

➤ Drug conversations could also require this important terminology:

dealer	**el droguero** *(ehl droh-'geh-roh)*
drug addict	**el drogadicto** *(ehl drohg-ah-'deek-toh)*
drug traffic	**el narcotráfico** *(ehl nahr-koh-'trah-fee-koh)*
habit	**el hábito** *(ehl 'ah-bee-toh)*
illegal possession	**la posesión ilegal** *(lah poh-seh-see-'ohn ee-leh-'gahl)*
informant	**el informante** *(ehl een-fohr-'mahn-teh)*
overdose	**la sobredosis** *(lah soh-breh-'doh-sees)*

➤ You should now have enough language to make the arrest:

I am going to...	**Voy a ...** *('voh-ee ah ...)*
arrest you	**arrestarlo** *(ah-rreh-'stahr-loh)*
frisk you	**registrarlo** *(reh-hee-'strahr-loh)*
handcuff you	**esposarlo** *(eh-spoh-'sahr-loh)*
use a police dog	**usar un perro policía** *(oo-'sahr oon 'peh-rroh poh-lee-'see-ah)*

I'm an official from (the)...	**Soy oficial de...** *('soh-ee oh-fee-see-'ahl deh...)*
city	**la ciudad** *(lah see-oo-'dahd)*
county	**el condado** *(ehl kohn-'dah-doh)*
federal government	**el gobierno federal** *(ehl goh-bee-'ehr-noh feh-deh-'rahl)*
state	**el estado** *(ehl eh-'stah-doh)*
vice squad	**la brigada contra el vicio** *(lah bree-'gah-dah 'kohn-trah ehl 'vee-see·oh)*

WHAT'S THAT?

¿Qué es eso? *(keh ehs -'eh-soh)*

Most words related to narcotics and drug paraphernalia can easily be translated into Spanish. Almost all of these terms are names for common objects around the house:

It's (the)...   **Es...** *(ehs...)*

    ammonia
        el amoníaco *(ehl ah-moh-'nee-ah-koh)*

    baking soda
        el bicarbonato *(ehl bee-kahr-boh-'nah-toh)*

    capsule
        la cápsula *(lah 'kahp-soo-lah)*

    chemical
        el producto químico *(ehl proh-'dook-toh 'kee-mee-koh)*

    cigarette
        el cigarrillo *(ehl see-gah-'rree-yoh)*

    injection
        la inyección *(lah een-yehk-see-'ohn)*

    leaf
        la hoja *(lah 'oh-hah)*

    liquid
        el líquido *(ehl 'lee-kee-doh)*

    match
        el fósforo *(ehl 'fohs-foh-roh)*

    needle
        la aguja *(lah ah-'goo-hah)*

    outfit
        el estuche *(ehl eh-'stoo-cheh)*

    pill
        la píldora *(lah 'peel-doh-rah)*

    pipe
        la pipa *(lah 'pee-pah)*

    plant
        la planta *(lah 'plahn-tah)*

    powder
        el polvo *(ehl 'pohl-voh)*

    razor
        la navaja *(lah nah-'vah-hah)*

    rock
        la piedra *(lah pee-'eh-drah)*

    spoon
        la cuchara *(lah koo-'chah-rah)*

    sugar cube
        el cubo de azúcar *(ehl 'koo-boh deh ah-'soo-kahr)*

    syringe
        la jeringa *(lah heh-'reen-gah)*

| tablet | **la tableta** (*lah tah-'bleh-tah*) |
| vial | **el frasco** (*ehl' frah-skoh*) |

It's…	**Es…** (*ehs…*)
pure	**puro** (*'poo-roh*)
diluted	**diluído** (*dee-loo-'ee-doh*)

HOW MUCH DO YOU HAVE?
¿Cuánto tiene? (*'kwahn-toh tee-'eh-neh*)

I have (the)…	**Tengo…** (*'tehn-goh…*)
bag	**la bolsa** (*lah 'bohl-sah*)
balloon	**el globo** (*ehl 'gloh-boh*)
bindle	**el paquetito** (*ehl pah-keh-'tee-toh*)
brick	**el ladrillo** (*ehl lah-'dree-yoh*)
can	**la lata** (*lah 'lah-tah*)
gram	**el gramo** (*ehl 'grah-moh*)
half	**la mitad** (*lah mee-'tahd*)
kilogram	**el kilo** (*ehl 'kee-loh*)
ounce	**la onza** (*lah 'ohn-sah*)
piece	**el pedazo** (*ehl peh-'dah-soh*)
pound	**la libra** (*lah 'lee-brah*)
quarter	**el cuarto** (*ehl 'kwahr-toh*)
tablespoon	**la cucharada** (*lah koo-chah-'rah-dah*)
teaspoon	**la cucharadita** (*lah koo-chah-rah-'dee-tah*)

Drugs come in all kinds of shapes and sizes:

The shape is (the)…	**La forma es…** (*lah 'fohr-mah ehs…*)
circle	**el círculo** (*ehl 'seer-koo-loh*)
diamond	**el diamante** (*ehl dee-ah-'mahn-teh*)
oval	**el óvalo** (*ehl 'oh-vah-loh*)
rectangle	**el rectángulo** (*ehl rehk-'tahn-goo-loh*)
round	**redondo** (*reh-'dohn-doh*)
square	**el cuadrado** (*ehl kwah-'drah-doh*)
star	**la estrella** (*lah eh-'streh-yah*)
triangle	**el triángulo** (*ehl tree-'ahn-goo-loh*)

THE DRUG ADDICT

El drogadicto *(ehl droh-gah-'deek-toh)*

Describe the suspect at the time of arrest:

He/she has... or
You have...   **Tiene...** *(tee-'eh-neh...)*

a fever	**una fiebre** *('oo-nah fee-'eh-breh)*
brain damage	**daño cerebral** *('dah-nyoh seh-reh-'brahl)*
breathing problems	**problemas para respirar** *(proh-'bleh-mahs 'pah-rah reh-spee-'rahr)*
convulsions	**convulsiones** *(kohn-vool-see-'oh-nehs)*
delusions	**delirio** *(deh-'lee-ree·oh)*
distorted senses	**los sentidos entorpecidos** *(lohs sehn-'tee-dohs ehn-tohr-peh-'see-dohs)*
dilated pupils	**pupilas dilatadas** *(poo-'pee-lahs dee-lah-'tah-dahs)*
dry mouth	**boca seca** *('boh-kah 'seh-kah)*
malnutrition	**desnutrición** *(dehs-noo-tree-see-'ohn)*
memory loss	**pérdida de memoria** *('pehr-dee-dah deh meh-'moh-ree·ah)*
nervous breakdown	**postración nerviosa** *(poh-strah-see-'ohn nehr-vee-'oh-sah)*
nausea	**náusea** *('now-seh-ah)*
nose tissue damage	**daño en el tejido nasal** *('dah-nyoh ehn ehl teh-'hee-doh nah-'sahl)*
palpitations	**palpitaciones** *(pahl-pee-tah-see-'oh-nehs)*
paranoia	**paranoia** *(pah-rah-'noh·ee-yah)*
personality change	**cambio de personalidad** *('kahm-bee·oh deh pehr-soh-nah-lee-'dahd)*
poor coordination	**mala coordinación** *('mah-lah koh-ohr-dee-nah-see-'ohn)*
rashes	**salpullidos** *(sahl-poo-'yee-dohs)*
red eyes	**ojos rojos** *('oh-hohs 'roh-hohs)*
schizophrenia	**esquizofrenia** *(ehs-keet-soh-'freh-nee·ah)*
seizures	**ataques** *(ah-'tah-kehs)*
shakes	**temblores** *(tehm-'bloh-rehs)*
slow mental reactions	**reacciones mentales lentas** *(reh-ahk-see-'oh-nehs mehn-'tah-lehs 'lehn-tahs)*
slurred speech	**pronunciación indistinta** *(proh-noon-see-ah-see-'ohn een-dee-'steen-tah)*

suicidal tendencies	**tendencias suicidas** *(tehn-'dehn-see·ahs soo-ee-'see-dee·ahs)*	
unstable emotions	**inestabilidad emocional** *(een-eh-stah-bee-lee-'dahd eh-moh-see·oh-'nahl)*	
violent behavior	**comportamiento violento** *(kohm-pahr-tah-mee-'ehn-toh vee-oh-'lehn-toh)*	

¡A MIS ÓRDENES!

The trouble is, many drug-related cases are dangerous, and need to be handled with extreme caution and proper procedure. Stay alert as you confront the suspect with the *Command Words*. Careful! You may need to show your weapon:

Come here!	**¡Venga aquí!** *('vehn-gah ah-'kee)*
Lie down!	**¡Acuéstese!** *(ah-'kweh-steh-seh)*
Raise your hands!	**¡Levante las manos!** *(leh-'vahn-teh lahs 'mah-nohs)*
Sit down!	**¡Siéntese!** *(see-'ehn-teh-seh)*
Turn around!	**¡Dése vuelta!** *('deh-seh 'vwehl-tah)*

Here are more command phrases that we practiced earlier:

Empty your pockets!	**¡Vacíe los bolsillos!** *(vah-'see-eh lohs bohl-'see-yohs)*
Give it to me!	**¡Démelo!** *('deh-meh-loh)*
Show me your hands!	**¡Muéstreme las manos!** *('mweh-streh-meh lahs 'mah-nohs)*
Take out your I.D.!	**¡Saque su identificación!** *('sah-keh soo ee-dehn-tee-fee-kah-see-'ohn)*

Ready for a few new ways to give orders? Read carefully as you say each word aloud:

Carry	**Lleve**	**Lleve esto** *('yeh-veh 'eh-stoh)*
Drink	**Beba**	**Beba el agua** *('beh-bah ehl 'ah-gwah)*
Drop	**Suelte**	**Suelte la llave** *('swehl-teh lah 'yah-veh)*
Eat	**Coma**	**Coma la comida** *('koh-mah lah koh-'mee-dah)*
Extend	**Extienda**	**Extienda los brazos** *(ehks-tee-'ehn-dah lohs 'brah-sohs)*
Interlace	**Entrelace**	**Entrelace los dedos** *(ehn-treh-'lah-seh lohs 'deh-dohs)*
Keep	**Guarde**	**Guarde el papel** *('gwahr-deh ehl pah-'pehl)*
Look	**Mire**	**Mire aquí** *('mee-reh ah-'kee)*

Pull	**Jale**	**Jale la puerta** *('hah-leh lah 'pwehr-tah)*
Push	**Empuje**	**Empuje el carro** *(ehm-'poo-heh ehl 'kah-rroh)*
Separate	**Separe**	**Separe los pies** *(seh-'pah-reh lohs 'pee-ehs)*
Throw	**Tire**	**Tire la bolsa** *('tee-reh lah 'bohl-sah)*

Dry your hands!	**¡Séquese las manos!** *('seh-keh-seh lahs 'mah-nohs)*
Kneel!	**¡Arrodíllese!** *(ah-rroh-'dee-yeh-seh)*
Touch your nose!	**¡Tóquese la nariz!** *('toh-keh-seh lah nah-'rees)*
Wake up!	**¡Despiértese!** *(dehs-pee-'ehr-teh-seh)*
Wash your face!	**¡Lávese la cara!** *('lah-veh-seh lah 'kah-rah)*

¡No beba de ese vaso! ¡Es la orina del sospechoso!

ROOM TO ROOM

De cuarto a cuarto *(deh 'kwahr-toh ah 'kwahr-toh)*

When your job takes you into a household in search of drugs, weapons, or stolen property, listen for those terms that describe the important items around you.

First, get an overall picture of the building in question:

It's (the)...	**Es...** *(ehs...)*
apartment	**el apartamento** *(ehl ah-pahr-tah-'mehn-toh)*
cabin	**la cabaña** *(lah kah-'bah-nah)*
condominium	**el condominio** *(ehl kohn-doh-'mee-nee·oh)*
hotel	**el hotel** *(ehl oh-'tehl)*
house	**la casa** *(lah 'kah-sah)*
mansion	**la mansión** *(lah mahn-see-'ohn)*
mobile home	**la casa rodante** *(lah 'kah-sah roh-'dahn-teh)*
motel	**el motel** *(ehl moh-'tehl)*

Where's the...	¿Dónde está... *('dohn-deh eh-'stah...)*
attic	**el desván?** *(ehl dehs-'vahn)*
backyard	**el patio?** *(ehl 'pah-tee·oh)*
basement	**el sótano?** *(ehl 'soh-tah-noh)*
bathroom	**el baño?** *(ehl 'bah-nyoh)*
bedroom	**el dormitorio?** *(ehl dohr-mee-'toh-ree·oh)*
dining room	**el comedor?** *(ehl koh-meh-'dohr)*
garage	**el garaje?** *(ehl gah-'rah-heh)*
garden	**el jardín?** *(ehl hahr-'deen)*
hallway	**el pasillo?** *(ehl pah-'see-yoh)*
kitchen	**la cocina?** *(lah koh-'see-nah)*
living room	**la sala?** *(lah 'sah-lah)*
porch	**el porche?** *(ehl 'pohr-cheh)*

Can you see the...?	¿Puede ver... *('pweh-deh vehr...)*
ceiling	**el cielo raso?** *(ehl see-'eh-loh 'rah-soh)*
chimney	**la chimenea?** *(lah chee-meh-'neh-ah)*
door	**la puerta?** *(lah 'pwehr-tah)*
driveway	**la entrada para carros?** *(lah ehn-'trah-dah 'pah-rah 'kah-rrohs)*
fence	**la cerca?** *(lah 'sehr-kah)*
fireplace	**el fogón?** *(ehl foh-'gohn)*
floor	**el piso?** *(ehl 'pee-soh)*
gate	**el portón?** *(ehl pohr-'tohn)*
pool	**la piscina?** *(lah pee-'see-nah)*
roof	**el techo?** *(ehl 'teh-choh)*
room	**el cuarto?** *(ehl 'kwahr-toh)*
wall	**la pared?** *(lah pah-'rehd)*
window	**la ventana?** *(lah vehn-'tah-nah)*

Walk over to one of the neighbors and ask for "inside" information:

Which room?	¿Cuál cuarto? *(kwahl 'kwahr-toh)*
How many people?	¿Cuántas personas? *('kwahn-tahs pehr-'soh-nahs)*
Who lives there?	¿Quién vive allí? *(kee-'ehn 'vee-veh ah-'yee)*
Where is the back door?	¿Dónde está la puerta trasera? *('dohn-deh eh-'stah lah 'pwehr-tah trah-'seh-rah)*
Are they inside?	¿Están adentro? *(eh-'stahn ah-'dehn-troh)*
Do they have a dog?	¿Tienen un perro? *(tee-'eh-nehn oon 'peh-rroh)*
Is it accessible?	¿Está accesible? *(eh-'stah ahk-seh-'see-bleh)*
I'm looking for (the)...	Estoy buscando... *(eh-'stoh-ee boo-'skahn-doh...)*
alarm	**la alarma** *(lah ah-'lahr-mah)*
fuse box	**la caja de fusibles** *(lah 'kah-hah deh foo-'see-blehs)*

gas meter	**el medidor de gas** *(ehl meh-dee-'dohr deh gahs)*
security system	**el sistema de seguridad** *(ehl see-'steh-mah deh seh-goo-ree-'dahd)*
smoke alarm	**el detector de humo** *(ehl deh-tehk-'tohr deh 'oo-moh)*
water valve	**la válvula de agua** *(lah 'vahl-voo-lah deh 'ah-gwah)*

Outdoor objects may provide clues:

awning	**el toldo** *(ehl 'tohl-doh)*
balcony	**el balcón** *(ehl bahl-'kohn)*
bench	**la banca** *(lah 'bahn-kah)*
deck	**la terraza** *(lah teh-'rrah-sah)*
fountain	**la fuente** *(lah 'fwehn-teh)*
Jacuzzi	**el jacuzzi** *(ehl yah-'koo-see)*
lawn	**el césped** *(ehl 'sehs-pehd)*
light post	**el farol** *(ehl fah-'rohl)*
patio	**el patio** *(ehl 'pah-tee-oh)*
planter	**el macetero** *(ehl mah-seh-'teh-roh)*
ramp	**la rampa** *(lah 'rahm-pah)*
shed	**el cobertizo** *(ehl koh-behr-'tee-soh)*
spa	**el balneario** *(ehl bahl-neh-'ah-ree-oh)*
steps	**los escalones** *(lohs ehs-kah-'loh-nehs)*
tower	**la torre** *(lah 'toh-rreh)*
trellis	**el enrejado** *(ehl ehn-reh-'hah-doh)*
walkway	**el sendero** *(ehl sehn-'deh-roh)*

THE RAID

La incursión *(lah een-koor-see-'ohn)*

Knock on the door and let the suspect know that you mean business:

This is the police	**Somos la policía** *('soh-mohs lah poh-lee-'see-ah)*
Give up now	**Ríndase ahora mismo** *('reen-dah-seh ah-'oh-rah 'mees-moh)*
This is your last chance	**Esta es su última oportunidad** *('ehs-tah ehs soo 'ool-tee-mah oh-pohr-too-nee-'dahd)*
Come out with your hands up	**Salga con las manos arriba** *('sahl-gah kohn lahs 'mah-nohs ah-'rree-bah)*

Do not try to escape	**No trate de escapar** *(noh 'trah-teh deh ehs-kah-'pahr)*
You are surrounded	**Está rodeado** *(eh-'stah roh-deh-'ah-doh)*
We have a warrant	**Tenemos una orden de la corte** *(teh-'meh-nohs 'oo-nah 'ohr-dehn deh lah 'kohr-teh)*
We are coming into the building	**Estamos entrando al edificio** *(ehs-'tah-mohs ehn-'trahn-doh ahl eh-dee-'fee-see-oh)*
Lie face down	**Acuéstese boca abajo** *(ah-'kweh-steh-seh 'boh-kah ah-'bah-hoh)*
Put your hands behind your head	**Ponga las manos detrás de la cabeza** *('pohn-gah lahs 'mah-nohs deh-'trahs deh lah kah-'beh-sah)*
Keep your hands where I can see them	**Mantenga las manos donde las puedo ver** *(mahn-'tehn-gah lahs 'mah-nohs 'dohn-deh lahs 'pweh-doh vehr)*

THE SEARCH
El registro *(ehl reh-'hees-troh)*

You are not obliged to consent to the search	**No está obligado/a a consentir a ser registrado/a** *(noh ehs-'tah oh-blee-'gah-doh/ah ah kohn-sehn-'teer ah sehr reh-hees-'trah-doh/ah)*
If you refuse to sign I will have to arrest you	**Si se niega a firmar tendré que arrestarlo/a** *(see seh nee-'eh-gah ah feer-'mahr tehn-'dreh keh ah-rrehs-'tahr-loh/ah)*
I have a search warrant	**Tengo la orden de registro** *('tehn-goh lah 'ohr-dehn deh reh-'hees-troh)*
I will be back with a warrant	**Volveré cuando tenga la orden** *(vohl-veh-'reh 'kwahn-doh 'tehn-gah lah 'ohr-dehn)*

INFORMACIÓN PRIVADA

➤ Situations like this might require some kind of an explanation to family and friends. Are any of these words useful?

He is...	**El está...** *(ehl eh-'stah...)*
accused	**acusado** *(ah-koo-'sah-doh)*
arrested	**arrestado** *(ah-rreh-'stah-doh)*
captured	**capturado** *(kahp-too-'rah-doh)*

216

charged	**denunciado** *(deh-noon-see-'ah-doh)*
detained	**detenido** *(deh-teh-'nee-doh)*
jailed	**encarcelado** *(ehn-kahr-seh-'lah-doh)*

AROUND THE HOUSE

Alrededor de la casa *(ahl-reh-deh-'dohr deh lah 'kah-sah)*

Once you get inside, look around you. These things are everywhere:

Look at (the)…	**Mire...** *('mee-reh…)*
Move (the)…	**Mueva...** *('mweh-vah…)*
Bring (the)…	**Traiga...** *('trah·ee-gah…)*
armchair	**el sillón** *(ehl see-'yohn)*
armoire	**el armario** *(ehl ahr-'mah-ree·oh)*
bed	**la cama** *(lah 'kah-mah)*
bookshelf	**el librero** *(ehl lee-'breh-roh)*
chair	**la silla** *(lah 'see-yah)*
chest	**el baúl** *(ehl bah-'ool)*
desk	**el escritorio** *(ehl eh-skree-'toh-ree·oh)*
dresser	**el tocador** *(ehl toh-kah-'dohr)*
furniture	**el mueble** *(ehl 'mweh-bleh)*
nightstand	**la mesa de noche** *(lah 'meh-sah deh 'noh-cheh)*
piano	**el piano** *(ehl pee-'ah-noh)*
sofa	**el sofá** *(ehl soh-'fah)*
stool	**el banquillo** *(ehl bahn-'kee-yoh)*
table	**la mesa** *(lah 'meh-sah)*

It's next to the...	**Está al lado de...** *(eh-'stah ahl 'lah-doh deh...)*
air conditioning	**el aire acondicionado** *(ehl 'ah·ee-reh ah-kohn-dee-see·oh-'nah-doh)*
bathroom	**el baño** *(ehl 'bah-nyoh)*
bathtub	**la tina** *(lah 'tee-nah)*
blind	**la persiana** *(lah pehr-see-'ah-nah)*
cabinet	**el gabinete** *(ehl gah-bee-'neh-teh)*
closet	**el ropero** *(ehl roh-'peh-roh)*
counter	**el mostrador** *(ehl moh-strah-'dohr)*
curtain	**la cortina** *(lah kohr-'tee-nah)*
drawer	**el cajón** *(ehl kah-'hohn)*
electrical outlet	**el enchufe** *(ehl ehn-'choo-feh)*
faucet	**el grifo** *(ehl 'gree-foh)*
fireplace	**la chimenea** *(lah chee-meh-'neh-ah)*
heating	**la calefacción** *(lah kah-leh-fahk-see-'ohn)*
kitchen sink	**el fregadero** *(ehl freh-gah-'deh-roh)*
lampshade	**la pantalla** *(lah pahn-'tah-yah)*
light	**la luz** *(lah loos)*
light switch	**el interruptor** *(ehl een-teh-rroop-'tohr)*
medicine chest	**el botiquín** *(ehl boh-tee-'keen)*
plumbing	**la tubería** *(lah too-beh-'ree-ah)*
rug	**la alfombra** *(lah ahl-'fohm-brah)*
shelf	**la repisa** *(lah reh-'pee-sah)*
shower	**la ducha** *(lah 'doo-chah)*
step	**el escalón** *(ehl eh-skah-'lohn)*
toilet	**el excusado** *(ehl ehks-koo-'sah-doh)*

Are you putting labels on your own home furnishings? It will help you remember the words!

Not all home furnishing stay indoors. You may want to consider labeling some outdoor pieces as well:

barbeque grill	**la parrilla** *(lah pah-'rree-yah)*
beach chair	**la silla de playa** *(lah 'see-yah deh 'plah-yah)*
hammock	**la hamaca** *(lah ah-'mah-kah)*
lawn chair	**la silla de césped** *(lah 'see-yah deh 'sehs-pehd)*
umbrella	**la sombrilla** *(lah sohm-'bree-yah)*

"Search and seizure" in Spanish is **El registro y la incautación** *(ehl reh-'hee-stroh ee lah een-kow-tah-see-'ohn)*.

ELECTRICAL APPLIANCES
Los electrodomésticos
(lohs eh-lehk-troh-doh-'meh-stee-kohs)

Have you considered how many common housewares and furnishings are popular targets in grand theft, burglary, and robbery incidents? Electrical appliances, for example, have excellent resale value on the streets. Read each word twice as you continue:

air conditioner	**el acondicionador de aire** *(ehl ah-kohn-dee-see·oh-nah-'dohr deh 'ah·ee-reh)*
answering machine	**la grabadora telefónica** *(lah grah-bah-'doh-rah teh-leh-'foh-nee-kah)*
audio system	**el sistema de audio** *(ehl sees-'teh-mah deh 'ah-oo-dee-oh)*
CD player	**el tocadiscos** *(ehl toh-kah-'dees-kohs)*
clock	**el reloj** *(ehl reh-'loh)*
computer	**la computadora** *(lah kohm-poo-tah-'doh-rah)*
cordless phone	**el teléfono inalámbrico** *(ehl teh-'leh-foh-noh ee-nah-'lahm-bree-koh)*
digital camera	**la cámara digital** *(lah 'kah-mah-rah dee-hee-'tahl)*
dryer	**la secadora** *(lah seh-kah-'doh-rah)*
DVD player	**el tocador de DVDs** *(ehl toh-kah-'dohr deh deh veh dehs)*
entertainment center	**el centro de entretenciones** *(ehl 'sehn-troh deh ehn-treh-tehn-see-'oh-nehs)*
fan	**el ventilador** *(ehl vehn-tee-lah-'dohr)*
hairdryer	**el secador de pelo** *(ehl seh-kah-'dohr deh 'peh-loh)*
heater	**el calentador** *(ehl kah-lehn-tah-'dohr)*
home theater	**el cine de hogar** *(ehl 'see-neh deh oh-'gahr)*
lamp	**la lámpara** *(lah 'lahm-pah-rah)*
laptop	**la computadora portátil** *(lah kohm-poo-tah-'doh-rah pohr-'tah-teel)*
monitor	**el monitor** *(ehl moh-nee-'tohr)*
radio	**el radio** *(ehl 'rah-dee·oh)*
receiver	**el receptor** *(ehl reh-sehp-'tohr)*
recorder	**la grabadora** *(lah grah-bah-'doh-rah)*
scale	**la balanza** *(lah bah-'lahn-sah)*
scanner	**el escáner** *(ehl ehs-'kah-nehr)*
security system	**el sistema de seguridad** *(ehl see-'steh-mah deh seh-goo-ree-'dahd)*

sewing machine	**la máquina de coser** *(lah 'mah-kee-nah deh koh-'sehr)*
speaker	**el altoparlante** *(ehl ahl-toh-pahr-'lahn-teh)*
stereo	**el estéreo** *(ehl eh-'steh-reh-oh)*
telephone	**el teléfono** *(ehl teh-'leh-foh-noh)*
TV	**el televisor** *(ehl teh-leh-vee-'sohr)*
VCR	**la videocasetera** *(lah vee-deh-oh-kah-seh-'teh-rah)*

Don't forget these kitchen appliances:

dishwasher	**el lavaplatos** *(ehl lah-vah-'plah-tohs)*
freezer	**el congelador** *(ehl kohn-heh-lah-'dohr)*
microwave	**el microondas** *(ehl mee-kroh-'ohn-dahs)*
oven	**el horno** *(ehl 'ohr-noh)*
refrigerator	**el refrigerador** *(ehl reh-free-heh-rah-'dohr)*
stove	**la estufa** *(lah ehs-'too-fah)*

INFORMACIÓN PRIVADA

➤ However, many technical items are referred to by their English names:

el TV
el DVD
el iPod
el DVR
el TiVO

➤ The following words may come in handy when handling a burglary:

chain	**la cadena** *(lah kah-'deh-nah)*
deadbolt	**el pestillo** *(ehl peh-'stee-yoh)*
handle	**el tirador** *(ehl tee-rah-'dohr)*
key	**la llave** *(lah 'yah-veh)*
latch	**el cerrojo** *(ehl seh-'rroh-hoh)*
lock	**la cerradura** *(lah seh-rah-'doo-rah)*
padlock	**el candado** *(ehl kahn-'dah-doh)*

Tengo cerrojo, candado, cadena y pestillo, ¡pero no tengo las llaves!

REPASO

A. Translate:

Have you been arrested before?

_____

Where did you buy it?

_____

When did you start using drugs?

_____

B. Connect each word with its opposite:

lávese *('lah-veh-seh)*   beba *('beh-bah)*

triste *('trees-teh)*   cuadrado *(kwah-'drah-doh)*

enfermo *(ehn-'fehr-moh)*   feliz *(feh-'lees)*

círculo *('seer-koo-loh)*   séquese *('seh-keh-seh)*

coma *('koh-mah)*   bien *('bee·ehn)*

C. In Spanish,

what are three physical characteristics of a heavy drug user:

_____   _____   _____

name three rooms in a typical home:

_____   _____   _____

name three standard pieces of furniture:

_____   _____   _____

name three common electrical appliances:

_____   _____   _____

name three forms of drug paraphernalia:

_____   _____   _____

ANSWERS

coma – beba
círculo – cuadrado
enfermo – bien   ¿Cuándo comenzó a tomar drogas?
triste – feliz   ¿Dónde lo compró?
B. lávese – séquese   A. ¿Ha estado arrestado antes?

THE BURGLARY
El robo *(ehl 'roh-boh)*

Utilize the following patterns and vocabulary to file a report or begin an investigation. Visualize a scene where these phrases can be practiced. Some things always attract intruders:

They stole (the)...	**Robaron...** *(roh-'bah-rohn...)*
antiques	**las antigüedades** *(lahs ahn-tee-gweh-'dah-dehs)*
bicycle	**la bicicleta** *(lah bee-see-'kleh-tah)*
camera	**la cámara** *(lah 'kah-mah-rah)*

credit card	**la tarjeta de crédito** *(lah tahr-'heh-tah deh 'kreh-dee-toh)*
equipment	**el equipaje** *(ehl eh-kee-'pah-heh)*
firearm	**el arma de fuego** *(ehl 'ahr-mah de 'fweh-goh)*
furniture	**el mueble** *(ehl 'mweh-bleh)*
instrument	**el instrumento** *(ehl een-stroo-'mehn-toh)*
jewelry	**la joya** *(lah 'hoh-yah)*
machine	**la máquina** *(lah 'mah-kee-nah)*
money	**el dinero** *(ehl dee-'neh-roh)*
painting	**el cuadro** *(ehl 'kwah-droh)*
stereo	**el estéreo** *(ehl eh-'steh-reh-oh)*
TV	**el televisor** *(ehl teh-leh-vee-'sohr)*
tool	**la herramienta** *(lah eh-'rrah-mee-'ehn-tah)*
vehicle	**el vehículo** *(ehl veh-'ee-koo-loh)*

IN THE SAFE

En la caja fuerte *(ehn lah 'kah-hah 'fwehr-teh)*

I can't find (the)...	**No puedo encontrar...** *(noh 'pweh-doh ehn-kohn-'trahr...)*
bracelet	**la pulsera** *(lah pool-'seh-rah)*
brooch	**el broche** *(ehl 'broh-cheh)*
collection	**la colección** *(lah koh-lehk-see-'ohn)*
earring	**el arete** *(ehl ah-'reh-teh)*
necklace	**el collar** *(ehl koh-'yahr)*
pendant	**el pendiente** *(ehl pehn-dee-'ehn-teh)*
wrist watch	**el reloj de pulsera** *(ehl reh-'loh deh pool-'seh-rah)*
They took the...	**Llevaron...** *(yeh-'vah-rohn...)*
agate	**la ágata** *(lah 'ah-gah-tah)*
diamond	**el diamante** *(ehl dee-ah-'mahn-teh)*
emerald	**la esmeralda** *(lah ehs-meh-'rahl-dah)*
jade	**el jade** *(ehl 'hah-deh)*
pearl	**la perla** *(lah 'pehr-lah)*
precious stone	**la piedra preciosa** *(lah pee-'eh-drah preh-see-'oh-sah)*
ruby	**el rubí** *(ehl roo-'bee)*
topaz	**el topacio** *(ehl toh-'pah-see·oh)*
sapphire	**el safiro** *(ehl sah-'fee-roh)*
turquoise	**la turquesa** *(lah toor-'keh-sah)*

➤ Not only homes get hit by thieves. Add to this list if you like:

They broke into the...	**Forzaron a...** *(fohr-'sah-rohn ah...)*
bank	**el banco** *(ehl 'bahn-koh)*
museum	**el museo** *(ehl moo-'seh-oh)*
office building	**el edificio de oficinas** *(ehl eh-dee-'fee-see·oh deh oh-fee-'see-nahs)*
school	**la escuela** *(lah eh-'skweh-lah)*
store	**la tienda** *(lah tee-'ehn-dah)*

➤ Collections can be valuable, too:

coins	**las monedas** *(lahs moh-'neh-dahs)*
dolls	**las muñecas** *(lahs moo-'nyeh-kahs)*
stamps	**las estampillas** *(lahs eh-stahm-'pee-yahs)*

I NEED A WITNESS

Necesito un testigo *(neh-seh-'see-toh oon teh-'stee-goh)*

You're in luck. Somebody saw what happened:

What was the plate number?	**¿Cuál fue el número de la placa?** *(kwahl fweh ehl 'noo-meh-roh deh lah 'plah-kah)*
Did you see anything strange?	**¿Vio algo raro?** *('vee·oh 'ahl-goh 'rah-roh)*
Where were you?	**¿Dónde estaba?** *('dohn-deh eh-'stah-bah)*
When did it happen?	**¿Cuándo pasó?** *('kwahn-doh pah-'soh)*
Between what hours?	**¿Entre qué horas?** *('ehn-treh keh 'oh-rahs)*
What did you see?	**¿Qué vio?** *(keh 'vee·oh)*
In what direction?	**¿En cuál dirección?** *(ehn kwahl dee-rehk-see-'ohn)*
Can you...?	**¿Puede...** *('pweh-deh...)*
identify the stolen property	**identificar la propiedad robada?** *(ee-dehn-tee-fee-'kahr lah proh-pee-eh-'dahd roh-'bah-dah)*
make a list	**hacer una lista?** *(ah-'sehr 'oo-nah 'lee-stah)*
remember that make and model	**recordar la marca y el modelo?** *(reh-kohr-'dahr lah 'mahr-kah ee ehl moh-'deh-loh)*

write the serial number	**escribir el número de serie?** *(eh-skree-'beer ehl 'noo-meh-roh deh 'seh-ree·eh)*
find the receipt	**encontrar el recibo?** *(ehn-kohn-'trahr ehl reh-'see-boh)*
prove that you bought it	**probar que usted lo compró?** *(proh-'bahr keh oo-'stehd loh kohm-'proh)*
give a description	**dar una descripción?** *(dahr 'oo-nah deh-skrep-see-'ohn)*
tell me the year	**decirme el año?** *(deh-'seer-meh ehl 'ah-nyoh)*
explain with more details	**explicar con más detalles?** *(ehk-splee-'kahr kohn mahs deh-'tah-yehs)*
recognize the label	**reconocer la etiqueta?** *(reh-koh-noh-'sehr lah eh-tee-'keh-tah)*

Take extra time to quiz the owner about the stolen property:

Where and when...?	**¿Dónde y cuándo...** *('dohn-deh ee 'kwahn-doh...)*
did you use it	**lo usó?** *(loh oo-'soh)*
did you get it	**lo consiguió?** *(loh kohn-see-gee-'oh)*
did you buy it	**lo compró?** *(loh kohm-'proh)*
did you sell it	**lo vendió?** *(loh vehn-dee-'oh)*
did you loan it	**lo prestó?** *(loh preh-'stoh)*
did you find it	**lo encontró?** *(loh ehn-kohn-'troh)*
did you rent it	**lo alquiló?** *(loh ahl-kee-'loh)*
There was/were...	**Había(n)...**
a group	**un grupo** *(oon 'groo-poh)*
another person	**otra persona** *('oh-trah pehr-'soh-nah)*
only one person	**sólo una persona** *('soh-loh 'oo-nah pehr-'soh-nah)*
several people	**varias personas** *('vah-ree·ahs pehr-'soh-nahs)*
Do you know who..?	**¿Sabe quién...** *('sah-beh kee-'ehn...)*
did it	**lo hizo?** *(loh 'ee-soh)*
the person was	**fue la persona?** *(fweh lah pehr-'soh-nah)*
was there	**estaba allí?** *(eh-'stah-bah ah-'yee)*
said that	**dijo eso?** *('dee-hoh 'eh-soh)*
the suspect is	**es el sospechoso?** *(ehs ehl soh-speh-'choh-soh)*
lives here	**vive aquí?** *('vee-veh ah-'kee)*
saw what happened	**vio lo que pasó?** *('vee·oh loh keh pah-'soh)*

INFORMACIÓN PRIVADA

➤ Get the names and addresses of everyone! Use "who" and "whose":

Whose is it?	**¿De quién es?** *(deh kee-'ehn ehs)*
With whom?	**¿Con quién?** *(kohn kee-'ehn)*
To whom?	**¿A quién?** *(ah kee-'ehn)*
From whom?	**¿De quién?** *(deh kee-'ehn)*
For whom?	**¿Para quién?** *('pah-rah kee-'ehn)*

Who is the...?	**¿Quién es...** *(kee-'ehn ehs...)*
bandit	**el bandido?** *(ehl bahn-'dee-doh)*
friend	**el amigo?** *(ehl ah-'mee-goh)*
intruder	**el intruso?** *(ehl een-'troo-soh)*
neighbor	**el vecino?** *(ehl veh-'see-noh)*
owner	**el dueño?** *(ehl 'dweh-nyoh)*
relative	**el pariente?** *(ehl pah-ree-'ehn-teh)*
stranger	**el extraño?** *(ehl eks-'trah-nyoh)*
suspect	**el sospechoso?** *(ehl soh-speh-'choh-soh)*
thief	**el ladrón?** *(ehl lah-'drohn)*
victim	**la víctima?** *(lah 'veek-tee-mah)*
visitor	**cl visitante?** *(ehl vee-see-'tahn-teh)*
witness	**el testigo?** *(ehl teh-'stee-goh)*

➤ You can't stop now! Keep rolling with those "question words":

How much did it cost?	**¿Cuánto costó?** *('kwahn-toh koh-'stoh)*
How much is it worth?	**¿Cuánto vale?** *('kwahn-toh 'vah-leh)*
How many were there?	**¿Cuántos habían?** *('kwahn-tohs ah-'bee-ahn)*
How many are left?	**¿Cuántos quedan?** *('kwahn-tohs 'keh-dahn)*

When...?	¿Cuándo... *('kwahn-doh...)*
did you finish	**terminó?** *(tehr-mee-'noh)*
did you start	**empezó?** *(ehm-peh-'soh)*
did you leave	**salió?** *(sah-lee-'oh)*
did you return	**regresó?** *(reh-greh-'soh)*
did you arrive	**llegó?** *(yeh-'goh)*
did you come	**vino?** *('vee-noh)*

Which...?	¿Cuál... *(kwahl...)*
day	**día?** *('dee-ah)*
item	**cosa?** *('koh-sah)*
person	**persona?** *(pehr-'soh-nah)*
place	**lugar?** *(loo-'gahr)*
time	**hora?** *('oh-rah)*

 TEMAS CULTURALES

Trust, honor, and respect are very important in the Hispanic culture. Never forget that what you say, and how you say it, will be taken seriously, and that a firm, professional, and fair approach to each situation is always best.

Remember, also, that men and women relate to each other very differently. To learn more about interaction between the sexes, observe a mixed group of Spanish-speaking adults in a neighborhood setting. Facial expressions, touch, changes in tone, and hand signals are a few of the many nonverbal differences between the Latin American and U.S. cultures. For more information, consider taking a course in cultural diversity.

WE FOUND IT

Lo encontramos *(loh ehn-kohn-'trah-mohs)*

Once you receive the news, give the victim an update:

It was...	Fue... *(fweh...)*
bought	**comprado** *(kohm-'prah-doh)*
broken	**roto** *('roh-toh)*
cut	**cortado** *(kohr-'tah-doh)*
destroyed	**destruido** *(deh-stroo-'ee-doh)*
disassembled	**desarmado** *(dehs-ahr-'mah-doh)*
examined	**examinado** *(ehk-sah-mee-'nah-doh)*

identified	**identificado** (ee-dehn-tee-fee-'kah-doh)
lost	**perdido** (pehr-'dee-doh)
marked	**marcado** (mahr-'kah-doh)
moved	**movido** (moh-'vee-doh)
painted	**pintado** (peen-'tah-doh)
recorded	**grabado** (grah-'bah-doh)
recovered	**recuperado** (reh-koo-peh-'rah-doh)
ruined	**arruinado** (ah-rroo·ee-'nah-doh)
scratched	**rayado** (rah-'yah-doh)
sold	**vendido** (vehn-'dee-doh)
stained	**manchado** (mahn-'chah-doh)
stolen	**robado** (roh-'bah-doh)

We found it at (the)...	**Lo encontramos en...** (loh ehn-kohn-'trah-mohs ehn...)
garage	**el garaje** (ehl gah-'rah-heh)
market	**el mercado** (ehl mehr-'kah-doh)
pawnshop	**la casa de empeños** (lah 'kah-sah deh ehm-'pehn-yohs)
store	**la tienda** (lah tee-'ehn-dah)
swap meet	**el mercado abierto** (ehl mehr-'kah-doh ah-bee-'ehr-toh)
warehouse	**el almacén** (ehl ahl-mah-'sehn)

Do you have insurance?	**¿Tiene seguro?** (tee-'eh-neh seh-'goo-roh)
What's the estimated loss?	**¿Cuál es la pérdida estimada?** (kwahl ehs lah 'pehr-dee-dah eh-stee-'mah-dah)
How long did you have it?	**¿Por cuánto tiempo lo tenía?** (pohr 'kwahn-toh tee-'ehm-poh loh teh-'nee-ah)

Occasionally, you get some bogus information. Attempt to explain it in Spanish:

It was...	**Fue...** (fweh...)
a false alarm	**una falsa alarma** ('oo-nah 'fahl-sah ah-'lahr-mah)
a hoax	**un engaño** (oon ehn-'gah-nyoh)
a joke	**un chiste** (oon 'chee-steh)
a lie	**una mentira** ('oo-nah mehn-'tee-rah)
a prank	**una travesura** ('oo-nah trah-veh-'soo-rah)

228

Encontramos
dos partes
del carro.

THE INVESTIGATION

La investigación *(lah een-veh-stee-'gah-see-'ohn)*

If a full investigation is in order, don't back away from using your new Spanish skills. Lots can be said with only a few words. As usual, open with a brief series of statements and questions:

We'll need fingerprints	**Necesitaremos las huellas digitales** *(neh-seh-see-tah-'reh-mohs lahs 'weh-yahs dee-hee-'tah-lehs)*
I'm going to talk to your neighbors	**Voy a hablar con sus vecinos** *('voh-ee ah ah-'blahr kohn soos veh-'see-nohs)*
Where is the alarm box?	**¿Dónde está la caja de alarma?** *('dohn-deh eh-'stah lah 'kah-hah deh ah-'lahr-mah)*
Did you lock it?	**¿Lo cerró con llave?** *(loh seh-'rroh kohn 'yah-veh)*
Were they open or closed?	**¿Estaban abiertos o cerrados?** *(eh-'stah-bahn ah-bee-'ehr-tohs oh seh-'rrah-dohs)*
Who has the key?	**¿Quién tiene la llave?** *(kee-'ehn tee-'eh-neh lah 'yah-veh)*
Did anyone call you?	**¿Lo llamó alguien?** *(loh yah-'moh 'ahl-gee·ehn)*
Were the lights on?	**¿Estaban prendidas las luces?** *(eh-'stah-bahn prehn-'dee-dahs lahs 'loo-sehs)*
Were you asleep?	**¿Estaba dormido?** *(eh-'stah-bah dohr-'mee-doh)*
Was it dark?	**¿Estaba oscuro?** *(eh-'stah-bah oh-'skoo-roh)*
Were you out of town?	**¿Estaba de viaje?** *(eh-'stah-bah deh vee-'ah-heh)*
Where...?	**¿Dónde...** *('dohn-deh...)*
did they break in	**forzaron?** *(fohr-'sah-rohn)*
enter	**entraron?** *(ehn-'trah-rohn)*
exit	**salieron?** *(sah-lee-'eh-rohn)*

What did they...?	**¿Qué...** *(keh...)*
break	**quebraron?** *(keh-'brah-rohn)*
do	**hicieron?** *(ee-see-'eh-rohn)*
move	**movieron?** *(moh-vee-'eh-rohn)*
open	**abrieron?** *(ah-bree-'eh-rohn)*
remove	**sacaron?** *(sah-'kah-rohn)*
steal	**robaron?** *(roh-'bah-rohn)*
touch	**tocaron?** *(toh-'kah-rohn)*
use	**usaron?** *(oo-'sah-rohn)*

Care to share your professional opinion?

It was planned	**Fue planeado** *(fweh plah-neh-'ah-doh)*
They were professionals	**Eran profesionales** *('eh-rahn proh-feh-see·oh-'nah-lehs)*
They used plastic gloves	**Usaron guantes de plástico** *(oo-'sah-rohn 'gwahn-tehs deh 'plah-stee-koh)*
They cut the cable	**Cortaron el cable** *(kohr-'tah-rohn ehl 'kah-bleh)*
There isn't much evidence	**No hay mucha evidencia** *(noh 'ah·ee 'moo-chah eh-vee-'dehn-see·ah)*
It happened very quickly	**Ocurrió bien rápido** *(oh-koo-rree-'oh bee-'ehn 'rah-pee-doh)*
They came in through (the)...	**Entraron por...** *(ehn-'trah-rohn pohr...)*
cellar	**el sótano** *(ehl 'soh-tah-noh)*
window	**la ventana** *(lah vehn-'tah-nah)*
roof	**el techo** *(ehl 'teh-choh)*

INFORMACIÓN PRIVADA

➤ Have you inquired about the building?

Was it vacant?	**¿Estaba vacante?** *(eh-'stah-bah vah-'kahn-teh)*
How long did they occupy it?	**¿Por cuánto tiempo lo ocuparon?** *(pohr 'kwahn-toh tee-'ehm-poh loh oh-koo-'pah-rohn)*

➤ Business-related burglaries and robberies often include the following:

They took (the)...	**Llevaron...** *(yeh-'vah-rohn...)*
answering machine	**la grabadora telefónica** *(lah grah-bah-'doh-rah teh-leh-'foh-nee-kah)*
computer	**la computadora** *(lah kohm-poo-tah-'doh-rah)*

copier	**la copiadora** *(lah koh-pee·ah-'doh-rah)*
fax	**el fax** *(ehl fahks)*
keyboard	**el teclado** *(ehl teh-'klah-doh)*
monitor	**el monitor** *(ehl moh-nee-'tohr)*
printer	**la impresora** *(lah eem-preh-'soh-rah)*
scanner	**el escáner** *(ehl ehs-'kah-nehr)*
telephone	**el teléfono** *(ehl teh-'leh-foh-noh)*
typewriter	**la máquina de escribir** *(lah 'mah-kee-nah deh eh-skree-'beer)*

➤ Don't forget the parts of the house and its furnishings. Review:

Which...?	**¿Cuál...** *(kwahl...)*
door	**puerta?** *('pwehr-tah)*
drawer	**cajón?** *(kah-'hohn)*
lock	**cerradura?** *(seh-rrah-'doo-rah)*
room	**cuarto?** *('kwahr-toh)*
window	**ventana?** *(vehn-'tah-nah)*

➤ And how did they get in?

They used (the)...	**Usaron...** *(oo-'sah-rohn...)*
bar	**la barra** *(lah 'bah-rrah)*
brick	**el ladrillo** *(ehl lah-'dree-yoh)*
explosive	**el explosivo** *(ehl ehk-sploh-see-voh)*
hammer	**el martillo** *(ehl mahr-'tee-yoh)*
hatchet	**el hacha** *(ehl 'ah-chah)*
knife	**el cuchillo** *(ehl koo-'chee-yoh)*
pliers	**el alicate** *(ehl ah-lee-'kah-teh)*
razor	**la navaja** *(lah nah-'vah-hah)*
rock	**la piedra** *(lah pee-'eh-drah)*
saw	**el serrucho** *(ehl seh-'rroo-choh)*
stick	**el palo** *(ehl 'pah-loh)*

LEAVING THE SCENE
Al dejar la escena *(ahl deh-'hahr lah eh-'seh-nah)*

As you finish your initial investigation, you may need a closing remark:

Are you going to stay here tonight?	**¿Se va a quedar aquí esta noche?** *(seh vah ah keh-'dahr ah-'kee 'eh-stah 'noh-cheh)*
Do you need help cleaning up everything?	**¿Necesita ayuda con la limpieza de todo?** *(neh-seh-'see-tah ah-'yoo-dah kohn lah leem-pee-'eh-sah deh 'toh-doh)*

Here's your case number	**Aquí tiene el número de su caso** (ah-'kee tee-'eh-neh ehl 'noo-meh-roh deh soo 'kah-sah)
Call this number	**Llame a este número** ('yah-meh ah 'eh-steh 'noo-meh-roh)
Where else can we reach you?	**¿Dónde más podemos ponernos en contacto con usted?** ('dohn-deh mahs poh-'deh-mohs poh-'nehr-nohs ehn kohn-'tahk-toh kohn oo-'stehd)
We will call you if we have more information	**Lo llamaremos si tenemos más información** (loh yah-mah-'reh-mohs see teh-'neh-mohs mahs een-fohr-mah-see-'ohn)
We'll do everything possible	**Haremos todo lo posible** (ah-'reh-mohs 'toh-doh loh poh-'see-bleh)
I can't promise anything	**No puedo prometer nada** (noh 'pweh-doh proh-meh-'tehr 'nah-dah)
We will look for it	**Vamos a buscarlo** ('vah-mohs ah boo-'skahr-loh)

SHOPLIFTING
La ratería en las tiendas (lah rah-teh-'ree-ah ehn lahs tee-'ehn-dahs)

All businesses are hit by shoplifters. Clothing, housewares, and food items are usually the prime targets, but people are known to steal just about anything. Here's a list of miscellaneous objects that you might want to know. Practice by using the labeling method:

They stole (the)…	**Robaron...** (roh-'bah-rohn…)
batteries	**las pilas** (lahs 'pee-lahs)
blow dryer	**la secadora de pelo** (lah seh-kah-'doh-rah deh 'peh-loh)
CD	**el disco compacto** (ehl 'dee-skoh kohm-'pahk-toh)
cigarrettes	**los cigarrillos** (lohs see-gah-'rree-yohs)
cologne	**la colonia** (lah koh-'loh-nee·ah)
combination lock	**el candado** (ehl kahn-'dah-doh)
cosmetics	**los cosméticos** (lohs kohs-'meh-tee-kohs)
deodorant	**el desodorante** (ehl dehs-oh-doh-'rahn-teh)
DVD	**el DVD** (ehl deh veh deh)
feminine napkins	**los paños** (lohs 'pah-nyohs)
greeting cards	**las tarjetas de saludo** (lahs tahr-'heh-tahs deh sah-'loo-doh)
hairbrush	**el cepillo de pelo** (ehl seh-'pee-yoh deh 'peh-loh)
luggage	**el equipaje** (ehl eh-kee-'pah-heh)
magazines	**las revistas** (lahs reh-'vee-stahs)

makeup	**el maquillaje** *(ehl mah-kee-'yah-heh)*
medicine	**la medicina** *(lah meh-dee-'see-nah)*
newspapers	**los periódicos** *(lohs peh-ree-'oh-dee-kohs)*
notebook	**el cuaderno** *(ehl kwah-'dehr-noh)*
paper	**el papel** *(ehl pah-'pehl)*
pen	**la pluma** *(lah 'ploo-mah)*
pencil	**el lápiz** *(ehl 'lah-pees)*
perfume	**el perfume** *(ehl pehr-'foo-meh)*
pin	**el alfiler** *(ehl ahl-fee-'lehr)*
postcards	**las tarjetas postales** *(lahs tahr-'heh-tahs poh-'stah-lehs)*
razor blades	**las navajas para afeitar** *(lahs nah-'vah-hahs 'pah-rah ah-feh·ee-'tahr)*
rolls of film	**los rollos de foto** *(lohs 'roh-yohs deh 'foh-toh)*
scissors	**las tijeras** *(lahs tee-'heh-rahs)*
shaver	**la afeitadora** *(lah ah-feh·ee-tah-'doh-rah)*
sunglasses	**los lentes del sol** *(lohs 'lehn-tehs dehl sohl)*
suntan lotion	**el bronceador** *(ehl brohn-seh-ah-'dohr)*
television	**el televisor** *(ehl teh-leh-vee-'sohr)*
thread	**el hilo** *(ehl 'ee-loh)*
tools	**las herramientas** *(lahs eh-rrah-mee-'ehn-tahs)*
toothbrush	**el cepillo de dientes** *(ehl seh-'pee-yoh deh dee-'ehn-tehs)*
toothpaste	**la pasta de dientes** *(lah 'pah-stah deh dee-'ehn-tehs)*
umbrella	**la sombrilla** *(lah sohm-'bree-yah)*

Fue fácil. Ella robó un televisor con pantalla grande.

233

G.T.A.

El robo de un vehículo *(ehl 'roh-boh deh oon veh-'ee-koo-loh)*

There is big business in auto theft, so prepare yourself for an interview with the victim. Some of these words should look familiar:

Who is the legal owner?

¿Quién es el dueño legal? *(kee-'ehn ehs ehl 'dweh-nyoh leh-'gahl)*

Where did you park the vehicle?

¿Dónde estacionó el vehículo? *('dohn-deh eh-stah-see·oh-'noh ehl veh-'ee-koo-loh)*

When did you park?

¿Cuándo estacionó? *('kwahn-doh eh-stah-see·oh-'noh)*

Who has keys to the vehicle?

¿Quién tiene las llaves del vehículo? *(kee-'ehn tee-'eh-neh lahs 'yah-vehs dehl veh-'ee-koo-loh)*

What is the license plate number?

¿Cuál es el número de la placa? *(kwahl ehs ehl 'noo-meh-roh deh lah 'plah-kah)*

From what state?

¿De cuál estado? *(deh kwahl eh-'stah-doh)*

What is the make and model?

¿Cuál es la marca y el modelo? *(kwahl ehs lah 'mahr-kah ee ehl moh-'deh-loh)*

What year is it?

¿De qué año? *(deh keh 'ah-nyoh)*

Did you lock the vehicle?

¿Cerró con llave el vehículo? *(seh-'rroh kohn 'yah-veh ehl veh-'ee-koo-loh)*

Were all the windows closed?

¿Estaban cerradas las ventanas? *(eh-'stah-bahn seh-'rrah-dahs lahs vehn-'tah-nahs)*

Does it have a security system?

¿Tiene un sistema de seguridad? *(tee-'eh-neh oon see-'steh-mah deh seh-goo-ree-'dahd)*

Are your payments current?

¿Están los pagos al día? *(eh-'stahn lohs 'pah-gohs ahl 'dee-ah)*

What color is the vehicle?

¿Cuál es el color del vehículo? *(kwahl ehs ehl koh-'lohr dehl veh-'ee-koo-loh)*

Do you know the VIN number?

¿Sabe el número de identificación del vehículo? *('sah-beh ehl 'noo-meh-roh deh ee-dehn-tee-fee-kah-see-'ohn dehl veh-'ee-koo-loh)*

What size is the engine?

¿Cuál es el tamaño del motor? *(kwahl ehs ehl tah-'mah-nyoh dehl moh-'tohr)*

Does it have a radio or tape deck?

¿Tiene radio o grabadora de casetes? *(tee-'eh-neh 'rah-dee·oh oh grah-bah-'doh-rah deh kah-'seh-tehs)*

What is the value of the vehicle?

¿Cuánto vale el vehículo? *('kwahn-toh 'vah-leh ehl veh-'ee-koo-loh)*

What condition is it in?

¿En qué condición está el vehículo? *(ehn keh kohn-dee-see-'ohn ehs-'tah ehl veh-'ee-koo-loh)*

| How many doors? | **¿Cuántas puertas tiene?** *('kwahn-tahs 'pwehr-tahs tee-'eh-neh)* |
| Does it have any special features? | **¿Tiene alguna característica especial?** *(tee-'eh-neh ahl-'goo-nah kah-rahk-the-'rees-tee-kah ehs-peh-see-'ahl)* |

Does it have...?	**Tiene...** *(tee-'eh-neh...)*
broken lights	**luces rotas** *('loo-sehs 'roh-tahs)*
dents	**abolladuras** *(ah-boh-yah-'doo-rahs)*
scratches	**rayas** *('rah-yahs)*
shiny rims	**aros cromados** *('ah-rohs kroh-'mah-dohs)*
stickers	**calcomanías** *(kahl-koh-mah-'nee-ahs)*
wide tires	**neumáticos anchos** *(neh-oo-'mah-tee-kohs 'ahn-chohs)*

WHAT DID THEY DO TO IT?
¿Qué le hicieron? *(keh leh ee-see-'eh-rohn)*

It was...	**Fue...** *(fweh...)*
burned	**quemado** *(keh-'mah-doh)*
in good condition	**en buena condición** *(ehn 'bweh-nah kohn-dee-see-'ohn)*
modified	**modificado** *(moh-dee-fee-'kah-doh)*
painted	**pintado** *(peen-'tah-doh)*
recovered	**recuperado** *(reh-koo-peh-'rah-doh)*
stolen	**robado** *(roh-'bah-doh)*
stripped	**desarmado** *(dehs-ahr-'mah-doh)*
wrecked	**destruido** *(deh-stroo-'ee-doh)*

| The plates were switched | **Cambiaron las placas** *(kahm-bee-'ah-rohn lahs 'plah-kahs)* |
| Some parts were missing | **Faltaron algunas piezas** *(fahl-'tah-rohn ahl-'goo-nahs pee-'eh-sahs)* |

A. Use the names for expensive items in Spanish to complete the following sentences:

No puedo encontrar _____ *(noh 'pweh-doh ehn-kohn-'trahr*

_____ *)*

Me robaron _____ *(meh roh-'bah-rohn)*

Llevaron _____ *(yeh-'vah-rohn)*

B. Translate:

Can you identify the stolen property?

_____

¿Sabe quién lo hizo?

_____

How much is it worth?

_____

Es una Ford SUV de dos mil siete con placas de California

_____

We'll need fingerprints

_____

¿Dónde forzaron?

_____

There isn't much evidence

_____

Haremos todo lo posible

_____

C. Name five items that are often stolen by shoplifters:

_____   _____   _____

_____   _____

D. What are some one-liners in Spanish that you can use at a scene involving auto theft?

_____

_____

_____

ANSWERS

We'll do everything we can
No hay mucha evidencia
Where did they break in?
Necesitaremos las huellas digitales
It's a 2007 Ford SUV with California plates
¿Cuánto vale?
Do you know who did it?
B. ¿Puede identificar la propiedad robada?

READY FOR ACTION
Listo para la acción _('lee-stoh 'pah-rah lah ahk-see-'ohn)_

Present and future _Action Word_ forms allow us to say a lot in Spanish, but no investigation could take place without past tense verbs. Begin by practicing the most commonly used past tense pattern, the preterit. Carefully read the following examples, and just as you did with the present and future action forms, make the necessary changes to each word:

–Ar verbs

to speak (**hablar**) _(ah-'blahr)_	Preterit
I spoke Spanish	**Hablé español** _(ah-'bleh eh-spah-'nyohl)_
You/He/She spoke Spanish	**Habló español** _(ah-'bloh eh-spah-'nyohl)_
They/You (pl.) spoke Spanish	**Hablaron español** _(uh-'blah-rohn eh-spah-'nyohl)_
We spoke Spanish	**Hablamos español** _(ah-'blah-mohs eh-spah-'nyohl)_

237

Now you try it:

to drive (**manejar**)
   (*mah-neh-'hahr*)

Preterit

I drove the car
      Manejé el carro (*mah-neh-'heh ehl 'kah-rroh*)

You/He/She drove the car
      _____

They/You (pl.) drove the
   car
      _____

We drove the car
      _____

–Er/Ir verbs

to drink (**beber**) (*beh-'behr*)
to leave (**salir**) (*sah-'leer*)

I left at eight   **Salí a los ocho** (*sah-'lee ah lahs 'oh-choh*)
I drank the water   **Bebí el agua** (*beh-'bee ehl 'ah-gwah*)

You/He/She left at eight   **Salió a las ocho** (*sah-lee-'oh ah lahs 'oh-choh*)
You/He/She drank the
   water   **Bebió el agua** (*beh-bee-'oh ehl 'ah-gwah*)

They left at eight   **Salieron a las ocho** (*sah-lee-'eh-rohn ah lahs 'oh-choh*)
They drank the water   **Bebieron el agua** (*beh-bee-'eh-rohn ehl 'ah-gwah*)
We left at eight   **Salimos a las ocho** (*sah-'lee-mohs ah lahs 'oh-choh*)
We drank the water   **Bebimos el agua** (*beh-'bee-mohs ehl 'ah-gwah*)

Your turn:

to write (**escribir**)
   (*eh-skree-'beer*)

Preterit

I wrote the report
      Escribí el informe (*eh-skree-'bee ehl een-'fohr-meh*)
You/He/She wrote the
   report
      _____

They/You (pl.) wrote the
   report
      _____

We wrote the report
      _____

Some common verbs have irregular past tenses, so be on the look out! This one is basic:

To have (**tener**)		Preterit
I had	**tuve** *('too-veh)*	**Tuve un accident** *('too-veh oon ahk-see-'dehn-teh)*
You/He/She had	**tuvo** *('too-voh)*	**Tuvo una fiesta** *('too-voh 'oo-nah fee-'eh-stah)*
They/You (pl.) had	**tuvieron** *(too-vee-'eh-rohn)*	**Tuvieron el dinero** *(too-vee-'eh-rohn ehl dee-'neh-roh)*
We had	**tuvimos** *(too-'vee-mohs)*	**Tuvimos un carro blanco** *(too-'vee-mohs oon 'kah-rroh 'blahn-koh)*

This past tense action form is probably the most frequently spoken tense in law enforcement. To get the conversation started, use the question **¿Qué pasó?** *(keh pah-'soh)* which means "What happened?"

He stole the stereo	**Robó el estéreo** *(roh-'boh ehl eh-'steh-reh-oh)*
She drank beer	**Bebió cerveza** *(beh-bee-'oh lah sehr-'veh-sah)*
They arrested the man	**Arrestaron al hombre** *(ah-rreh-'stah-rohn ahl 'ohm-breh)*

A. Follow the pattern below:

I speak	Hablo *('ah-bloh)*
I spoke	Hablé *(ah-'bleh)*
I work	Trabajo *(trah-'bah-hoh)*
I worked	_____
I drive	Manejo *(mah-'neh-oh)*
I drove	_____
I run	Corro *('koh-rroh)*
I ran	_____
I eat	Como *('koh-moh)*
I ate	_____
I write	Escribo *(eh-'skree-boh)*
I wrote	_____

ANSWERS

A. Trabajé
Manejé
Corrí
Comí
Escribí

INFORMACIÓN PRIVADA

➤ This past tense (preterit) isn't the only past tense verb form that you are going to need. The "imperfect" form is pretty common also. Notice how it only has three forms:

–Ar verbs
to buy (**comprar**) *(kohm-'prahr)*	Imperfect
You/He/She used to buy	**compraba** *(kohm-'prah-bah)*
They/You (pl.) used to buy	**compraban** *(kohm-'prah-bahn)*
We used to buy	**comprábamos** *(kohm-'prah-bah-mohs)*

–Er, Ir verbs

to sell (**vender**) *(vehn-'dehr)*	Imperfect
You/He/She used to sell	**vendía** *(vehn-'dee-ah)*
They/You (pl.) used to sell	**vendían** *(vehn-'dee-ahn)*
We used to sell	**vendíamos** *(vehn-'dee-ah-mohs)*

➤ What is the difference between the preterit and the imperfect? In the former you just did something (e.g., I bought), whereas in the latter you used to do something (e.g., I used to buy).

GRANDES HABILIDADES

Look over this new list of crime-related verbs, and then add a sample sentence to the right. Study these examples:

to break in	**forzar** *(fohr-'sahr)*	_____
to buy	**comprar** *(kohm-'prahr)*	_____
to destroy	**destruir** *(deh-stroo-'eer)*	**Las drogas pueden destruir la vida** *(lahs 'droh-gahs 'pweh-dehn deh-stroo-'eer lah 'veeh-dah)*
to drink	**beber** *(beh-'behr)*	
to eat	**comer** *(koh-'mehr)*	**No comía mucho** *(noh koh-'mee-ah 'moo-choh)*
to empty	**vaciar** *(vah-see-'ahr)*	_____
to fall	**caer** *(kah-'ehr)*	_____
to frisk	**registrar** *(reh-hee-'strahr)*	_____
to guess	**adivinar** *(ah-dee-vee-'nahr)*	_____
to hide	**esconder** *(eh-skohn-'dehr)*	**Escondieron el alcohol** *(eh-skohn-dee-'eh-rohn ehl ahl-koh-'ohl)*
to inhale	**inhalar** *(een-ah-'lahr)*	_____
to inject	**inyectar** *(een-yehk-'tahr)*	_____
to lend	**prestar** *(preh-'stahr)*	_____
to occupy	**ocupar** *(oh-koo-'pahr)*	_____
to paint	**pintar** *(peen-'tahr)*	_____
to protect	**proteger** *(proh-teh-'hehr)*	**Estoy protegiendo la casa** *(eh-'stoh-ee proh-teh-hee-'ehn-doh lah 'kah-sah)*

241

to prove	**probar** *(proh-'bahr)*	_____
to put	**poner** *(poh-'nehr)*	_____
to recognize	**reconocer** *(reh-koh-noh-'sehr)*	_____
to record	**grabar** *(grah-'bahr)*	_____
to recover	**recuperar** *(reh-koo-peh-'rahr)*	_____
to remember	**recordar** *(reh-kohr-'dahr)*	_____
to rent	**alquilar** *(ahl kee-'lahr)*	_____
to sell	**vender** *(vehn-'dehr)*	_____
to smoke	**fumar** *(foo-'mahr)*	<u>**¿Fuma usted?**</u> *('foo-mah oo-'stehd)*
to stay	**quedar** *(keh-'dahr)*	_____
to steal	**robar** *(roh-'bahr)*	_____

CHAPTER SIX
Capítulo Seis
(kah-'pee-too-loh 'seh·ees)

CRIME SCENE
(Part 2)

La escena del crimen

(Segunda parte)

(lah eh-'seh-nah dehl 'kree-mehn)

(seh-'goon-dah 'pahr-teh)

ASSAULT AND BATTERY

El asalto y la agresión *(ehl ah-'sahl-toh ee lah ah-greh-see-'ohn)*

It's a case involving assault and battery, and no one involved speaks any English. First, get everyone's name and personal information using your basic Spanish skills. Next, take care of the victim's needs:

What's your name and address?	**¿Cuál es su nombre y dirección?** *(kwahl ehs soo 'nohm-breh ee dee-rehk-see-'ohn)*
Did you call for our help?	**¿Pidió nuestra ayuda?** *(pee-dee-'oh 'nweh-strah ah-'yoo-dah)*
Are you OK?	**¿Está bien?** *(eh-'stah 'bee·ehn)*
Can you walk?	**¿Puede caminar?** *('pweh-deh kah-mee-'nahr)*
Do you need an ambulance?	**¿Necesita una ambulancia?** *(neh-seh-'see-tah 'oo-nah ahm-boo-'lahn-see·ah)*

Use your commands if you have to:

Please calm down	**Cálmese, por favor** *('kahl-meh-seh, pohr fah-'vohr)*
Tell me what happened	**Dígame qué pasó** *('dee-gah-meh keh pah-'soh)*
Sit down here	**Siéntese aquí** *(see-'ehn-teh-seh ah-'kee)*

Now, pull out all those question words to start the investigation:

How many were there?	**¿Cuántos habían?** *('kwahn-tohs ah-'bee-ahn)*
Which way did they go?	**¿En cuál dirección fueron?** *(ehn kwahl dee-rehk-see-'ohn 'fweh-rohn)*
What did they do to you?	**¿Qué le hicieron?** *(keh leh ee-see-'eh-rohn)*
How long ago?	**¿Hace cuánto?** *('ah-seh 'kwahn-toh)*
Where did it happen?	**¿Dónde le pasó?** *('dohn-deh leh pah-'soh)*

Try to figure out what happened. Here's a story you've heard before:

It was dark	**Estaba oscuro** *(eh-'stah-bah oh-'skoo-roh)*
They surprised me	**Me sorprendieron** *(meh sohr-prehn-dee-'eh-rohn)*
They knocked me down	**Me tumbaron** *(meh toom-'bah-rohn)*
They stole (the)...	**Me robaron...** *(meh roh-'bah-rohn...)*
backpack	**la mochila** *(lah moh-'chee-lah)*
bag	**la bolsa** *(lah 'bohl-sah)*
box	**la caja** *(lah 'kah-hah)*
bracelet	**el brazalete** *(ehl brah-sah-'leh-teh)*

briefcase	**el maletín** *(ehl mah-leh-'teen)*
camera	**la cámara** *(lah 'kah-mah-rah)*
chain	**la cadena** *(lah kah-'deh-nah)*
check	**el cheque** *(ehl 'cheh-keh)*
checkbook	**la chequera** *(lah cheh-'keh-rah)*
coin	**la moneda** *(lah moh-'neh-dah)*
coin case	**el monedero** *(ehl moh-neh-'deh-roh)*
credit card	**la tarjeta de crédito** *(lah tahr-'heh-tah deh 'kreh-dee-toh)*
document	**el documento** *(ehl doh-koo-'mehn-toh)*
duffel bag	**la talega** *(lah tah-'leh-gah)*
gift	**el regalo** *(ehl reh-'gah-loh)*
mail	**el correo** *(ehl koh-'rreh-oh)*
money	**el dinero** *(ehl dee-'neh-roh)*
necklace	**el collar** *(ehl koh-'yahr)*
paycheck	**el cheque de sueldo** *(ehl 'cheh-keh deh 'swehl-doh)*
purse	**la cartera** *(lah kahr-'teh-rah)*
wallet	**la billetera** *(lah bee-yeh-'teh-rah)*
watch	**el reloj** *(ehl reh-'loh)*

 INFORMACIÓN PRIVADA

➤ Street robberies may include expensive clothing:

They removed (the)...	**Me sacaron...** *(meh sah-'kah-rohn...)*
jacket	**la chaqueta** *(lah chah-'keh-tah)*
overcoat	**el abrigo** *(ehl ah-'bree-goh)*
shoe	**el zapato** *(ehl sah-'pah-toh)*
suit	**el traje** *(ehl 'trah-heh)*
sweater	**el suéter** *(ehl 'sweh-tehr)*

THE ALTERCATION
El altercado *(ehl ahl-tehr-'kah-doh)*

Get to the bottom of the confrontation:

How did it start?	**¿Cómo empezó?** *('koh-moh ehm-peh-'soh)*
Who started it?	**¿Quién lo empezó?** *(kee-'ehn loh ehm-peh-'soh)*
What were they doing?	**¿Qué estaban haciendo?** *(keh eh-'stah-bahn ah-see-'ehn-doh)*

Take a few moments to add any new *Action Words* to your Spanish verb list:

They were...	**Estaban...** *(eh-'stah-bahn...)*
arguing	**discutiendo** *(dee-skoo-tee-'ehn-doh)*
chasing him	**persiguiéndole** *(pehr-see-gee-'ehn-doh-leh)*
doing drugs	**tomando drogas** *(toh-'mahn-doh 'droh-gahs)*
drinking	**tomando alcohol** *(toh-'mahn-doh ahl-koh-'ohl)*
fighting	**peleando** *(peh-leh-'ahn-doh)*
jostling him	**empujándole** *(ehm-poo-'hahn-doh-leh)*
resisting arrest	**resistiendo el arresto** *(reh-see-stee-'ehn-doh ehl ah-'rreh-stoh)*
taunting him	**burlándose de él** *(boor-'lahn-doh-seh deh ehl)*
wrestling	**luchando** *(loo-'chan-doh)*
yelling	**gritando** *(gree-'tahn-doh)*

It happened at (the)...	**Pasó en...** *(pah-'soh ehn...)*
bar	**el bar** *(ehl bahr)*
brothel	**el burdel** *(ehl boor-'dehl)*
casino	**el casino** *(ehl kah-'see-noh)*
concert	**el concierto** *(ehl kohn-see-'ehr-toh)*
dance	**el baile** *(ehl 'bah·ee-leh)*
fair	**la feria** *(lah 'feh-ree·ah)*
festival	**el festival** *(ehl feh-stee-'vahl)*
game	**el juego** *(ehl 'hweh-goh)*
horse race	**la carrera de caballos** *(lah kah-'rreh-rah deh kah-'bah-yohs)*
massage parlor	**la sala de masajes** *(lah 'sah-lah deh mah-'sah-hehs)*
meeting	**la reunión** *(lah reh-oo-nee-'ohn)*
nightclub	**el club nocturno** *(ehl kloob nohk-'toor-noh)*
parade	**el desfile** *(ehl dehs-'fee-leh)*
party	**la fiesta** *(lah fee-'eh-stah)*

picnic	**la comida campestre** *(lah koh-'mee-dah kahm-'peh-streh)*
pool hall	**la sala de billar** *(lah 'sah-lah deh bee-'yahr)*
racetrack	**el hipódromo** *(ehl ee-'poh-droh-moh)*
show	**el espectáculo** *(ehl eh-spehk-'tah-koo-loh)*
stadium	**el estadio** *(ehl eh-'stah-dee·oh)*
strike	**la huelga** *(lah 'wehl-gah)*
wedding	**la boda** *(lah 'boh-dah)*

INFORMACIÓN PRIVADA

➤ What did they fight over? It could be anything, but here's what usually happens:

It was about (the)...	**Fue acerca de...** *(fweh ah-'sehr-kah deh...)*
child	**el niño** *(ehl 'nee-nyoh)*
drugs	**las drogas** *(lahs 'droh-gahs)*
girlfriend	**la novia** *(lah 'noh-vee·ah)*
money	**el dinero** *(ehl dee-'neh-roh)*
property	**la propiedad** *(lah proh-pee-eh-'dahd)*

➤ What can you say about fiestas? *(fee-'eh-stahs)*

anniversary	**el aniversario** *(ehl ah-nee-vehr-'sah-ree·oh)*
baby shower	**el "baby shower"**
baptism	**el bautismo** *(ehl bow-'tees-moh)*
birthday	**el cumpleaños** *(ehl koom-pleh-'ah-nyohs)*
celebration	**la celebración** *(lah seh-leh-brah-see-'ohn)*
graduation	**la graduación** *(lah grah-doo-ah-see-'ohn)*
holiday	**el día de fiesta** *(ehl 'dee-ah deh fee-'eh-stah)*

TEMAS CULTURALES

Learn all you can about the special days of the year. Most cultures differ on how they celebrate U.S. holidays, and try to keep hold of traditions from their native countries. Most of our holidays are easy to translate:

It's (the)...	Es... *(ehs...)*
Christmas	**la Navidad** *(lah nah-vee-'dahd)*
Easter	**la Pascua** *(lah 'pah-skwah)*
Independence Day	**el Día de Independencia** *(ehl 'dee-ah deh een-deh-pehn-'dehn-see·ah)*
New Year's	**el Año Nuevo** *(ehl 'ah-nyoh 'nweh-voh)*
a 15-year-old girl's "coming out" party	**la Quinceañera** *(lah keen-seh-ah-'nyeh-rah)*

¡A MIS ÓRDENES!

Continue to add words to your law enforcement command list. Here are some new one-liners that work well at a crime scene. Do any of these verb forms look familiar?

Answer me	**Contésteme** *(kohn-'teh-steh-meh)*
Ask him	**Pregúntele** *(preh-'goon-teh-leh)*
Bend over	**Inclínese** *(een-'klee-neh-seh)*
Check it out	**Revíselo** *(reh-'vee-seh-loh)*
Cover yourself	**Cúbrase** *('koo-brah-seh)*
Cross them	**Crúcelos** *('kroo-seh-lohs)*
Describe it	**Descríbalo** *(deh-'skree-bah-loh)*
Do it	**Hágalo** *('ah-gah-loh)*
Drop it	**Suéltelo** *('swehl-teh-loh)*
Get dressed	**Vístase** *('vee-stah-seh)*
Get inside	**Entre** *('ehn-treh)*
Join them	**Júntelos** *('hoon-teh-lohs)*
Let me	**Déjeme** *('deh-heh-meh)*
Look at me	**Míreme** *('mee-reh-meh)*
Point	**Señale** *(seh-'nyah-leh)*
Raise them up	**Levántelos** *(leh-'vahn-teh-lohs)*
Spread them	**Sepárelos** *(seh-'pah-reh-lohs)*
Stop him	**Deténgalo** *(deh-'tehn-gah-loh)*
Tell him	**Dígale** *('dee-gah-leh)*
Throw it	**Tírelo** *('tee-reh-loh)*
Unload it	**Descárguelo** *(deh-'skahr-geh-loh)*

Learn how to add vocabulary to the command words. As you know, enforcement personnel spend much of their time telling people what to do:

Stop or I'll shoot	**Párese o disparo** *('pah-reh-seh oh dee-'spah-roh)*
Keep your hands...	**Mantenga las manos...** *(mahn-'tehn-gah lahs 'mah-nohs...)*
on the ground	**en el suelo** *(ehn ehl 'sweh-loh)*
where I can see them	**donde las puedo ver** *('dohn-deh lahs 'pweh-doh vehr)*
on top of your head	**encima de la cabeza** *(ehn-'see-mah deh lah kah-'beh-sah)*
behind your neck	**detrás del cuello** *(deh-'trahs dehl 'kweh-yoh)*
with the palms up	**con las palmas arriba** *(kohn lahs 'pahl-mahs ah-'rree-bah)*
Get out with your hands up	**Salga con las manos arriba** *('sahl-gah kohn lahs 'mah-nohs ah-'rree-bah)*
Put your weapon on the ground	**Ponga el arma en el suelo** *('pohn-gah ehl 'ahr-mah ehn ehl 'sweh-loh)*
Move very slowly	**Muévase muy despacio** *('mweh-vah-seh 'moo·ee deh-'spah-see·oh)*
Kneel down and stay there	**Arrodíllese y quédese allí** *(ah-rroh-'dee-yeh-seh ee 'keh-deh-seh ah-'yee)*
Lie on your stomach	**Acuéstese en el estómago** *(ah-'kweh-steh-seh ehn ehl eh-'stoh-mah-goh)*
Spread your legs	**Separe las piernas** *(seh-'pah-reh lahs pee-'ehr-nahs)*
Turn around and walk backwards	**Dése vuelta y camine hacia atrás** *('deh-seh 'vwehl-tah ee kah-'mee-neh 'ah-see·ah ah-'trahs)*
Put your knees together	**Junte las rodillas** *('hoon-teh lahs roh-'dee-yahs)*
Cross your feet	**Cruce los pies** *('kroo-seh lohs 'pee-ehs)*
Put one hand behind your back.	**Ponga una mano detrás de la espalda** *('pohn-gah 'oo-nah 'mah-noh deh-'trahs deh lah ehs-'pahl-dah)*
Now the other one	**Ahora la otra** *(ah-'oh-rah lah 'oh-trah)*
Lie on the ground	**Échese en el suelo** *('eh-cheh-seh ehn ehl 'sweh-loh)*

249

➤ Get firm in the negative:

Don't do that.	**No haga eso.** *(noh 'ah-gah 'eh-soh)*
Don't interfere.	**No se entrometa.** *(noh seh ehn-troh-'meh-tah)*
Don't lie.	**No mienta.** *(noh mee-'ehn-tah)*
Don't move.	**No se mueva.** *(no se 'mweh-vah)*
Don't run.	**No corra.** *(noh 'koh-rrah)*
Don't shoot.	**No dispare.** *(noh dee-'spah-reh)*
Don't speak.	**No hable.** *(noh 'ah-bleh)*

➤ Use commands to interrogate the suspect:

Point to the person	**Señale a la persona** *(sch-'nyahl-leh ah lah pehr-'soh-nah)*
Answer yes or no	**Conteste sí o no** *(kohn-'teh-steh see oh noh)*
Tell me the truth	**Dígame la verdad** *('dee-gah-meh lah vehr-'dahd)*

➤ Did you know that you can create your own command phrases in Spanish? First, select any **–ar, –er,** or **–ir** base verb, and then drop the last two letters of the infinitive form and replace them as follows.

ar as in **hablar** (to speak)	**Hable** *('ah-bleh)*	**Hable más despacio** *('ah-bleh mahs deh-'spah-see·oh)*
er as in **leer** (to read)	**Lea** *('leh-ah)*	**Lea el papel** *('leh-ah ehl pah-'pehl)*
ir as in **escribir** (to write)	**Escriba** *(eh-'skree-bah)*	**Escriba el número** *(eh-'skree-bah ehl 'noo-meh-roh)*

➤ Beware. Some verbs are strange and simply have to be memorized:

to go	**ir** *(eer)*	Go!	**¡Vaya!** *('vah'yah)*
to come	**venir** *(veh-'neer)*	Come!	**¡Venga!** *('vehn-gah)*
to tell	**decir** *(deh-'seer)*	Tell!	**¡Diga!** *('dee-gah)*

THE ASSAILANT
El asaltante *(ehl ah-sahl-'tahn-teh)*

Piece together what transpired between the suspects and the victim. Study the consistent pattern in this past tense verb form (preterit), as you take note of any new Spanish *Action Words*:

Did they...you?	¿Lo... (loh...)
attack	**atacaron** (ah-tah-'kah-rohn)
bite	**mordieron** (mohr-dee-'eh-rohn)
chase	**persiguieron** (pehr-see-gee-'eh-rohn)
cut	**cortaron** (kohr-'tah-rohn)
follow	**siguieron** (see-gee-'eh-rohn)
grab	**agarraron** (ah-gah-'rrah-rohn)
insult	**insultaron** (een-sool-'tah-rohn)
intimidate	**intimidaron** (een-tee-mee-'dah-rohn)
kick	**patearon** (pah-teh-'ah-rohn)
punch	**golpearon** (gohl-peh-'ah-rohn)
push	**empujaron** (ehm-poo-'hah-rohn)
rape	**violaron** (vee·oh-'lah-rohn)
rob	**robaron** (roh-'bah-rohn)
scratch	**arañaron** (ah-rah-'nyah-rohn)
shoot	**dispararon** (dee-spah-'rah-rohn)
slap	**abofetearon** (ah-boh-feh-teh-'ah-rohn)
stab	**apuñalaron** (ah-poon-yah-'lah-rohn)
surprise	**sorprendieron** (sohr-prehn-dee-'eh-rohn)
threaten	**amenazaron** (ah-meh-nah-'sah-rohn)
touch	**tocaron** (toh-'kah-rohn)
trip	**tropezaron** (troh-peh-'sah-rohn)
wound	**hirieron** (ee-ree-'eh-rohn)

Did he/she...?	¿Le... (leh...)
cause physical harm	**causó daño físico** (kah-oo-'soh 'dah-nyoh 'fee-see-koh)
curse at you	**dijo groserías** ('dee-hoh groh-seh-'ree-ahs)
make obscene gestures	**hizo gestos obscenos** ('ee-soh 'hehs-tohs oh-'bseh-nohs)
yell at you	**gritó** (gree-'toh)

You can't catch the suspect without accurate information. Listen carefully to their answers when you ask the questions below:

Where have you seen him before?	¿**Dónde lo ha visto antes?** ('dohn-deh loh ah 'vee-stoh 'ahn-tehs)
What did he break?	¿**Qué rompió?** (keh rohm-pee-'oh)
Were there witnesses?	¿**Había testigos?** (ah-'bee-ah teh-'stee-gohs)
Did you recognize anyone?	¿**Reconoció a alguien?** (reh-koh-noh-see-'oh ah 'ahl-gee·ehn)
Do they live in this neighborhood?	¿**Viven en este vecindario?** ('vee-vehn ehn 'eh-steh veh-seen-'dah-ree·oh)
Where do you think he could be?	¿**Dónde cree que pueda estar?** ('dohn-deh 'kreh-eh keh 'pweh-dah eh-'stahr)

WHAT DID HE LOOK LIKE?
¿Cómo era? *('koh-moh 'eh-rah)*

Shoot for both general information as well as specific details. Practice:

Was it a child, teen, or adult?	**¿Fue un niño, adolescente o adulto?** *(fweh oon 'nee-nyoh, ah-doh-leh-'sehn-teh oh ah-'dool-toh)*
Was it a man or a woman?	**¿Fue hombre o mujer?** *(fweh oon 'ohm-breh ho moo-'hehr)*
Was the face covered?	**¿Estaba cubierta la cara?** *(eh-'stah-bah koo-bee-'ehr-tah lah 'kah-rah)*

Can you tell me (the)...?	**¿Puede decirme...** *('pweh-deh deh-'seer-meh...)*
age	**la edad?** *(lah eh-'dahd)*
eye color	**el color de los ojos?** *(ehl koh-'lohr deh lohs 'oh-hohs)*
hair color	**el color del pelo?** *(ehl koh-'lohr dehl 'peh-loh)*
height	**la estatura?** *(lah eh-stah-'too-rah)*
race	**la raza?** *(lah 'rah-sah)*
size	**el tamaño?** *(ehl tah-'mah-nyoh)*
skin color	**el color de piel?** *(ehl koh-'lohr deh pee-'ehl)*
weight	**el peso?** *(ehl 'peh-soh)*

Did you see (the)...	**¿Vio...** *('vee·oh...)*
birthmark	**la marca de nacimiento?** *(lah 'mahr-kah deh nah-see-mee-'ehn-toh)*
deformity	**la deformidad?** *(lah deh-fohr-mee-'dahd)*
freckle	**la peca?** *(lah 'peh-kah)*
mark	**la marca?** *(lah 'mahr-kah)*
mole	**el lunar?** *(ehl loo-'nahr)*

252

scar	**la cicatriz?** *(lah see-kah-'trees)*
spot	**la mancha?** *(lah 'mahn-chah)*
tattoo	**el tatuaje?** *(ehl tah-too-'ah-heh)*
wart	**la verruga?** *(lah veh-'rroo-gah)*

Where was he standing?	**¿Dónde estaba parado?** *('dohn-deh eh-'stah-bah pah-'rah-doh)*
Did he touch anything?	**¿Tocó algo?** *(toh-'koh 'ahl-goh)*
Did you see the vehicle?	**¿Vio el vehículo?** *('vee·oh ehl veh-'ee-koo-loh)*
Was anyone with him?	**¿Había otra persona con él?** *(ah-'bee-ah 'oh-trah pehr-'soh-nah kohn ehl)*
Did you see the driver?	**¿Vio al chofer?** *('vee·oh ahl choh-'fehr)*
What was the plate number?	**¿Cuál fue el número de la placa?** *(kwahl fweh ehl 'noo-meh-roh deh lah 'plah-kah)*
Tell me what he said	**Dígame lo que dijo** *('dee-gah-meh loh keh 'dee-hoh)*
Tell me the exact words	**Dígame sus palabras exactas** *('dee-gah-meh soos pah-'lah-brahs ehk-'sahk-tahs)*
Did he have an accent?	**¿Tenía acento?** *(teh-'nee-ah ah-'sehn-toh)*

Describe (the)...	**Describa...** *(deh-'skree-bah...)*
attitude	**la actitud** *(lah ahk-tee-'tood)*
breathing	**la respiración** *(lah reh-spee-rah-see-'ohn)*
complexion	**el cutis** *(ehl 'koo-tees)*
facial expression	**la expresión** *(lah ehk-spreh-see-'ohn)*
feature	**la facción** *(lah fahk-see-'ohn)*
gesture	**el gesto** *(ehl 'heh-stoh)*
hair	**el pelo** *(ehl 'peh-loh)*
laugh	**la risa** *(lah 'ree-sah)*
mannerisms	**los hábitos** *(lohs 'ah-bee-tohs)*
movement	**el movimiento** *(ehl moh-vee-mee-'ehn-toh)*
shape	**la forma** *(lah 'fohr-mah)*
smell	**el olor** *(ehl oh-'lohr)*
sound	**el sonido** *(ehl soh-'nee-doh)*
speech	**el habla** *(ehl 'ah-blah)*
style	**el estilo** *(ehl eh-'stee-loh)*
tooth	**el diente** *(ehl dee-'ehn-teh)*
voice	**la voz** *(lah vohs)*
walk	**la forma de caminar** *(lah 'fohr-mah deh kah-mee-'nahr)*

➤ Press the witness for a good description:

Can you draw it?	**¿Puede dibujarlo?** *('pweh-deh dee-boo-'hahr-loh)*
Can you identify it?	**¿Puede identificarlo?** *('pweh-deh ee-dehn-tee-fee-'kahr-loh)*
Can you remember it?	**¿Puede recordarlo?** *('pweh-deh reh-kohr-'dahr-loh)*

➤ Say "more or less" (**más o menos**) when folks have trouble remembering each detail.

A GOOD MEMORY
Una buena memoria *('oo-nah 'bweh-nah meh-'moh-ree·ah)*

Some folks are able to remember everything. Take notes as you study this detailed selection of personal characteristics. Note that we use **era** and/or **estaba** for "was." This happens because, again, we are dealing with the two "to be" verbs, **ser** or **estar** (see pages 24–27). **Era** indicates a steady, continuous condition (**él era bajo,** "he was short") whereas **estaba** implies a temporary state (**él estaba ocupado,** "he was busy"). Using plain logic, you will see that both **era** and **estaba** can be used sometimes for the same adjective, as in **él era cojo** (he was lame today or he always was lame). Be sure to make the necessary changes if you are referring to a female.

He was...

abnormal	**Era** or **Estaba anormal** *('eh-rah / eh-'stah-bah ah-nohr-'mahl)*
a dwarf	**Era enano** *('eh-rah eh-'nah-noh)*
a stutterer	**Era tartamudo** *('eh-rah tahr-tah-'moo-doh)*
albino	**Era albino** *('eh-rah ahl-'bee-noh)*
average	**Era de apariencia normal** *('eh-rah deh ah-pah-ree-'ehn-see-ah nohr-'mahl)*
bald	**Era** or **Estaba calvo** *('eh-rah / eh-'stah-bah 'kahl-voh)*
big	**Era grande** *('eh-rah 'grahn-deh)*
black	**Era negro** *('eh-rah 'neh-groh)*
blind	**Era ciego** *('eh-rah see-'eh-goh)*
blonde	**Era rubio** *('eh-rah 'roo-bee-oh)*
bright	**Era inteligente** *('eh-rah een-teh-lee-'hehn-teh)*

brunette	**Era moreno** *('eh-rah moh-'reh-noh)*
busy	**Estaba ocupado** *(eh-'stah-bah oh-koo-'pah-doh)*
clean	**Estaba limpio** *(eh-'stah-bah 'leem-pee·oh)*
clean-shaven	**Estaba bien afeitado** *(ehs-'tah-bah bee-'ehn ah-feh-ee-'tah-doh)*
crazy	**Era or Estaba loco** *(eh-rah / eh-'stah-bah 'loh-koh)*
cross-eyed	**Era bizco** *('eh-rah 'bee-skoh)*
cruel	**Era cruel** *('eh-rah kroo-'ehl)*
curly-haired	**Era de pelo rizado** *('eh-rah deh 'peh-loh ree-'sah-doh)*
dark-skinned	**Era prieto** *('eh-rah pree-'eh-toh)*
deaf	**Era or Estaba sordo** *(eh-rah / eh-'stah-bah 'sohr-doh)*
dirty	**Estaba sucio** *(eh-'stah-bah 'soo-see·oh)*
disabled	**Era or Estaba incapacitado** *('eh-rah / eh-'stah-bah een-kah-pah-see-'tah-doh)*
drugged	**Estaba drogado** *(eh-'stah-bah droh-'gah-doh)*
drunk	**Estaba borracho** *(eh-'stah-bah boh-'rrah-choh)*
far-sighted	**Era présbita** *('eh-rah 'prehs-bee-tah)*
fast	**Era rápido** *('eh-rah 'rah-pee-doh)*
fat	**Era gordo** *('eh-rah 'gohr-doh)*
____ feet tall	**Era de ____ pies de alto** *('eh-rah deh ___ pee-'ehs deh 'ahl-toh)*
friendly	**Era amistoso** *('eh-rah ah-mee-'stoh-soh)*
funny	**Estaba chistoso** *(eh-'stah-bah chee-'stoh-soh)*
good-looking	**Era bien parecido** *('eh-rah 'bee·ehn pah-reh-'see-doh)*
gray-haired	**Estaba canoso** *(eh-'stah-bah kah-'noh-soh)*
hairy	**Era peludo** *('eh-rah peh-'loo-doh)*
handsome	**Era guapo** *('eh-rah 'gwah-poh)*
happy	**Estaba feliz** *(eh-'stah-bah feh-'lees)*
healthy	**Estaba saludable** *(eh-'stah-bah sah-loo-'dah-bleh)*
heavy-set	**Era grueso** *('eh-rah groo-'eh-soh)*
hunchback	**Era jorobado** *('eh-rah hoh-roh-'bah-doh)*
impatient	**Era or Estaba impaciente** *('eh-rah / eh-'stah-bah eem-pah-see-'ehn-teh)*
injured	**Estaba herido** *(eh-'stah-bah eh-'ree-doh)*
lazy	**Era perezoso** *('eh-rah peh-reh-'soh-soh)*
left-handed	**Era zurdo** *('eh-rah 'soor-doh)*
light-skinned	**Era de piel clara** *('eh-rah deh pee-'ehl 'klah-rah)*
loud	**Estaba ruidoso** *(eh-'stah-bah roo-ee-'doh-soh)*
medium-build	**Era de tamaño mediano** *('eh-rah deh tah-'mah-nyoh meh-dee-'ah-noh)*

middle-aged	**Era de edad mediana** *('eh-rah deh eh-'dahd meh-dee-'ah-nah)*
muscular	**Era musculoso** *('eh-rah moos-koo-'loh-soh)*
mute	**Era mudo** *('eh-rah 'moo-doh)*
near-sighted	**Era miope** *('eh-rah mee-'oh-peh)*
nice	**Era** or **Estaba simpático** *('eh-rah / eh-'stah-bah seem-'pah-tee-koh)*
obese	**Era muy gordo** *('eh-rah 'moo-ee 'gohr-doh)*
old	**Era viejo** *('eh-rah vee-'eh-hoh)*
older	**Era mayor** *('eh-rah mah-'yohr)*
one-eyed	**Era tuerto** *('eh-rah 'twehr-toh)*
pale	**Era** or **Estaba pálido** *('eh-rah / eh-'stah-bah 'pah-lee-doh)*
polite	**Era** or **Estaba cortés** *('eh-rah / eh-'stah-bah kohr-'tehs)*
poor	**Era** or **Estaba pobre** *('eh-rah / eh-'stah-bah 'poh-breh)*
professional	**Era profesional** *('eh-rah pro-feh-see·oh-'nahl)*
quiet	**Era** or **Estaba quieto** *(eh-rah / eh-'stah-bah kee-'eh-toh)*
red-haired	**Era pelirojo** *('eh-rah peh-lee-'roh-hoh)*
rich	**Era** or **Estaba rico** *('eh-rah / eh-'stah-bah 'ree-koh)*
right-handed	**Era diestro** *('eh-rah dee-'eh-stroh)*
rough	**Era tosco** *('eh-rah-'toh-skoh)*
rude	**Era rudo** *('eh-rah 'roo-doh)*
short	**Era bajo** *('eh-rah 'bah-hoh)*
shy	**Era** or **Estaba tímido** *('eh-rah / eh-'stah-bah 'tee-mee-doh)*
sickly	**Era enfermizo** *('eh-rah ehn-fehr-'mee-soh)*
slender	**Era** or **Estaba delgado** *('eh-rah / eh-'stah-bah dehl-'gah-doh)*
slow	**Era** or **Estaba lento** *('eh-rah / eh-'stah-bah 'lehn-toh)*
small	**Era pequeño** *('eh-rah peh-'keh-nyoh)*
smart	**Era inteligente** *('eh-roh een-teh-lee-'hehn-teh)*
straight-haired	**Era de pelo lacio** *('eh-rah deh 'peh-loh 'lah-see·oh)*
strange	**Era** or **Estaba extraño** *('eh-rah / eh-'stah-bah eks-'trah-nyoh)*
strong	**Era fuerte** *('eh-rah 'fwehr-teh)*
tall	**Era alto** *('eh-rah 'ahl-toh)*
ugly	**Era feo** *('eh-rah 'feh-oh)*
uncombed	**Estaba despeinado** *(eh-'stah-bah dehs-peh·ee-'nah-doh)*
vicious	**Era vicioso** *('eh-rah vee-see-'oh-soh)*
weak	**Era** or **Estaba débil** *('eh-rah / eh-'stah-bah 'deh-beel)*
well-mannered	**Era de buenos modales** *('eh-rah deh 'bweh-nohs moh-'dah-lehs)*

white	**Era blanco** *('eh-rah 'blahn-koh)*
young	**Era joven** *('eh-rah 'hoh-vehn)*
younger	**Era menor** *('eh-rah meh-'nohr)*

He/She had (the)...	**Tenía...** *(teh-'nee-ah...)*
beard	**la barba** *(lah 'bahr-bah)*
braces	**el corrector dental** *(ehl koh-rrehk-'tohr dehn-'tahl)*
contact lenses	**los lentes de contacto** *(lohs 'lehn-tehs deh kohn-'tahk-toh)*
dentures	**la dentadura postiza** *(lah dehn-tah-'doo-rah poh-'stee-sah)*
full beard	**la barba llena** *(lah 'bahr-bah 'yeh-nah)*
glasses	**los anteojos** *(lohs ahn-teh-'oh-hohs)*
goatee	**la perita** *(lah peh-'ree-tah)*
jewelry	**las joyas** *(lahs 'hoh-yahs)*
long hair	**el pelo largo** *(ehl 'peh-loh 'lahr-goh)*
moustache	**el bigote** *(ehl bee-'goh-teh)*
pimples	**los granos** *(lohs 'grah-nohs)*
pony tail	**la coleta** *(lah koh-'leh-tah)*
short hair	**el pelo corto** *(ehl 'peh-loh 'kohr-toh)*
side burns	**las patillas** *(lahs pah-'tee-yahs)*
sunglasses	**los lentes de sol** *(lohs 'lehn-tehs deh sohl)*
wig	**la peluca** *(lah peh-'loo-kah)*
wrinkles	**las arrugas** *(lahs ah-'rroo-gahs)*

Era alto, fuerte, cortés, inteligente, simpático, amistoso . . .
¡y muy guapo!

SUSPECT IDENTIFICATION
La identificación del sospechoso
(lah ee-dehn-tee-fee-kah-see-'ohn dehl sohs-peh-'choh-soh)

He/She had...	**Tenía...** *(teh-'nee-ah)*
baggy pants	**los pantalones anchos** *(lohs pahn-tah-'loh-nehs 'ahn-chohs)*
bags under the eyes	**bolsas debajo de los ojos** *('bohl-sahs deh-'bah-hoh deh lohs 'oh-hohs)*
blue eyes	**los ojos azules** *(lohs 'oh-hohs ah-'soo-lehs)*
brown eyes	**los ojos marrones** *(lohs 'oh-hohs mah-'rroh-nehs)*
braids	**las trenzas** *(lahs 'trehn-sahs)*
bushy hair	**el pelo espeso** *(ehl 'peh-loh ehs-'peh-soh)*
coarse hair	**el pelo grueso** *(ehl 'peh-loh groo-'eh-soh)*
crooked teeth	**los dientes torcidos** *(lohs dee-'ehn-tehs tohr-'see-dohs)*
dirty teeth	**los dientes sucios** *(lohs dee-'ehn-tehs 'soo-see-ohs)*
fine hair	**el pelo fino** *(ehl 'peh-loh 'fee-noh)*
gold teeth	**los dientes dorados** *(lohs dee-'ehn-tehs doh-'rah-dohs)*
high cheekbones	**las mejillas altas** *(lahs meh-'hee-yahs 'ahl-tahs)*
a hook nose	**la nariz aguileña** *(lah nah-'rees ah-gee-'leh-nyah)*
a limp	**una cojera** *('oo-nah koh-'heh-rah)*
a military haircut	**el corte de pelo militar** *(ehl 'kohr-teh deh 'peh-loh mee-lee-'tahr)*
pockmarks	**las marcas de viruela** *(lahs 'mahr-kahs deh vee-roo-'eh-lah)*
spiked hair	**los cabellos en punta** *(lohs kah-'beh-yohs ehn 'poon-tah)*

His/her face was...	**Tenía la cara...** *(teh-'nee-ah lah 'kah-rah)*
broad	**ancha** *('ahn-chah)*
long	**larga** *('lahr-gah)*
oval	**ovalada** *(oh-vah-'lah-dah)*
round	**redonda** *(reh-'dohn-dah)*
square	**cuadrada** *(kwah-'drah-dah*

His/her voice was...	**Su voz era...** *(soo vohs 'eh-rah)*
deep	**baja** *('bah-hah)*
high	**alta** *('ahl-tah)*
loud	**ruidosa** *(roo-ee-'doh-sah)*
monotone	**monótona** *(moh-'noh-toh-nah)*

pleasant	**agradable** *(ah-grah-'dah-bleh)*
raspy	**chillona** *(chee-'yoh-nah)*
very nasal	**muy nasal** *('moo-ee nah-'sahl)*
with an accent	**con acento** *(kohn ah-'sehn-toh)*

His/Her clothing had...	**Su ropa tenía...** *(soo 'roh-pah teh-'nee-ah)*
checks	**cuadros** *('kwah-drohs)*
colors	**colores** *(koh-'loh-rehs)*
designs	**diseños** *(dee-'seh-nyohs)*
dots	**lunares** *(loo-'nah-rehs)*
letters	**letras** *('leh-trahs)*
numbers	**números** *('noo-meh-rohs)*
stains	**manchas** *('mahn-chahs)*
stripes	**rayas** *('rah-yahs)*

INFORMACIÓN PRIVADA

➤ Countless "descriptive words" in Spanish look a lot like English. Can you guess at the meanings of these?

necesario *(neh-seh-'sah-ree·oh)*
horrible *(oh-'rree-bleh)*
terrible *('teh-'rree-bleh)*
posible *(poh-'see-bleh)*
probable *(proh-'bah-bleh)*
magnífico *(mahg-'nee-fee-koh)*
fantástico *(fahn-'tah-stee-koh)*
maravilloso *(mah-rah-vee-'yoh-soh)*

➤ Not all descriptive words change because of the "o" or "a" endings. For example:

It's a big man	**Es un hombre <u>grande</u>** *(ehs oon 'ohm-breh 'grahn-deh)*
It's a big woman	**Es una mujer <u>grande</u>** *(ehs 'oo-nah moo-'hehr 'grahn-deh)*

➤ Description words that begin with "des" or "in" often refer to an opposite:

correct **correcto** *(koh-'rrehk-toh)*	incorrect **incorrecto** *(een-koh-'rrehk-toh)*
combed **peinado** *(peh·ee-'nah-doh)*	uncombed **despeinado** *(dehs-peh·ee-'nah-doh)*

➤ Be specific about the eyewear.

The glasses were...	**Los lentes eran...** *(lohs 'lehn-tehs 'eh-rahn)*
bifocals	**bifocales** *(bee-foh-'kah-lehs)*
colored	**con color** *(kohn koh-'lohr)*
metallic	**metálicos** *(meh-'tah-lee-kohs)*
mirrored	**con espejos** *(kohn ehs-'peh-hohs)*
tinted	**con tinte** *(kohn 'teen-teh)*

RACE AND NATIONALITY

La raza y la nacionalidad *(lah 'rah-sah ee lah nah-see·oh-nah-lee-'dahd)*

It would be an advantage to know the suspect's nationality or race. Most Hispanics will answer using the sample list below:

He was...	**Era...** *('eh-rah...)*
African-American	**africano-americano** *(ah-free-'kah-noh ah-meh-ree-'kah-noh)*
Anglo-Saxon	**anglosajón** *(ahn-gloh-sah-'hohn)*
Arab	**árabe** *('ah-rah-beh)*
Asian-American	**asiático-americano** *(ah-see-'ah-tee-koh ah-meh-ree-'kah-noh)*
black	**negro** *('neh-groh)*
Canadian	**canadiense** *(kah-nah-dee-'ehn-seh)*
Chinese	**chino** *('chee-noh)*
Cuban	**cubano** *(koo-'bah-noh)*
English	**inglés** *(een-'glehs)*
French	**francés** *(frahn-'sehs)*
German	**alemán** *(ah-leh-'mahn)*
Hispanic	**hispano** *(ee-'spah-noh)*
Indian	**indio** *('een-dee·oh)*
Italian	**italiano** *(ee-tah-lee-'ah-noh)*
Japanese	**japonés** *(hah-poh-'nehs)*
Latin American	**latinoamericano** *(lah-tee-noh-ah-meh-ree-'kah-noh)*
Mexican	**mejicano** *(meh-hee-'kah-noh)*
mulatto	**mulato** *(moo-'lah-toh)*
Polynesian	**polinesio** *(poh-lee-'neh-see·oh)*
Puerto Rican	**puertorriqueño** *(pwehr-toh-rree-'keh-nyoh)*
Spanish	**español** *(eh-spah-'nyohl)*
Vietnamese	**vietnamés** *(vee-eht-nah-'mehs)*
white	**blanco** *('blahn-koh)*

➤ Review your body parts in Spanish before you ask any more questions:

He had...	**Tenía...** *(teh-'nee-ah...)*
bad teeth	**los dientes malos** *(lohs dee-'ehn-tehs 'mah-lohs)*
long legs	**las piernas largas** *(lahs pee-'ehr-nahs 'lahr-gahs)*
strong arms	**los brazos fuertes** *(lohs 'brah-sohs 'fwehr-tehs)*

➤ Use "very" (**muy**) *('moo·ee)* or "a little" (**un poco**) *(oon 'poh-koh)* to clarify each description:

Era <u>muy</u> alto *('eh-rah 'moo·ee 'ahl-toh)*

Era <u>un poco</u> bajo *('eh-rah oon 'poh-koh 'bah-hoh)*

➤ Get as detailed as you can. The suspect is still at large!

He had...	**Tenía...** *(teh-'nee-ah...)*
faded shirt	**la camisa descolorida** *(lah kah-'mee-sah deh-skoh-loh-'ree-dah*
scuffed shoes	**los zapatos rayados** *(lohs sah-'pah-tohs rah-'yah-dohs)*
stained pants	**los pantalones manchados** *(lohs pahn-tah-'loh-nehs mahn-'chah-dohs)*

➤ For your information, "short" in length is **corto** *('kohr-toh)* in Spanish.

➤ Again, bear in mind that descriptions of a female change:

He's tall   **Es alto** *(ehs 'ahl-toh)*   She's tall   **Es alta** *(ehs 'ahl-tah)*

HOW DID HE BEHAVE?
¿Cómo se portó? *('koh-moh seh pohr-'toh)*

He seemed..	**Parecía...** *(pah-reh-'see-ah...)*
aggressive	**agresivo** *(ah-greh-'see-voh)*
angry	**enojado** *(eh-noh-'hah-doh)*
anxious	**ansioso** *(ahn-see-'oh-soh)*
bored	**aburrido** *(ah-boo-'rree-doh)*
busy	**ocupado** *(oh-koo-'pah-doh)*
calm	**calmado** *(kahl-'mah-doh)*

confident	**seguro de sí** *(seh-'goo-roh deh see)*
confused	**confundido** *(kohn-foon-'dee-doh)*
courteous	**cortés** *(kohr-'tehs)*
crude	**vulgar** *(vool-'gahr)*
determined	**determinado** *(deh-tehr-mee-'nah-doh)*
excited	**emocionado** *(eh-moh-see·oh-'nah-doh)*
friendly	**amistoso** *(ah-mees-'toh-soh)*
furious	**furioso** *(foo-ree-'oh-soh)*
happy	**feliz** *(feh-'lees)*
indecisive	**indeciso** *(een-deh-'see-soh)*
nervous	**nervioso** *(nehr-vee-'oh-soh)*
ready	**listo** *('lee-stoh)*
relaxed	**relajado** *(reh-lah-'hah-doh)*
sad	**triste** *('tree-steh)*
scared	**espantado** *(eh-spahn-'tah-doh)*
shy	**tímido** *('tee-mee-doh)*
surprised	**sorprendido** *(sohr-prehn-'dee-doh)*
tired	**cansado** *(kahn-'sah-doh)*
uncomfortable	**incómodo** *(een-'koh-moh-doh)*
uneasy	**inquieto** *(een-kee-'eh-toh)*
unsure	**inseguro** *(een-seh-'goo-roh)*
upset	**molesto** *(moh-'lehs-toh)*
violent	**violento** *(vee-oh-'lehn-toh)*
worried	**preocupado** *(preh-oh-koo-'pah-doh)*

MORE DESCRIPTIONS!
¡Más descripciones! *(mahs deh-skreep-see-'oh-nehs)*

Ask about everything related to the crime. Listen for common descriptive words. It helps to review these terms as opposites:

better	**mejor** *(meh-'hohr)*
cheap	**barato** *(bah-'rah-toh)*
closed	**cerrado** *(seh-'rrah-doh)*
cold	**frío** *('free-oh)*
dangerous	**peligroso** *(peh-lee-'groh-soh)*
difficult	**difícil** *(dee-'fee-seel)*
down	**abajo** *(ah-'bah-hoh)*
dry	**seco** *('seh-koh)*

dull	**romo** *('roh-moh)*
easy	**fácil** *('fah-seel)*
empty	**vacío** *(vah-'see-oh)*
expensive	**caro** *('kah-roh)*
full	**lleno** *('yeh-noh)*
hard	**duro** *('doo-roh)*
heavy	**pesado** *(peh-'sah-doh)*
hot	**caliente** *(kah-lee-'ehn-teh)*
light	**ligero** *(lee-'heh-roh)*
loose	**flojo** *('floh-hoh)*
narrow	**estrecho** *(eh-'streh-choh)*
open	**abierto** *(ah-bee-'ehr-toh)*
right	**correcto** *(koh-'rrehk-toh)*
safe	**seguro** *(seh-'goo-roh)*
sharp	**afilado** *(ah-fee-'lah-doh)*
soft	**suave** *('swah-veh)*
thick	**grueso** *(groo-'eh-soh)*
thin	**delgado** *(dehl-'gah-doh)*
tight	**apretado** *(ah-preh-'tah-doh)*
up	**arriba** *(ah-'rree-bah)*
wet	**mojado** *(moh-'hah-doh)*
wide	**ancho** *('ahn-choh)*
worse	**peor** *(peh-'ohr)*
wrong	**equivocado** *(eh-kee-voh-'kah-doh)*

INFORMACIÓN PRIVADA

➤ Use these lines to confirm the facts:

Is this correct?	**¿Es correcto esto?** *(ehs koh-'rrehk-toh 'eh-stoh)*
Do you have a doubt?	**¿Tiene una duda?** *(tee-'eh-neh 'oo-nah 'doo-dah)*
Are you sure?	**¿Está seguro?** *(eh-'stah seh-'goo-roh)*

A. Name three items that are often stolen in robberies involving assault and battery:

_____   _____   _____

B. Find out who committed the crime. Complete the phrases:

¿Cuál es el color de su _____? *(kwahl ehs ehl koh-'lohr deh soo _____)*
Describa su _____ *(deh-'skree-bah soo _____)*
Tenía _____ *(teh-'nee-ah _____)*
Era _____ *('eh-rah_____)*
¿Se veía _____? *('seh veh-'ee-ah _____)*

C. Translate:

Tell him   _____
Look at me   _____
Drop it   _____

264

D. Match these opposites:

estrecho *(eh-'streh-choh)*   feo *('feh-oh)*
contento *(kohn-'tehn-toh)*   ancho *('ahn-choh)*
joven *('hoh-vehn)*   delgado *(dehl-'gah-doh)*
sucio *('soo-see·oh)*   viejo *(vee-'eh-hoh)*
gordo *('gohr-doh)*   limpio *('leem-pee·oh)*
mojado *(moh-'hah-doh)*   alto *('ahl-toh)*
guapo *('gwah-poh)*   triste *('tree-steh)*
bajo *('bah-hoh)*   seco *('seh-koh)*

ANSWERS

bajo – alto	sucio – limpio	
guapo – feo	joven – viejo	C. Dígale
mojado – seco	contento – triste	Míreme
gordo – delgado	D. estrecho – ancho	Suéltelo

WHAT WERE THEY WEARING?

¿Qué llevaban? *(keh yeh-'vah-bahn)*

Law enforcement officials agree that it is much easier to apprehend suspects if they have valid information about what the suspects were wearing at the crime scene. Start with the face:

He/She had (the)...over	**Tenía...sobre la cara** *(teh-'nee-ah...'soh-breh lah 'kah-rah)*
the face	
handkerchief	**el pañuelo** *(ehl pah-nyoo-'eh-loh)*
mask	**la máscara** *(lah 'mah-skah-rah)*
scarf	**la bufanda** *(lah boo-'fahn-dah)*

Now, ask "yes" or "no" questions:

Was he...?	**Estaba...** *(eh-'stah-bah...)*
barefoot	**descalzo?** *(deh-'skahl-soh)*
dressed funny	**mal vestido?** *(mahl veh-'stee-doh)*
in a costume	**disfrazado?** *(dees-frah-'sah-doh)*
in style	**de moda?** *(deh 'moh-dah)*
lightly dressed	**con poca ropa?** *(kohn 'poh-kah 'roh-pah)*
neatly dressed	**bien vestido?** *('bee·ehn veh-'stee-doh)*
sloppy	**desaliñado?** *(dehs-ah-lee-'nyah-doh)*
warmly dressed	**muy arropado?** *('moo·ee ah-rroh-'pah-doh)*

Continue the questioning about specific articles of clothing:

Describe the...	**Describa...** (deh-'skree-bah...)
beret	**la boina** (lah boh-'ee-nah)
bathing suit	**el traje de baño** (ehl 'trah-heh deh 'bah-nyoh)
bathrobe	**la bata de baño** (lah 'bah-tah deh 'bah-nyoh)
belt	**el cinturón** (ehl seen-too-'rohn)
blouse	**la blusa** (lah 'bloo-sah)
boots	**las botas** (lahs 'boh-tahs)
bra	**el sostén** (ehl soh-'stehn)
cap	**la gorra** (lah 'goh-rrah)
dress	**el vestido** (ehl veh-'stee-doh)
girdle	**la faja** (lah 'fah-hah)
gloves	**los guantes** (lohs 'gwahn-tehs)
hat	**el sombrero** (ehl sohm-'breh-roh)
jacket	**la chaqueta** (lah chah-'keh-tah)
mittens	**los mitones** (lohs mee-'toh-nehs)
overcoat	**el abrigo** (ehl ah-'bree-goh)
pajamas	**la pijama** (lah pee-'hah-mah)
panties	**las bragas** (lahs 'brah-gahs)
pants	**los pantalones** (lohs pahn-tah-'loh-nehs)
raincoat	**el impermeable** (ehl eem-pehr-meh-'ah-bleh)
sandals	**las sandalias** (lahs sahn-'dah-lee·ahs)
shirt	**la camisa** (lah kah-'mee-sah)
shoes	**las zapatos** (lohs sah-'pah-tohs)
shorts	**los calzoncillos** (lohs kahl-sohn-'see-yohs)
skirt	**la falda** (lah 'fahl-dah)
slip	**la combinación** (lah kohm-bee-nah-see-'ohn)
slippers	**las zapatillas** (lahs sah-pah-'tee-yahs)
socks	**los calcetines** (lohs kahl-seh-'tee-nehs)
sportcoat	**el saco** (ehl 'sah-koh)
stockings	**las medias** (lahs 'meh-dee·ahs)
suit	**el traje** (ehl 'trah-heh)
sweater	**el suéter** (ehl 'sweh-tehr)
sweatsuit	**la sudadera** (lah soo-dah-'deh-rah)
T-shirt	**la camiseta** (lah kah-mee-'seh-tah)
tennis shoes	**los tenis** (lohs 'teh-nees)
tie	**la corbata** (lah kohr-'bah-tah)
underpants	**los calzoncillos** (lohs kahl-sohn-'see-yohs)
underwear	**la ropa interior** (lah 'roh-pah een-teh-ree-'ohr)
uniform	**el uniforme** (ehl oo-nee-'fohr-meh)
vest	**el chaleco** (ehl chah-'leh-koh)

WORD SEARCH 3

e	t	r	a	j	e	a	v	a	r	r	o	g
a	m	s	i	o	j	e	l	n	e	g	m	a
o	n	r	e	a	s	c	a	m	i	s	a	f
o	n	l	o	t	e	l	c	r	m	u	i	i
o	i	e	i	f	n	p	b	z	p	l	a	e
r	a	d	b	s	i	a	n	u	e	n	t	o
e	o	i	o	a	t	n	u	f	r	p	e	s
r	c	e	t	n	e	t	u	g	m	l	u	a
b	l	b	a	d	c	a	r	z	e	m	q	g
m	a	t	s	a	l	l	i	t	a	p	a	z
o	a	d	u	l	a	o	c	b	b	a	h	o
s	o	l	l	i	c	n	o	z	l	a	c	n
r	e	u	b	a	d	e	a	g	e	b	e	e
c	a	o	s	s	f	s	o	t	a	p	a	z

saco
blusa
gorra
botas
vestido
guantes
sombrero
chaqueta
abrigo
pantalones
impermeable
sandalias
camisa
zapatos
calzoncillos
falda
zapatillas
calcetines
traje
uniforme

AND THE COLOR?
¿Y el color? *(ee ehl koh-'lohr)*

Not only will knowing all the colors in Spanish allow you to identify a suspect, but it can also help to describe any stolen object. Some of these words were introduced in Chapter One, so it should be easy to try them out in practice phrases:

What color is it?	**¿De qué color es?** *(deh keh koh-'lohr ehs)*
What color was it?	**¿De qué color era?** *(deh keh koh-'lohr 'eh-rah)*
Do you remember the color?	**¿Recuerda el color?** *(reh-'kwehr-dah ehl koh-'lohr)*

Some of this is review material. Come up with more sample sentences:

beige	**beige** *('beh-eesh)*	**El carro es beige** *(ehl 'kah-rroh ehs'beh·eesh)*

267

black	**negro** *('neh-groh)*	<u>**El pelo es negro**</u> *(ehl 'peh-loh ehs 'neh-groh)*
blue	**azul** *(ah-'sool)*	_____
brown	**café** *('kah-feh)*	_____
copper	**cobrizo** *(koh-'bree-soh)*	_____
cream	**color de crema** *(koh-'lohr deh 'kreh-mah)*	_____
dark	**oscuro** *(oh-'skoo-roh)*	_____
gold	**oro** *('oh-roh)*	_____
gray	**gris** *(grees)*	_____
green	**verde** *('vehr-deh)*	_____
light	**claro** *('klah-roh)*	_____
maroon	**marrón** *(mah-'rrohn)*	
olive green	**de color oliva** *(deh koh-'lohr oh-'lee-vah)*	<u>**Su camisa es de color oliva**</u> *(soo kah-'mee-sah ehs deh koh-'lohr oh-'lee-vah)*
orange	**anaranjado** *(ah-nah-rahn-'hah-doh)*	_____
pink	**rosado** *(roh'-sah-doh)*	_____
red	**rojo** *('roh-hoh)*	_____
silver	**plateado** *(plah-teh-'ah-doh)*	_____
tan	**café claro** *(kah-'feh 'klah-roh)*	_____
turquoise	**turquesa** *(toor-'keh-sah)*	_____
violet	**violeta** *(vee-oh-'leh-tah)*	_____
white	**blanco** *('blahn-koh)*	_____
yellow	**amarillo** *(ah-mah-'rree-yoh)*	_____

WEAPONS
Las armas *(lahs 'ahr-mahs)*

People can attack each other with just about any object, so this list isn't really complete. However, the following words pop up more often when weapons are at the scene:

Drop...	**Suelte...** *('swehl-teh...)*
Give me...	**Déme...** *('deh-meh...)*
bat	**el palo de béisbol** *(ehl 'pah-loh deh 'beh·ees-bohl)*
belt	**el cinturón** *(ehl seen-too-'rohn)*
billiard cue	**el taco de billar** *(ehl 'tah-koh deh bee-'yahr)*

billy club	**el garrote** (ehl gah-'rroh-teh)
blade	**la navaja** (lah nah-'vah-hah)
bomb	**la bomba** (lah 'bohm-bah)
bottle	**la botella** (lah boh-'teh-yah)
bow and arrow	**el arco y la flecha** (ehl 'ahr-koh ee lah 'fleh-chah)
brass knuckles	**las manoplas** (lahs mah-'noh-plahs)
brick	**el ladrillo** (ehl lah-'dree-yoh)
broomstick	**el palo de escoba** (ehl 'pah-loh deh eh-'skoh-bah)
car jack	**el gato del carro** (ehl 'gah-toh dehl 'kah-rroh)
chain	**la cadena** (lah kah-'deh-nah)
chair	**la silla** (lah 'see-yah)
dagger	**la daga** (lah 'dah-gah)
dynamite	**la dinamita** (lah dee-nah-'mee-tah)
explosive	**el explosivo** (ehl ehk-sploh-'see-voh)
file	**la lima** (lah 'lee-mah)
firearm	**el arma de fuego** (ehl 'ahr-mah deh 'fweh-goh)
grenade	**la granada** (lah grah-'nah-dah)
hammer	**el martillo** (ehl mahr-'tee-yoh)
hatchet	**el hacha** (ehl 'ah-chah)
hook	**el gancho** (ehl 'gahn-choh)
ice pick	**el picahielos** (ehl pee-kah-'yeh-lohs)
knife	**el cuchillo** (ehl koo-'chee-yoh)
metal bar	**la barra de metal** (lah 'bah-rrah deh meh-'tahl)
machine gun	**la ametralladora** (lah ah-meh-trah-yah-'doh-rah)
pick	**el pico** (ehl 'pee-koh)
pin	**el alfiler** (ehl ahl-fee-'lehr)
pipe	**el tubo** (ehl 'too-boh)
pistol	**la pistola** (lah pee-'stoh-lah)
pitchfork	**la horquilla** (lah ohr-'kee-yah)
revolver	**el revólver** (ehl reh-'vohl-vehr)
rifle	**el rifle** (ehl 'ree-fleh)
rock	**la piedra** (lah pee-'eh-drah)
rope	**la soga** (lah 'soh-gah)
saw	**el serrucho** (ehl seh-'rroo-choh)
scissors	**las tijeras** (lahs tee-'heh-rahs)
screwdriver	**el atornillador** (ehl ah-tohr-nee-yah-'dohr)
semi-automatic	**la semiautomática** (lah seh-mee-ow-toh-'mah-tee-kah)
shotgun	**la escopeta** (lah eh-skoh-'peh-tah)
shovel	**la pala** (lah 'pah-lah)
spear	**la lanza** (lah 'lahn-sah)

stick	**el palo** *(ehl 'pah-loh)*
sword	**la espada** *(lah eh-'spah-dah)*
tool	**la herramienta** *(lah eh-rrah-mee-'ehn-tah)*
torch	**la antorcha** *(lah ahn-'tohr-chah)*
whip	**el látigo** *(ehl 'lah-tee-goh)*
wire	**el alambre** *(ehl ah-'lahm-breh)*
wrench	**la llave inglesa** *(lah 'yah-veh een-'gleh-sah)*

If there are guns around, ask individuals about their firearms:

Do you have a concealed firearm?	**¿Tiene un arma de fuego escondida?** *(tee-'eh-neh oon 'ahr-mah deh 'fweh-goh eh-skohn-'dee-dah)*
Where did you get the firearm?	**¿Dónde consiguió el arma de fuego?** *('dohn-deh kohn-see-gee-'oh ehl 'ahr-mah deh 'fweh-goh)*
Are you the owner of the firearm?	**¿Es el dueño del arma de fuego?** *(ehs ehl 'dweh-nyoh dehl 'ahr-mah deh 'fweh-goh)*
Do you have a license for the firearm?	**¿Tiene una licencia para el arma de fuego?** *(tee-'eh-neh 'oo-nah lee-'sehn-see·ah 'pah-rah ehl 'ahr-mah deh 'fweh-goh)*
Is it loaded?	**¿Está cargada?** *(eh-'stah kahr-'gah-dah)*

Question the witness:

What kind of sound?	**¿Qué tipo de sonido?** *(keh 'tee-poh deh soh-'nee-doh)*
In which direction did he shoot?	**¿En cuál dirección disparó?** *(ehn kwahl dee-rehk-see-'ohn dees-pah-'roh)*
Was it a hold-up?	**¿Le robó con un arma?** *(leh roh-'boh kohn oon 'ahr-mah)*

270

➤ Get right to the point:

Were they armed?	**¿Estaban armados?** *(eh-'stah-bahn ahr-'mah-dohs)*
What weapon did he use?	**¿Cuál arma usó?** *(kwahl 'ahr-mah oo-'soh)*
How many were there?	**¿Cuántas habían?** *('kwahn-tohs ah-'bee-ahn)*

➤ Special terminology follows:

blank	**el cartucho sin bala** *(ehl kahr-'too-choh seen 'bah-lah)*
bullet	**la bala** *(lah 'bah-lah)*
caliber	**el calibre** *(ehl kah-'lee-breh)*
carbine	**la carabina** *(lah kah-rah-'bee-nah)*
cartridge belt	**la cartuchera** *(lah kahr-too-'cheh-rah)*
double barreled	**de dos cañones** *(deh dohs kah-'nyoh-nehs)*
holster	**la funda de pistola** *(lah 'foon-dah deh pee-'stoh-lah)*
magazine	**la recámara** *(lah reh-'kah-mah-rah)*
powder	**la pólvora** *(lah 'pohl-voh-rah)*
round	**el número de tiros** *(ehl 'noo-meh-roh deh 'tee-rohs)*
safety	**el seguro** *(ehl seh-'goo-roh)*
shell casing	**el cartucho** *(ehl kahr-'too-choh)*
silencer	**el silenciador** *(ehl see-lehn-see·ah-'dohr)*

FORENSIC SCIENCE
La ciencia legal *(lah see-'ehn-see·ah leh-'gahl)*

Specialists are used whenever a firearm is used in a crime. If a Spanish-speaking suspect is in custody, add the following words to your language skills:

What kind of firearm?	**¿Qué tipo de arma?** *('keh 'tee-poh deh 'ahr-mah)*
Which caliber?	**¿Cuál calibre?** *(kwahl kah-'lee-breh)*
Which shell casing?	**¿Cuál cartucho?** *(kwahl kahr-'too-choh)*
How many rounds?	**¿Cuántos tiros?** *('kwahn-tohs 'tee-rohs)*

Now speak directly to the suspect:

Are you left-handed or right-handed?	**¿Es zurdo o diestro?** *(ehs 'soor-doh oh dee-'eh-stroh)*

When did you wash your hands?	**¿Cuándo se lavó las manos?** *('kwahn-doh seh lah-'voh lahs 'mah-nohs)*
I'm looking for blood and particles	**Estoy buscando sangre y partículas** *(eh-'stoh-ee boo-'skahn-doh 'sahn-greh ee pahr-'tee-koo-lahs)*
I am going to take pictures	**Voy a tomar fotos** *('voh-ee ah toh-'mahr 'foh-tohs)*
This bag contains evidence	**Esta bolsa contiene evidencia** *('eh-stah 'bohl-sah kohn-tee-'eh-neh eh-vee-'dehn-see·ah)*
I need a sample	**Necesito una muestra** *(neh-seh-'see-toh 'oo-nah 'mweh-strah)*
I'm going to put (the) …on you	**Voy a ponerle...** *('voh-ee ah poh-'nehr-leh...)*
spray	**el aerosol** *(ehl ah-eh-roh-'sohl)*
drop	**la gota** *(lah 'goh-tah)*
sticky disk	**el disco pegajoso** *(ehl 'dee-skoh peh-gah-'hoh-soh)*
plastic bag	**la bolsa de plástico** *(lah 'bohl-sah deh 'plah-stee-koh)*
powder	**el polvo** *(ehl 'pohl-voh)*
chemical	**la substancia química** *(lah soob-'stahn-see·ah 'kee-mee-kah)*

THE HOMICIDE

El homicidio *(ehl oh-mee-'see-dee·oh)*

Once the cause of death has been determined, use some of these key vocabulary words to discuss all necessary homicide procedures. Keep in mind, however, that when it comes to witness interrogations, the search for clues, and other case-related activities, *always* make sure you are accompanied by a qualified bilingual interpreter.

For starters, calm everyone down and then try to figure out what happened:

Calm down	**Cálmese** *('kahl-meh-seh)*
Please, let us through	**Por favor, déjenos pasar** *(pohr fah-'vohr, 'deh-heh-nohs pah-'sahr)*
Where's the victim?	**¿Dónde está la víctima?** *('dohn-deh eh-'stah lah 'veek-tee-mah)*
Do you need (the)...?	**¿Necesita a...** *(neh-seh-'see-tah ah...)*
ambulance	**la ambulancia?** *(lah ahm-boo-'lahn-see·ah)*
coroner	**el médico legista?** *(ehl 'meh-dee-koh leh-'hee-stah)*
lawyer	**el abogado?** *(ehl ah-boh-'gah-doh)*
minister	**el ministro?** *(ehl mee-'nee-stroh)*

mortician	**el agente funerario?** *(ehl ah-'hehn-teh foo-neh-'rah-ree·oh)*
next of kin	**el pariente más cercano?** *(ehl pah-ree-'ehn-teh mahs sehr-'kah-noh)*
priest	**el sacerdote?** *(ehl sah-sehr-'doh-teh)*
rabbi	**el rabino?** *(ehl rah-'bee-noh)*

We will take care of everyhing	**Vamos a cuidar de todo** *('vah-mohs ah kwee-'dahr deh 'toh-doh)*
Stay behind the yellow tape	**Quédese detrás de la cinta amarilla** *('keh-deh-seh deh-'trahs deh lah 'seen-tah ah-mah-'ree-yah)*
I want to speak with the family	**Quiero hablar con la familia** *(kee-'eh-roh ah-'blahr kohn lah fah-'mee-lee·ah)*
Are there witnesses?	**¿Hay testigos?** *('ah·ee teh-'stee-gohs)*
Who was here at the time?	**¿Quién estaba aquí cuando pasó esto?** *(kee-'ehn eh-'stah-bah ah-'kee 'kwahn-doh pah-'soh 'eh-stoh)*
Did anyone touch the dead body?	**¿Alguien tocó el cadáver?** *('ahl-gee·ehn toh-'koh ehl kah-'dah-vehr)*
Do you know who killed him?	**¿Sabe quién lo mató?** *('sah-beh kee-'ehn loh mah-'toh)*

Focus on a variety of explanations and descriptions:

It was...	**Fue...** *(fweh...)*
a crime of passion	**un crimen pasional** *(oon 'kree-mehn pah-see·oh-'nahl)*
a drive-by	**un disparo de un carro** *(oon dee-'spah-roh deh oon 'kah-rroh)*
a massacre	**una matanza** *('oo-nah mah-'tahn-sah)*
a murder	**un asesinato** *(oon ah-seh-see-'nah-toh)*
a shooting	**un disparo** *(oon dee-'spah-roh)*
a shot	**un balazo** *(oon bah-'lah-soh)*
a sniper	**un francotirador** *(oon frahn-koh-tee-rah-'dohr)*
a suicide	**un suicidio** *(oon soo-ee-'see-dee·oh)*
an accident	**un accidente** *(oon ahk-see-'dehn-teh)*
bloody	**sangriento** *(sahn-gree-'ehn-toh)*
fatal	**fatal** *(fah-'tahl)*
first degree	**del primer grado** *(dehl pree-'mehr 'grah-doh)*
in cold blood	**a sangre fría** *(ah 'sahn-greh 'free-ah)*
manslaughter	**homicidio involuntario** *(oh-mee-'see-dee·oh een-voh-loon-'tah-ree·oh)*
premeditated	**premeditado** *(preh-meh-dee-'tah-doh)*
second degree	**del segundo grado** *(dehl seh-'goon-doh 'grah-doh)*

Don't forget about a cause or motive:

It was...   **Fue...** *(fweh...)*
  love   **el amor** *(ehl ah-'mohr)*
  hate   **el odio** *(ehl 'oh-dee·oh)*
  jealousy   **los celos** *(lohs 'seh-lohs)*
  passion   **la pasión** *(lah pah-see-'ohn)*
  revenge   **la venganza** *(lah vehn-'gahn-sah)*
  racism   **el racismo** *(ehl rah-'sees-moh)*
  insanity   **la locura** *(lah loh-'koo-rah)*

La comida fue su amor. Comió y comió y se murió. Fue un crimen pasional.

INFORMACIÓN PRIVADA

➤ These key phrases need to be acquired as soon as possible:

  He's dead   **Está muerto** *(eh-'stah 'mwehr-toh)*
  He's dying   **Se está muriendo** *(seh eh-'stah moo-ree-'ehn-doh)*
  He died   **Se murió** *(seh moo-ree-'oh)*

➤ You should be exposed to some words that relate to death in general:

  autopsy   **la autopsia** *(lah ow-'tohp-see·ah)*
  cadaver   **el cadáver** *(ehl kah-'dah-vehr)*
  cemetery   **el cementerio** *(ehl seh-mehn-'teh-ree·oh)*
  coffin   **el ataúd** *(ehl ah-tah-'ood)*
  funeral   **el funeral** *(ehl foo-neh-'rahl)*
  funeral home   **la funeraria** *(lah foo-neh-'rah-ree·ah)*
  morgue   **la morgue** *(lah mohr-geh)*

CRUCIGRAMA 3

Across

3 pistol
5 hook
7 dagger
8 shotgun
13 dynamite
14 explosive
15 bomb

Down

1 brass knuckles
2 saw
4 sword
6 blade
9 ice pick
10 billy club
11 knife
12 hammer

SEX CRIMES

Los crímenes sexuales *(lohs 'kree-meh-nehs sehk-soo-'ah-lehs)*

Tough jobs require tough language, so don't hold back on this next group of Spanish words.

It's...	Es... *(ehs...)*
beastiality	**la bestialidad** *(lah beh-stee-ah-lee-'dahd)*
bisexual	**el bisexual** *(ehl bee-sehk-soo-'ahl)*
breast	**el seno** *(ehl 'seh-noh)*
brothel	**el burdel** *(ehl boor-'dehl)*
buttock	**la nalga** *(lah 'nahl-gah)*
copulation	**la cópula** *(lah 'kohp-oo-lah)*
gay	**el gay** *(ehl 'gah·ee)*
harassment	**el acosamiento** *(ehl ah-koh-sah-mee-'ehn-toh)*
homosexual	**el homosexual** *(ehl oh-moh-sehk-soo-'ahl)*
immoral conduct	**la conducta inmoral** *(lah kohn-'dook-tah een-moh-'rahl)*
incest	**el incesto** *(ehl een-'seh-stoh)*
intercourse	**el coito** *(ehl 'koh-ee-toh)*
lesbian	**la lesbiana** *(lah lehs-bee-'ah-nah)*
lewd behavior	**el comportamiento indecente** *(ehl kohm-pohr-tah-mee-'ehn-toh een-deh-'sehn-teh)*
masturbation	**la masturbación** *(lah mah-stoor-bah-see-'ohn)*
molestation	**el abuso sexual** *(ehl ah-'boo-soh sehk-soo-'ahl)*
nudity	**la desnudez** *(lah dehs-noo-'dehs)*
obscene phone call	**la llamada obscena** *(lah yah-'mah-dah ohb-'seh-nah)*
penis	**el pene** *(ehl 'peh-neh)*
pervert	**el pervertido** *(ehl pehr-vehr-'tee-doh)*
pimp	**el cafiche** *(ehl kah-'fee-cheh)*
polygamy	**la poligamia** *(lah poh-lee-'gah-mee-ah)*
pornography	**la pornografía** *(lah pohr-noh-grah-'fee-ah)*
prostitution	**la prostitución** *(lah proh-stee-too-see-'ohn)*
rape	**la violación** *(lah vee-oh-lah-see-'ohn)*
sexual act	**el acto sexual** *(ehl 'ahk-toh sehk-soo-'ahl)*
sodomy	**la sodomía** *(lah soh-doh-'mee-ah)*
solicitation	**la incitación** *(lah een-see-tah-see-'ohn)*
transexual	**el transexual** *(ehl trahn-sehk-soo-'ahl)*
transvestite	**el transvestista** *(ehl trahns-veh-'stee-stah)*
vagina	**la vagina** *(lah vah-'hee-nah)*
vulgarity	**la vulgaridad** *(lah vool-gah-ree-'dahd)*

MORE CRIMINALS AND CRIMES

Más criminales y crímenes *(mahs kree-mee-'nah-lehs ee 'kree-meh-nehs)*

Who's...?	**¿Quién es...** *(kee-'ehn ehs...)*
bookie	**el corredor de apuestas?** *(ehl koh-rreh-'dohr deh ah-'pweh-stahs)*
bunco artist	**el estafador?** *(ehl eh-stah-fah-'dohr)*
forger	**el falsificador?** *(ehl fahl-see-fee-kah-'dohr)*
loiterer	**el holgazán?** *(ehl ohl-gah-'sahn)*
murderer	**el asesino?** *(ehl ah-seh-'see-noh)*
pickpocket	**el carterista?** *(ehl kahr-teh-'ree-stah)*
racketeer	**el extorsionador?** *(ehl ehks-tohr-see·oh-nah-'dohr)*
rapist	**el violador?** *(ehl vee-oh-lah-'dohr)*
smuggler	**el contrabandista?** *(ehl kohn-trah-bahn-'dee-stah)*
vagrant	**el vagabundo?** *(ehl vah-gah-'boon-doh)*
He was arrested for...	**Fue arrestado por...** *(fweh ah-rreh-'stah-doh pohr...)*
arson	**el incendio premeditado** *(ehl een-'sehn-dee·oh preh-meh-dee-'tah-doh)*
bribery	**el soborno** *(ehl soh-'bohr-noh)*
child neglect	**el descuido de los niños** *(ehl dehs-'koo-ee-doh deh lohs 'nee-nyohs)*
counterfeiting	**la falsificación** *(lah fahl-see-fee-kah-see-'ohn)*
disorderly conduct	**el desorden público** *(ehl deh-'sohr-dehn 'poo-blee-koh)*
embezzling	**el desfalco** *(ehl dehs-'fahl-koh)*
extortion	**la extorsión** *(lah ehks-tohr-see-'ohn)*
fraud	**el fraude** *(ehl 'frow-deh)*
gambling	**el juego de apuestas** *(ehl 'hweh-goh deh ah-'pweh-stahs)*
grand theft	**el robo de mayor cuantía** *(ehl 'roh-boh deh mah-'yohr kwahn-'tee-ah)*
hijacking	**el robo en tránsito** *(ehl 'roh-boh ehn 'trahn-see-toh)*
kidnapping	**el secuestro** *(ehl seh-'kweh-stroh)*
larceny	**el hurto** *(ehl 'oor-toh)*
spousal abuse	**el abuso conyugal** *(ehl ah-'boo-soh kohn-yoo-'gahl)*
trespassing	**la intrusión** *(lah een-troo-see-'ohn)*
vagrancy	**el vagabundeo** *(ehl vah-gah-boon-'deh-oh)*
vandalism	**el vandalismo** *(ehl vahn-dah-'lees-moh)*

CRIME INVESTIGATION

La investigación del crimen *(lah een-veh-stee-gah-see-'ohn dehl 'kree-mehn)*

Every crime involves some investigative work, and the process or procedures seldom move quickly. During this time, officials will have to explain what's going on to witnesses, suspects, or victims, along with their families, neighbors, and friends. When the case includes Spanish speakers, use the words below:

It was (the)…	**Fue…** *(fweh…)*
bullet	**la bala** *(lah 'bah-lah)*
drug	**la droga** *(lah 'droh-gah)*
poison	**el veneno** *(ehl veh-'neh-noh)*
strangulation	**la estrangulación** *(lah eh-strahn-goo-lah-see-'ohn)*
unknown	**desconocido** *(dehs-koh-noh-'see-doh)*
We know (the)…	**Sabemos…** *(sah-'beh-mohs…)*
cause	**la causa** *(lah 'kow-sah)*
motive	**el motivo** *(ehl moh-'tee-voh)*
place	**el sitio** *(ehl 'see-tee·oh)*
purpose	**el propósito** *(ehl proh-'poh-see-toh)*
reason	**la razón** *(lah rah-'sohn)*
time	**la hora** *(lah 'oh-rah)*
There is (the)…	**Allí está…** *(ah-'yee eh-'stah…)*
I'm looking for (the)…	**Estoy buscando…** *(eh-'stoh-ee boo-'skahn-doh…)*
I found (the)…	**Encontré…** *(ehn-kohn-'treh…)*
ash	**la ceniza** *(lah seh-'nee-sah)*
blood	**la sangre** *(lah 'sahn-greh)*
corrosion	**la corrosión** *(lah koh-rroh-see-'ohn)*
crack	**la grieta** *(lah gree-'eh-tah)*
damage	**el daño** *(ehl 'dah-nyoh)*
dirt	**la tierra** *(lah tee-'eh-rrah)*
dust	**el polvo** *(ehl 'pohl-voh)*
hair	**el pelo** *(ehl 'peh-loh)*
hole	**el agujero** *(ehl ah-goo-'heh-roh)*
mark	**la marca** *(lah 'mahr-kah)*
mold	**el moho** *(ehl 'moh-oh)*
mud	**el lodo** *(ehl 'loh-doh)*
odor	**el olor** *(ehl oh-'lohr)*
print	**la huella** *(lah 'weh-yah)*
puddle	**el charco** *(ehl 'chahr-koh)*
residue	**el residuo** *(ehl reh-'see-doo-oh)*

smoke	**el humo** *(ehl 'oo-moh)*
soot	**el tizne** *(ehl 'tees-neh)*
stain	**la mancha** *(lah 'mahn-chah)*
track	**la pisada** *(lah pee-'sah-dah)*

It's all over (the)...	**Está por todo ...** *(eh-'stah pohr 'toh-doh...)*
asphalt	**el asfalto** *(ehl ahs-'fahl-toh)*
bedspread	**el cubrecama** *(ehl coo-breh-'kah-mah)*
blanket	**la cobija** *(lah koh-'bee-hah)*
branch	**la rama** *(lah 'rah-mah)*
brick	**el ladrillo** *(ehl lah-'dree-yoh)*
cement	**el cemento** *(ehl seh-'mehn-toh)*
drape	**la cortina** *(lah kohr-'tee-nah)*
floor	**el piso** *(ehl 'pee-soh)*
garden	**el jardín** *(ehl hahr-'deen)*
glass	**el vidrio** *(ehl 'vee-dree·oh)*
ground	**el suelo** *(ehl 'sweh-loh)*
leaf	**la hoja** *(lah 'oh-hah)*
linoleum	**el linóleo** *(ehl lee-'noh-leh-oh)*
marble	**el mármol** *(ehl 'mahr-mohl)*
mattress	**la colcha** *(lah 'kohl-chah)*
napkin	**la servilleta** *(lah sehr-vee-'yeh-tah)*
pavement	**el pavimento** *(ehl pah-vee-'mehn-toh)*
pillow	**la almohada** *(lah ahl-moh-'ah-dah)*
pillowcase	**la funda** *(lah 'foon-dah)*
rug	**el tapete** *(ehl tah-'peh-teh)*
sheet	**la sábana** *(lah 'sah-bah-nah)*
tile	**la loceta** *(lah loh-'seh-tah)*
towel	**la toalla** *(lah toh-'ah-yah)*
wallpaper	**el empapelado** *(ehl ehm-pah-peh-'lah-doh)*

279

➤ Some evidence may be on pieces of clothing:

buckle	**la hebilla** *(lah eh-'bee-yah)*
button	**el botón** *(ehl boh-'tohn)*
collar	**el cuello** *(ehl 'kweh-yoh)*
cuff	**el puño** *(ehl 'poo-nyoh)*
embroidery	**el bordado** *(ehl bohr-'dah-doh)*
pocket	**el bolsillo** *(ehl bohl-'see-yoh)*
shoulder pad	**la hombrera** *(lah ohm-'breh-rah)*
sleeve	**la manga** *(lah 'mahn-gah)*
strap	**la correa** *(lah koh-'rreh-ah)*
zipper	**el cierre** *(ehl see-'eh-rreh)*

➤ Use **¿Cuál?** questions when you need specific details:

What's the size?	**¿Cuál es la talla?** *(kwahl ehs lah 'tah-yah)*
What's the shape?	**¿Cuál es la forma?** *(kwahl ehs lah 'fohr-mah)*
What's the amount?	**¿Cuál es la cantidad?** *(kwahl ehs lah kahn-tee-'dahd)*
What's the length?	**¿Cuál es el largo?** *(kwahl ehs ehl 'lahr-goh)*
What's the height?	**¿Cuál es la estatura?** *(kwahl ehs lah eh-stah-'too-rah)*
What's the weight?	**¿Cuál es el peso?** *(kwahl ehs ehl 'peh-soh)*
What's the width?	**¿Cuál es el ancho?** *(kwahl ehs ehl 'ahn-choh)*

DETECTIVE WORK
El trabajo del detective *(ehl trah-'bah-hoh dehl deh-tehk-'tee-veh)*

There's so much to say about the investigation. Does everyone who speaks Spanish understand what you are doing?

I'm looking for clues	**Estoy buscando indicios** *(eh-'stoh-ee boo-'skahn-doh een-'dee-see·ohs)*
We are offering a reward	**Estamos ofreciendo una recompensa** *(eh-'stah-mohs oh-freh-see-'ehn-doh 'oo-nah reh-kohm-'pehn-sah)*
I'm using (the)...	**Estoy usando...** *(eh-'stoh-ee oo-'sahn-doh...)*
bag	**la bolsa** *(lah 'bohl-sah)*
bottle	**la botella** *(lah boh-'teh-yah)*
brush	**el cepillo** *(ehl seh-'pee-yoh)*

glove	**el guante** (ehl 'gwahn-teh)
liquid	**el líquido** (ehl 'lee-kee-doh)
mask	**la máscara** (lah 'mah-skah-rah)
rag	**el trapo** (ehl 'trah-poh)
scissors	**las tijeras** (lahs tee-'heh-rahs)
sponge	**la esponja** (lah eh-'spohn-hah)
tweezers	**las pinzas** (lahs 'peen-sahs)

I am removing (the)...	**Estoy sacando...** (eh-'stoh-ee sah-'kahn-doh...)
It's made of...	**Está hecho de...** (eh-'stah 'eh-choh deh...)
brass	**el latón** (ehl lah-'tohn)
cardboard	**el cartón** (ehl kahr-'tohn)
cotton	**el algodón** (ehl ahl-goh-'dohn)
fabric	**la tela** (lah 'teh-lah)
iron	**el hierro** (ehl 'yeh-rroh)
leather	**el cuero** (ehl 'kweh-roh)
metal	**el metal** (ehl meh-'tahl)
plastic	**el plástico** (ehl 'plah-stee-koh)
rubber	**la goma** (lah 'goh-mah)
steel	**el acero** (ehl ah-'seh-roh)
stone	**la piedra** (lah pee-'eh-drah)
wood	**la madera** (lah mah-'deh-rah)
wool	**la lana** (lah 'lah-nah)

MEASUREMENTS
Las medidas (lahs meh-'dee-dahs)

Officials need to communicate precise information in order to avoid any confusion between legal agencies and the general public. When it comes to investigation and research, record all results in full detail. Let others know "how much" is actually involved:

It's...	**Es...** (ehs...)
a centimeter	**un centímetro** (oon sehn-'tee-meh-troh)
a dozen	**una docena** ('oo-nah doh-'seh-nah)
a foot	**un pie** (oon pee-'eh)
a gallon	**un galón** (oon gah-'lohn)
a gram	**un gramo** (oon 'grah-moh)
a kilogram	**un kilo** (oon 'kee-loh)
a liter	**un litro** (oon 'lee-troh)
a meter	**un metro** (oon 'meh-troh)
a mile	**una milla** ('oo-nah 'mee-yah)

a millimeter	**un milímetro** *(oon mee-'lee-meh-troh)*
a pair	**un par** *(oon pahr)*
a percent	**un por ciento** *(oon pohr see-'ehn-toh)*
a pinch	**una pizca** *('oo-nah 'pee-skah)*
a pint	**una pinta** *('oo-nah 'peen-tah)*
a portion	**una porción** *('oo-nah pohr-see-'ohn)*
a quart	**un cuarto** *(oon 'kwahr-toh)*
a quarter	**un cuarto** *(oon 'kwahr-toh)*
a tablespoon	**una cucharada** *('oo-nah koo-chah-'rah-dah)*
a teaspoon	**una cucharadita** *('oo-nah koo-chah-rah-'dee-tah)*
a third	**un tercero** *(oon tehr-'seh-roh)*
a yard	**una yarda** *('oo-nah 'yahr-dah)*
an inch	**una pulgada** *('oo-nah pool-'gah-dah)*
an ounce	**una onza** *('oo-nah 'ohn-sah)*

INFORMACIÓN PRIVADA

➤ These words indicate the amount as well:

double	**el doble** *(ehl 'doh-bleh)*
enough	**suficiente** *(soo-fee-see-'ehn-teh)*
half	**la mitad** *(lah mee-'tahd)*

➤ Get really specific!

corner	**la esquina** *(lah eh-'skee-nah)*
crooked	**torcido** *(tohr-'see-doh)*
dot	**el punto** *(ehl 'poon-toh)*
edge	**el borde** *(ehl 'bohr-deh)*
end	**la punta** *(lah 'poon-tah)*
front	**el frente** *(ehl 'frehn-teh)*
groove	**la ranura** *(lah rah-'noo-rah)*
line	**la línea** *(lah 'lee-neh-ah)*
long	**largo** *('lahr-goh)*
low	**bajo** *('bah-hoh)*
middle	**el medio** *(ehl 'meh-dee·oh)*
parallel	**paralelo** *(pah-rah-'leh-loh)*
short	**corto** *('kohr-toh)*
straight	**derecho** *(deh-'reh-choh)*
tall	**alto** *('ahl-toh)*

JUMBLE PUZZLE 2

oicntovc

racimlin

acrifsaildof

aodlienlrp

dsrescuretoa

rnoepsorii

postttuari

secshooops

eioartstrr

ssieaon

TEMAS CULTURALES

Do you know the metric system?

5/8 mi. = **un kilómetro** *(oon kee-'loh-meh-troh)*
2.2 lbs. = **un kilogramo** *(oon kee-loh-'grah-moh)*
32° F = **0°C** *('seh-roh 'grah-dohs 'sehl-see-oos)*

El informante dijo que ese sospechoso tiene diez kilos de heroína, pero, ¿dónde?

 REPASO

A. In Spanish,

name five common items of clothing

_____ _____ _____

_____ _____

name as many colors as you can

_____ _____ _____ _____ _____

_____ _____ _____ _____ _____

name three different kinds of firearms

_____ _____ _____

name three words that refer to sex crimes

_____ _____ _____

name three terms related to measurements

_____ _____ _____

B. Finish these statements. They are used throughout the investigation:

Fue arrestado por... *(fweh ah-rreh-'stah-doh pohr...)*_____

Estoy buscando... *(eh-'stoh-ee boo-'skahn-doh ...)*_____

Está hecho de... *(eh-'stah 'eh-choh deh...)*_____

Estoy usando... *(eh-'stoh-ee oo-'sahn-doh ...)*_____

la bala *(lah 'bah-lah)* _____

el cartucho *(ehl kahr-'too-choh)* _____

el arma *(ehl 'ahr-mah)* _____

el disparo *(ehl dee-'spah-roh)* _____

el asesinato *(ehl ah-seh-see-'nah-toh)* _____

ANSWERS

murder
gunshot
weapon
cartridge
C. bullet

THE BOOKING

La inscripción del arrestado *(lah een-skreep-see-'ohn dehl ah-rreh-'stah-doh)*

Walk through the procedures with the suspect in custody. Take your time, and ask an interpreter for assistance:

You are at _____	**Está en** _____ *('eh-stah ehn _____)*
Take your hands out of your pockets	**Saque las manos de los bolsillos** *('sah-keh lahs 'mah-nohs deh lohs bohl-'see-yohs)*
Stand here for your picture	**Párese aquí para su foto** *('pah-reh-seh ah-'kee 'pah-rah soo 'foh-toh)*
Hold this board up next to your chest with both hands	**Ponga esta tabla contra su pecho con las dos manos** *('pohn-gah 'ehs-tah 'tah-blah 'kohn-trah soo 'peh-choh kohn lahs dohs 'mah-nohs)*
Face in that direction	**Mire en aquella dirección** *('mee-reh ehn ah-'keh-yah dee-rehk-see-'ohn)*
Roll up your sleeves	**Remánguese** *(reh-'mahn-geh-seh)*
I'm going to take your fingerprints	**Voy a tomarle las huellas digitales** *('voh-ee ah toh-'mahr-leh lahs 'weh-yahs dee-hee-'tah-lehs)*
Give me your hand	**Déme la mano** *('deh-meh lah 'mah-noh)*
Hold your palms like this	**Sostenga las palmas así** *(soh-'stehn-gah lahs 'pahl-mahs ah-'see)*
Relax your fingers	**Relaje los dedos** *(reh-'lah-heh lohs 'deh-dohs)*
Clean yourself with this	**Límpiese con esto** *('leem-pee·eh-seh kohn 'eh-stoh)*

Sign here and keep this copy	**Firme aquí y guarde esta copia** *('feer-meh ah-'kee ee 'gwahr-deh 'eh-stah 'koh-pee·ah)*
You have the right to make three phone calls	**Tiene el derecho de hacer tres llamadas** *(tee-'eh-neh ehl deh-'reh-choh deh ah-'sehr trehs yah-'mah-dahs)*
Who are you calling?	**¿A quién está llamando?** *(ah kee-'ehn eh-'stah yah-'mahn-doh)*
Tell them where you are now	**Dígales dónde está ahora** *('dee-gah-lehs 'dohn-deh eh-'stah ah-'oh-rah)*
Do you want me to call?	**¿Quiere que yo llame?** *(kee-'eh-reh keh yoh 'yah-meh)*
You have been arrested for _____	**Ha sido arrestado por** _____ *(ah 'see-doh ah-rreh-'stah-doh pohr)*
Your bail is _____	**Su fianza es** _____ *(soo fee-'ahn-sah ehs)*
The bail bondsmen are in the phone book	**Los fiadores están en la guía telefónica** *(lohs fee-ah-'doh-rehs eh-'stahn ehn lah 'gee-ah teh-leh-'foh-nee-kah)*
Do you need a lawyer?	**¿Necesita un abogado?** _____ *(neh-seh-'see-tah oon ah-boh-'gah-doh)*

CUSTODY SEARCH

Rebuscar al arrestado *(reh-boo-'skahr ahl ah-rreh-'stah-doh)*

No one is incarcerated without a complete inspection. Start with the accessories:

Take off (the)...	**Quítese...** *('kee-teh-seh...)*
bandana	**el pañuelo** *(ehl pah-nyoo-'eh-loh)*
cap	**la gorra** *(lah 'goh-rrah)*
clothes	**la ropa** *(lah 'roh-pah)*
glasses	**los lentes** *(lohs 'lehn-tehs)*
hair net	**la red del pelo** *(lah rehd dehl 'peh-loh)*
hat	**el sombrero** *(ehl sohm-'breh-roh)*
jewelry	**las joyas** *(lahs 'hoh-yahs)*
watch	**el reloj** *(ehl reh-'loh)*
wig	**la peluca** *(lah peh-'loo-kah)*

Lift (your) ...	**Levante(n)...** *(leh-'vahn-teh[n])*
arms	**los brazos** *(lohs 'brah-sohs)*
tongue	**la lengua** *(lah lehn-gwah)*
testicles	**los testículos** *(lohs tehs-'tee-koo-lohs)*
breasts	**los senos** *(lohs 'seh-nohs)*
hair	**el cabello** *(ehl kah-'beh-yoh)*

Now combine commands, questions, and statements to complete the rest of the procedures:

What do you have in your hair?	**¿Qué tiene en el pelo?** *(keh tee-'eh-neh ehn ehl 'peh-loh)*
Open your mouth and lift your tongue	**Abra la boca y levante la lengua** *('ah-brah lah 'boh-kah ee leh-'vahn-teh lah 'lehn-gwah)*
Put the chewing gum in here	**Ponga el chicle aquí** *('pohn-gah ehl 'chee-kleh ah-'kee)*
Lift your arms	**Levante los brazos** *(leh-'vahn-teh lohs 'brah-sohs)*
Bend over and spread your buttocks	**Dóblese y separe las nalgas con los dedos** *('doh-bleh-seh ee seh-'pah-reh lahs 'nahl-gahs kohn lohs 'deh-dohs)*
I will give you a new tampon	**Voy a darle un tampón nuevo** *('voh-ee ah 'dahr-leh oon tahm-'pohn noo-'eh-voh)*
Show me the bottoms of your feet	**Muéstreme las plantas de los pies** *('mweh-streh-meh lahs 'plahn-tahs deh lohs pee-'ehs)*
You may get dressed now	**Puede vestirse ahora** *('pweh-deh veh-'steer-seh ah-'oh-rah)*
They will be kept with your property	**Serán guardados con sus pertenencias** *('seh-rahn gwahr-'dah-dohs kohn soos pehr-teh-'nehn-see·ahs)*

TEMAS CULTURALES

You're going to hear plenty of curses from the people you have to deal with. It will be very helpful to befriend a Spanish speaker in your area, and discuss the foul side of foreign language learning.

PRISONER RELEASE
La liberación del preso *(lah lee-beh-rah-see-'ohn dehl 'preh-soh)*

Send folks home with the phrases below:

Sign here	**Firme aquí** *('feer-meh ah-'kee)*
This form shows that you have received your property	**Este formulario indica que usted ha recibido sus pertenencias** *('eh-steh fohr-moo-'lah-ree·oh een-'dee-kah keh oo-'stehd ah reh-see-'bee-doh soos pehr-teh-'nehn-see·ahs)*

It explains why you were arrested	**Explica por qué usted fue arestado** *(ehks-'plee-kah pohr keh oo-'stehd fue ah-rreh-'stah-doh)*
This is the date you are to appear in court	**Esta es la fecha para presentarse en la corte** *('eh-stah ehs lah 'feh-chah 'pah-rah preh-sehn-'tahr-seh ehn lah 'kohr-teh)*
This is where your car is	**Aquí es dónde está su carro** *(ah-'kee ehs 'dohn-deh eh-'stah soo 'kah-rroh)*
Do you have all your property?	**¿Tiene usted todas sus pertenencias?** *(tee-'eh-neh oo-'stehd 'toh-dahs soos pehr-teh-'nehn-see·ahs)*
You may leave through that door	**Puede irse por esa puerta** *('pweh-deh 'eer-seh pohr 'eh-sah 'pwehr-tah)*
This is your booking slip	**Este es el documento de su proceso** *('eh-steh ehs ehl doh-koo-'mehn-toh deh soo proh-'seh-soh)*
This is your booking number	**Este es el número de su proceso** *('eh-steh ehs ehl 'noo-meh-roh deh soo proh-'seh-soh)*
This is the name of your probation officer	**Este es el nombre del oficial que vigilará su libertad provisional** *('eh-steh ehs ehl 'nohm-breh dehl oh-fee-see-'ahl keh vee-hee-lah-'rah soo lee-behr-'tahd proh-vee-see·oh-'nahl)*
If you don't go to court, a warrant will be issued for your arrest.	**Si usted no se presenta en la corte, se pedirá una orden de arresto.** *(see oos-'tehd noh seh preh-'sehn-tah ehn lah 'kohr-teh seh peh-dee-'rah 'oo-nah 'ohr-dehn deh ah-'rrehs-toh)*

INFORMACIÓN PRIVADA

➤ Guide them through the fingerprinting process:

Give me the...	**Deme...** *('deh-meh...)*
thumb	**el dedo pulgar** *(ehl 'deh-doh pool-'gahr)*
index finger	**el dedo índice** *(ehl 'deh-doh 'een-dee-seh)*
right hand	**la mano derecha** *(lah 'mah-noh deh-'reh-chah)*
left hand	**la mano izquierda** *(lah 'mah-noh ees-kee-'ehr-dah)*
other one	**el otro** *(ehl 'oh-troh)*

➤ Have you ever interrogated a suspect in Spanish?

...did you do it?	**¿...lo hizo?** *(...loh 'ee-soh)*
How	**Cómo** *('koh-moh)*
Where	**Dónde** *('dohn-deh)*
When	**Cuándo** *('kwahn-doh)*

| Why | **Por qué** *(pohr keh)* |
| With whom | **Con quién** *(kohn kee-'ehn)* |

➤ Use Spanish to talk about the prison:

cell	**la celda** *(lah 'sehl-dah)*
fugitive	**el fugitivo** *(ehl foo-hee-'tee-voh)*
guard	**el guardia** *(ehl 'gwahr-dee·ah)*
inmate	**el preso** *(ehl 'preh-soh)*
prison	**la prisión** *(lah pree-see-'ohn)*
prisoner	**el prisionero** *(ehl pree-see·oh-'neh-roh)*
trustee	**el prisionero con privilegios** *(ehl pree-see-oh-'neh-roh kohn pree-vee-'leh-hee·ohs)*
visiting room	**el salón de visitantes** *(ehl sah-'lohn deh vee-see-'tahn-tehs)*
warden	**el carcelero** *(ehl kahr-seh-'leh-roh)*

ACCIÓN

The verbs below are usually needed at the scene of a serious crime. How can they be changed to make appropriate questions and answers?

to abandon	**abandonar** *(ah-bahn-doh-'nahr)*	**¿Abandonó a su hijo?** *(ah-bahn-doh-'noh ah soo 'ee-hoh)*
to accuse	**acusar** *(ah-koo-'sahr)*	_____
to bet	**apostar** *(ah-poh-'stahr)*	_____
to catch	**apresar** *(ah-preh-'sahr)*	_____
to chase	**perseguir** *(pehr-seh-'geer)*	_____
to detain	**detener** *(deh-teh-'nehr)*	_____
to escape	**escapar** *(eh-skah-'pahr)*	_____
to fight	**pelear** *(peh-leh-'ahr)*	_____
to fornicate	**fornicar** *(fohr-nee-'kahr)*	_____
to incarcerate	**encarcelar** *(ehn-kahr-seh-'lahr)*	_____
to knock down	**tumbar** *(toom-'bahr)*	_____
to lie	**mentir** *(mehn-'teer)*	_____
to murder	**matar** *(mah-'tahr)*	_____
to play	**jugar** *(hoo-'gahr)*	_____
to pray	**rezar** *(reh-'sahr)*	_____
to release	**liberar** *(lee-beh-'rahr)*	_____

to seize	**apresar** *(ah-preh-'sahr)*	_____
to shoot	**disparar** *(dee-spah-'rahr)*	_____
to stab	**apuñalar** *(ah-poo-nyah-'lahr)*	_____
to threaten	**amenazar** *(ah-meh-nah-'sahr)*	_____
to weigh	**pesar** *(peh-'sahr)*	_____
to wound	**herir** *(eh-'reer)*	_____
to yell	**gritar** *(gree-'tahr)*	_____

Prisionero
con
privilegios

GRANDES HABILIDADES

Check out the structure of this important question:

What have you done?   **¿Qué ha hecho?** *(keh ah 'eh-choh)*

Study this powerful two-part verb pattern. It's extremely important in law enforcement conversations because it refers to actions that have already taken place. It's a "past action" pattern used frequently in everyday communication, so pay close attention to each example.

The first part consists of forms of the verb **haber.** The second part consists of the past participle of the *Action Word*. Both parts must be used together.

I've	**(He)**	gone	**(ido)** *('ee-doh)*
		eaten	**(comido)** *(koh-'mee-doh)*
You've/She's/He's	**(Ha)**	fought	**(peleado)** *(peh-leh-'ah-doh)*
		played	**(jugado)** *(hoo-'gah-doh)*
They've/You've (pl.)	**(Han)**	worked	**(trabajado)** *(trah-bah-'hah-doh)*
		driven	**(manejado)** *(mah-neh-'hah-doh)*

We've	(**Hemos**) called (**llamado**) *(yah-'mah-doh)*
I've called many times	**He llamado muchas veces** *(eh yah-'mah-doh 'moo-chahs 'veh-sehs)*
She's driven a truck	**Ella ha manejado un camión** *('eh-yah ah mah-neh-'hah-doh oon kah-mee-'ohn)*
They've gone home	**Han ido a la casa** *(ahn 'ee-doh ah 'kah-sah)*
We've worked at night	**Hemos trabajado en la noche** *('eh-mohs trah-bah-'hah-doh ehn lah 'noh-cheh)*

Now memorize as many past participles as possible!

arrested	**arrestado**	**Han arrestado a muchos latinos** *(ahn ah-rreh-'stah-doh ah 'moo-chohs lah-'tee-nohs)*
done	**hecho**	**¿Qué ha hecho?** *(keh ah-'eh-choh)*
gone	**ido**	**¿Adónde ha ido?** *(ah-'dohn-deh ah 'ee-doh)*
heard	**oído**	**¿Dónde he oído esto?** *('dohn-deh oh-'ee-doh 'eh-stoh)*
killed	**matado**	**Yo sé que ha matado antes** *(yoh seh keh ah mah-'tah-doh 'ahn-tehs)*
seen	**visto**	**¿Cuándo lo ha visto?** *('kwahn-doh loh ah 'vee-stoh)*
spoken	**hablado**	**He hablado con él** *(eh ah-'blah-doh kohn ehl)*
thought	**pensado**	**No hemos pensado en eso** *(noh 'eh-mohs pehn-'sah-doh ehn 'eh-soh)*

REPASO

A. Conjugate these *Action Words* according to the following five time references. Follow this example:

Manejar *(mah-neh-'hahr)*

Ahora <u>estoy manejando</u> *(ah-'oh-rah eh-'stoh-ee mah-neh-'hahn-doh)*
Hoy <u>manejo</u> *('oh-ee mah-'neh-hoh)*
Mañana <u>manejaré</u> *(mah-'nyah-nah mah-neh-hah-'reh)*
Ayer <u>manejé</u> *(ah-'yehr mah-neh-'heh)*
Antes <u>he manejado</u> *('ahn-tehs eh mah-neh-'hah-doh)*

291

Trabajar *(trah-bah-'hahr)*

_____

_____

_____

_____

_____

Investigar *(een-veh-stee-'gahr)*

_____

_____

_____

_____

_____

ANSWERS

A. estoy trabajando   estoy investigando

trabajo   investigo

trabajaré   investigaré

trabajé   investigué

he trabajado   he investigado

CHAPTER SEVEN
Capítulo Siete
(kah-'pee-too-loh see-'eh-teh)

TO SERVE AND PROTECT

Para servir y proteger

('pah-rah sehr-'veer ee proh-teh-'hehr)

PREPARE YOURSELF
Prepárese *(preh-'pah-reh-seh)*

To know the Spanish names of your uniform and equipment will not only be useful, but it will also boost your self-confidence.

This is (the)…	**Esto es...** *('eh-stoh ehs...)*
badge	**el emblema** *(ehl ehm-'bleh-mah)*
billy club	**el garrote** *(ehl gah-'rroh-teh)*
bullet	**la bala** *(lah 'bah-lah)*
bullet-proof vest	**el chaleco a prueba de bala** *(ehl chah-'leh-koh ah proo-'eh-bah deh 'bah-lah)*
bullhorn	**el altavoz** *(ehl ahl-tah-'vohs)*
cartridge belt	**la cartuchera** *(lah kahr-too-'cheh-rah)*
cartridge	**el cartucho** *(ehl kahr-'too-choh)*
computer	**la computadora** *(lah kohm-poo-tah-'doh-rah)*
equipment belt	**la correa de equipaje** *(lah koh-'rreh-ah deh eh-kee-'pah-heh)*
flashlight	**la linterna** *(lah leen-'tehr-nah)*
gas mask	**la máscara de gas** *(lah 'mah-skah-rah deh gahs)*
handcuff	**la esposa** *(lah eh-'spoh-sah)*
helmet	**el casco** *(ehl 'kah-skoh)*
holster	**la funda de revólver** *(lah 'foon-dah deh reh-'vohl-vehr)*
radio transmitter	**el radiotransmisor** *(ehl rah-dee·oh-trahns-mee-'sohr)*
revolver	**el revólver** *(ehl reh-'vohl-vehr)*
shield	**el escudo** *(ehl eh-'skoo-doh)*
siren	**la sirena** *(lah see-'reh-nah)*
spray gun	**la rociadora** *(lah roh-see·ah-'doh-rah)*
tazer gun	**el tazer** *(ehl tah-'sehr)*
tear gas	**el gas lacrimógeno** *(ehl gahs lah-kree-'moh-heh-noh)*
uniform	**el uniforme** *(ehl oo-nee-'fohr-meh)*
whistle	**el silbato** *(ehl seel-'bah-toh)*

CALL THE POLICE!

¡Llame la policía! *('yah-meh lah poh-lee-'see-ah)*

Problems in the home: lost children, abuse, and domestic violence are always common themes, and officers often find themselves caught up in cases involving very *sensitive* issues.

When your Spanish skills are needed, use good judgment. Serious problems could result if complex messages are communicated inaccurately, so be on the safe side—when situations get a little touchy, ask for a qualified bilingual translator and interpreter to lend you a hand.

Here are just a few of the many cases where more advanced skills in Spanish will probably be required:

child abuse	**el abuso de menores** *(ehl ah-'boo-soh deh meh-'noh-rehs)*
child negligence	**el descuido de menores** *(ehl dehs-'kwee-doh deh meh-'noh-rehs)*
domestic violence	**la violencia doméstica** *(lah vee·oh-'lehn-see·ah doh-'meh-stee-kah)*
family dispute	**el argumento en la famila** *(ehl ahr-goo-'mehn-toh ehn lah fah-'mee-lee·ah)*
homelessness	**la gente desamparada** *(lah 'hehn-teh dehs-ahm-pah-'rah-dah)*
incest	**el incesto** *(ehl een-'seh-stoh)*
juvenile delinquency	**la delicuencia juvenil** *(lah deh-leen-'kwehn-see·ah hoo-veh-'neel)*
kidnapping	**el secuestro** *(ehl seh-'kweh-stroh)*
lost child	**el niño desaparecido** *(ehl 'nee-nyoh dehs-ah-pah-reh-'see-doh)*
rape	**la violación** *(lah vee-oh-lah-see-'ohn)*
run-away child	**el niño fugitivo** *(ehl 'nee-nyoh foo-hee-'tee-voh)*
sexual assault	**el asalto sexual** *(ehl ah-'sahl-toh sehk-soo-'ahl)*
sexual harassment	**el acosamiento sexual** *(ehl ah-koh-sah-mee-'ehn-toh sehk-soo-'ahl)*
spousal abuse	**el abuso conyugal** *(ehl ah-'boo-soh kohn-yoo-'gahl)*

Can you think of any more?

_____

_____

_____

_____

Yo voy a trabajar aquí el resto de mi vida.

¡Yo he trabajado aquí toda mi vida!

INFORMACIÓN PRIVADA

➤ Although you're already aware of the names for family members in Spanish, you still lack all of the other terms that refer to people and relationships. Come up with sentences for all of these new words:

adolescent	**el adolescente** (ehl ah-doh-leh-'sehn-teh)
adopted child	**el niño adoptado** (ehl 'nee-nyoh ah-dohp-'tah-doh)
adoption	**la adopción** (lah ah-dohp-see-'ohn)
adult	**el adulto** (ehl ah-'dool-toh)
bachelor	**el soltero** (ehl sohl-'teh-roh)
bride	**la novia** (lah 'noh-vee·ah)
bridegroom	**el novio** (ehl 'noh-vee·oh)
childhood	**la niñez** (lah nee-'nyehs)
dependent	**el dependiente** (ehl deh-pehn-dee-'ehn-teh)
divorced person	**el divorciado** (ehl dee-vohr-see-'ah-doh)
fiancee	**el prometido** (ehl proh-meh-'tee-doh)
finance	**la prometida** (lah proh-meh-'tee-dah)
foster child	**el ahijado** (ehl ah-ee-'hah-doh)
guardian	**el guardián** (ehl gwahr-dee-'ahn)

296

lover	**el amante** *(ehl ah-'mahn-teh)*
marriage	**el matrimonio** *(ehl mah-tree-'moh-nee·oh)*
married	**el casado** *(ehl kah-'sah-doh)*
newlywed	**el recién casado** *(ehl reh-see-'ehn kah-'sah-doh)*
old age	**la vejez** *(lah veh-'hehs)*
older child	**el hijo mayor** *(ehl 'ee-hoh mah-'yohr)*
orphan	**el huérfano** *(ehl 'wehr-fah-noh)*
parenthood	**la paternidad** *(lah pah-tehr-nee-'dahd)*
puberty	**la pubertad** *(lah poo-behr-'tahd)*
twin	**el gemelo** *(ehl heh-'meh-loh)*
widow	**la viuda** *(lah vee-'oo-dah)*
widower	**el viudo** *(ehl vee-'oo-doh)*
younger child	**el hijo menor** *(ehl 'ee-hoh meh-'nohr)*
youth	**la juventud** *(lah hoo-vehn-'tood)*

TEMAS CULTURALES

Family crisis seems to draw people closer to their religious faith. Most of Latin America is Roman Catholic, so you may notice the religious influence during your association with some Hispanics. Using God (**Dios**) or prayers (**los rezos,** *lohs 'reh-sohs*) in conversation, attending daily Mass (**la misa,** *lah 'mee-sah*) or observing Catholic traditions are common traits among Hispanics. Remember that respect and sensitivity are always in demand when topics center around such beliefs.

DOMESTIC VIOLENCE
La violencia doméstica *(lah vee-oh-'lehn-see·ah doh-'meh-stee-kah)*

Because the majority of violent crimes committed take place in the victim's home, most law enforcement employees receive extensive training in handling crimes related to family disputes. Get things started using some of the lines below. Most of the words you have seen before:

Is this the correct address?	**¿Es correcta la dirección?** *(ehs koh-'rrehk-tah lah dee-rehk-see-'ohn)*
Which one of you called?	**¿Cuál de ustedes llamó?** *(kwahl deh oo-'steh-dehs yah-'moh)*

Is anyone hurt?	**¿Hay alguien herido?** *('ah·ee 'ahl-gee·ehn eh-'ree-doh)*
Do you need help?	**¿Necesita ayuda?** *(neh-seh-'see-tah ah-'yoo-dah)*
What happened?	**¿Qué pasó?** *(keh pah-'soh)*
Who started it?	**¿Quién lo empezó?** *(kee-'ehn loh ehm-peh-'soh)*
What is the problem?	**¿Cuál es el problema?** *(kwahl ehs ehl proh-'bleh-mah)*
Is he a violent person?	**¿Es él una persona violenta?** *(ehs ehl 'oo-nah pehr-'soh-nah vee-oh-'lehn-tah)*
Who is inside?	**¿Quién está adentro?** *(kee-'ehn eh-'stah ah-'dehn-troh)*
Is he still here?	**¿Está él aquí todavía?** *(eh-'stah ehl ah-'kee toh-dah-'vee-ah)*
What's your relation?	**¿Cómo está relacionado con él (ella)?** *('koh-moh eh-'stah reh-lah-see-oh-'nah-doh kohn ehl) ('eh-yah)*
Is he drunk or on drugs?	**¿Está borracho o drogado?** *(eh-'stah boh-'rrah-choh oh droh-'gah-doh)*
Are there any firearms inside?	**¿Hay armas de fuego adentro?** *('ah·ee 'ahr-mahs deh 'fweh-goh ah-'dehn-troh)*
What did he do to you?	**¿Qué le hizo a usted?** *(keh leh 'ee-soh ah oo-'stehd)*
Are there any children?	**¿Hay niños?** *('ah·ee 'nee-nyohs)*
Who was involved?	**¿Quién estaba envuelto?** *(kee-'ehn eh-'stah-bah ehn-'vwehl-toh)*
Where is everyone?	**¿Dónde está todo el mundo?** *('dohn-deh eh-'stah 'toh-doh ehl 'moon-doh)*
When...?	**¿Cuándo...** *('kwahn-doh...)*
did he arrive	**llegó?** *(yeh-'goh)*
did he leave	**salió?** *(sah-lee-'oh)*
did he return	**regresó?** *(reh-greh-'soh)*

Now, get a little background information:

Has this happened before?	**¿Ha pasado antes esto?** *(ah pah-'sah-doh 'ahn-tehs 'eh-stoh)*
Have you called before?	**¿Ha llamado antes?** *(ah yah-'mah-doh 'ahn-tehs)*
How often?	**¿Cuán a menudo?** *(kwahn ah meh-'noo-doh)*
How many times?	**¿Cuántas veces?** *('kwahn-tahs 'veh-sehs)*
Are you...?	**¿Están...** *(eh-'stahn...)*
living together	**viviendo juntos?** *(vee-vee-'ehn-doh 'hoon-tohs)*
married	**casados?** *(kah-'sah-dohs)*
divorced	**divorciados?** *(dee-vohr-see-'ah-dohs)*
separated	**separados?** *(seh-pah-'rah-dohs)*
alone	**solos?** *('soh-lohs)*

Keep asking questions!

Do you want...?	**¿Quiere...** *(kee-'eh-reh...)*
a court order	**una orden del tribunal?** *('oo-nah 'ohr-dehn dehl tree-boo-'nahl)*
to press charges	**hacerle cargos?** *(ah-'sehr-leh 'kahr-gohs)*
me to arrest him	**que le arreste?** *(keh leh ah-'rreh-steh)*

¡A MIS ÓRDENES!

You can't live without these *Command Words*!

Don't yell	**No grite** *(noh 'gree-teh)*
Calm down	**Cálmese** *('kahl-meh-seh)*
Come here	**Venga acá** *('vehn-gah ah-'kah)*
Call this number	**Llame ese número** *('yah-meh 'eh-seh 'noo-meh-roh)*
Put that down	**Baje eso** *('bah-heh 'eh-soh)*

Combine your skills to talk at a more personal level:

Let's go to the other room	**Vamos al otro cuarto** *('vah-mohs ahl 'oh-troh 'kwahr-toh)*
Will you be OK if I leave?	**¿Estará bien si me voy?** *(eh-stah-'rah 'bee·ehn see meh-'voh-ee)*
Who's going to accompany you?	**¿Quién lo va a acompañar?** *(kee-'ehn loh vah ah ah-kohm-pah-'nyahr)*
Can I come back later?	**¿Puedo regresar más tarde?** *('pweh-doh reh-greh-'sahr mahs 'tahr-deh)*
Do you have a place to go?	**¿Tiene un lugar adónde ir?** *(tee-'eh-neh oon loo-'gahr ah-'dohn-deh eer)*
What do you want me to do?	**¿Qué quiere que haga?** *(keh kee-'eh-reh keh 'ah-gah)*

299

Do you have your own place?	**¿Tiene su propio sitio?** *(tee-'eh-neh soo 'proh-pee·oh 'see-tee·oh)*
Can you...?	**¿Puede...** *('pweh-deh...)*
go to another house	**ir a otra casa?** *(eer ah 'oh-trah 'kah-sah)*
resolve this problem	**resolver este problema?** *(reh-sohl-'vehr 'eh-steh proh-'bleh-mah)*
make up	**hacer las paces?** *(ah-'sehr lahs 'pah-sehs)*
call this agency	**llamar a esta agencia?** *(yah-'mahr ah 'eh-stah ah-'hehn-see·ah)*
wait until tomorrow	**esperar hasta mañana?** *(eh-speh-'rahr 'ah-stah mah-'nyah-nah)*
separate for awhile	**separarse por un rato?** *(seh-pah-'rahr-seh pohr oon 'rah-toh)*
move	**mudarse?** *(moo-'dahr-seh)*
think about the children	**pensar en los niños?** *(pehn-'sahr ehn lohs 'nee-nyohs)*

Pick out any key word or phrase that will help you in the field:

It is criminal conduct	**Es conducta criminal** *(ehs kohn-'dook-tah kree-mee-'nahl)*
It will not be tolerated	**No será tolerada** *(noh seh-'rah toh-leh-'rah-dah)*
This is a criminal complaint	**Es una denuncia criminal** *(ehs 'oo-nah deh-'noon-see·ah kree-mee-'nahl)*
It is a civil lawsuit	**Es una demanda civil** *(ehs 'oo-nah deh-'mahn-dah see-'veel)*
You need a restraining order	**Necesita una orden de restricción** *(neh-seh-'see-tah 'oo-nah 'ohr-dehn deh reh-streek-see-'ohn)*
You need legal protection	**Necesita protección legal** *(neh-seh-'see-tah proh-tehk-see-'ohn leh-'gahl)*
We will take necessary measures	**Tomaremos las medidas necesarias** *(toh-mah-'reh-mohs lahs meh-'dee-dahs neh-seh-'sah-ree·ahs)*

THE CHILDREN
Los niños *(lohs 'nee-nyohs)*

To discuss matters concerning children, you'll need a variety of basic terms and phrases. As you pronounce each of the following baby words, envision a scenario where you'll be using it:

Where's the...?	**¿Dónde está...** *('dohn-deh eh-'stah...)*
ball	**la pelota?** *(lah peh-'loh-tah)*
balloon	**el globo?** *(ehl 'gloh-boh)*

bassinet	**la cuna portátil?** *(lah 'koo-nah pohr-'tah-teel)*
blanket	**la cobija?** *(lah koh-'bee-hah)*
cartoon	**el dibujo animado?** *(ehl dee-'boo-hoh ah-nee-'mah-doh)*
costume	**el disfraz?** *(ehl dees-'frahs)*
crayon	**el lápiz de color?** *(ehl 'lah-pees deh koh-'lohr)*
crib	**la cuna?** *(lah 'koo-nah)*
diaper	**el pañal?** *(ehl pah-'nyahl)*
doll	**la muñeca?** *(lah moo-'nyeh-kah)*
game	**el juego?** *(ehl 'hweh-goh)*
infant car seat	**el asiento para infantes?** *(ehl ah-see-'ehn-toh 'pah-rah een-'fahn-tehs)*
joke	**el chiste?** *(ehl 'chee-steh)*
kite	**la cometa?** *(lah koh-'meh-tah)*
marble	**la canica?** *(lah kah-'nee-kah)*
pacifier	**el chupete?** *(ehl choo-'peh-teh)*
puppet	**el títere?** *(ehl 'tee-teh-reh)*
puzzle	**el rompecabezas?** *(ehl rohm-peh-kah-'beh-sahs)*
skateboard	**la patineta?** *(lah pah-tee-'neh-tah)*
skate	**el patín?** *(ehl pah-'teen)*
sled	**el trineo?** *(ehl tree-'neh-oh)*
slide	**el resbalador?** *(ehl rehs-bah-lah-'dohr)*
song	**la canción?** *(lah kahn-see-'ohn)*
story	**el cuento?** *(ehl 'kwehn-toh)*
stroller	**el cochecillo?** *(ehl koh-cheh-'see-yoh)*
swing	**el columpio?** *(ehl koh-'loom-pee·oh)*
top	**el trompo?** *(ehl 'trohm-poh)*
toy	**el juguete?** *(ehl hoo-'geh-teh)*
trick	**el truco?** *(ehl 'troo-koh)*
tricycle	**el triciclo?** *(ehl tree-'see-kloh)*
wagon	**el carretón?** *(ehl kah-rreh-'tohn)*

SPORTS
Los deportes *(lohs deh-'pohr-tehs)*

Kids love sports, too! Are you saying "hi" at all the parks and playgrounds? Notice that these words sound a lot like English!

They want to play...	**Quieren jugar...** *(kee-'eh-rehn hoo-'gahr...)*
baseball	**el béisbol** *(ehl 'beh·ees-bohl)*
basketball	**el básquetbol** *(ehl 'bahs-keht-bohl)*
bowling	**el boliche** *(ehl boh-'lee-cheh)*

boxing	**el boxeo** *(ehl bohk-'seh-oh)*
football	**el fútbol americano** *(ehl 'foot-bohl ah-meh-ree-'kah-noh)*
golf	**el golf** *(ehl gohlf)*
hockey	**el hockey** *(ehl 'hoh-kee)*
lacrosse	**el lacrosse** *(ehl lah-'krohs)*
soccer	**el fútbol** *(ehl 'foot-bohl)*
tennis	**el tenis** *(ehl 'teh-nees)*
volleyball	**el vóleibol** *(ehl 'voh-leh·ee-bohl)*
They go to the...	**Van a...** *(vahn ah...)*
court	**la cancha** *(lah 'kahn-chah)*
field	**el campo** *(ehl 'kahm-poh)*
golf course	**el campo de golf** *(ehl 'kahm-poh deh gohlf)*
gymnasium	**el gimnasio** *(ehl heem-'nah-see·oh)*
ice rink	**la pista de patinaje** *(lah 'pee-stah deh pah-tee-'nah-heh)*
match	**el partido** *(ehl pahr-'tee-doh)*
playground	**el campo de recreo** *(ehl 'kahm-poh deh reh-'kreh-oh)*
pool	**la piscina** *(lah pee-'see-nah)*
practice	**la práctica** *(lah 'prahk-tee-kah)*
stadium	**el estadio** *(ehl eh-'stah-dee·oh)*

INFORMACIÓN PRIVADA

➤ Here are two more concerns that involve young people:

Lost Child	**El niño perdido** *(ehl 'nee-nyoh pehr-'dee-doh)*
How did you get here?	**¿Cómo llegaste por aquí?** *('koh-moh yeh-'gahs-teh pohr ah-'kee)*
What is near where you live?	**¿Qué hay cerca de donde vives?** *(keh 'ah-ee 'sehr-kah deh 'dohn-deh 'vee-vehs)*
What are your parents' names?	**¿Cuáles son los nombres de tus padres?** *('kwah-lehs sohn lohs 'nohm-brehs deh toos 'pah-drehs)*
Loud Party	**La fiesta ruidosa** *(lah fee-'ehs-tah roo-ee-'doh-sah)*
You cannot make noise after _____	**No puede hacer ruido después de las _____** *(noh 'pweh-deh ah-'sehr roo-'ee-doh dehs-'pwehs deh lahs _____)*

| There are too many people at the party | **Hay demasiada gente en la fiesta** *('ah-ee deh-mah-see-'ah-dah 'hehn-teh ehn lah fee-'ehs-tah)* |
| Please lower the volume | **Baje el volumen, por favor.** *('bah-heh ehl voh-'loo-mehn pohr fah-'vohr)* |

TEMAS CULTURALES

Be aware that *Action Words* change a bit when you chat with children. Hispanics use the "informal" or **tú** *(too)* form:

Come here	**Ven acá** *(vehn ah-'kah)*
Don't be afraid	**No tengas miedo** *(noh 'tehn-gahs mee-'eh-doh)*
Don't cry	**No llores** *(noh 'yoh-rehs)*
Give me a hug	**Dame un abrazo** *('dah-meh oon ah-'brah-soh)*
It's for you	**Es para ti** *(ehs 'pah-rah tee)*

When kids are around, communicate with brief, direct statements. Read over the following sentence patterns and figure out ways to substitute phrases with other key vocabulary. Notice the "informal" approach:

You have to...	**Tienes que...** *(tee-'eh-nehs keh...)*
You need to...	**Necesitas...** *(neh-seh-'see-tahs...)*
You should...	**Debes...** *('deh-behs...)*
ask for permission	**pedir permiso** *(peh-'deer pehr-'mee-soh)*
be careful	**tener cuidado** *(te-'nehr kwee-'dah-doh)*
behave	**portarte bien** *(pohr-'tahr-teh bee-'ehn)*
calm down	**calmarte** *(kahl-'mahr-teh)*
clean up the mess	**limpiar la basura** *(leem-pee-'ahr lah bah-'soo-rah)*
cross at the corner	**cruzar en la esquina** *(kroo-'sahr ehn lah eh-'skee-nah)*
go home	**ir a casa** *(eer ah 'kah-sah)*
obey the rules	**obedecer las reglas** *(oh-beh-deh-'sehr lahs 'reh-glahs)*
rest	**descansar** *(dehs-kahn-'sahr)*
stay here	**quedarte aquí** *(keh-'dahr-teh ah-'kee)*
stop fighting	**dejar de pelear** *(deh-'hahr deh peh-leh-'ahr)*
tell me	**decirme** *(deh-'seer-meh)*
tell our parents	**decirle a los padres** *(deh-'seer-leh ah lohs 'pah-drehs)*
try	**tratar** *(trah-'tahr)*
wear a helmet	**llevar el casco** *(yeh-'vahr ehl 'kah-skoh)*

| wait for the light | **esperar la luz** *(eh-speh-'rahr lah loos)* |
| walk | **caminar** *(kah-mee-'nahr)* |

You cannot...	**No puedes...** *(noh 'pweh-dehs...)*
enter	**entrar** *(ehn-'trahr)*
fight	**pelear** *(peh-leh-'ahr)*
hit or kick	**golpear o patear** *(gohl-peh-'ahr oh pah-teh-'ahr)*
play with that	**jugar con eso** *(hoo-'gahr kohn 'eh-soh)*
run in the street	**correr en la calle** *(koh-'rrehr ehn lah 'kah-yeh)*
say bad words	**decir groserías** *(deh-'seer groh-seh-'ree-ahs)*
steal	**robar** *(roh-'bahr)*
throw rocks	**tirar piedras** *(tee-'rahr pee-'eh-drahs)*
write on the walls	**escribir en las paredes** *(eh-skree-'beer ehn lahs pah-'reh-dehs)*
yell	**gritar** *(gree-'tahr)*

Working with children usually involves plenty of activity. Add this group of verbs to your growing list of Spanish *Action Words*:

to cry	**llorar** *(yoh-'rahr)*
to feed	**alimentar** *(ah-lee-mehn-'tahr)*
to frighten	**asustar** *(ah-soo-'stahr)*
to grow	**crecer** *(kreh-'sehr)*
to hug	**abrazar** *(ah-brah-'sahr)*
to kiss	**besar** *(beh-'sahr)*
to laugh	**reír** *(reh-'eer)*
to love	**querer** *(keh-'rehr)*
to play	**jugar** *(hoo-'gahr)*
to provide	**proveer** *(proh-veh-'ehr)*
to punish	**castigar** *(kah-stee-'gahr)*
to scold	**regañar** *(reh-gah-'nyahr)*

A. In Spanish,

...name three pieces of equipment familiar to most police officers.

_____ _____ _____

...name three particularly sensitive areas of criminal activity that often require the help of a fluent bilingual interpreter.

_____ _____ _____

B. Finish these one-liners that are directed at the children:

Tienes que... *(tee-'eh-nehs keh...)*_____

No puedes... *(noh 'pweh-dehs...)*_____

Necesitas... *(neh-seh-'see-tahs...)*_____

C. What's this conversation all about? Translate:

¿Cuál es el problema? *(kwahl ehs ehl proh-'bleh-mah)*

_____

¿Ha llamado antes? *(ah yah-'mah-doh 'ahn-tehs)*

_____

¿Quiere que lo arreste? *(kee-'eh-reh keh loh ah-'rreh-steh)*

_____

D. Connect each vocabulary item with its translation:

doll	el fútbol *(ehl 'foot-bohl)*
game	el juego *(ehl 'hweh-goh)*
song	el baile *(ehl 'bah·ee-leh)*
toy	la canción *(lah kahn-see-'ohn)*
soccer	la muñeca *(lah moo-'nyeh-kah)*
dancing	el juguete *(ehl hoo-'geh-teh)*

THE SCHOOL

La escuela *(lah eh-skweh-lah)*

Troubled kids everywhere get a head start in crime at a very early age. To learn more about Spanish in a school environment, hang around a campus and listen for the words below:

absent	**ausente** *(ow-'sehn-teh)*	**No puede estar ausente** *(noh 'pweh-deh eh-'stahr ow-'sehn-teh)*
academic grade	**la calificación** *(lah kah-lee-fee-kah-see-'ohn)*	**Tiene buenas calificaciones** *(tee-'eh-neh 'bweh-nahs kah-lee-fee-kah-see-'oh-nehs)*
attendance	**la asistencia** *(lah ah-sees-'tehn-see·ah)*	**Su asistencia es importante** *(soo ah-sees-'tehn-see·ah ehs eem-pohr-'tahn-teh)*
class	**la clase** *(lah 'klah-seh)*	**Tiene una clase grande** *(tee-'eh-neh 'oo-nah 'klah-seh 'grahn-deh)*
counselor	**el consejero** *(ehl kohn-seh-'heh-roh)*	**¿Quién es su consejero?** *(kee-'ehn ehs soo kohn-seh-'heh-roh)*
grade level	**el grado** *(ehl 'grah-doh)*	**Está en el segundo grado** *(eh-'stah ehn ehl seh-'goon-doh 'grah-doh)*
homework	**la tarea** *(lah tah-'reh-ah)*	**Tiene que hacer su tarea** *(tee-'eh-neh keh ah-'sehr soo tah-'reh-ah)*
meeting	**la reunión** *(lah reh-oo-nee-'ohn)*	**Está en la reunión** *(eh-'stah ehn lah reh-oo-nee-'ohn)*
notebook	**el cuaderno** *(ehl kwah-'dehr-noh)*	**Escribe en el cuaderno** *(eh-'skree-beh ehn ehl kwah-'dehr-noh)*
playground	**el campo de recreo** *(ehl 'kahm-poh deh reh-'kreh-oh)*	**El campo de recreo es bueno** *(ehl 'kahm-poh deh reh-'kreh-oh ehs 'bweh-noh)*

principal	**el director** *(ehl dee-rehk-'tohr)*	**Necesito llamar al director** *(neh-seh-'see-toh yah-'mahr ahl dee-rehk-'tohr)*
school	**la escuela** *(lah eh-'skweh-lah)*	**Su escuela está muy cerca** *(soo eh-'skweh-lah eh-'stah 'moo·ee 'sehr-kah)*
student	**el estudiante** *(ehl eh-stoo-dee-'ahn-teh)*	**Es un estudiante inteligente** *(ehs oon eh-stoo-dee-'ahn-teh een-teh-lee-'hehn-teh)*
subject	**la asignatura** *(lah ah-seeg-nah-'too-rah)*	**Es su asignatura favorita** *(ehs soo ah-seeg-nah-'too-rah fah-voh-'ree-tah)*
teacher	**el maestro** *(ehl mah-'eh-stroh)*	**El Sr. Smith es su maestro** *(ehl seh-'nyohr Smith ehs soo mah-'eh-stroh)*
test	**el examen** *(ehl ehk-'sah-mehn)*	**El examen es importante** *(ehl ehk-'sah-mehn ehs eem-pohr-'tahn-teh)*

 TEMAS CULTURALES

While dropping by the schoolyard, don't be afraid to shake hands with the students. In some Spanish-speaking countries, people believe that children can get sick if you stare at them without making physical contact. It is also considered rude. A brief pat or handshake will make everyone feel more comfortable.

KIDS IN TROUBLE
Los niños con problemas *(lohs 'nee-nyohs kohn proh-'bleh-mahs)*

Is the child causing problems at school? This is what the teachers are trying to say:

It's (the)...	**Es...** *(ehs...)*
behavior	**el comportamiento** *(ehl koh-pohr-tah-mee-'ehn-toh)*
curfew	**el toque de queda** *(ehl 'toh-keh deh 'keh-dah)*
cutting class	**no asistir a clase** *(noh ah-see-'steer ah 'klah-seh)*
delinquent	**el delincuente** *(ehl deh-leen-'kwehn-teh)*
detention	**la detención** *(lah deh-tehn-see-'ohn)*

discipline	**la disciplina** (lah dee-see-'plee-nah)
disobedience	**la desobediencia** (lah dehs-oh-beh-dee-'ehn-see·ah)
expulsion	**la expulsión** (lah ehks-pool-see-'ohn)
gang	**la pandilla** (lah pahn-'dee-yah)
graffiti, tagging	**el grafiti, las pintadas** (ehl grah-'fee-tee, lahs peen-'tah-dahs)
mischief	**la travesura** (lah trah-veh-'soo-rah)
nickname	**el apodo** (ehl ah-'poh-doh)
punishment	**el castigo** (ehl kah-'stee-goh)
security guard	**el guardia de seguridad** (ehl 'gwahr-dee·ah deh seh-goo-ree-'dahd)
suspension	**la suspensión** (lah soo-spehn-see-'ohn)
vandalism	**el vandalismo** (ehl vahn-dah-'lees-moh)

Sit down with the parent or guardian and ask about the child in question. Notice the use of *Action Words*:

Does your child obey you?	**¿Le obedece su hijo?** (leh oh-beh-'deh-seh soo 'ee-hoh)
Does your child stay home much?	**¿Se queda en casa mucho su hijo?** (seh 'keh-dah ehn 'kah-sah 'moo-choh soo 'ee-hoh)
Does your child miss school?	**¿Falta a la escuela mucho su hijo?** ('fahl-tah ah lah eh-'skweh-lah 'moo-choh soo 'ee-hoh)
Does your child consume drugs or alcohol?	**¿Toma drogas o alcohol su hijo?** ('toh-mah 'droh-gahs oh ahl-koh-'ohl soo 'ee-hoh)
Does your child have problems with another family member?	**¿Tiene su hijo problemas con otro miembro de la familia?** (tee-'eh-neh soo 'ee-hoh proh-'bleh-mahs kohn 'oh-troh mee-'ehm-broh deh lah fah-'mee-lee·ah)
Does your child have problems at school?	**¿Tiene problemas su hijo en la escuela?** (tee-'eh-neh proh-'bleh-mahs soo 'ee-hoh ehn lah eh-'skweh-lah)
Does your child have emotional problems?	**¿Tiene problemas emocionales su hijo?** (tee-'eh-neh proh-'bleh-mahs eh-moh-see·oh-'nah-lehs soo 'ee-hoh)
Does your child have learning difficulties?	**¿Tiene dificultades para aprender su hijo?** (tee-'eh-neh dee-fee-kool-'tah-dehs 'pah-rah ah-prehn-'dehr soo 'ee-hoh)

Find out all you can:

Who are your child's friends?	**¿Quiénes son los amigos de su hijo?** (kee-'eh-nehs sohn lohs ah-'mee-gohs deh soo 'ee-hoh)
Who cares for the child when you're not home?	**¿Quién le cuida al niño cuando usted no está en casa?** (kee-'ehn leh 'kwee-dah ahl 'nee-nyoh 'kwahn-doh oo-'stehd noh eh-'stah ehn 'kah-sah)

Is your child in good health?	¿Tiene su niño buena salud? *(tee-'eh-neh soo 'nee-nyoh 'bweh-nah sah-'lood)*
Has your child had problems with the police?	¿Ha tenido problemas su hijo con la policía? *(ah-teh-'nee-doh soo 'ee-hoh proh-'bleh-mahs kohn lah poh-lee-'see-ah)*
Has your child been arrested?	¿Ha sido arrestado su hijo? *(ah 'see-doh ah-rreh-'stah-doh soo 'ee-hoh)*
What do you think is the problem?	¿Cuál cree que es el problema? *(kwahl 'kreh-eh key ehs ehl proh-'bleh-mah)*

TEMAS CULTURALES

Law enforcement agencies have found that gang-related crime is reduced when there is regular communication between schools, parents, and concerned community members. Experts have also discovered that the relationship between law enforcement officers and the gang members themselves is important. Much of the time, it's a matter of understanding and respect. Once there is a willingness to communicate, real solutions can be discussed. That is why Spanish-speaking officers are so critically needed in our country.

INFORMACIÓN PRIVADA

➤ At the district, school, or parent's meeting, hear what the experts are saying about the child's true feelings:

The child feels...	El niño se siente... *(ehl 'nee-nyoh seh see-'ehn-teh...)*
apathetic	**apático** *(ah-'pah-tee-koh)*
bitter	**amargado** *(ah-mahr-'gah-doh)*
confused	**confundido** *(kohn-foon-'dee-doh)*
depressed	**deprimido** *(deh-pree-'mee-doh)*
frustrated	**frustrado** *(froo-'strah-doh)*
guilty	**culpable** *(kool-'pah-bleh)*
helpless	**desamparado** *(dehs-ahm-pah-'rah-doh)*
hostile	**hostil** *(oh-'steel)*
insecure	**inseguro** *(een-seh-'goo-roh)*

restless	**inquieto** (een-kee-'eh-toh)
suicidal	**suicida** (soo-ee-'see-dah)
threatened	**amenazado** (ah-meh-nah-'sah-doh)

➤ When a child's behavior is headed in the wrong direction, some of these words and phrases surface in conversation. Take the ones you need:

child care	**el cuidado de los niños** (ehl kwee-'dah-doh deh lohs 'nee-nyohs)
community service	**el servicio para la comunidad** (ehl sehr-'vee-see·oh 'pah-rah lah koh-moo-nee-'dahd)
continuation school	**la escuela secundaria especial** (lah eh-'skweh-lah seh-koon-'dah-ree·ah eh-speh-see-'ahl)
county jail	**la cárcel del condado** (lah 'kahr-sehl dehl kohn-'dah-doh)
federal prison	**la prisión federal** (lah pree-see-'ohn feh-deh-'rahl)
house of correction	**la cárcel** (lah 'kahr-sehl)
institution	**la institución** (lah een-stee-too-see-'ohn)
juvenile court	**la corte de menores** (lah 'kohr-teh deh meh-'noh-rehs)
legal aid	**la ayuda legal** (lah ah-'yoo-dah leh-'gahl)
parole	**la libertad bajo palabra** (lah lee-behr-'tahd 'bah-hoh pah-'lah-brah)
probation officer	**el agente encargado de la libertad provisional** (ehl ah-'hehn-teh ehn-kahr-'gah-doh deh lah lee-behr-'tahd proh-vee-see·oh-'nahl)
reformatory	**el reformatorio** (ehl reh-fohr-mah-'toh-ree·oh)
rehabilitation	**la rehabilitación** (lah reh-ah-bee-lee-tah-see-'ohn)
shelter	**el alojamiento** (ehl ah-loh-hah-mee-'ehn-toh)
special program	**el programa especial** (ehl proh-'grah-mah eh-speh-see-'ahl)
state prison	**la prisión del estado** (lah pree-see-'ohn dehl eh-'stah-doh)
penitentiary	**la penitenciaría** (lah pehn-ee-tehn-see·ah-'ree-ah)

Do not use children as translators! Not only is there a chance that the message may be misunderstood, but there's also the risk of causing emotional damage to the kids.

SPECIAL SERVICES

Los servicios especiales *(lohs sehr-'vee-see·ohs eh-speh-see-'ah-lehs)*

When families are in need of special services and support, law enforcement often steps in to link them with the appropriate public or private agencies. The requests vary, so why not learn the following vocabulary:

They need (the)...	**Necesitan...** *(neh-seh-'see-tahn...)*
advice	**el consejo** *(ehl kohn-'seh-hoh)*
assistance	**la ayuda** *(lah ah-'yoo-dah)*
church program	**el programa de la iglesia** *(ehl proh-'grah-mah deh lah ee-'gleh-see·ah)*
counselor	**el consejero** *(ehl kohn-seh-'heh-roh)*
day care center	**la guardería infantil** *(lah gwahr-deh-'ree-ah een-fahn-'teel)*
donation	**la donación** *(lah doh-nah-see-'ohn)*
food stamp	**el cupón de alimentos** *(ehl koo-'pohn deh ah-lee-'mehn-tohs)*
home	**el hogar** *(ehl oh-'gahr)*
housing	**la vivienda** *(lah vee-vee-'ehn-dah)*
insurance	**el seguro** *(ehl seh-'goo-roh)*
legal service	**el servicio legal** *(ehl sehr-'vee-see·oh leh-'gahl)*
medical care	**el cuidado médico** *(ehl kwee-'dah-doh 'meh-dee-koh)*
nursing home	**el hogar para ancianos** *(ehl oh-'gahr 'pah-rah ahn-see-'ah-nohs)*
psychologist	**el psicólogo** *(ehl see-'koh-loh-goh)*
resource	**el recurso** *(ehl reh-'koor-soh)*
shelter	**el amparo** *(ehl ahm-'pah-roh)*
social worker	**el trabajador social** *(ehl trah-bah-hah-'dohr soh-see-'ahl)*
support	**el apoyo** *(ehl ah-'poh-yoh)*
therapy	**la terapia** *(lah teh-'rah-pee·ah)*
vaccination	**la vacunación** *(lah vah-koo-nah-see-'ohn)*
welfare	**el bienestar social** *(ehl bee·ehn-eh-'stahr soh-see-'ahl)*

They can help you with (the)...	**Pueden ayudarle con...** *('pweh-dehn ah-yoo-'dahr-leh kohn...)*
alimony	**la pensión para el ex-cónyugue** *(lah pehn-see-'ohn 'pah-rah ehl ehks-'kohn-yoo-eh)*
child custody	**la custodia del niño** *(lah koo-'stoh-dee·ah dehl 'nee-nyoh)*
child support	**la ayuda para el niño** *(lah ah-'yoo-dah 'pah-rah ehl 'nee-nyoh)*
sanitary condition	**la condición sanitaria** *(lah kohn-dee-see-'ohn sah-nee-'tah-ree·ah)*
unemployment	**el desempleo** *(ehl dehs-ehm-'pleh-oh)*

TEMAS CULTURALES

You can prevent potential problems with new immigrants by providing them with as much legal information as possible. By contacting a variety of service agencies, one can pick up literature in Spanish concerning citizenship, taxes, health care, education, transportation, and residence, as well as personal rights and privileges.

COMMUNITY MEETING

La reunión de la comunidad *(lah reh-oo-nee-'ohn deh lah koh-moo-nee-'dahd)*

One common activity that brings everyone together but often requires governmental agency support is the community meeting. Agenda topics are diverse, so feel free to add to the sample list below:

They talked about (the)...	**Hablaron de...** *(ah-'blah-rohn deh...)*
bankruptcy	**la bancarrota** *(lah bahn-kah-'rroh-tah)*
budget	**el presupuesto** *(ehl preh-soo-'pweh-stoh)*
chamber of commerce	**la cámara de comercio** *(lah 'kah-mah-rah deh koh-'mehr-see·oh)*
construction	**la construcción** *(lah kohn-strook-see-'ohn)*
crime	**el crimen** *(ehl 'kree-mehn)*
crime rate	**la proporción de crimen** *(lah proh-pohr-see-'ohn dehl 'kree-mehn)*
crisis	**la crisis** *(lah 'kree-sees)*
ecology	**la ecología** *(lah eh-koh-loh-'hee-ah)*
election	**la elección** *(lah eh-lehk-see-'ohn)*

hearing	**la audiencia** *(lah ow-dee-'ehn-see·ah)*
law and order	**la ley y el orden** *(lah 'leh·ee ee ehl 'ohr-dehn)*
population	**la población** *(lah poh-blah-see-'ohn)*
poverty	**la pobreza** *(lah poh-'breh-sah)*
property value	**el valor de la propiedad** *(ehl vah-'lohr deh lah proh-pee-eh-'dahd)*
public service	**el servicio público** *(ehl sehr-'vee-see·oh 'poo-blee-koh)*
public utility	**la empresa de servicio público** *(lah ehm-'preh-sah deh sehr-'vee-see·oh 'poo-blee-koh)*
transportation	**el transporte** *(ehl trahns-'pohr-teh)*
zoning	**la división en zonas** *(lah dee-vee-see-'ohn ehn 'soh-nahs)*

CRIME PREVENTION

La prevención del crimen *(lah preh-vehn-see-'ohn dehl 'kree-mehn)*

One of the most common themes at community meetings is crime prevention, and law enforcement agencies are often invited to discuss topics such as home security, personal protection, and community watch programs. Are you proficient enough in Spanish to participate in the discussion? Odds are you still need a few of these vocabulary items:

I'm going to talk about (the)...	**Voy a hablar de...** *('voh-ee ah ah-'blahr deh...)*
alarm system	**el sistema de alarmas** *(ehl see-'steh-mah deh ah-'lahr-mahs)*
community watch	**la vigilancia de la comunidad** *(lah vee-hee-'lahn-see·ah deh lah koh-moo-nee-'dahd)*
fight against crime	**la batalla contra el crimen** *(lah bah-'tah-yah 'kohn-trah ehl 'kree-mehn)*
street lighting	**la iluminación callejera** *(lah ee-loo-mee-nah-see-'ohn kah-yeh-'heh-rah)*
home security	**la seguridad del hogar** *(lah seh-goo-ree-'dahd dehl oh-'gahr)*
loss of property	**la pérdida de propiedad** *(lah 'pehr-dee-dah deh proh-pee-eh-'dahd)*
neighborhood care	**el cuidado del vecindario** *(ehl kwee-'dah-doh dehl veh-seen-'dah-ree·oh)*
preventive measures	**la medidas preventivas** *(lahs meh-'dee-dahs preh-vehn-'tee-vahs)*

risk reduction	**la reducción del riesgo** *(lah reh-dook-see-'ohn dehl ree-'ehs-goh)*
safety suggestions	**las sugerencias sobre protección** *(lahs soo-heh-'rehn-see·ahs 'soh-breh proh-tehk-see-'ohn)*
security inspection	**la inspección de seguridad** *(lah een-spehk-see-'ohn deh seh-goo-ree-'dahd)*
self-defense	**la autodefensa** *(lah ow-toh-deh-'fehn-sah)*
suspicious persons	**las personas sospechosas** *(lahs pehr-'soh-nahs soh-speh-'choh-sahs)*
the special lock	**la cerradura especial** *(lah seh-rrah-'doo-rah eh-speh-see-'ahl)*

No sé por qué el niño se siente amargado y hostil.

INFORMACIÓN PRIVADA

➤ Sometimes it's easier to learn expressions in a different language when they follow a certain pattern. Try these out in complete sentences:

office security	**la seguridad en la oficina** *(lah seh-goo-ree-'dahd ehn lah oh-fee-'see-nah)*
personal security	**la seguridad personal** *(lah seh-goo-ree-'dahd pehr-soh-'nahl)*
vehicle security	**la seguridad del carro** *(lah seh-goo-ree-'dahd dehl 'kah-rroh)*

314

identification	**la identificación** *(lah ee-dehn-tee-fee-kah-see-'ohn)*
precaution	**la precaución** *(lah preh-kow-see-'ohn)*
protection	**la protección** *(lah proh-tehk-see-'ohn)*
way to avoid trouble	**el modo de evitar problemas** *(ehl 'moh-doh deh eh-vee-'tahr proh-'bleh-mahs)*
way to carry a handbag	**el modo de portar la cartera** *(ehl 'moh-doh deh pohr-'tahr lah kahr-'teh-rah)*
way to report a crime	**el modo de reportar un crimen** *(ehl 'moh-doh deh reh-pohr-'tahr oon 'kree-mehn)*

TEMAS CULTURALES

Generally, most immigrants in the United States tend to reside near those who come from their same cultural and language background. Since families remain in the same areas for years, it's not uncommon for communities to take pride in their local neighborhoods. By getting neighbors to work together, this concept can help in the development of numerous city projects. Using Spanish in certain vicinities is quite an advantage to law enforcement officers. Just a few words will help you become more familiar with Hispanic leaders at local churches, schools, and businesses.

MORE HELP
Más ayuda *(mahs ah-'yoo-dah)*

No single Spanish guidebook could cover every job that is linked to law enforcement. The only solution is to mention a few general areas, along with some support vocabulary. Hopefully, all of the language skills that have been presented thus far can be incorporated into your specific field of employment. Use these lists as a reference:

STATE AND FEDERAL POLICE OFFICERS
La policía estatal y federal
(lah poh-lee-'see-ah eh-stah-'tahl ee feh-deh-'rahl)

assassination	**el asesinato** *(ehl ah-seh-see-'nah-toh)*
bomb	**la bomba** *(lah 'bohm-bah)*
civil disorder	**la desobediencia civil** *(lah dehs-oh-beh-dee-'ehn-see·ah see-'veel)*

315

deportation	**la deportación** *(lah deh-pohr-tah-see-'ohn)*
fugitive	**el fugitivo** *(ehl foo-hee-'tee-voh)*
hostage	**el rehén** *(ehl reh-'ehn)*
illegal immigration	**la inmigración ilegal** *(lah een-mee-grah-see-'ohn ee-leh-'gahl)*
looting	**el saqueo** *(ehl sah-'keh-oh)*
mass murder	**la masacre** *(lah mah-'sah-kreh)*
military	**el militar** *(ehl mee-lee-'tahr)*
ransom	**el rescate** *(ehl reh-'skah-teh)*
reinforcement	**el refuerzo** *(ehl reh-'fwehr-soh)*
riot	**el tumulto** *(ehl too-'mool-toh)*
smuggling	**el contrabando** *(ehl kohn-trah-'bahn-doh)*
sniper	**el francotirador** *(ehl frahn-koh-tee-rah-'dohr)*
strike	**la huelga** *(lah 'wehl-gah)*
terrorism	**el terrorismo** *(ehl teh-rroh-'rees-moh)*

THE HARBOR PATROL AND COAST GUARD
La patrulla de la bahía y el cuerpo de guardacostas
(lah pah-'troo-yah deh lah bah-'ee-ah ee ehl 'kwehr-poh deh gwahr-dah-'koh-stahs)

boat	**el barco** *(ehl 'bahr-koh)*
canoe	**la canoa** *(lah kah-'noh-ah)*
lifeboat	**el bote salvavidas** *(ehl 'boh-teh sahl-vah-'vee-dahs)*
life buoy	**la boya salvavidas** *(lah 'boh-yah sahl-vah-'vee-dahs)*
life guard	**el guardia salvavidas** *(ehl 'gwahr-dee·ah sahl-vah-'vee-dahs)*
life jacket	**el chaleco salvavidas** *(ehl chah-'leh-koh sahl-vah-'vee-dahs)*
life line	**la cuerda salvavidas** *(lah 'kwehr-dah sahl-vah-'vee-dahs)*
life preserver	**el salvavidas** *(ehl sahl-vah-'vee-dahs)*
parachute	**el paracaídas** *(ehl pah-rah-kah-'ee-dahs)*
raft	**la balsa** *(lah 'bahl-sah)*
rowboat	**el bote de remos** *(ehl 'boh-teh deh 'reh-mohs)*
sailboat	**el velero** *(ehl veh-'leh-roh)*
search	**la búsqueda** *(lah 'boos-keh-dah)*
shipwreck	**el naufragio** *(ehl now-'frah-hee·oh)*
speedboat	**la lancha de motor** *(lah 'lahn-chah deh moh-'tohr)*
voyage	**el viaje** *(ehl vee-'ah-heh)*
yacht	**el yate** *(ehl 'yah-teh)*

THE PARK RANGER
El guardabosques (ehl gwahr-dah-'boh-skehs)

backpack	**la mochila** (lah moh-'chee-lah)
butane gas	**el gas butano** (ehl gahs boo-'tah-noh)
campfire	**el fuego de campamento** (ehl 'fweh-goh deh kahm-pah-'mehn-toh)
campground	**el campamento** (ehl kahm-pah-'mehn-toh)
camping trailer	**la caravana** (lah kah-rah-'vah-nah)
drinking water	**el agua potable** (ehl 'ah-gwah poh-'tah-bleh)
firewood	**la leña** (lah 'leh-nyah)
fishing rod	**la caña de pesca** (lah 'kah-nyah deh 'pehs-kah)
hike	**la caminata** (lah kah-mee-'nah-tah)
litter	**la basura** (lah bah-'soo-rah)
matches	**los fósforos** (lohs 'fohs-foh-rohs)
permit	**el permiso** (ehl pehr-'mee-soh)
rescue	**el salvamento** (ehl sahl-vah-'mehn-toh)
sleeping bag	**el saco para dormir** (ehl 'sah-koh 'pah-rah dohr-'meer)
tent	**la tienda** (lah tee-'ehn-dah)
trail	**la senda** (lah 'sehn-dah)
trap	**la trampa** (lah 'trahm-pah)
wild animal	**el animal salvaje** (ehl ah-nee-'mahl sahl-'vah-heh)
I am a fish and game warden	**Soy agente de caza y pesca** ('soh-ee ah-'hehn-teh deh 'kah-sah ee 'pehs-kah)
Beware of the animals	**Tenga cuidado con los animales** ('tehn-gah koo-ee-'dah-doh kohn lohs ah-nee-'mah-lehs)
You are in violation of the code	**Está en violación del código** (ehs-'tah ehn vee-oh-lah-see-'ohn dehl 'koh-dee-goh)
Do you have a camping permit?	**¿Tiene permiso para acampar?** (tee-'eh-neh pehr-'mee-soh 'pah-rah ah-kahm-'pahr)
What are you hunting?	**¿Qué está cazando?** (keh ehs-'tah kah-'sahn-doh)
What are you fishing?	**¿Qué está pescando?** (keh ehs-'tah pehs-'kahn-doh)
May I see your hunting license?	**¿Puedo ver su licencia de caza?** ('pweh-doh vehr soo lee-'sehn-see-ah deh 'kah-sah)
May I see your fishing license?	**¿Puedo ver su licencia de pesca?** ('pweh-doh vehr soo lee-'sehn-see-ah deh 'pehs-kah)
This animal is illegal	**Este animal es ilegal** (ehs-teh ah-nee-'mahl ehs ee-leh-'gahl)
This fish is illegal	**Este pez es ilegal** (ehs-teh pehs ehs ee-leh-'gahl)

Do you have permission from the landowner?	¿Tiene permiso del dueño de la propiedad? *(tee-'eh-neh pehr-'mee-soh dehl 'dweh-nyoh deh lah proh-pee-eh 'dahd)*
Did you see the "No Hunting" or "No Trespassing" sign?	¿Vio el aviso que dice "Prohibido Cazar" o "Prohibido Pasar"? *(vee-'oh ehl ah-'vee-soh keh 'dee-seh proh-ee-'bee-doh kah-'sahr oh proh-ee-'bee-doh pah-'sahr)*
It's against the law to fish here.	Es contra la ley pescar aquí. *(ehs 'kohn-trah lah 'leh-ee pehs-'kahr ah-'kee)*
Is this your equipment/ firearm?	¿Es este su equipo/arma de fuego? *(ehs ehs-teh soo eh-'kee-poh / ahr-mah deh 'fweh-goh)*

SECURITY GUARDS
Los guardias *(lohs 'gwahr-dee·ahs)*

The... is closed	...está cerrado/a *(...eh-'stah seh-'rrah-doh / ah)*
amusement park	el parque de diversiones *(ehl 'pahr-keh deh dee-vehr-see-'oh-nehs)*
beach	la playa *(lah 'plah-yah)*
booth	la caseta *(lah kah-'seh-tah)*
building	el edificio *(ehl eh-dee-'fee-see·oh)*
concert	el concierto *(ehl kohn-see-'ehr-toh)*
fair	la feria *(lah 'feh-ree·ah)*
gate	el portón *(ehl pohr-'tohn)*
museum	el museo *(ehl moo-'seh-oh)*
park	el parque *(ehl 'pahr-keh)*
parking lot	el estacionamiento *(ehl eh-stah-see·oh-nah-mee-'ehn-toh)*
stadium	el estadio *(ehl eh-'stah-dee·oh)*
theater	el teatro *(ehl teh-'ah-troh)*
zoo	el zoológico *(ehl soh-oh-'loh-hee-koh)*

LEGAL TERMINOLOGY
Terminología legal *(tehr-mee-noh-loh-'hee-ah leh-'gahl)*

Explain in Spanish what's going on in the courtroom:

It's (the)...	Es... *(ehs...)*
accessory	el cómplice *(ehl 'kohm-plee-seh)*
accused	el acusado *(ehl ah-koo-'sah-doh)*

acquital	**la absolución** *(lah ahb-soh-loo-see-'ohn)*
affidavit	**la declaración jurada** *(lah deh-klah-rah-see-'ohn hoo-'rah-dah)*
alibi	**la coartada** *(lah koh-ahr-'tah-dah)*
allegation	**la acusación** *(lah ah-koo-sah-see-'ohn)*
arraignment	**la denuncia** *(lah deh-'noon-see·ah)*
arrest	**el arresto/la detención** *(ehl ah-'rrehs-toh / lah deh-tehn-see-'ohn)*
autopsy	**la autopsia** *(lah ah-oo-'tohp-see-ah)*
bail	**la fianza** *(lah fee-'ahn-sah)*
bail bond	**la escritura de fianza** *(lah eh-skree-'too-rah deh fee-'ahn-sah)*
bailiff	**el alguacil** *(ehl ah-gwah-'seel)*
charge	**el cargo** *(ehl 'kahr-goh)*
claim	**la demanda** *(lah deh-'mahn-dah)*
complaint	**la queja** *(lah 'keh-hah)*
confession	**la confesión** *(lah kohn-feh-see-'ohn)*
consent	**el permiso** *(ehl pehr-'mee-soh)*
constitution	**la constitución** *(lah kohn-stee-too-see-'ohn)*
court	**el tribunal** *(ehl tree-boo-'nahl)*
court order	**la orden de la corte** *(lah 'ohr-dehn deh lah 'kohr-teh)*
cross-examination	**la interrogación** *(lah een-teh-rroh-gah-see-'ohn)*
custody	**la custodia** *(lah koos-'toh-dee-ah)*
defendant	**el demandado, el acusado** *(ehl deh-mahn-'dah-doh, ehl ah-koo-'sah-doh)*
defense	**la defensa** *(lah deh-'fehn-sah)*
dispute	**la disputa** *(lah dee-'spoo-tah)*
District Attorney	**el fiscal del distrito** *(ehl fees-'kahl dehl dee-'stree-toh)*
effective date	**la fecha en efecto** *(lah 'feh-chah ehn eh-'fehk-toh)*
evidence	**la evidencia** *(lah eh-vee-'dehn-see·ah)*
execution	**la ejecución** *(lah eh-heh-koo-see-'ohn)*
eyewitness	**el/la testigo ocular** *(ehl / lah tehs-'tee-goh oh-koo-'lahr)*
felony	**el delito mayor** *(ehl deh-'lee-toh mah-'yohr)*
fine	**la multa** *(lah 'mool-tah)*
government	**el gobierno** *(ehl goh-bee-'ehr-noh)*
grand jury	**el gran jurado** *(ehl grahn hoo-'rah-doh)*
guilt	**la culpabilidad** *(lah kool-pah-bee-lee-'dahd)*
guilty	**el culpable** *(ehl kool-'pah-bleh)*
hearing	**la audiencia** *(lah ah-oo-dee-'ehn-see-ah)*
incarceration	**el encarcelamiento** *(ehl ehn-kahr-seh-lah-mee-'ehn-toh)*

indictment	**la acusación** *(lah ah-koo-sah-see-'ohn)*
infraction	**la infracción** *(lah een-frahk-see-'ohn)*
injunction	**el entredicho** *(ehl ehn-treh-'dee-choh)*
inmate	**el preso** *(ehl 'preh-soh)*
innocence	**la inocencia** *(lah ee-noh-'sehn-see·ah)*
innocent	**el inocente** *(ehl ee-noh-'sehn-teh)*
inquiry	**la investigación** *(lah een-veh-stee-gah-see-'ohn)*
intent	**el intento** *(ehl een-'tehn-toh)*
interrogation	**el interrogatorio** *(ehl een-teh-rroh-gah-'toh-ree-oh)*
investigation	**la investigación** *(lah een-vehs-tee-gah-see-'ohn)*
jail	**la cárcel** *(lah 'kahr-sehl)*
judge	**el juez** *(ehl hoo-'ehs)*
jurisdiction	**la jurisdicción** *(lah hoo-rees-deek-see-'ohn)*
jury	**el jurado** *(ehl hoo-'rah-doh)*
justice	**la justicia** *(lah hoo-'stee-see·ah)*
lawsuit	**el pleito** *(ehl 'pleh·ee-toh)*
lawyer	**el abogado** *(ehl ah-boh-'gah-doh)*
legal aid	**la asistencia legal** *(lah ah-sees-'tehn-see-ah leh-'gahl)*
lie detector	**el detector de mentiras** *(ehl deh-tehk-'tohr deh meh-'tee-rahs)*
misdemeanor	**el delito menor** *(ehl deh-'lee-toh meh-'nohr)*
motion	**la moción** *(lah moh-see-'ohn)*
motive	**el motivo** *(ehl moh-'tee-voh)*
oath	**el juramento** *(ehl hoo-rah-'mehn-toh)*
offense	**la ofensa** *(lah oh-'fehn-sah)*
parole	**la libertad provisional** *(lah lee-behr-'tahd proh-vee-see·oh-'nahl)*
perjury	**el perjurio** *(ehl pehr-'hoo-ree·oh)*
plea	**el alegato** *(ehl ah-leh-'gah-toh)*
prior conviction	**la condena anterior** *(lah kohn-'deh-nah ahn-teh-ree-'ohr)*
priors	**el archivo de antecedentes anteriores** *(ehl ahr-'chee-voh deh ahn-teh-seh-'dehn-tehs ahn-teh-ree-'oh-rehs)*
prison	**la prisión** *(lah pree-see-'ohn)*
probation	**la libertad vigilada** *(lah lee-behr-'tahd vee-hee-'lah-dah)*
proof	**la prueba** *(lah proo-'eh-bah)*
punishment	**la pena** *(lah 'peh-nah)*
release	**la libertad** *(lah lee-behr-'tahd)*

restraining order	**la orden de retiro y restricción** *(lah 'ohr-dehn deh reh-'tee-roh ee rehs-treek-see-'ohn)*
rights	**los derechos** *(lohs deh-'reh-chohs)*
sentence	**la sentencia** *(lah sehn-'tehn-see·ah)*
subpoena	**el apercibimiento** *(ehl ah-pehr-see-bee-mee-'ehn-toh)*
surveillance	**la vigilancia** *(lah vee-hee-'lahn-see·ah)*
term	**el término** *(ehl 'tehr-mee-noh)*
testimony	**el testimonio** *(ehl tehs-tee-'moh-nee·oh)*
trial	**el juicio** *(ehl 'hoo·ee-see·oh)*
verdict	**el veredicto** *(ehl veh-reh-'deek-toh)*
warrant	**la orden** *(lah 'ohr-dehn)*
witness	**el testigo** *(ehl teh-'stee-goh)*

Add more actions that relate to legal affairs:

appeal	**apelar** *(ah-peh-'lahr)*
promise	**prometer** *(proh-meh-'tehr)*
refuse	**rehusar** *(reh-oo-'sahr)*
share	**repartir** *(reh-pahr-'teer)*
suppose	**suponer** *(soo-poh-'nehr)*
testify	**testificar** *(teh-stee-fee-'kahr)*

...court	**El tribunal de...** *(ehl tree-boo-'nahl deh...)*
civil	**casos civiles** *('kah-sohs see-'vee-lehs)*
justice	**justicia** *(hoo-'stee-see·ah)*
juvenile	**menores** *(meh-'noh-rehs)*
night	**noche** *('noh-cheh)*
superior	**superior** *(soo-peh-ree-'ohr)*
traffic	**tráfico** *('trah-fee-koh)*

CRUCIGRAMA 4

Across

1 el juicio
6 el culpable
7 el demandado
9 el acusado
10 la evidencia
12 la denuncia
14 el tribunal
16 el inocente
18 la fianza
20 el delito mayor

Down

2 el encarcelamiento
3 la custodia
4 la coartada
5 el juez
8 el gobierno
11 el permiso
13 el jurado
15 la disputa
17 el cargo
19 la multa

FINAL WORDS
Las palabras finales *(lahs pah-'lah-brahs fee-'nah-lehs)*

This final series of statements in Spanish can be used as a powerful resource when you need to inform others of their legal rights and responsibilities. Certain comments must be precise, according to the law, so take extra time to practice each of the following sentences. You might even have to say them twice!

You have the right to remain silent
   Usted tiene el derecho de no decir nada *(oo-'stehd tee-'eh-neh ehl deh-'reh-choh deh noh deh-'seer 'nah-dah)*
Anything you say can and will be used against you in a court of law
   Cualquier cosa que usted diga puede ser usada contra usted y será usada en su contra en un tribunal *(kwahl-kee-'ehr 'koh-sah keh oo-'stehd 'dee-gah 'pweh-deh sehr oo-'sah-dah 'kohn-trah oo-'stehd ee seh-'rah oo-'sah-dah ehn soo 'kohn-trah ehn oon tree-boo-'nahl)*

You have the right to talk to a lawyer and have him present before and during questioning
   Usted tiene el derecho de hablar con un abogado y tenerlo presente, antes y durante cualquier interrogatorio *(oo-'stehd tee-'eh-neh ehl deh-'reh-choh deh ah-'blahr kohn oon ah-boh-'gah-doh ee teh-'nehr-loh preh-'sehn-teh 'ahn-tehs ee doo-'rahn-teh kwahl-kee-'ehr een-teh-rroh-gah-'toh-ree·oh)*

If you cannot afford to hire a lawyer, one will be appointed free of charge before or during questioning, if you wish
   Si usted no puede pagar por un abogado, uno le será nombrado gratis antes o durante cualquier interrogatorio, si usted lo desea *(see oo-'stehd noh 'pweh-deh pah-'gahr pohr oon ah-boh-'gah-doh, 'oo-noh leh seh-'rah nohm-'brah-doh 'grah-tees 'ahn-tehs oh doo-'rahn-teh kwahl-kee-'ehr een-teh-rroh-gah-'toh-ree·oh, see oo-'stehd loh deh-'seh-ah)*

Do you understand each of these rights I have explained to you?
   ¿Entiende usted cada uno de estos derechos que le acabo de explicar? *(ehn-tee-'ehn-deh oo-'stehd 'kah-dah 'oo-noh deh 'eh-stohs deh-'reh-chohs keh leh ah-'kah-boh deh ehk-splee-'kahr)*

Having these rights in mind, do you wish to talk to me now?
   Teniendo en cuenta estos derechos, ¿desea hablar conmigo ahora? *(teh-nee-'ehn-doh ehn 'kwehn-tah 'eh-stohs deh-'reh-chohs, deh-'seh-ah ah-'blahr kohn-'mee-goh ah-'oh-rah)*

I am declaring this an unlawful assembly and order you to leave this area immediately

Estoy declarando que esta asamblea es ilegal, y ordeno que se retiren de esta área inmediatamente *(eh-'stoh-ee deh-klah-'rahn-doh keh 'eh-stah ah-sahm-'bleh-ah ehs ee-leh-'gahl, ee ohr-'deh-noh keh seh reh-'tee-rehn deh 'eh-stah 'ah-reh-ah een-meh-dee-ah-tah-'mehn-teh)*

If you do not leave, you will be arrested for failure to disperse

Si no se retiran, serán arrestados por no cumplir con esta orden *(see noh seh reh-'tee-rahn, seh-'rahn ah-rreh-'stah-dohs pohr noh koom-'pleer kohn 'eh-stah 'ohr-dehn)*

Do you certify under penalty of perjury that the foregoing is true and correct?

¿Certifica bajo la pena de perjurio que lo anterior es verdadero y correcto? *(sehr-tee-'fee-kah 'bah-hoh lah 'peh-nah deh pehr-'hoo-ree·oh keh loh ahn-teh-ree-'ohr ehs vehr-dah-'deh-roh ee koh-'rrehk-toh)*

Do you understand that failure to comply may result in court action?

¿Entiende que por no acatar las reglas, la corte puede tomar medidas contra usted? *(ehn-tee-'ehn-deh keh pohr noh ah-kah-'tahr lahs 'reh-glahs, lah 'kohr-teh 'pweh-deh toh-'mahr meh-'dee-dahs 'kohn-trah oo-'stehd)*

I am going to show you a person who may or may not be responsible for the crime. You are not obligated to make an identification

Le voy a mostrar una persona que podría o no podría ser responsable del crimen. No tiene obligación de hacer una identificación *(leh 'voh-ee ah moh-'strahr 'oo-nah pehr-'soh-nah keh poh-'dree-ah oh noh poh-'dree-ah sehr reh-spohn-'sah-bleh dehl 'kree-mehn. noh tee-'eh-neh ohb-lee-gah-see-'ohn deh ah-'sehr 'oo-nah ee-dehn-tee-fee-kah-see-'ohn)*

 REPASO

A. In Spanish, name three...

...words associated with public schools

_____   _____   _____

...terms and phrases related to problem children

_____   _____   _____

324

...special service agencies who assist families in need

_____   _____   _____

...popular topics of discussion at a traditional city council meeting

_____   _____   _____

...legal terms or expressions frequently heard in a local courtroom

_____   _____   _____

INFORMACIÓN PRIVADA

➤ After you've read through this guidebook, go back and review those words or phrases that you thought were the most important. Don't try to take in too much at one sitting! Be patient with yourself, and practice your new skills as often as you can. If possible, keep a record of what you've learned, and share the information with family, friends, or co-workers. Have fun while you learn, relax, and always pay special attention to cultural differences.

ANSWERS

WORD SEARCH 1

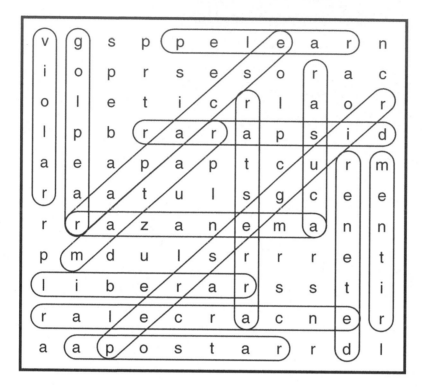

acusar
apostar
violar
perseguir
detener
escapar
pelear
arrestar
encarcelar
mentir
matar
liberar
disparar
amenazar
golpear

WORD SEARCH 2

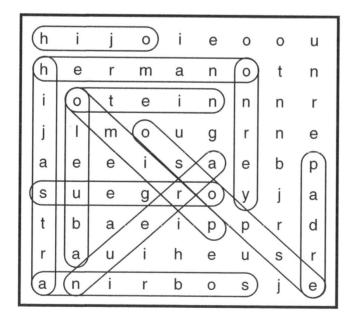

hermano
primo
nuera
padre
suegro
abuelo
esposo
sobrina
yerno
hijo
hijastra
nieto

CRUCIGRAMA 1

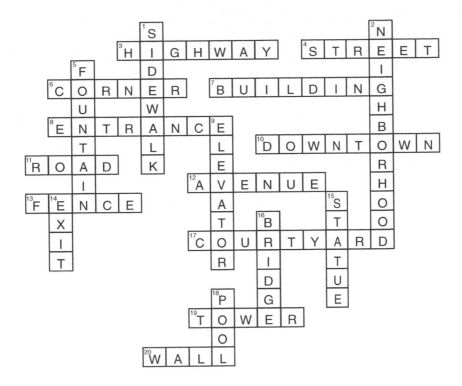

CRUCIGRAMA 2

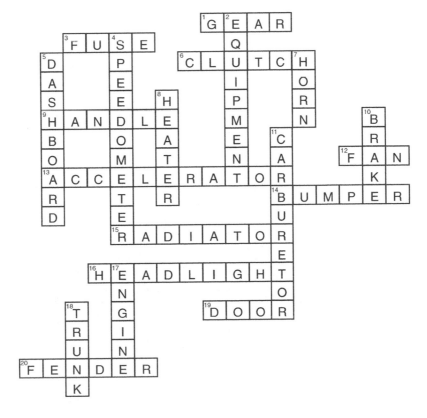

JUMBLE PUZZLE 1

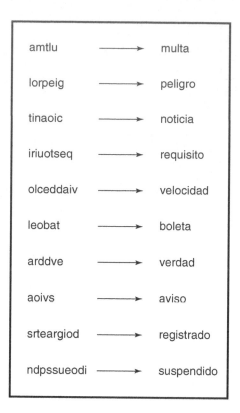

amtlu	⟶	multa
lorpeig	⟶	peligro
tinaoic	⟶	noticia
iriuotseq	⟶	requisito
olceddaiv	⟶	velocidad
leobat	⟶	boleta
arddve	⟶	verdad
aoivs	⟶	aviso
srteargiod	⟶	registrado
ndpssueodi	⟶	suspendido

WORD SEARCH 3

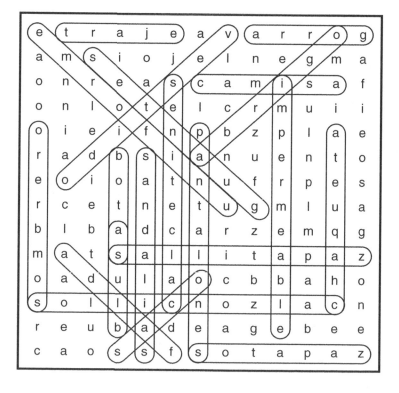

saco
blusa
gorra
botas
vestido
guantes
sombrero
chaqueta
abrigo
pantalones
impermeable
sandalias
camisa
zapatos
calzoncillos
falda
zapatillas
calcetines
traje
uniforme

CRUCIGRAMA 3

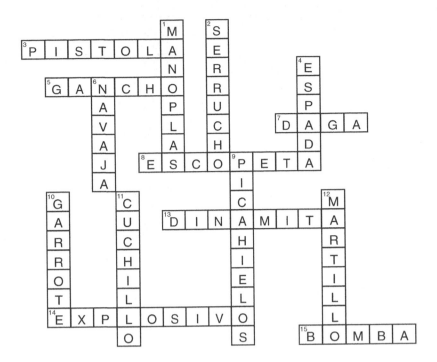

JUMBLE PUZZLE 2

oicntovc	⟶	convicto
racimlin	⟶	criminal
acrifsaildof	⟶	falsificador
aodlienlrp	⟶	pandillero
dsrescuretoa	⟶	secuestrador
rnoepsorii	⟶	prisionero
postttuari	⟶	prostituta
secshooops	⟶	sospechoso
eioartstrr	⟶	terrorista
ssieaon	⟶	asesino

CRUCIGRAMA 4

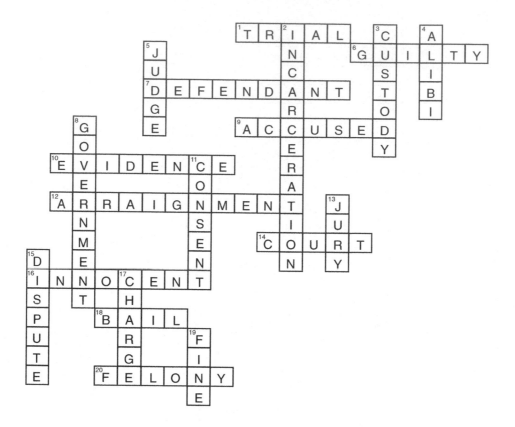

ENGLISH-SPANISH GLOSSARY

Spanish feminine nouns are preceded by the article **la,** and the masculine nouns are preceded by the article **el** (or the plural articles **las** or **los,** respectively). The gender of adjectives and pronouns is masculine in this glossary, but it should be changed to feminine when the sentence requires it. Useful expressions are preceded by an asterisk.

A

English	Spanish	Pronunciation
a, an	un	*(oon)*
a little	poco	*('poh-koh)*
a lot	mucho	*('moo-choh)*
abandon (to)	abandonar	*(ah-bahn-doh-'nahr)*
above	encima	*(ehn-'see-mah)*
absent	ausente	*(ow-'sehn-teh)*
abuse	abuso, el	*(ehl ah-'boo-soh)*
academic grade	calificación, la	*(lah kah-lee-fee-kah-see-'ohn)*
accelerator	acelerador, el	*(ehl ah-seh-leh-rah-'dohr)*
accident	accidente, el	*(ehl ahk-see-'dehn-teh)*
accomplice	cómplice, el	*(ehl 'kohm-plee-seh)*
accountant	contador, el	*(ehl kohn-tah-'dohr)*
accurate	correcto	*(koh-'rrehk-toh)*
accuse (to)	acusar	*(ah-koo-'sahr)*
acid	ácido, el	*(ehl 'ah-see-doh)*
acquaintance	conocido, el	*(ehl koh-noh-'see-doh)*
action	acción, la	*(lah ahk-see-'ohn)*
addict	adicto, el	*(ehl ah-'deek-toh)*
address	dirección, la	*(lah dee-rehk-see-'ohn)*
administrator	administrador, el	*(ehl ahd-mee-nee-strah-'dohr)*
adolescent	adolescente, el	*(ehl ah-doh-leh-'sehn-teh)*
adult	adulto, el	*(ehl ah-'dool-toh)*
advice	consejo, el	*(ehl kohn-'seh-hoh)*
affection	afecto, el	*(ehl ah-'fehk-toh)*
affidavit	declaración jurada, la	*(lah deh-klah-rah-see-'ohn hoo-'rah-dah)*
African-American	afroamericano, el	*(ehlah-froh-ah-meh-ree-'kah-noh)*
after	después	*(deh-'spwehs)*
again	otra vez	*('oh-trah vehs)*
*****Against the wall!**	¡Contra la pared!	*('kohn-trah lah pah-'rehd)*
age	edad, la	*(lah eh-'dahd)*
agency	agencia, la	*(lah ah-'hehn-see·ah)*
agent	agente, el	*(ehl ah-'hehn-teh)*
aggressor	agresor, el	*(ehl ah-greh-'sohr)*
ago	hace	*('ah-seh)*
AIDS	SIDA, el	*(ehl 'see-dah)*
air conditioner	acondicionador de aire, el	*(ehl ah-kohn-dee-see-oh-nah-'dohr deh 'ah·ee-reh)*

air conditioning	aire acondicionado, el	*(ehl 'ah·ee-reh ah-kohn-dee-see·oh-'nah-doh)*
airport	aeropuerto, el	*(ehl ah-eh-roh-'pwehr-toh)*
alarm	alarma, la	*(lah ah-'lahr-mah)*
alcohol	alcohol, el	*(ehl ahl-koh-'ohl)*
alcoholic	alcohólico, el	*(ehl ahl-koh-'oh-lee-koh)*
alert	alerta	*(ah-'lehr-tah)*
alias (a.k.a)	alias, el	*(ehl 'ah-lee-ahs)*
alibi	coartada, la	*(lah koh-ahr-'tah-dah)*
alimony	pensión para el ex-conyugue, la	*(lah pehn-see-'ohn 'pah-rah ehl ehks-kohn-'yoo-geh)*
alive	vivo	*('vee-voh)*
all	todo	*('toh-doh)*
allergic	alérgico	*(ah-'lehr-hee-koh)*
alley	callejón, el	*(ehl kah-yeh-'hohn)*
alone	solo	*('soh-loh)*
altered	alterado	*(ahl-teh-'rah-doh)*
always	siempre	*(see-'ehm-preh)*
ambulance	ambulancia, la	*(lah ahm-boo-'lahn-see·ah)*
American	americano	*(ah-meh-ree-'kah-noh)*
amusement park	parque de diversiones, el	*(ehl 'pahr-keh deh dee-vehr-see-'oh-nehs)*
and	y	*(ee)*
Anglo-Saxon	anglosajón	*(ahn-gloh-sah-'hohn)*
angry	enojado	*(eh-noh-'hah-doh)*
animal shelter	refugio de animales, el	*(ehl reh-'foo-hee·oh deh ah-nee-'mah-lehs)*
ankle	tobillo, el	*(ehl toh-'bee-yoh)*
anniversary	aniversario, el	*(ehl ah-nee-vehr-'sah-ree·oh)*
answering machine	grabadora telefónica, la	*(lah grah-bah-'doh-rah teh-leh-'foh-nee-kah)*
answer (to)	contestar	*(kohn-teh-'stahr)*
antenna	antena, la	*(lah ahn-'teh-nah)*
antibiotic	antibiótico, el	*(ehl ahn-tee-bee-'oh-tee-koh)*
antique	antigüedad, la	*(lah ahn-tee-gweh-'dahd)*
anxious	ansioso	*(ahn-see·oh-soh)*
apartment	apartamento, el	*(ehl ah-pahr-tah-'mehn-toh)*
appeal (to)	apelar	*(ah-peh-'lahr)*
appendix	apéndice, el	*(ehl ah-'pehn-dee-seh)*
apple	manzana, la	*(lah mahn-'sah-nah)*
appliances (electric)	electrodomésticos, los	*(lohs eh-lehk-troh-doh-'mehs-tee-kohs)*
appointment	cita, la	*(lah 'see-tah)*
approval	aprobación, la	*(lah ah-proh-bah-see-'ohn)*
approve (to)	aprobar	*(ah-proh-'bahr)*
approximately	aproximadamente	*(ah-prohk-see-mah-dah-'mehn-teh)*
April	abril	*(ah-'breel)*
Arab	árabe, el	*(ehl 'ah-rah-beh)*

area	área, el	*(ehl 'ah-reh-ah)*
arm	brazo, el	*(ehl 'brah-soh)*
armchair	sillón, el	*(ehl see-'yohn)*
armoire	armario, el	*(ehl ahr-'mah-ree·oh)*
armored car	carro blindado, el	*(ehl 'kah-rroh bleen-'dah-doh)*
arraignment	denuncia, la	*(lah deh-'noon-see·ah)*
arrange (to)	arreglar	*(ah-rreh-'glahr)*
arrest (to)	arrestar	*(ah-rreh-'stahr)*
arrive (to)	llegar	*(yeh-'gahr)*
arrow	flecha, la	*(lah 'fleh-chah)*
arson	incendio premeditado, el	*(ehl een-'sehn-dee·oh preh-meh-dee-'tah-doh)*
arsonist	incendiario, el	*(ehl een-sehn-dee-'ah-ree-oh)*
artist	artista, el	*(ehl ahr-'tee-stah)*
ashtray	cenicero, el	*(ehl seh-nee-'seh-roh)*
ask (to)	preguntar	*(preh-goon-'tahr)*
asleep	dormido	*(dohr-'mee-doh)*
asphalt	asfalto, el	*(ehl ahs-'fahl-toh)*
asphyxiated	asfixiado	*(ahs-feek-see-'ah-doh)*
aspirin	aspirina, la	*(lah ah-spee-'ree-nah)*
assailant	asaltante, el	*(ehl ah-sahl-'tahn-teh)*
assault	asalto, el	*(ehl ah-'sahl-toh)*
assistance	ayuda, la	*(lah ah-'yoo-dah)*
assistant	asistente, el	*(ehl ah-see-'stehn-teh)*
at	en	*(ehn)*
attend (to)	asistir	*(ah-see-'steer)*
attendance	asistencia, la	*(lah ah-see-'stehn-see·ah)*
attic	desván, el	*(ehl dehs-'vahn)*
attitude	actitud, la	*(lah ahk-tee-'tood)*
August	agosto	*(ah-'goh-stoh)*
aunt	tía, la	*(lah 'tee-ah)*
authorities	autoridades, las	*(lahs ow-toh-ree-'dah-dehs)*
auto parts	piezas de auto, las	*(lahs pee-'eh-sahs deh 'ow-toh)*
autopsy	autopsia, la	*(lah ow-'tohp-see·ah)*
autumn	otoño, el	*(ehl oh-'toh-nyoh)*
available	disponible	*(dees-poh-'nee-bleh)*
avenue	avenida, la	*(lah ah-veh-'nee-dah)*
awake	despierto	*(dehs-pee-'ehr-toh)*
awhile	rato, el	*(ehl 'rah-toh)*
axle	eje, el	*(ehl 'eh-heh)*

B

baby	bebé, el	*(ehl beh-'beh)*
babysitter	niñero, el	*(ehl nee-'nyeh-roh)*
bachelor	soltero, el	*(ehl sohl-'teh-roh)*
back	espalda, la	*(lah eh-'spahl-dah)*
back seat	asiento trasero, el	*(ehl ah-see-'ehn-toh trah-'seh-roh)*
back up (to)	retroceder	*(reh-troh-seh-'dehr)*
backache	dolor de espalda, el	*(ehl doh-'lohr deh eh-'spahl-dah)*

backpack	mochila, la	*(lah moh-'chee-lah)*
backyard	patio, el	*(ehl 'pah-tee·oh)*
bad	mal	*(mahl)*
badge	emblema, el	*(ehl ehm-'bleh-mah)*
bag	bolsa, la	*(lah 'bohl-sah)*
bail	fianza, la	*(lah fee-'ahn-sah)*
bail bond	escritura de fianza, la	*(lah eh-skree-'too-rah deh fee-'ahn-sah)*
bailiff	alguacil, el	*(ehl ahl-gwah-'seel)*
baker	panadero, el	*(ehl pah-nah-'deh-roh)*
balance	equilibrio, el	*(ehl eh-kee-'lee-bree·oh)*
bald	calvo	*('kahl-voh)*
ball	pelota, la	*(lah peh-'loh-tah)*
balloon	globo, el	*(ehl 'gloh-boh)*
banana	plátano, el	*(ehl 'plah-tah-noh)*
bandage	vendaje, el	*(ehl vehn-'dah-heh)*
Band-Aid	curita, la	*(lah koo-'ree-tah)*
bank	banco, el	*(ehl 'bahn-koh)*
bank account	cuenta de banco, la	*(lah 'kwehn-tah deh 'bahn-koh)*
bar	bar, el	*(ehl bahr)*
barefoot	descalzo	*(deh-'skahl-soh)*
bargain	ganga, la	*(lah 'gahn-gah)*
barrier	barrera, la	*(lah bah-'rreh-rah)*
bartender	cantinero, el	*(ehl kahn-tee-'neh-roh)*
baseball	béisbol, el	*(ehl 'beh·ees-bohl)*
basement	sótano, el	*(ehl 'soh-tah-noh)*
basket	canasta, la	*(lah kah-'nah-stah)*
basketball	básquetbol, el	*(ehl 'bah-skeht-bohl)*
bat (baseball)	bate, el	*(ehl 'bah-teh)*
bathing suit	traje de baño, el	*(ehl 'trah-heh deh 'bah-nyoh)*
bathrobe	bata de baño, la	*(lah 'bah-tah deh 'bah-nyoh)*
bathroom	baño, el	*(ehl 'bah-nyoh)*
bathtub	tina, la	*(lah 'tee-nah)*
batteries	pilas, las	*(lahs 'pee-lahs)*
battery	agresión, la	*(lah ah-greh-see-'ohn)*
be able (to)	poder	*(poh-'dehr)*
beach	playa, la	*(lah 'plah-yah)*
beans	frijoles, los	*(lohs free-'hoh-lehs)*
bear	oso, el	*(ehl 'oh-soh)*
beard	barba, la	*(lah 'bahr-bah)*
beautician	cosmetólogo, el	*(ehl kohs-meh-'toh-loh-goh)*
beautiful	bello	*('beh-yoh)*
beauty salon	salón de belleza, el	*(ehl sah-'lohn deh beh-'yeh-sah)*
because	porque	*('pohr-keh)*
bed	cama, la	*(lah 'kah-mah)*
bedroom	dormitorio, el	*(ehl dohr-mee-'toh-ree·oh)*
bedspread	cubrecama, el	*(ehl koo-breh-'kah-mah)*
beer	cerveza, la	*(lah sehr-'veh-sah)*

before	antes	(´ahn-tehs)
beggar	limosnero, el	(ehl lee-mohs-´neh-roh)
begin (to)	empezar	(ehm-peh-´sahr)
behave (to)	portarse	(pohr-´tahr-seh)
behavior	comportamiento, el	(ehl kohm-pohr-tah-mee-´ehn -toh)
behind	detrás	(deh-´trahs)
belt	cinturón, el	(ehl seen-too-´rohn)
bend (to)	doblar	(doh-´blahr)
beneficial	beneficioso	(beh-neh-fee-see-´oh-soh)
bet (to)	apostar	(ah-poh-´stahr)
better	mejor	(meh-´hohr)
between	entre	(´ehn-treh)
beverage	bebida, la	(lah beh-´bee-dah)
bicycle	bicicleta, la	(lah bee-see-´kleh-tah)
bicyclist	ciclista, el	(ehl see-´klee-stah)
big	grande	(´grahn-deh)
bill (currency)	billete, el	(ehl bee-´yeh-teh)
billboard	letrero, el	(ehl leh-´treh-roh)
billion	mil millones	(meel mee-´yoh-nehs)
billy club	garrote, el	(ehl gah-´rroh-teh)
birth	nacimiento, el	(ehl nah-see-mee-´ehn-toh)
birthday	cumpleaños, el	(ehl koom-pleh-´ah-nyohs)
black	negro, el	(ehl ´neh-groh)
bladder	vejiga, la	(lah veh-´hee-gah)
blanket	cobija, la	(lah koh-´bee-hah)
bleed (to)	sangrar	(sahn-´grahr)
*Bless you!	¡Salud!	(sah-´lood)
blind	ciego	(see-´eh-goh)
blonde	rubio	(´roo-bee·oh)
blood	sangre, la	(lah ´sahn-greh)
bloody	sangriento	(sahn-gree-´ehn-toh)
blouse	blusa, la	(lah ´bloo-sah)
blow (to)	soplar	(soh-´plahr)
blue	azul	(ah-´sool)
board	tabla, la	(lah ´tah-blah)
boat	bote, el	(ehl ´boh-teh)
body	cuerpo, el	(ehl ´kwehr-poh)
body (dead)	cadáver, el	(ehl kah-´dah-vehr)
bodyguard	guardaespaldas, el	(ehl gwahr-dah-eh-´spahl-dahs)
bomb	bomba, la	(lah ´bohm-bah)
bondsman	fiador, el	(ehl fee-ah-´dohr)
bone	hueso, el	(ehl ´weh-soh)
book	libro, el	(ehl ´lee-broh)
bookshelf	librero, el	(ehl lee-´breh-roh)
boot	bota, la	(lah ´boh-tah)
booth	caseta, la	(lah kah-´seh-tah)
bored	aburrido	(ah-boo-´rree-doh)

bother (to)	molestar	*(moh-leh-'stahr)*
bottle	botella, la	*(lah boh-'teh-yah)*
bottom	fondo, el	*(ehl 'fohn-doh)*
boulevard	bulevar, el	*(ehl boo-leh-'vahr)*
bowling	boliche, el	*(ehl boh-'lee-cheh)*
box	caja, la	*(lah 'kah-hah)*
boxing	boxeo, el	*(ehl bohk-'seh-oh)*
boy	niño, el	*(ehl 'nee-nyoh)*
bracelet	brazalete, el	*(ehl brah-sah-'leh-teh)*
braces	corrector dental, el	*(ehl koh-rrehk-'tohr dehn-'tahl)*
brain	cerebro, el	*(ehl seh-'reh-broh)*
brake	freno, el	*(ehl 'freh-noh)*
brake light	luz de parada, la	*(lah loos deh pah-'rah-dah)*
brass knuckles	manoplas, las; nudillera, la	*(lahs mah-'noh-plahs, lah noo-dee-'yeh-rah)*
brassiere	sostén, el	*(ehl soh-'stehn)*
break in (to)	forzar	*(fohr-'sahr)*
break (to)	quebrar	*(keh-'brahr)*
breakfast	desayuno, el	*(ehl deh-sah-'yoo-noh)*
breast	seno, el	*(ehl 'seh-noh)*
breath	aliento, el	*(ehl ah-lee-'ehn-toh)*
breathe (to)	respirar	*(reh-spee-'rahr)*
brick	ladrillo, el	*(ehl lah-'dree-yoh)*
bridge	puente, el	*(ehl 'pwehn-teh)*
briefcase	maletín, el	*(ehl mah-leh-'teen)*
bright	brillante	*(bree-'yahn-teh)*
broken	roto	*('roh-toh)*
brooch	broche, el	*(ehl 'broh-cheh)*
brothel	burdel, el	*(ehl boor-'dehl)*
brother	hermano, el	*(ehl ehr-'mah-noh)*
brother-in-law	cuñado, el	*(ehl koo-'nyah-doh)*
brown	café	*(kah-'feh)*
bruise	contusión, la	*(lah kohn-too-see-'ohn)*
brunette	moreno	*(moh-'reh-noh)* NOTE: For Central Americans, moreno often is an euphemism for "African-American" or "mulatto."
brush	cepillo, el	*(ehl seh-'pee-yoh)*
buckle	hebilla, la	*(lah eh-'bee-yah)*
Buddhist	budista	*(boo-'dee-stah)*
budget	presupuesto, el	*(ehl preh-soo-'pweh-stoh)*
building	edificio, el	*(ehl eh-dee-'fee-see·oh)*
bulldozer	niveladora, la	*(lah nee-veh-lah-'doh-rah)*
bullet	bala, la	*(lah 'bah-lah)*
bullet-proof vest	chaleco a prueba de bala, el	*(ehl chah-'leh-koh ah proo-'eh-bah deh 'bah-lah)*
bullhorn	altavoz, el	*(ehl ahl-tah-'vohs)*
bumper	parachoques, el	*(ehl pah-rah-'choh-kehs)*
burn	quemadura, la	*(lah keh-mah-'doo-rah)*
bus	autobús, el	*(ehl ow-tow-'boos)*

bus stop	parada de autobús, la	*(lah pah-'rah-dah deh ow-toh-'boos)*
busboy	ayudante de camarero, el	*(ehl ah-yoo-'dahn-teh deh kah-mah-'reh-roh)*
bush	arbusto, el	*(ehl ahr-'boo-stoh)*
business	negocio, el	*(ehl neh-'goh-see·oh)*
busy	ocupado	*(oh-koo-'pah-doh)*
but	pero	*('peh-roh)*
butcher	carnicero, el	*(ehl kahr-nee-'seh-roh)*
buttock	nalga, la	*(lah 'nahl-gah)*
button	botón, el	*(ehl boh-'tohn)*
buy (to)	comprar	*(kohm-'prahr)*
by	por	*(pohr)*
bystander	espectador, el	*(ehl eh-spehk-tah-'dohr)*

C

cabin	cabaña, la	*(lah kah-'bah-nyah)*
cabinet	gabinete, el	*(ehl gah-bee-'neh-teh)*
cable	cable, el	*(ehl 'kah-bleh)*
cadaver	cadáver, el	*(ehl kah-'dah-vehr)*
cafeteria	cafetería, la	*(lah kah-feh-teh-'ree-ah)*
cage	jaula, la	*(lah 'how-lah)*
cake	torta, la	*(lah 'tohr-tah)*
calendar	calendario, el	*(ehl kah-lehn-'dah-ree·oh)*
caliber	calibre, el	*(ehl kah-'lee-breh)*
call	llamada, la	*(lah yah-'mah-dah)*
call (to)	llamar	*(yah-'mahr)*
calm	calmado	*(kahl-'mah-doh)*
calm (to)	calmar	*(kahl-'mahr)*
camera	cámara, la	*(lah 'kah-mah-rah)*
campground	campamento, el	*(ehl kahm-pah-'mehn-toh)*
can	lata, la	*(lah 'lah-tah)*
cancel (to)	cancelar	*(kahn-seh-'lahr)*
cap	gorra, la	*(lah 'goh-rrah)*
capsule	cápsula, la	*(lah 'kahp-soo-lah)*
captain	capitán, el	*(ehl kah-pee-'tahn)*
car	carro, el	*(ehl 'kah-rroh)*
car lot	lote de carros, el	*(ehl 'loh-teh deh 'kah-rrohs)*
carbine	carabina, la	*(lah kah-rah-'bee-nah)*
carburetor	carburador, el	*(ehl kahr-boo-rah-'dohr)*
card	tarjeta, la	*(lah tahr-'heh-tah)*
cardboard	cartón, el	*(ehl kahr-'tohn)*
carpenter	carpintero, el	*(ehl kahr-peen-'teh-roh)*
carrot	zanahoria, la	*(lah sah-nah-'oh-ree·ah)*
carry (to)	llevar	*(yeh-'vahr)*
cartilage	cartílago, el	*(ehl kahr-'tee-lah-goh)*
cartridge	cartucho, el	*(ehl kahr-'too-choh)*
case	caso, el	*(ehl 'kah-soh)*

cash	dinero al contado, el	(ehl dee-'neh-roh ahl kohn-'tah-doh)
cashier	cajero, el	(ehl kah-'heh-roh)
cassette	casete, el	(ehl kah-'seh-teh)
cast	armadura de yeso, la	(lah ahr-mah-'doo-rah deh'yeh-soh)
cat	gato, el	(ehl 'gah-toh)
catch (to)	coger	(koh-'hehr)
Catholic	católico	(kah-'toh-lee-koh)
cause	causa, la	(lah 'kow-sah)
ceiling	cielo raso, el	(ehl see-'eh-loh 'rah-soh)
cell	celda, la	(lah 'sehl-dah)
cement	cemento, el	(ehl seh-'mehn-toh)
cement truck	mezclador de cemento, el	(ehl meh-sklah-'dohr deh seh-'mehn-toh)
cemetery	cementerio, el	(ehl seh-mehn-'teh-ree·oh)
cent	centavo, el	(ehl sehn-'tah-voh)
certificate	certificado, el	(ehl sehr-tee-fee-'kah-doh)
chain	cadena, la	(lah kah-'deh-nah)
chair	silla, la	(lah 'see-yah)
chamber of commerce	cámara de comercio, la	(lah 'kah-mah-rah deh koh-'mehr-see·oh)
champagne	champaña, la	(lah chahm-'pah-nyah)
change	cambio, el	(ehl 'kahm-bee·oh)
change (to)	cambiar	(kahm-bee-'ahr)
chaplain	capellán, el	(ehl kah-peh-'yahn)
charge	cargo, el; acusación, la	(ehl 'kahr-goh; lah ah-koo-sah-see-'ohn)
charge (to)	denunciar	(deh-noon-see-'ahr)
chase (to)	perseguir	(pehr-seh-'geer)
cheap	barato	(bah-'rah-toh)
check	cheque, el	(ehl 'cheh-keh)
check (to)	verificar	(veh-ree-fee-'kahr)
checkbook	chequera, la	(lah cheh-'keh-rah)
cheek	mejilla, la	(lah meh-'hee-yah)
cheese	queso, el	(ehl 'keh-soh)
chemical	producto químico, el	(ehl proh-'dook-toh 'kee-mee-koh)
chest	pecho, el	(ehl 'peh-choh)
chicken	pollo, el	(ehl 'poh-yoh)
chief	jefe, el	(ehl 'heh-feh)
child	niño, el	(ehl 'nee-nyoh)
child abuse	abuso de menores, el	(ehl ah-'boo-soh deh meh-'noh-rehs)
child care	cuidado del niño, el	(ehl kwee-'dah-doh dehl 'nee-nyoh)
child support	ayuda para el niño, la	(lah ah-'yoo-dah 'pah-rah ehl'nee-nyoh)
childhood	niñez, la	(lah nee-'nyehs)

chimney	chimenea, la	*(lah chee-meh-'neh-ah)*
chin	barbilla, la	*(lah bahr-'bee-yah)*
choose (to)	elegir	*(eh-leh-'heer)*
Christian	cristiano	*(kree-stee-'ah-noh)*
Christmas	navidad, la	*(lah nah-vee-'dahd)*
church	iglesia, la	*(lah ee-'gleh-see·ah)*
cigar	puro, el	*(ehl 'poo-roh)*
cigarette	cigarrillo, el	*(ehl see-gah-'rree-yoh)*
circle	círculo, el	*(ehl 'seer-koo-loh)*
circus	circo, el	*(ehl 'seer-koh)*
citation	citación, la	*(lah see-tah-see-'ohn)*
citizen	ciudadano, el	*(ehl see-oo-dah-'dah-noh)*
city	ciudad, la	*(lah see-oo-'dahd)*
city block	cuadra, la	*(lah 'kwah-drah)*
city hall	municipio, el	*(ehl moo-nee-'see-pee·oh)*
civic	cívico	*('see-vee-koh)*
claim	petición, la	*(lah peh-tee-see-'ohn)*
class	clase, la	*(lah 'klah-seh)*
classification	clasificación, la	*(lah klah-see-fee-kah-see-'ohn)*
clean	limpio	*('leem-pee·oh)*
clean (to)	limpiar	*(leem-pee-'ahr)*
clerk	dependiente, el	*(ehl deh-pehn-dee-'ehn-teh)*
client	cliente, el	*(ehl klee-'ehn-teh)*
climate	clima, el	*(ehl 'klee-mah)*
clock	reloj, el	*(ehl reh-'loh)*
close (to)	cerrar	*(seh-'rrahr)*
closed	cerrado	*(seh-'rrah-doh)*
closet	ropero, el	*(ehl roh-'peh-roh)*
cloud	nube, la	*(lah 'noo-beh)*
cloudy	nublado	*(noo-'blah-doh)*
clutch	embrague, el	*(ehl ehm-'brah-geh)*
cocaine	cocaína, la	*(lah koh-kah-'ee-nah)*
cocktail	cóctel, el	*(ehl 'kohk-tehl)*
code	código, el	*(ehl 'koh-dee-goh)*
coffee	café, el	*(ehl kah-'feh)*
coffin	ataúd, el	*(ehl ah-tah-'ood)*
coin	moneda, la	*(lah moh-'neh-dah)*
coin case	monedero, el	*(ehl moh-neh-'deh-roh)*
cold	frío	*('free-oh)*
cold (illness)	resfrío, el	*(ehl rehs-'free-oh)*
collection	colección, la	*(lah koh-lehk-see-'ohn)*
college	colegio, el	*(ehl koh-'leh-hee·oh)*
colonel	coronel, el	*(ehl koh-roh-'nehl)*
color	color, el	*(ehl koh-'lohr)*
comb	peine, el	*(ehl 'peh·ee-neh)*
comfortable	cómodo	*('koh-moh-doh)*
command	orden, la	*(lah 'ohr-dehn)*
commercial	comercial	*(koh-mehr-see·ahl)*

compact disc	disco compacto, el	*(ehl 'dee-skoh kohm-'pahk-toh)*
companion	compañero, el	*(ehl kohm-pah-'nyeh-roh)*
complaint	queja, la	*(lah 'keh-hah)*
complete	completo	*(kohm-'pleh-toh)*
computer	computadora, la	*(lah kohm-poo-tah-'doh-rah)*
concert	concierto, el	*(ehl kohn-see-'ehr-toh)*
condominium	condominio, el	*(ehl kohn-doh-'mee-nee·oh)*
cone	cono, el	*(ehl 'koh-noh)*
conference	conferencia, la	*(lah kohn-feh-'rehn-see·ah)*
confess (to)	confesar	*(kohn-feh-'sahr)*
confession	confesión, la	*(lah kohn-feh-see-'ohn)*
conflict	conflicto, el	*(ehl kohn-'fleek-toh)*
confused	confundido	*(kohn-foon-'dee-doh)*
congested	congestionado	*(kohn-heh-stee·oh-'nah-doh)*
* **Congratulations!**	¡Felicitaciones!	*(feh-lee-see-tah-see-'oh-nehs)*
consent	permiso, el	*(ehl pehr-'mee-soh)*
construction	construcción, la	*(lah kohn-strook-see-'ohn)*
consume (to)	tomar	*(toh-'mahr)*
contact lenses	lentes de contacto, los	*(lohs 'lehn-tehs deh kohn-'tahk-toh)*
contagious	contagioso	*(kohn-tah-hee-'oh-soh)*
continue (to)	seguir	*(seh-'geer)*
control	control, el	*(ehl kohn-'trohl)*
convertible	descapotable, el	*(ehl dehs-kah-poh-'tah-bleh)*
convict	convicto, el	*(ehl kohn-'veek-toh)*
cook	cocinero, el	*(ehl koh-see-'neh-roh)*
cookie	galleta, la	*(lah gah-'yeh-tah)*
cool	fresco	*('freh-skoh)*
coordinator	coordinador, el	*(ehl koh-ohr-dee-mah-'dohr)*
copier	copiadora, la	*(lah koh-pee·ah-'doh-rah)*
copy	copia, la	*(lah 'koh-pee·ah)*
corn	maíz, el	*(ehl mah-'ees)*
corner	esquina, la	*(lah eh-'skee-nah)*
coroner	médico legista, el	*(ehl 'meh-dee-koh leh-'hee-stah)*
corporal (army)	cabo, el	*(ehl 'kah-boh)*
corporal (body)	corporal	*(kohr-poh-'rahl)*
cosmetics	cosméticos, los	*(lohs kohs-'meh-tee-kohs)*
cost	costo, el	*(ehl 'koh-stoh)*
costume	disfraz, el	*(ehl dees-'frahs)*
cotton	algodón, el	*(ehl ahl-goh-'dohn)*
cough	tos, la	*(lah tohs)*
counselor	consejero, el	*(ehl kohn-seh-'heh-roh)*
counterfeiting	falsificación, la	*(lah fahl-see-fee-kah-see-'ohn)*
country	país, el	*(ehl pah-'ees)*
county	condado, el	*(ehl kohn-'dah-doh)*
coupon	cupón, el	*(ehl koo-'pohn)*
court	tribunal, el	*(ehl tree-boo-'nahl)*
courtesy	cortesía, la	*(lah kohr-teh-'see-ah)*

courthouse	corte, la	(lah 'kohr-teh)
courtyard	patio, el	(ehl 'pah-tee·oh)
cousin	primo, el	(ehl 'pree-moh)
cow	vaca, la	(lah 'vah-kah)
CPR	respiración artificial, la	(lah reh-spee-rah-see-'ohn ahr-tee-fee-see-'ahl)
cracker	galleta salada, la	(lah gah-'yeh-tah sah-'lah-dah)
crash (to)	chocar	(choh-'kahr)
crazy	loco	('loh-koh)
credit card	tarjeta de crédito, la	(lah tahr-'heh-tah deh 'kreh-dee-toh)
crib	cuna, la	(lah 'koo-nah)
crime	crimen, el	(ehl 'kree-mehn)
criminal	criminal, el	(ehl kree-mee-'nahl)
critical	crítico	('kree-tee-koh)
crop	cosecha, la	(lah koh-'seh-chah)
cross (to)	cruzar	(kroo-'sahr)
cross-examination	interrogación, la	(lah een-teh-rroh-gah-see-'ohn)
crosswalk	cruce de peatones, el	(ehl 'kroo-seh deh peh-ah-'toh-nehs)
crowd	muchedumbre, la	(lah moo-cheh-'doom-breh)
crutch	muleta, la	(lah moo-'leh-tah)
cry (to)	llorar	(yoh-'rahr)
Cuban	cubano	(koo-'bah-noh)
cul-de-sac	calle sin salida, la	(lah 'kah-yeh seen sah-'lee-dah)
curb	orilla, la	(lah oh-'ree-yah)
curfew	toque de queda, el	(ehl 'toh-keh deh 'keh-dah)
curtain	cortina, la	(lah kohr-'tee-nah)
curve	curva, la	(lah 'koor-vah)
custody	custodia, la	(lah koo-'stoh-dee·ah)
custom	costumbre, la	(lah koh-'stoom-breh)
customer	cliente, el	(ehl klee-'ehn-teh)
cut	cortada, la	(lah kohr-'tah-dah)
cut (to)	cortar	(kohr-'tahr)
cyclist	ciclista, el	(ehl see-'klee-stah)

D

dagger	daga, la	(lah 'dah-gah)
dam	represa, la	(lah reh-'preh-sah)
damage	daño, el	(ehl 'dah-nyoh)
damaged	dañado	(dah-'nyah-doh)
dance	baile, el	(ehl 'bah·ee-leh)
* Danger!	¡Peligro!	(peh-'lee-groh)
danger	peligro, el	(ehl peh-'lee-groh)
dangerous	peligroso	(peh-lee-'groh-soh)
dashboard	tablero de instrumentos, el	(ehl tah-'bleh-roh deh een-stroo-'mehn-tohs)
date	fecha, la	(lah 'feh-chah)

daughter	hija, la	*(lah 'ee-hah)*
daughter-in-law	nuera, la	*(lah 'nweh-rah)*
day	día, el	*(ehl 'dee-ah)*
day care center	guardería infantil, la	*(lah gwahr-deh-'ree-ah een-fahn-'teel)*
dead	muerto	*('mwehr-toh)*
dead bolt	pestillo, el	*(ehl peh-'stee-yoh)*
deaf	sordo	*('sohr-doh)*
dealer (drug)	droguero, el	*(ehl droh-'geh-roh)*
death	muerte, la	*(lah 'mwehr-teh)*
December	diciembre	*(dee-see-'ehm-breh)*
defective	defectuoso	*(deh-fehk-too-'oh-soh)*
defendant	demandado, el	*(ehl deh-mahn-'dah-doh)*
defense	defensa, la	*(lah deh-'fehn-sah)*
dehydration	deshidratación, la	*(lah dehs-ee-drah-tah-see-'ohn)*
delay	tardanza, la	*(lah tahr-'dahn-sah)*
delinquency	delincuencia, la	*(lah deh-leen-'kwehn-see·ah)*
delinquent	delincuente, el	*(ehl deh-leen-'kwehn-teh)*
delivery truck	camión de reparto, el	*(ehl kah-mee-'ohn deh reh-'pahr-toh)*
delusions	delirios, los	*(lohs deh-'lee-ree·ohs)*
dented	abollado	*(ah-boh-'yah-doh)*
dentist	dentista, el	*(ehl dehn-'tee-stah)*
dentures	dentadura postiza, la	*(lah dehn-tah-'doo-rah poh-'stee-sah)*
deny (to)	negar	*(neh-'gahr)*
deodorant	desodorante, el	*(ehl dehs-oh-doh-'rahn-teh)*
department	departamento, el	*(ehl deh-pahr-tah-'mehn-toh)*
deportation	deportación, la	*(lah deh-pohr-tah-see-'ohn)*
deputy	diputado, el	*(ehl dee-poo-'tah-doh)*
desert	desierto, el	*(ehl deh-see-'ehr-toh)*
desk	escritorio, el	*(ehl eh-skree-'toh-ree·oh)*
dessert	postre, el	*(ehl 'poh-streh)*
destroy (to)	destruir	*(deh-stroo-'eer)*
detain (to)	detener	*(deh-teh-'nehr)*
detained	detenido	*(deh-teh-'nee-doh)*
detective	detective, el	*(ehl deh-tehk-'tee-veh)*
detour	desvío, el	*(ehl dehs-'vee-oh)*
diamond	diamante, el	*(ehl dee-ah-'mahn-teh)*
diaper	paño, el	*(ehl 'pah-nyoh)*
die (to)	morir	*(moh-'reer)*
different	diferente	*(dee-feh-'rehn-teh)*
difficult	difícil	*(dee-'fee-seel)*
dining room	comedor, el	*(ehl koh-meh-'dohr)*
dinner	cena, la	*(lah 'seh-nah)*
direction	dirección, la	*(lah dee-rehk-see-'ohn)*
directions	instrucciones, las	*(lahs eens-trook-see-'oh-nehs)*
dirt	tierra, la	*(lah tee-'eh-rrah)*

dirty	sucio	('soo-see·oh)
disability	incapacidad, la	(lah een-kah-pah-see-'dahd)
disabled	incapacitado	(een-kah-pah-see-'tah-doh)
discipline	disciplina, la	(lah dee-see-'plee-nah)
discount	descuento, el	(ehl dehs-kwehn-toh)
dishwasher	lavaplatos, el	(ehl lah-vah-'plah-tohs)
dispatcher	despachador, el	(ehl deh-spah-chah-'dohr)
dispute	disputa, la	(lah dees-'poo-tah)
distributor	distribuidor, el	(ehl dees-tree-boo-ee-'dohr)
district	distrito, el	(ehl dee-'stree-toh)
district attorney	fiscal del distrito, el	(ehl fee-'skahl dehl dee-'stree-toh)
ditch	zanja, la	(lah 'sahn-hah)
divider	divisoria, la	(lah dee-vee-'soh-ree·ah)
divorced	divorciado	(dee-vohr-see-'ah-doh)
dizzy	mareado	(mah-reh-'ah-doh)
DMV	departamento de vehículos , el	(ehl deh-pahr-tah-'mehn-toh deh veh-'ee-koo-lohs)
do (to)	hacer	(ah-'sehr)
*Do you desire...?	¿Desea...?	(deh-'seh-ah...)
*Do you like...?	¿Le gusta...?	(leh 'goo-stah...)
doctor	médico, el	(ehl 'meh-dee·koh)
document	documento, el	(ehl doh-koo-'mehn-toh)
dog	perro, el	(ehl 'peh-rroh)
doghouse	perrera, la	(lah peh-'rreh-rah)
dollar	dólar, el	(ehl 'doh-lahr)
domestic violence	violencia doméstica, la	(lah vee-oh-'lehn-see·ah doh-'meh-stee-kah)
*Don't worry!	¡No se preocupe!	(noh seh preh-oh-'koo-peh)
door	puerta, la	(lah 'pwehr-tah)
double	doble	('doh-bleh)
down	abajo	(ah-'bah-hoh)
downtown	centro, el	(ehl 'sehn-troh)
dozen	docena, la	(lah doh-'seh-nah)
drainage	drenaje, el	(ehl dreh-'nah-heh)
drawer	cajón, el	(ehl kah-'hohn)
dress	vestido, el	(ehl veh-'stee-doh)
dressmaker	modisto, el	(ehl moh-'dee-stoh)
dresser	tocador, el	(ehl toh-kah-'dohr)
drink	bebida, la	(lah beh-'bee-dah)
drink (to)	beber	(beh-'behr)
drive (to)	manejar	(mah-neh-'hahr)
driver	chofer, el	(ehl choh-'fehr)
driveway	entrada para carros, la	(lah ehn-'trah-dah 'pah-rah'kah-rrohs)
drop	gota, la	(lah 'goh-tah)
drug abuse	abuso de las drogas, el	(ehl ah-'boo-soh deh lahs'droh-gahs)
drug addict	drogadicto, el	(ehl drohg-ah-'deek-toh)

drug dealer	vendedor de drogas, el	*(ehl vehn-deh-'dohr deh'droh-gahs)*
drug traffic	narcotráfico, el	*(ehl nahr-koh-'trah-fee-koh)*
drugged	drogado	*(droh-'gah-doh)*
drunk	borracho	*(boh-'rrah-choh)*
drunkard	borracho, el	*(ehl boh-'rrah-choh)*
dry	seco	*('seh-koh)*
dry (to)	secar	*(seh-'kahr)*
dryer	secadora, la	*(lah seh-kah-'doh-rah)*
duffel bag	talega, la	*(lah tah-'leh-gah)*
dull	romo	*('roh-moh)*
dump	basural, el	*(ehl bah-soo-'rahl)*
dump truck	volquete, el	*(ehl vohl-'keh-teh)*
dust	polvo, el	*(ehl 'pohl-voh)*
dynamite	dinamita, la	*(lah dee-nah-'mee-tah)*

E

ear	oreja, la	*(lah oh-'reh-hah)*
early	temprano	*(tehm-'prah-noh)*
earring	arete, el	*(ehl ah-'reh-teh)*
earthquake	terremoto, el	*(ehl teh-rreh-'moh-toh)*
east	este	*('eh-steh)*
Easter	Pascua, la	*(lah 'pahs-kwah)*
easy	fácil	*('fah-seel)*
eat (to)	comer	*(koh-'mehr)*
education	educación, la	*(lah eh-doo-kah-see-'ohn)*
egg	huevo, el	*(ehl 'weh-voh)*
eight	ocho	*('oh-choh)*
eighteen	dieciocho	*(dee-ehs-ee-'oh-choh)*
eighth	octavo	*(ohk-'tah-voh)*
eighty	ochenta	*(oh-'chehn-tah)*
elbow	codo, el	*(ehl 'koh-doh)*
elderly	anciano, el	*(ehl ahn-see-'ah-noh)*
electrician	electricista, el	*(ehl eh-lehk-tree-'sees-tah)*
electrical outlet	enchufe, el	*(ehl ehn-'choo-feh)*
electricity	electricidad, la	*(lah eh-lehk-tree-see-'dahd)*
elevator	ascensor, el	*(ehl ah-sehn-'sohr)*
eleven	once	*('ohn-seh)*
embezzling	desfalco, el	*(ehl dehs-'fahl-koh)*
emergency	emergencia, la	*(lah eh-mehr-'hehn-see·ah)*
emigrant	emigrante, el	*(ehl eh-mee-'grahn-teh)*
employee	empleador, el	*(ehl ehm-pleh-ah-'dohr)*
employer	empresario, el	*(ehl ehm-preh-'sah-ree·oh)*
employment	empleo, el	*(ehl ehm-'pleh-oh)*
empty	vacío	*(vah-'see-oh)*
empty (to)	vaciar	*(vah-see-'ahr)*
end	punta, la	*(lah 'poon-tah)*
end (to)	terminar	*(tehr-mee-'nahr)*
engine	motor, el	*(ehl moh-'tohr)*

engineer	ingeniero, el	*(ehl een-heh-nee-'eh-roh)*
enough	suficiente	*(soo-fee-see-'ehn-teh)*
entrance	entrada, la	*(lah ehn-'trah-dah)*
envelope	sobre, el	*(ehl 'soh-breh)*
epidemic	epidemia, la	*(lah eh-pee-'deh-mee·ah)*
equipment	equipaje, el	*(ehl eh-kee-'pah-heh)*
escalator	escalera mecánica, la	*(lah eh-skah-'leh-rah meh-'kah-nee-kah)*
escape (to)	escapar	*(eh-skah-'pahr)*
* **Everyone get back!**	¡Todos hacia atrás!	*('toh-dohs 'ah-see·ah ah-'trahs)*
everything	todo	*('toh-doh)*
everywhere	por todas partes	*(pohr 'toh-dahs 'pahr-tehs)*
evidence	evidencia, la	*(lah eh-vee-'dehn-see·ah)*
examine (to)	examinar	*(ehk-sah-mee-'nahr)*
examiner	examinador, el	*(ehl ehk-sah-mee-nah-'dohr)*
example	ejemplo, el	*(ehl eh-'hehm-ploh)*
excited	emocionado	*(eh-moh-see·oh-'nah-doh)*
* **Excuse me!**	¡Con permiso!	*(kohn pehr-'mee-soh)*
	¡Perdón!	*(pehr-'dohn)*
	¡Disculpe!	*(dee-'skool-peh)*
execution	ejecución, la	*(lah eh-heh-koo-see-'ohn)*
executive	gerente, el	*(ehl heh-'rehn-teh)*
exhaust	tubo de escape, el	*(ehl 'too-boh deh eh-'skah-peh)*
exhausted	agotado	*(ah-goh-'tah-doh)*
exit	salida, la	*(lah sah-'lee-dah)*
expensive	caro	*('kah-roh)*
experience	experiencia, la	*(lah ehk-speh-ree-'ehn-see·ah)*
explanation	explicación, la	*(lah ehk-splee-kah-see-'ohn)*
explosive	explosivo, el	*(ehl ehk-sploh-'see-voh)*
expression	expresión, la	*(lah ehk-spreh-see-'ohn)*
extended	extendido	*(ehks-tehn-'dee-doh)*
extension	extensión, la	*(lah ehk-stehn-see-'ohn)*
exterior	exterior	*(ehks-teh-ree-'ohr)*
extortion	extorsión, la	*(lah ehks-tohr-see-'ohn)*
eye	ojo, el	*(ehl 'oh-hoh)*
eyebrow	ceja, la	*(lah 'seh-hah)*
eyelash	pestaña, la	*(lah peh-'stah-nyah)*
F		
face	cara, la	*(lah 'kah-rah)*
factory	fábrica, la	*(lah 'fah-bree-kah)*
faint (to)	desmayarse	*(dehs-mah-'yahr-seh)*
fair	feria, la	*(lah 'feh-ree·ah)*
fake	falso	*('fahl-soh)*
fall (to)	caer	*(kah-'ehr)*
fan	ventilador, el	*(ehl vehn-tee-lah-'dohr)*
fan belt	correa del ventilador, la	*(lah koh-'rreh-ah dehl vehn-tee-lah-'dohr)*

far	lejos	(ʹleh-hohs)
farsighted	présbita	(ʹprehs-bee-tah)
farmer	granjero, el	(ehl grahn-ʹheh-roh)
fast	rápido	(ʹrah-pee-doh)
fasten (to)	amarrar	(ah-mah-ʹrrahr)
fat	gordo	(ʹgohr-doh)
fatal	fatal	(fah-ʹtahl)
father	padre, el	(ehl ʹpah-dreh)
father-in-law	suegro, el	(ehl ʹsweh-groh)
fatigue	fatiga, la	(lah fah-ʹtee-gah)
faucet	grifo, el	(ehl ʹgree-foh)
fault	culpa la	(lah ʹkool-pah)
fax	fax, el	(ehl fahks)
fear	miedo, el	(ehl mee-ʹeh-doh)
February	febrero	(feh-ʹbreh-roh)
fee	honorario, el	(ehl oh-noh-ʹrah-ree·oh)
feed (to)	alimentar	(ah-lee-mehn-ʹtahr)
felony	delito mayor, el	(ehl deh-ʹlee-toh mah-ʹyohr)
fence	cerca, la	(lah ʹsehr-kah)
fender	guardabarro, el	(ehl gwahr-dah-ʹbah-rroh)
ferocious	feroz	(feh-ʹrohs)
festival	festival, el	(ehl feh-stee-ʹvahl)
fever	fiebre, la	(lah fee-ʹeh-breh)
few	pocos	(ʹpoh-kohs)
field	campo, el	(ehl ʹkahm-poh)
fifteen	quince	(ʹkeen-seh)
fifth	quinto	(ʹkeen-toh)
fifty	cincuenta	(seen-ʹkwehn-tah)
fight	pelea, la	(lah peh-ʹleh-ah)
fight (to)	pelear	(peh-leh-ʹahr)
file (instrument)	lima, la	(lah ʹlee-mah)
files	archivos, los	(lohs ahr-ʹchee-vohs)
find (to)	encontrar	(ehn-kohn-ʹtrahr)
fine (good)	bien	(ʹbee·ehn)
fine (penalty)	multa, la	(lah ʹmool-tah)
finger	dedo, el	(ehl ʹdeh-doh)
finish (to)	acabar	(ah-kah-ʹbahr)
* Fire!	¡Fuego!	(ʹfweh-goh)
fire	fuego, el	(ehl ʹfweh-goh)
fire department	departamento de bomberos, el	(ehl deh-pahr-tah-ʹmehn-toh deh bohm-ʹbeh-rohs)
firefighter	bombero, el	(ehl bohm-ʹbeh-roh)
fire hydrant	llave de incendios, la	(lah ʹyah-veh deh een-ʹsehn-dee-ohs)
firearm	arma de fuego, el	(ehl ʹahr-mah deh ʹfweh-goh)
fireplace	fogón, el	(ehl foh-ʹgohn)
fire truck	camión de bomberos, el	(ehl kah-mee-ʹohn deh bohm-ʹbeh-rohs)

fireworks	fuegos artificiales, los	*(lohs 'fweh-gohs ahr-tee-fee-see-'ah-lehs)*
first	primero	*(pree-'meh-roh)*
first aid	primeros auxilios, los	*(lohs pree-'meh-rohs owk-'see-lee·ohs)*
first aid kit	botiquín, el	*(ehl boh-tee-'keen)*
fish	pescado, el	*(ehl peh-'skah-doh)*
fish (to)	pescar	*(peh-'skahr)*
fisherman	pescador, el	*(ehl peh-skah-'dohr)*
fist	puño, el	*(ehl 'poo-nyoh)*
five	cinco	*('seen-koh)*
five hundred	quinientos	*(kee-nee-'ehn-tohs)*
flag	bandera, la	*(lah bahn-'deh-rah)*
flame	llama, la	*(lah 'yah-mah)*
flare	antorcha, la	*(lah ahn-'tohr-chah)*
flashing	relampagueante	*(ehl reh-lahm-pah-geh-'ah-teh)*
flashlight	linterna, la	*(lah leen-'tehr-nah)*
flat (airless)	desinflado	*(dehs-een-'flah-doh)*
flatbed truck	camión de plataforma, el	*(ehl kah-mee-'ohn deh plah-tah-'fohr-mah)*
flight	vuelo, el	*(ehl 'vweh-loh)*
flood	inundación	*(lah een-oon-dah-see-'ohn)*
floodlight	reflector, el	*(ehl reh-flehk-'tohr)*
floor	piso, el	*(ehl 'pee-soh)*
florist	floristería, la	*(lah floh-ree-steh-'ree-ah)*
flower	flor, la	*(lah flohr)*
flu	influenza, la	*(lah een-floo-'ehn-sah)*
fly	mosca, la	*(lah 'moh-skah)*
fog	neblina, la	*(lah neh-'blee-nah)*
foliage	follaje, el	*(ehl foh-'yah-heh)*
follow (to)	seguir	*(seh-'geer)*
following (the)	siguiente, el	*(ehl see-gee-'ehn-teh)*
food	comida, la	*(lah koh-'mee-dah)*
foot	pie, el	*(ehl 'pee-eh)*
football	fútbol americano, el	*(ehl 'foot-bohl ah-meh-ree-'kah-noh)*
for	para	*('pah-rah)*
foreman	capataz, el	*(ehl kah-pah-'tahs)*
forensic science	ciencia forense, la	*(lah see-'ehn-see·ah foh-'rehn-seh)*
forest	bosque, el	*(ehl 'boh-skeh)*
forger	falsificador, el	*(ehl fahl-see-fee-kah-'dohr)*
form	formulario, el	*(ehl fohr-moo-'lah-ree·oh)*
formality	formalidad, la	*(lah fohr-mah-lee-'dahd)*
forty	cuarenta	*(kwah-'rehn-tah)*
fountain	fuente, la	*(lah 'fwehn-teh)*
four	cuatro	*('kwah-troh)*
fourteen	catorce	*(kah-'tohr-seh)*

fourth	cuarto	(´kwahr-toh)
fracture	fractura, la	(lah frahk-´too-rah)
fraud	fraude, el	(ehl ´frow-deh)
free	libre	(´lee-breh)
freeway	autopista, la	(lah ow-toh-´pee-stah)
freezer	congelador, el	(ehl kohn-heh-lah-´dohr)
Friday	viernes	(vee-´ehr-nehs)
friend	amigo, el	(ehl ah-´mee-goh)
friendly	amistoso	(ah-mee-´stoh-soh)
frighten (to)	asustar	(ah-soo-´stahr)
frisk (to)	registrar	(reh-hee-´strahr)
front	frente, el	(ehl ´frehn-teh)
frost	escarcha, la	(lah eh-´skahr-chah)
frostbite	congelamiento, el	(ehl kohn-heh-lah-mee-´ehn-toh)
fugitive	fugitivo, el	(ehl foo-hee-´tee-voh)
full	lleno	(´yeh-noh)
funeral	funeral, el	(ehl foo-neh-´rahl)
funeral home	funeraria, la	(lah foo-neh-´rah-ree·ah)
funny	chistoso	(chee-´stoh-soh)
furious	furioso	(foo-ree-´oh-soh)
furniture	muebles, los	(los ´mweh-blehs)
fuse	fusible, el	(ehl foo-´see-bleh)
fuse box	caja de fusibles, la	(lah ´kah-hah deh foo-´see-blehs)

G

gallbladder	vesícula, la	(lah veh-´see-koo-lah)
gallon	galón, el	(ehl gah-´lohn)
gambler	apostador, el; jugador, el	(ehl ah-pohs-tah-´dohr; ehl hoo-gah-´dohr)
gambling	juego de apuestas, el	(ehl ´hweh-goh deh ah-´pweh-stahs)
game	juego, el	(ehl ´hweh-goh)
gang	pandilla, la	(lah pahn-´dee-yah)
gang member	pandillero, el	(ehl pahn-dee-´yeh-roh)
garage	garaje, el	(ehl gah-´rah-heh)
garden	jardín, el	(ehl hahr-´deen)
gardener	jardinero, el	(ehl hahr-dee-´neh-roh)
gas	gas, el	(ehl gahs)
gas cap	tapón del tanque, el	(ehl tah-´pohn dehl ´tahn-keh)
gas mask	máscara de gas, la	(lah ´mah-skah-rah deh gahs)
gas station	gasolinera, la	(lah gah-soh-lee-´neh-rah)
gasoline	gasolina, la	(lah gah-soh-´lee-nah)
gate	portón, el	(ehl pohr-´tohn)
gauge	indicador, el	(ehl een-dee-kah-´dohr)
gay	gay, el	(ehl geh)
gear	engranaje, el	(ehl ehn-grah-´nah-heh)
gesture	gesto, el	(ehl ´heh-stoh)
gift	regalo, el	(ehl reh-´gah-loh)
gin	ginebra, la	(lah hee-´neh-brah)

girl	niña, la	(lah 'nee-nyah)
give (to)	dar	(dahr)
glass	vidrio, el	(ehl 'vee-dree·oh)
glass (drinking)	vaso, el	(ehl 'vah-soh)
glasses	anteojos, los	(lohs ahn-teh-'oh-hohs)
glove	guante, el	(ehl 'gwahn-teh)
glove compartment	guantera, la	(lah gwahn-'teh-rah)
glue	pegamento, el	(ehl peh-gah-'mehn-toh)
* Go ahead!	¡Pase!	('pah-seh)
go (to)	ir	(eer)
* Go with God!	¡Vaya con Dios!	('vah-yah kohn 'dee-ohs)
God	Dios	('dee-ohs)
godparents	padrinos, los	(lohs pah-'dree-nohs)
good	bueno	('bweh-noh)
* Good afternoon!	¡Buenas tardes!	('bweh-nahs 'tahr-dehs)
* Good evening!	¡Buenas noches!	('bweh-nahs 'noh-chehs)
* Good idea!	¡Buena idea!	('bweh-nah ee-'deh-ah)
* Good luck!	¡Buena suerte!	('bweh-nah 'swehr-teh)
* Good morning!	¡Buenos días!	('bweh-nohs 'dee-ahs)
* Good night!	¡Buenas noches!	('bweh-nahs 'noh-chehs)
* Good-bye!	¡Adiós!	('ah-dee-'ohs)
government	gobierno, el	(ehl goh-bee-'ehr-noh)
governor	gobernador, el	(ehl goh-behr-nah-'dohr)
grade	grado, el	(ehl 'grah-doh)
graffiti	grafiti, el; pintadas, las	(ehl grah-'fee-tee; lahs peen-'tah-dahs)
gram	gramo, el	(ehl 'grah-moh)
grand jury	gran jurado, el	(ehl grahn hoo-'rah-doh)
grand theft	robo de mayor cuantía, el; robo mayor, el	(ehl 'roh-boh deh mah-'yohr kwahn-'tee-ah; ehl 'roh-boh mah-'yohr)
granddaughter	nieta, la	(lah nee-'eh-tah)
grandfather	abuelo, el	(ehl ah-'bweh-loh)
grandmother	abuela, la	(lah ah-'bweh-lah)
grandson	nieto, el	(ehl nee-'eh-toh)
grape	uva, la	(lah 'oo-vah)
grass	césped, el	(ehl 'sehs-pehd)
grasshopper	saltamontes, el	(ehl sahl-tah-'mohn-tehs)
gravel	cascajo, el; grava, la	(ehl kahs-'kah-hoh; lah 'grah-vah)
gray	gris	(grees)
green	verde	('vehr-deh)
greet (to)	saludar	(sah-loo-'dahr)
grocery store	bodega, la	(lah boh-'deh-gah)
groin	ingle, la	(lah 'een-gleh)
ground	suelo, el	(ehl 'sweh-loh)
grove	arboleda, la	(lah ahr-boh-'leh-dah)
grow (to)	crecer	(kreh-'sehr)
guard	guardia, el	(ehl 'gwahr-dee·ah)

guess (to)	adivinar	*(ah-dee-vee-'nahr)*
guilty	culpable	*(kool-'pah-bleh)*
gulch	barranca, la	*(lah bah-'rrahn-kah)*
gum	encía, la	*(lah ehn-'see-ah)*
gymnasium	gimnasio, el	*(ehl heem-'nah-see·oh)*

H

habit	hábito, el	*(ehl 'ah-bee-toh)*
hail	granizo, el	*(ehl grah-'nee-soh)*
hair	cabello, el	*(ehl kah-'beh-yoh)*
hairbrush	cepillo de pelo, el	*(ehl seh-'pee-yoh deh 'peh-loh)*
hairdresser	peluquero, el	*(ehl peh-loo-'keh-roh)*
hair dryer	secador de pelo, el	*(ehl seh-kah-'dohr deh 'peh-loh)*
half	mitad, la	*(lah mee-'tahd)*
hallway	pasillo, el	*(ehl pah-'see-yoh)*
ham	jamón, el	*(ehl hah-'mohn)*
hamburger	hamburguesa, la	*(lah ahm-boor-'geh-sah)*
hammer	martillo, el	*(ehl mahr-'tee-yoh)*
hand	mano, la	*(lah 'mah-noh)*
handcuffs	esposas, las	*(lahs eh-'spoh-sahs)*
handicapped	minusválido, el	*(ehl mee-noos-'vah-lee-doh)*
handle	tirador, el	*(ehl tee-rah-'dohr)*
* **Hands up!**	¡Manos arriba!	*('mah-nohs ah-'rree-bah)*
handsome	guapo	*('gwah-poh)*
happen (to)	pasar	*(pah-'sahr)*
happy	feliz	*(feh-'lees)*
* **Happy Birthday!**	¡Feliz cumpleaños!	*(feh-'lees koom-pleh-'ah-nyohs)*
harassment	acosamiento, el	*(ehl ah-koh-sah-mee-'ehn-toh)*
hard	duro	*('doo-roh)*
harmless	inofensivo	*(een-oh-fehn-'see-voh)*
hat	sombrero, el	*(ehl sohm-'breh-roh)*
hatch	portillo, el	*(ehl pohr-'tee-yoh)*
hatchet	hacha, el	*(ehl 'ah-chah)*
hate	odio, el	*(ehl 'oh-dee·oh)*
* **Have a nice day!**	¡Qué tenga un buen día!	*(keh 'tehn-gah oon bwehn 'dee-ah)*
have (to)	tener	*(teh-'nehr)*
hawk	halcón, el	*(ehl ahl-'kohn)*
he	él	*(ehl)*
head	cabeza, la	*(lah kah-'beh-sah)*
headache	dolor de cabeza, el	*(ehl doh-'lohr deh kah-'beh-sah)*
headlight	faro delantero, el	*(ehl 'fah-roh deh-lahn-'teh-roh)*
hear (to)	oír	*(oh-'eer)*
hearing	audiencia, la	*(lah ow-dee-'ehn-see·ah)*
heart	corazón, el	*(ehl koh-rah-'sohn)*
heart attack	ataque al corazón, el	*(ehl ah-'tah-keh ahl koh-rah-'sohn)*

heater	calentador, el	*(ehl kah-lehn-tah-'dohr)*
heating	calefacción, la	*(lah kah-leh-fahk-see-'ohn)*
heavy	pesado	*(peh-'sah-doh)*
height	estatura	*(eh-stah-'too-rah)*
helicopter	helicóptero, el	*(ehl eh-lee-'kohp-teh-roh)*
helmet	casco, el	*(ehl 'kah-skoh)*
* Help!	¡Socorro!	*(soh-'koh-rroh)*
help	ayuda, la	*(lah ah-'yoo-dah)*
help (to)	ayudar	*(ah-yoo-'dahr)*
helper	ayudante, el	*(ehl ah-yoo-'dahn-teh)*
her	su	*(soo)*
here	aquí	*(ah-'kee)*
heroin	heroína, la	*(lah eh-roh-'ee-nah)*
hers	suyo; suya	*(soo-yoh; 'soo-yah)*
* Hi!	¡Hola!	*('oh-lah)*
hide (to)	esconder	*(eh-skohn-'dehr)*
high	alto	*('ahl-toh)*
high (drugged)	drogado	*(droh-'gah-doh)*
highway	carretera, la	*(lah kah-rreh-'teh-rah)*
hijacking	robo en tránsito, el	*(ehl 'roh-boh ehn 'trahn-see-toh)*
hill	cerro, el	*(ehl 'seh-rroh)*
hip	cadera, la	*(lah kah-'deh-rah)*
his	su; suyo; suya	*(soo; 'soo-yoh; 'soo-yah)*
hit (to)	pegar	*(peh-'gahr)*
hole	agujero, el	*(ehl ah-goo-'heh-roh)*
holiday	día de fiesta, el	*(ehl 'dee-ah deh fee-'eh-stah)*
holster	funda de pistola, la	*(lah 'foon-dah deh pee-'stoh-lah)*
home	hogar, el	*(ehl oh-'gahr)*
homeless	desamparado	*(dehs-ahm-pah-'rah-doh)*
homework	tarea, la	*(lah tah-'reh-ah)*
homicide	homicidio, el	*(ehl oh-mee-'see-dee·oh)*
honor	honor, el	*(ehl oh-'nohr)*
hood	capota, la	*(lah kah-'poh-tah)*
hook	gancho, el	*(ehl 'gahn-choh)*
horn	bocina, la	*(lah boh-'see-nah)*
horse	caballo, el	*(ehl kah-'bah-yoh)*
hospital	hospital, el	*(ehl oh-spee-'tahl)*
hostage	rehén, el	*(ehl reh-'ehn)*
hostile	hostil	*(oh-'steel)*
hot	caliente	*(kah-lee-'ehn-teh)*
hotel	hotel, el	*(ehl oh-'tehl)*
house	casa, la	*(lah 'kah-sah)*
house trailer	coche habitación, el	*(ehl 'koh-cheh ah-bee-tah-see-'ohn)*
housing	vivienda, la	*(lah vee-vee-'ehn-dah)*
how	cómo	*('koh-moh)*
* How are you?	¿Cómo está?	*('koh-moh eh-'stah)*
* How can I help you?	¿Cómo puedo ayudarle?	*('koh-moh 'pweh-doh ah-yoo-'dahr-leh)*

* **How do you feel?**	¿Cómo se siente?	*('koh-moh se see-'ehn-teh)*
* **How do you say it?**	¿Cómo se dice?	*('koh-moh seh 'dee-seh)*
* **How do you write it?**	¿Cómo se escribe?	*('koh-moh seh eh-'skree-beh)*
how many	cuántos	*('kwahn-tohs)*
how much	cuánto	*('kwahn-toh)*
* **How old are you?**	¿Cuántos años tiene?	*(kwahn-tohs 'ah-nyohs tee-'eh-neh)*
hubcap	tapacubo, el	*(ehl tah-pah-'koo-boh)*
hug (to)	abrazar	*(ah-brah-'sahr)*
humid	húmedo	*('oo-meh-doh)*
hungry	hambre	*('ahm-breh)*
hunt (to)	cazar	*(kah-'sahr)*
hurricane	huracán, el	*(ehl oo-rah-'kahn)*
hurry up (to)	apurarse	*(ah-poo-'rahr-seh)*
hurt	lastimado	*(lah-stee-'mah-doh)*
husband	esposo, el	*(ehl eh-'spoh-soh)*
I		
I	yo	*(yoh)*
* **I don't know!**	¡No sé!	*(noh seh)*
* **I don't understand!**	¡No entiendo!	*(noh ehn-tee-'ehn-doh)*
* **I hope so!**	¡Ojalá!	*(oh-hah-'lah)*
* **I just finished...**	Acabo de...	*(ah-'kah-boh deh...)*
* **I think so!**	¡Creo que sí!	*('kreh-oh keh see)*
* **I'll be right back!**	¡Ahora vengo!	*(ah-'oh-rah 'vehn-goh)*
* **I'm going to...**	Voy a...	*('voh-ee ah...)*
* **I'm (qualities, characteristics)**	soy	*('soh-ee)*
I'm (temporary state, location, condition)	estoy	*(eh-'stoh-ee)*
* **I'm sorry!**	¡Lo siento!	*(loh see-'ehn-toh)*
ice	hielo, el	*(ehl 'yeh-loh)*
ice cream	helado, el	*(ehl eh-'lah-doh)*
identification	identificación, la	*(lah ee-dehn-tee-fee-kah-see-'ohn)*
ignition	encendido, el	*(ehl ehn-seh-'dee-doh)*
illegal	ilegal	*(ee-leh-'gahl)*
immigrant	inmigrante, el	*(ehl een-mee-'grahn-teh)*
immigration	inmigración	*(lah een-mee-grah-see-'ohn)*
important	importante	*(eem-pohr-'tahn-teh)*
impound (to)	embargar	*(ehm-bahr-'gahr)*
in	en	*(ehn)*
incarcerate (to)	encarcelar	*(ehn-kahr-seh-'lahr)*
incarceration	encarcelamiento, el	*(ehl ehn-kahr-seh-lah-mee-'ehn-toh)*
incest	incesto, el	*(ehl een-'seh-stoh)*
inch	pulgada, la	*(lah pool-'gah-dah)*
income	ingreso, el	*(ehl een-'greh-soh)*
Indian	indio, el	*(ehl 'een-dee·oh)*

indictment	acusación, la	*(lah ah-koo-sah-see-'ohn)*
information	información, la	*(lah een-fohr-mah-see-'ohn)*
informer	informante, el	*(ehl een-fohr-'mahn-teh)*
infraction	infracción, la	*(lah een-frahk-see-'ohn)*
inhalant	inhalante, el	*(ehl een-ah-'lahn-teh)*
inhale (to)	inhalar	*(een-ah-'lahr)*
inject (to)	inyectar	*(een-yehk-'tahr)*
injection	inyección, la	*(lah een-yehk-see-'ohn)*
injunction	entredicho, el	*(ehl ehn-treh-'dee-choh)*
injure (to)	herir	*(eh-'reer)*
injury	herida, la	*(lah eh-'ree-dah)*
inmate	preso, el	*(ehl 'preh-soh)*
innocent	inocente	*(ee-noh-'sehn-teh)*
inquiry	investigación, la	*(lah een-veh-stee-gah-see-'ohn)*
insanity	locura, la	*(lah loh-'koo-rah)*
inside	adentro	*(ah-'dehn-troh)*
inspector	inspector, el	*(ehl een-spehk-'tohr)*
instruction	instrucción, la	*(lah een-strook-see-'ohn)*
instrument	instrumento, el	*(ehl een-stroo-'mehn-toh)*
insulin	insulina, la	*(lah een-soo-'lee-nah)*
insurance	seguro, el	*(ehl seh-'goo-roh)*
insurance company	compañía de seguros, la	*(lah kohm-pah-'nyee-ah deh seh-'goo-rohs)*
interior	interior, el	*(ehl een-teh-ree-'ohr)*
interpreter	intérprete, el	*(ehl een-'tehr-preh-teh)*
intersection	bocacalle, la	*(lah boh-kah-'kah-yeh)*
interview	entrevista, la	*(lah ehn-treh-'vee-stah)*
intoxicated	intoxicado	*(een-tohk-see-'kah-doh)*
intruder	intruso, el	*(ehl een-'troo-soh)*
investigate (to)	investigar	*(een-veh-stee-'gahr)*
investigation	investigación, la	*(lah een-veh-stee-gah-see-'ohn)*
investigator	investigador, el	*(ehl een-veh-stee-gah-'dohr)*
invoice	factura, la	*(lah fahk-'too-rah)*
irrigation	irrigación, la	*(lah ee-rree-gah-see-'ohn)*
is (qualities, characteristics)	es	*(ehs)*
is (temporary state, condition, location)	está	*(eh-'stah)*
island	isla, la	*(lah 'ees-lah)*
* **It's the law!**	¡Es la ley!	*(ehs lah 'leh·ee)*
J		
jack	gata, la	*(lah 'gah-tah)*
jacket	chaqueta, la	*(lah chah-'keh-tah)*
jail	cárcel, la	*(lah 'kahr-sehl)*
January	enero	*(eh-'neh-roh)*
jaw	mandíbula, la	*(lah mahn-'dee-boo-lah)*
jealousy	celo, el	*(ehl 'seh-loh)*

jewelry	joyas, las	*(lahs 'hoh-yahs)*
Jewish	judío	*(hoo-'dee-oh)*
job	trabajo, el	*(ehl trah-'bah-hoh)*
joke	chiste, el	*(ehl 'chee-steh)*
judge	juez, el	*(ehl hoo·'ehs)*
juice	jugo, el	*(ehl 'hoo-goh)*
July	julio	*('hoo-lee·oh)*
June	junio	*('hoo-nee·oh)*
jungle	selva, la	*(lah 'sehl-vah)*
jurisdiction	jurisdicción, la	*(lah hoo-rees-deek-see-'ohn)*
jury	jurado, el	*(ehl hoo-'rah-doh)*
just	justo	*('hoo-stoh)*
justice	justicia, la	*(lah hoo-'stee-see·ah)*
juvenile	menor de edad, el	*(ehl meh-'nohr deh eh-'dahd)*
juvenile delinquency	delincuencia juvenil, la	*(lah deh-leen-'kwehn-see·ah hoo-veh-'neel)*

K

key	llave, la	*(lah 'yah-veh)*
kidnapper	secuestrador, el	*(ehl seh-kweh-strah-'dohr)*
kidnapping	secuestro, el	*(ehl seh-'kweh-stroh)*
kidney	riñón, el	*(ehl ree-'nyohn)*
kill (to)	matar	*(mah-'tahr)*
killer	asesino, el	*(ehl ah-seh-'see-noh)*
kiss (to)	besar	*(beh-'sahr)*
kitchen	cocina, la	*(lah koh-'see-nah)*
kitchen sink	fregadero, el	*(ehl freh-gah-'deh-roh)*
kite	cometa, la	*(lah koh-'meh-tah)*
knee	rodilla, la	*(lah roh-'dee-yah)*
knife	cuchillo, el	*(ehl koo-'chee-yoh)*
knock down (to)	tumbar	*(toom-'bahr)*
know someone (to)	conocer	*(koh-noh-'sehr)*
know something (to)	saber	*(sah-'behr)*

L

labor pains	dolores de parto, los	*(lohs doh-'loh-rehs deh 'pahr-toh)*
laboratory	laboratorio, el	*(ehl lah-boh-rah-'toh-ree·oh)*
laborer	obrero, el	*(ehl oh-'breh-roh)*
ladder	escalera, la	*(lah eh-skah-'leh-rah)*
lake	lago, el	*(ehl 'lah-goh)*
lamp	lámpara, la	*(lah 'lahm-pah-rah)*
lamp shade	pantalla, la	*(lah pahn-'tah-yah)*
land	terreno, el	*(ehl teh-'rreh-noh)*
landslide	avalancha, la	*(lah ah-vah-'lahn-chah)*
lane	pista, la	*(lah pee-'stah)*
language	idioma, el	*(ehl ee-dee-'oh-mah)*
larceny	hurto, el	*(ehl 'oor-toh)*
last name	apellido	*(ah-peh-'yee-doh)*

latch	cerrojo, el	*(ehl seh-'rroh-hoh)*
late	tarde	*('tahr-deh)*
later	luego	*('lweh-goh)*
Latino	latino, el	*(ehl lah-'tee-noh)*
laugh (to)	reír	*(reh-'eer)*
law	ley, la	*(lah 'leh·ee)*
lawn	césped, el	*(ehl 'sehs-pehd)*
lawsuit	pleito, el	*(ehl 'pleh·ee-toh)*
lawyer	abogado, el	*(ehl ah-boh-'gah-doh)*
lazy	perezoso	*(peh-reh-'soh-soh)*
leader	líder, el	*(ehl 'lee-dehr)*
leak	gotera, la	*(lah goh-'teh-rah)*
leash	correa, la	*(lah koh-'rreh-ah)*
leave (to)	salir	*(sah-'leer)*
left-handed	zurdo, el	*(ehl 'soor-doh)*
leg	pierna, la	*(lah pee-'ehr-nah)*
legal	legal	*(leh-'gahl)*
legal aid	ayuda legal, la	*(lah ah-'yoo-dah leh-'gahl)*
legal guardian	tutor, el	*(ehl too-'tohr)*
lend (to)	prestar	*(preh-'stahr)*
less	menos	*('meh-nohs)*
* **Let's go!**	¡Vamos!	*('vah-mohs)*
* **Let's see!**	¡A ver!	*(ah vehr)*
liable	expuesto	*(ehks-'pweh-stoh)*
library	biblioteca, la	*(lah bee-blee-oh-'teh-kah)*
license	licencia, la	*(lah lee-'sehn-see·ah)*
lie	mentira, la	*(lah mehn-'tee-rah)*
lie (to)	mentir	*(mehn-'teer)*
lieutenant	teniente, el	*(ehl teh-nee-'ehn-teh)*
life	vida, la	*(lah 'vee-dah)*
lifeguard	salvavidas, el	*(ehl 'sahl-vah-'vee-dahs)*
lift (to)	levantar	*(leh-vahn-'tahr)*
light	luz, la	*(lah loos)*
light (not heavy)	ligero	*(lee-'heh-roh)*
lightbulb	foco, el	*(ehl 'foh-koh)*
light switch	interruptor, el	*(ehl een-teh-rroop-'tohr)*
lightning	relámpago, el	*(ehl reh-'lahm-pah-goh)*
line	línea, la	*(lah 'lee-neh-ah)*
lip	labio, el	*(ehl 'lah-bee·oh)*
liquid	líquido, el	*(ehl 'lee-kee-doh)*
liquor	licor, el	*(ehl lee-'kohr)*
listen (to)	escuchar	*(eh-skoo-'chahr)*
litter	basura, la	*(lah bah-'soo-rah)*
live (to)	vivir	*(vee-'veer)*
liver	hígado, el	*(ehl 'ee-gah-doh)*
living room	sala, la	*(lah 'sah-lah)*
load	carga, la	*(lah 'kahr-gah)*
lobby	salón, el	*(ehl sah-'lohn)*

lock	cerradura, la	*(lah seh-rrah-'doo-rah)*
lock (to)	cerrar con llave	*(seh-'rrahr kohn 'yah-veh)*
locksmith	cerrajero, el	*(ehl seh-rrah-'heh-roh)*
loiterer	holgazán, el	*(ehl ohl-gah-'sahn)*
long	largo	*('lahr-goh)*
long distance	larga distancia	*('lahr-gah dee-'stahn-see·ah)*
look (to)	mirar	*(mee-'rahr)*
loose	flojo	*('floh-hoh)*
lose (to)	perder	*(pehr-'dehr)*
loud	ruidoso	*(roo-ee-'doh-soh)*
love	amor, el	*(ehl ah-'mohr)*
love (to)	querer, amar	*(keh-'rehr, ah-'mahr)*
lover	amante, el	*(ehl ah-'mahn-teh)*
low	bajo	*('bah-hoh)*
luggage	equipaje, el	*(ehl eh-kee-'pah-heh)*
lumber	madera, la	*(lah mah-'deh-rah)*
lunch	almuerzo, el	*(ehl ahl-moo-'ehr-soh)*
lung	pulmón, el	*(ehl pool-'mohn)*

M

m.p.h.	millas por hora	*('mee-yahs pohr 'oh-rah)*
machine	máquina, la	*(lah 'mah-kee-nah)*
machine gun	ametralladora, la	*(lah ah-meh-trah-yah-'doh-rah)*
machinist	maquinista, el	*(ehl mah-kee-'nee-stah)*
magazine	revista, la	*(lah reh-'vee-stah)*
mail	correo, el	*(ehl koh-'rreh-oh)*
mail carrier	cartero, el	*(ehl kahr-'teh-roh)*
mailbox	buzón, el	*(ehl boo-'sohn)*
maintain (to)	mantener	*(mahn-teh-'nehr)*
make (to)	hacer	*(ah-'sehr)*
makeup	maquillaje, el	*(ehl mah-kee-'yah-heh)*
man	hombre, el	*(ehl 'ohm-breh)*
manager	administrador, el	*(ehl ahd-mee-nee-strah-'dohr)*
mansion	mansión, la	*(lah mahn-see-'ohn)*
many	muchos	*('moo-chohs)*
map	mapa, el	*(ehl 'mah-pah)*
March	marzo	*('mahr-soh)*
marijuana	marijuana, la	*(lah mah-ree-'wah-nah)*
marital status	estado civil, el	*(ehl eh-'stah-doh see-'veel)*
mark	marca, la	*(lah 'mahr-kah)*
market	mercado, el	*(ehl mehr-'kah-doh)*
marriage	matrimonio, el	*(ehl mah-tree-'moh-nee·oh)*
married	casado	*(kah-'sah-doh)*
marshal	alguacil, el	*(ehl ahl-goo-ah-'seel)*
Mass	misa, la	*(lah 'mee-sah)*
massage parlor	sala de masaje, la	*(lah 'sah-lah deh mah-'sah-heh)*
matches	fósforos, los	*(lohs 'fohs-foh-rohs)*

matter	asunto, el	*(ehl ah-'soon-toh)*
mattress	colcha, la	*(lah 'kohl-chah)*
May	mayo	*('mah-yoh)*
* May I come in?	¿Se puede?	*(seh 'pweh-deh)*
* May I help you?	¿Puedo ayudarle?	*('pweh-doh ah-yoo-'dahr-leh)*
maybe	quizás	*(kee-'sahs)*
mayor	alcalde, el	*(ehl ahl-'kahl-deh)*
meal	comida, la	*(lah koh-'mee-dah)*
measure (to)	medir	*(meh-'deer)*
measurements	medidas, las	*(lahs meh-'dee-dahs)*
meat	carne, la	*(lah 'kahr-neh)*
mechanic	mecánico, el	*(ehl meh-'kah-nee-koh)*
medicine	medicina, la	*(lah meh-dee-'see-nah)*
medicine chest	botiquín, el	*(ehl boh-tee-'keen)*
meeting	reunión, la	*(lah reh-oo-nee-'ohn)*
methedrine	metanfetamina, la	*(lah meh-tahn-feh-tah-'mee-nah)*
Mexican	mejicano	*(meh-hee-'kah-noh)*
microwave	microondas, el	*(ehl mee-kroh-'ohn-dahs)*
middle	medio, el	*(ehl 'meh-dee·oh)*
midnight	medianoche, la	*(lah meh-dee·ah-'noh-cheh)*
mile	milla, la	*(lah 'mee-yah)*
milk	leche, la	*(lah 'leh-cheh)*
million	millón	*(mee-'yohn)*
mine (possessive)	mío (or mía)	*('mee-oh, 'mee-ah)*
minister	ministro, el	*(ehl mee-'nee-stroh)*
minor	menor	*(meh-'nohr)*
mirror	espejo, el	*(ehl eh-'speh-hoh)*
mischief	travesura, la	*(lah trah-veh-'soo-rah)*
misdemeanor	delito menor, el	*(ehl deh-'lee-toh meh-'nohr)*
Miss	señorita (Srta.)	*(seh-nyoh-'ree-tah)*
miss (to)	faltar	*(fahl-'tahr)*
mobile home	casa rodante, la	*(lah 'kah-sah roh-'dahn-teh)*
model	modelo, el	*(ehl moh-'deh-loh)*
molestation	abuso sexual, el	*(ehl ah-'boo-soh sehk-soo-'ahl)*
Monday	lunes	*('loo-nehs)*
money	dinero, el	*(ehl dee-'neh-roh)*
month	mes, el	*(ehl mehs)*
moped	bicicleta motorizada, la	*(lah bee-see-'kleh-tah moh-toh-ree-'sah-dah)*
more	más	*(mahs)*
* More or less!	¡Más o menos!	*(mahs oh 'meh-nohs)*
* More slowly!	¡Más despacio!	*(mahs deh-'spah-see·oh)*
morgue	morgue, la	*(lah 'mohr-geh)*
mortician	agente funerario, el	*(ehl ah-'hehn-teh foo-neh-'rah-ree·oh)*
mortuary	mortuorio, el	*(ehl mohr-too-'oh-ree·oh)*
mosquito	zancudo, el	*(ehl sahn-'koo-doh)*
motel	motel, el	*(ehl moh-'tehl)*

mother	madre, la	(lah 'mah-dreh)
mother-in-law	suegra, la	(lah 'sweh-grah)
motion	moción, la	(lah moh-see-'ohn)
motive	motivo, el	(ehl moh-'tee-voh)
motorcycle	motocicleta, la	(lah moh-toh-see-'kleh-tah)
mountain	montaña, la	(lah mohn-'tah-nyah)
mouse	ratón, el	(ehl rah-'tohn)
moustache	bigote, el	(ehl bee-'goh-teh)
mouth	boca, la	(lah 'boh-kah)
movie theater	cine, el	(ehl 'see-neh)
Mr.	señor (Sr.)	(seh-'nyohr)
Mrs.	señora (Sra.)	(seh-'nyoh-rah)
mud	lodo, el	(ehl 'loh-doh)
muffler	silenciador, el	(ehl see-lehn-see·ah-'dohr)
murder	asesinato, el	(ehl ah-seh-see-'nah-toh)
murder (to)	matar	(mah-'tahr)
murderer	asesino, el	(ehl ah-seh-'see-noh)
muscle	músculo, el	(ehl 'moo-skoo-loh)
museum	museo, el	(ehl moo-'seh-oh)
musician	músico, el	(ehl 'moo-see-koh)
Muslim	musulmán	(moo-sool-'mahn)
my	mi	(mee)

N

nail	clavo, el	(ehl 'klah-voh)
naked	desnudo	(dehs-'noo-doh)
name	nombre	('nohm-breh)
narcotics	narcóticos, los	(lohs nahr-'koh-tee-kohs)
narrow	estrecho	(eh-'streh-choh)
National Guard	Guardia Nacional, la	(lah 'gwahr-dee·ah nah-see·oh-'nahl)
nationality	nacionalidad, la	(lah nah-see·oh-nah-lee-'dahd)
near	cerca	('sehr-kah)
nearsighted	miope	(mee-'oh-peh)
necessary	necesario	(neh-seh-'sah-ree·oh)
neck	cuello, el	(ehl 'kweh-yoh)
necklace	collar, el	(ehl koh-'yahr)
needle	aguja, la	(lah ah-'goo-hah)
negligence	descuido, el	(ehl dehs-'kwee-doh)
neighbor	vecino, el	(ehl veh-'see-noh)
neighborhood	barrio, el	(ehl 'bah-rree·oh)
nephew	sobrino, el	(ehl soh-'bree-noh)
nerve	nervio, cl	(ehl 'nehr-vee·oh)
nervous	nervioso	(nehr-vee-'oh-soh)
never	nunca	('noon-kah)
New Year's	nuevo año, el	(ehl noo-'eh-voh 'ah-nyoh)
newspaper	periódico, el	(ehl peh-ree-'oh-dee-koh)
next	próximo	('prohk-see-moh)

next to	al lado de	(ahl 'lah-doh deh)
nice	simpático	(seem-'pah-tee-koh)
* Nice to meet you!	¡Mucho gusto!	('moo-choh 'goo-stoh)
nickname	apodo, el	(ehl ah-'poh-doh)
niece	sobrina, la	(lah soh-'bree-nah)
nightclub	club nocturno, el	(ehl kloob nohk-'toor-noh)
nightstand	mesa de noche, la	(lah 'meh-sah deh 'noh-cheh)
nine	nueve	(noo-'eh-veh)
nine hundred	novecientos	(noh-veh-see-'ehn-tohs)
nineteen	diecinueve	(dee-ehs-ee-noo-'eh-veh)
ninety	noventa	(noh-'vehn-tah)
ninth	noveno	(noh-'veh-noh)
noise	ruido, el	(ehl roo-'ee-doh)
none	ninguno	(neen-'goo-noh)
noon	mediodía, el	(ehl meh-dee-oh-'dee-ah)
north	norte	('nohr-teh)
nose	nariz, la	(lah nah-'rees)
* Not bad!	¡Así-así!	(ah-'see, ah-'see)
* Not yet!	¡Todavía no!	(toh-dah-'vee-ah noh)
notary public	notario, el	(ehl noh-'tah-ree-oh)
notebook	cuaderno, el	(ehl kwah-'dehr-noh)
nothing	nada	('nah-dah)
notice	noticia, la	(lah noh-'tee-see-ah)
November	noviembre	(noh-vee-'ehm-breh)
nowadays	ahora	(ah-'oh-rah)
nowhere	por ninguna parte	(pohr neen-'goo-nah 'pahr-teh)
number	número, el	(ehl 'noo-meh-roh)
nurse	enfermero, el	(ehl ehn-fehr-'meh-roh)
nursing home	hogar para ancianos, el	(ehl oh-'gahr 'pah-rah ahn-see-'ah-nohs)
nut	tuerca, la	(lah 'twehr-kah)

O

obey (to)	obedecer	(oh-beh-deh-'sehr)
obscene	obsceno	(ohb-'seh-noh)
obscenities	groserías, las	(lahs groh-seh-'ree-ahs)
obstruct (to)	obstruir	(ohb-stroo-'eer)
occupant	inquilino el	(ehl een-kee-'lee-noh)
occupation	ocupación, la	(lah oh-koo-pah-see-'ohn)
occupy (to)	ocupar	(oh-koo-'pahr)
occur (to)	ocurrir	(oh-koo-'reer)
October	octubre	(ohk-'too-breh)
odometer	odómetro, el	(ehl oh-'doh-meh-troh)
of, from	de	(deh)
of the, from the	del	(dehl)
offense	ofensa, la	(lah oh-'fehn-sah)
offer	oferta, la	(lah oh-'fehr-tah)
office	oficina, la	(lah oh-fee-'see-nah)

officer	oficial, el	*(ehl oh-fee-see-'ahl)*
official	oficial	*(oh-fee-see-'ahl)*
often	frecuentemente	*(freh-kwehn-teh-'mehn-teh)*
oil	aceite, el	*(ehl ah-'seh·ee-teh)*
old	viejo	*(vee-'eh-hoh)*
older	mayor	*(mah-'yohr)*
on	en	*(ehn)*
one	uno	*('oo-noh)*
one hundred	cien	*('see-ehn)*
* One must...	Hay que...	*('ah·ee keh)*
onion	cebolla, la	*(lah seh-'boh-yah)*
open	abierto	*(ah-bee-'ehr-toh)*
open (to)	abrir	*(ah-'breer)*
operator	operador, el	*(ehl oh-peh-rah-'dohr)*
or	o	*(oh)*
orange	naranja, la	*(lah nah-'rahn-hah)*
orange (color)	anaranjado	*(ah-nah-rahn-'hah-doh)*
orchard	huerta, la	*(lah 'wehr-tah)*
order (command)	orden, la	*(lah 'ohr-dehn)*
order (condition)	orden, el	*(ehl 'ohr-dehn)*
Oriental	oriental, el	*(ehl oh-ree-ehn-'tahl)*
orphan	huérfano, el	*(ehl 'wehr-fah-noh)*
ounce	onza, la	*(lah 'ohn-sah)*
our	nuestro	*('nweh-stroh)*
outdoors	afueras, las	*(lahs ah-'fweh-rahs)*
outside	afuera	*(ah-'fweh-rah)*
oval	óvalo, el	*(ehl 'oh-vah-loh)*
oven	horno, el	*(ehl 'ohr-noh)*
over there	allá	*(ah-'yah)*
overcoat	abrigo, el	*(ehl ah-'bree-goh)*
overdose	sobredosis, la	*(lah soh-breh-'doh-sees)*
overdue	sobrevencido	*(soh-breh-vehn-'see-doh)*
owner	dueño, el	*(ehl 'dweh-nyoh)*
oxygen	oxígeno, el	*(ehl ohk-'see-heh-noh)*

P

padlock	candado, el	*(ehl kahn-'dah-doh)*
page	página, la	*(lah 'pah-hee-nah)*
pain	dolor, el	*(ehl doh-'lohr)*
paint	pintura, la	*(lah peen-'too-rah)*
paint (to)	pintar	*(peen-'tahr)*
painter	pintor, el	*(ehl peen-'tohr)*
painting	cuadro, el	*(ehl 'kwah-droh)*
pair	par, el	*(ehl pahr)*
panties	bragas, las	*(lahs 'brah-gahs)*
pants	pantalones, los	*(lohs pahn-tah-'loh-nehs)*
paper	papel, el	*(ehl pah-'pehl)*
paperwork	papeleo, el	*(ehl pah-peh-'leh-oh)*

parade	desfile, el	*(ehl dehs-'fee-leh)*
paramedic	paramédico, el	*(ehl pah-rah-'meh-dee-koh)*
park	parque, el	*(ehl 'pahr-keh)*
park (to)	estacionar	*(eh-stah-see·oh-'nahr)*
parking lot	lote de estacionamiento, el	*(ehl 'loh-teh deh eh-stah-see·oh-nah-mee-'ehn-toh)*
parking meter	parquímetro, el	*(ehl pahr-'kee-meh-troh)*
parole	libertad provisional, la	*(lah lee-behr-'tahd proh-vee-see·oh-'nahl)*
partner	socio, el	*(ehl 'soh-see·oh)*
party	fiesta, la	*(lah fee-'eh-stah)*
pass (to)	pasar	*(pah-'sahr)*
passenger	pasajero, el	*(ehl pah-sah-'heh-roh)*
passport	pasaporte, el	*(ehl pah-sah-'pohr-teh)*
path	senda, la	*(lah 'sehn-dah)*
patience	paciencia, la	*(lah pah-see-'ehn-see·ah)*
patient	paciente, el	*(ehl pah-see-'ehn-teh)*
patrol	patrulla, la	*(lah pah-'troo-yah)*
patrol car	patrullera, la	*(lah pah-troo-'yeh-rah)*
patrolman	patrullero, el	*(ehl pah-troo-'yeh-roh)*
pavement	pavimento, el	*(ehl pah-vee-'mehn-toh)*
pawnshop	casa de empeños, la	*(lah 'kah-sah deh ehm-'peh-nyohs)*
pay (to)	pagar	*(pah-'gahr)*
paycheck	cheque de sueldo, el	*(ehl 'cheh-keh deh 'swehl-doh)*
payment	pago, el	*(ehl 'pah-goh)*
pear	pera, la	*(lah 'peh-rah)*
pedal	pedal, el	*(ehl peh-'dahl)*
pedestrian	peatón, el	*(ehl peh-ah-'tohn)*
pen	pluma, la; bolígrafo, el	*(lah 'ploo-mah; ehl boh-'lee-grah-foh)*
pencil	lápiz, el	*(ehl 'lah-pees)*
pendant	pendiente, el	*(ehl pehn-dee-'ehn-teh)*
penicillin	penicilina, la	*(lah peh-nee-see-'lee-nah)*
penitentiary	penitenciaría, la	*(lah peh-nee-tehn-see-ah-'ree·ah)*
people	gente, la	*(lah 'hehn-teh)*
percent	por ciento, el	*(ehl pohr see-'ehn-toh)*
perjurer	perjuro, el	*(ehl pehr-'hoo-roh)*
perjury	perjurio, el	*(ehl pehr-'hoo-ree·oh)*
permit	permiso, el	*(ehl pehr-'mee-soh)*
person	persona, la	*(lah pehr-'soh-nah)*
pharmacy	farmacia, la	*(lah fahr-'mah-see·ah)*
phone	teléfono, el	*(ehl teh-'leh-foh-noh)*
phone call	llamada, la	*(lah yah-'mah-dah)*
piano	piano, el	*(ehl pee-'ah-noh)*
pick	pico, el	*(ehl 'pee-koh)*
pickpocket	carterista, el	*(ehl kahr-teh-'ree-stah)*
pickup	camioneta, la	*(lah kah-mee·oh-'neh-tah)*

picture	retrato, el	*(ehl reh-'trah-toh)*
pie	pastel, el	*(ehl pah-'stehl)*
piece	pedazo, el	*(ehl peh-'dah-soh)*
pier	muelle, el	*(ehl 'mweh-yeh)*
pig	cerdo, el	*(ehl 'sehr-doh)*
pill	píldora, la	*(lah 'peel-doh-rah)*
pillow	almohada, la	*(lah ahl-moh-'ah-dah)*
pilot	piloto, el	*(ehl pee-'loh-toh)*
pimp	cafiche, el	*(ehl kah-'fee-cheh)*
pin	alfiler, el	*(ehl ahl-fee-'lehr)*
pineapple	piña, la	*(lah 'pee-nyah)*
pipe	tubo, el	*(ehl 'too-boh)*
pistol	pistola, la	*(lah pee-'stoh-lah)*
pitcher	jarra, la	*(lah 'hah-rrah)*
place	sitio, el	*(ehl 'see-tee·oh)*
plaintiff	demandante, el	*(ehl deh-mahn-'dahn-teh)*
plane	avión, el	*(ehl ah-vee-'ohn)*
plant	planta, la	*(lah 'plahn-tah)*
plastic	plástico, el	*(ehl 'plah-stee-koh)*
plate	plato, el	*(ehl 'plah-toh)*
plates	placas, las	*(lahs 'plah-kahs)*
play (to)	jugar	*(hoo-'gahr)*
playground	campo de recreo, el	*(ehl 'kahm-poh deh reh-'kreh-oh)*
plea	alegato, el	*(ehl ah-leh-'gah-toh)*
* Please!	¡Por favor!	*(pohr fah-'vohr)*
pliers	pinzas, las	*(lahs 'peen-sahs)*
plumber	plomero, el	*(ehl ploh-'meh-roh)*
plumbing	tubería, la	*(lah too-beh-'ree-ah)*
pocket	bolsillo, el	*(ehl bohl-see-yoh)*
poison	veneno, el	*(ehl veh-'neh-noh)*
police dog	perro de la policía, el	*(ehl 'peh-rroh deh lah poh-lee-'see-ah)*
police (general)	policía, la	*(lah poh-lee-'see-ah)*
police officer	policía, el	*(ehl poh-lee-'see-ah)*
police station	estación de policía, la	*(lah eh-stah-see-'ohn deh poh-lee-'see-ah)*
policy	póliza, la	*(lah 'poh-lee-sah)*
polite	cortés	*(kohr-'tehs)*
pond	charca, la	*(lah 'chahr-kah)*
pool hall	sala de billar, la	*(lah 'sah-lah deh bee-'yahr)*
poor	pobre	*('poh-breh)*
population	población, la	*(lah poh-blah-see-'ohn)*
porch	porche, el	*(ehl 'pohr-cheh)*
pork	cerdo, el	*(ehl 'sehr-doh)*
pornography	pornografía, la	*(lah pohr-noh-grah-'fee-ah)*
port	puerto, el	*(ehl 'pwehr-toh)*
post	poste, el	*(ehl 'poh-steh)*
post office	correo, el	*(ehl koh-'rreh-oh)*

postcard	tarjeta postal, la	*(lah tahr-'heh-tah poh-'stahl)*
potato	papa, la	*(lah 'pah-pah)*
pound	libra, la	*(lah 'lee-brah)*
poverty	pobreza, la	*(lah poh-'breh-sah)*
powder	pólvora, la	*(lah 'pohl-voh-rah)*
practice	práctica, la	*(lah 'prahk-tee-kah)*
practice (to)	practicar	*(prahk-tee-'kahr)*
pray (to)	rezar	*(reh-'sahr)*
prayer	rezo, el	*(ehl 'reh-soh)*
precinct	distrito, el	*(ehl dee-'stree-toh)*
prefabricated home	casa prefabricada, la	*(lah 'kah-sah preh-fah-bree-'kah-dah)*
prefer (to)	preferir	*(preh-feh-'reer)*
pregnant	embarazada	*(ehm-bah-rah-'sah-dah)*
prescription	receta, la	*(lah reh-'seh-tah)*
president	presidente, el	*(ehl preh-see-'dehn-teh)*
prevention	prevención, la	*(lah preh-vehn-see-'ohn)*
price	precio, el	*(ehl 'preh-see·oh)*
priest	sacerdote, el	*(ehl sah-sehr-'doh-teh)*
principal	director, el	*(ehl dee-rehk-'tohr)*
prison	prisión, la	*(lah pree-see-'ohn)*
prisoner	prisionero, el	*(ehl pree-see·oh-'neh-roh)*
private	privado	*(pree-'vah-doh)*
probation	libertad provisional, la	*(lah lee-behr-'tahd proh-vee-see·oh-'nahl)*
probation officer	oficial a cargo de la libertad provisional, el	*(ehl oh-'fee-see-'ahl ah 'kahr-goh deh lah lee-behr-'tahd proh-vee-see·oh-'nahl)*
problem	problema, el	*(ehl proh-'bleh-mah)*
procedure	procedimiento, el	*(ehl proh-seh-dee-mee-'ehn-toh)*
promise (to)	prometer	*(proh-meh-'tehr)*
pronounce (to)	pronunciar	*(proh-noon-see-'ahr)*
proof	prueba, la	*(lah proo-'eh-bah)*
property	propiedad, la	*(lah proh-pee·eh-'dahd)*
prostitute	prostituta, la	*(lah proh-stee-'too-tah)*
prostitution	prostitución, la	*(lah proh-stee-too-see-'ohn)*
protect (to)	proteger	*(proh-teh-'hehr)*
Protestant	protestante	*(proh-teh-'stahn-teh)*
prove (to)	probar	*(proh-'bahr)*
provide (to)	proveer	*(proh-veh-'ehr)*
psychologist	psicólogo, el	*(ehl see-'koh-loh-goh)*
puberty	pubertad, la	*(lah poo-behr-'tahd)*
public	público, el	*(ehl 'poo-blee-koh)*
public defender	defensor público, el	*(ehl deh-fehn-'sohr 'poo-blee-koh)*
puddle	charca, la	*(lah 'chahr-kah)*
Puerto Rican	puertorriqueño	*(pwehr-toh-rree-'keh-nyoh)*
pull (to)	jalar	*(hah-'lahr)*
pump	bomba, la	*(lah 'bohm-bah)*

punctual	puntual	*(poon-too-'ahl)*
punish (to)	castigar	*(kah-stee-'gahr)*
punishment	castigo, el	*(ehl kah-'stee-goh)*
purple	morado	*(moh-'rah-doh)*
purpose	propósito, el	*(ehl proh-'poh-see-toh)*
purse	cartera, la	*(lah kahr-'teh-rah)*
push	empujón, el	*(ehl ehm-poo-'hohn)*
push (to)	empujar	*(ehm-poo-'hahr)*
put (to)	poner	*(poh-'nehr)*
puzzle	rompecabezas, el	*(ehl rohm-peh-kah-'beh-sahs)*

Q

quarter	cuarto, el	*(ehl 'kwahr-toh)*
question	pregunta, la	*(lah preh-'goon-tah)*
* **Quiet!**	¡Silencio!	*(see-'lehn-see·oh)*
quiet	quieto	*(kee-'eh-toh)*

R

rabbit	conejo, el	*(ehl koh-'neh-hoh)*
raccoon	mapache, el	*(ehl mah-'pah-cheh)*
race	raza, la	*(lah 'rah-sah)*
racism	racismo, el	*(ehl rah-'sees-moh)*
racketeer	extorsionador, el	*(ehl ehks-tohr-see·oh-nah-'dohr)*
radar	radar, el	*(ehl rah-'dahr)*
radiator	radiador, el	*(ehl rah-dee·ah-'dohr)*
radio	radio, el	*(ehl 'rah-dee·oh)*
radio transmitter	radio transmisor, el	*(ehl 'rah-dee·oh trahns-mee-'sohr)*
rag	trapo, el	*(ehl 'trah-poh)*
raid	incursión, la	*(lah een-koor-see-'ohn)*
railroad	ferrocarril, el	*(ehl feh-rroh-kah-'rreel)*
rain	lluvia, la	*(lah 'yoo-vee·ah)*
rain (to)	llover	*(yoh-'vehr)*
raincoat	impermeable, el	*(ehl eem-pehr-meh-'ah-bleh)*
ramp	rampa, la	*(lah 'rahm-pah)*
ranger	guardabosques, el	*(ehl gwahr-dah-'boh-skehs)*
ransom	rescate, el	*(ehl reh-'skah-teh)*
rape	violación, la	*(lah vee·oh-lah-see-'ohn)*
rape (to)	violar	*(vee-oh-'lahr)*
rapidly	rápidamente	*(rah-pee-dah-'mehn-teh)*
rapist	violador, el	*(ehl vee-oh-lah-'dohr)*
rat	rata, la	*(lah 'rah-tah)*
razor	navaja, la	*(lah nah-'vah-hah)*
reaction	reacción, la	*(lah reh-ahk-see-'ohn)*
read (to)	leer	*(leh-'ehr)*
ready	listo	*('lee-stoh)*
rearview mirror	espejo retrovisor, el	*(ehl eh-'speh-hoh reh-troh-vee-'sohr)*
reason	razón, la	*(lah rah-'sohn)*

receipt	recibo, el	*(ehl reh-'see-boh)*
receptionist	recepcionista, el	*(ehl reh-sehp-see·oh-'nee-stah)*
reckless	temerario	*(teh-meh-'rah-ree·oh)*
recognize (to)	reconocer	*(reh-koh-noh-'sehr)*
record player	tocadiscos, el	*(ehl toh-kah-'dee-skohs)*
record (to)	grabar	*(grah-'bahr)*
recorder	grabadora, la	*(lah grah-bah-'doh-rah)*
recover (to)	recuperar	*(reh-koo-peh-'rahr)*
recreation vehicle	vehículo de recreo, el	*(ehl veh-'ee-koo-loh deh reh-'kreh-oh)*
rectangle	rectángulo, el	*(ehl rehk-'tahn-goo-loh)*
red	rojo	*('roh-hoh)*
Red Cross	Cruz Roja, la	*(lah kroos 'roh-hah)*
refrigerator	refrigerador, el	*(ehl reh-free-heh-rah-'dohr)*
refugee	refugiado, el	*(ehl reh-foo-hee-'ah-doh)*
refuse (to)	rehusar	*(reh-oo-'sahr)*
region	región, la	*(lah reh-hee-'ohn)*
registration	registro, el	*(ehl reh-'hee-stroh)*
regulation	reglamento, el	*(ehl reh-glah-'mehn-toh)*
rehabilitation	rehabilitación, la	*(lah reh-ah-bee-lee-tah-see-'ohn)*
relationship	parentezco, el	*(ehl pah-rehn-'tehs-koh)*
relative	pariente, el	*(ehl pah-ree-'ehn-teh)*
relaxed	relajado	*(reh-lah-'hah-doh)*
release (to)	liberar	*(lee-beh-'rahr)*
religion	religión, la	*(lah reh-lee-hee-'ohn)*
remember (to)	recordar	*(reh-kohr-'dahr)*
renew (to)	renovar	*(reh-noh-'vahr)*
rent (to)	alquilar	*(ahl-kee-'lahr)*
repeat (to)	repetir	*(reh-peh-'teer)*
replace (to)	reemplazar	*(reh-ehm-plah-'sahr)*
report (to)	reportar	*(reh-pohr-'tahr)*
request	petición, la	*(lah peh-tee-see-'ohn)*
requirement	requisito, el	*(ehl reh-kee-'see-toh)*
rescue	salvamento, el	*(ehl sahl-vah-'mehn-toh)*
Reserve (Army)	Reserva, la	*(lah reh-'serh-vah)*
reserve (to)	reservar	*(reh-sehr-'vahr)*
reservist	reservista, el	*(ehl reh-sehr-'vee-stah)*
residence	residencia, la	*(lah reh-see-'dehn-see·ah)*
resident	residente, el	*(ehl reh-see-'dehn-teh)*
resource	recurso, el	*(ehl reh-'koor-soh)*
respect	respeto, el	*(ehl reh-'speh-toh)*
respond (to)	responder	*(reh-spohn-'dehr)*
response	respuesta, la	*(lah reh-'spweh-stah)*
responsible	responsable	*(reh-spohn-'sah-bleh)*
rest (to)	descansar	*(dehs-kahn-'sahr)*
restaurant	restaurante, el	*(ehl reh-stah·oo-'rahn-teh)*
restless	inquieto	*(een-kee-'eh-toh)*

restraining order	orden de restricción, la	*(lah 'ohr-dehn deh reh-streek-see-'ohn)*
restriction	restricción, la	*(lah reh-streek-see-'ohn)*
restrooms	servicios sanitarios, los	*(lohs sehr-'vee-see·ohs sah-nee-'tah-ree·ohs)*
result	resultado, el	*(ehl reh-sool-'tah-doh)*
return somebody (to)	volver	*(vohl-'vehr)*
return something (to)	devolver	*(deh-vohl-'vehr)*
revenge	venganza, la	*(lah vehn-'gahn-sah)*
revolver	revólver, el	*(ehl reh-'vohl-vehr)*
reward	recompensa, la	*(lah reh-kohm-'pehn-sah)*
rib	costilla, la	*(lah koh-'stee-yah)*
rice	arroz, el	*(ehl ah-'rrohs)*
rich	rico	*('ree-koh)*
rifle	rifle, el	*(ehl 'ree-fleh)*
right	correcto	*(koh-'rrehk-toh)*
* **Right away!**	¡En seguida!	*(ehn seh-'gee-dah)*
right now	ahorita	*(ah-oh-'ree-tah)*
right of way	derecho de vía, el	*(ehl deh-'reh-choh deh 'vee-ah)*
right-handed	diestro	*(dee-'eh-stroh)*
riot	tumulto, el	*(ehl too-'mool-toh)*
river	río, el	*(ehl 'ree-oh)*
road	camino, el	*(ehl kah-'mee-noh)*
roadblock (intentional)	barricada, la	*(lah bah-rree-'kah-dah)*
roadblock (natural)	obstáculo, el	*(ehl obs-'tah-koo-loh)*
rob (to)	robar	*(roh-'bahr)*
robbery	robo, el	*(ehl 'roh-boh)*
rock (small)	piedra, la	*(lah pee-'eh-drah)*
roof	techo, el	*(ehl 'teh-choh)*
room	cuarto, el	*(ehl 'kwahr-toh)*
rope	soga, la	*(lah 'soh-gah)*
round (number of bullets)	número de tiros, el	*(ehl 'noo-meh-roh deh 'tee-rohs)*
round (shape)	redondo	*(reh-'dohn-doh)*
route	ruta, la	*(lah 'roo-tah)*
routine	rutina, la	*(lah roo-'tee-nah)*
rubber	goma, la	*(lah 'goh-mah)*
rug	alfombra, la	*(lah ahl-'fohm-brah)*
rule	regla, la	*(lah 'reh-glah)*
run (to)	correr	*(koh-'rrehr)*

S

sad	triste	*('tree-steh)*
safe	seguro	*(seh-'goo-roh)*
safety belt	cinturón de seguridad, el	*(ehl seen-too-'rohn deh seh-goo-ree-'dahd)*
sail (to)	navegar	*(nah-veh-'gahr)*

sailing	navegación a vela, la	*(lah nah-veh-gah-see-'ohn ah 'veh-lah)*
salad	ensalada, la	*(lah ehn-sah-'lah-dah)*
sale	venta, la	*(lah 'vehn-tah)*
salesman	vendedor, el	*(ehl vehn-deh-'dohr)*
same	mismo	*('mees-moh)*
sand	arena, la	*(lah ah-'reh-nah)*
Saturday	sábado	*('sah-bah-doh)*
save (to)	salvar	*(sahl-'vahr)*
saw	serrucho, el	*(ehl seh-'rroo-choh)*
scale	balanza, la	*(lah bahl-'lahn-sah)*
scar	cicatriz, la	*(lah see-kah-'trees)*
scene	escena, la	*(lah eh-'seh-nah)*
schedule	horario, el	*(ehl oh-'rah-ree·oh)*
school	escuela, la	*(lah eh-'skweh-lah)*
school bus	autobús escolar, el	*(ehl ow-toh-'boos eh-skoh-'lahr)*
scissors	tijeras, las	*(lahs tee-'heh-rahs)*
scold (to)	regañar	*(reh-gah-'nyahr)*
screw	tornillo, el	*(ehl tohr-'nee-yoh)*
screwdriver	atornillador, el	*(ehl ah-tohr-nee-yah-'dohr)*
sea	mar, el	*(ehl mahr)*
seafood	marisco, el	*(ehl mah-'ree-skoh)*
search	búsqueda, la	*(lah 'boo-skeh-dah)*
search (to)	buscar	*(boo-'skahr)*
seat	asiento, el	*(ehl ah-see-'ehn-toh)*
seat belt	cinturón de seguridad, el	*(ehl seen-too-'rohn deh seh-goo-ree-'dahd)*
second	segundo	*(seh-'goon-doh)*
secret	secreto, el	*(ehl seh-'kreh-toh)*
secretary	secretario, el	*(ehl seh-kreh-'tah-ree·oh)*
section	sección, la	*(lah sehk-see-'ohn)*
secure	seguro	*(seh-'goo-roh)*
secure (to)	asegurar	*(ah-seh-goo-'rahr)*
security guard	guardia de seguridad, el	*(ehl 'gwahr-dee·ah deh seh-goo-ree-'dahd)*
security system	sistema de seguridad, el	*(ehl see-'steh-mah deh seh-goo-ree-'dahd)*
sedan	sedán, el	*(ehl seh-'dahn)*
see (to)	ver	*(vehr)*
seeing eye dog	perro guía, el	*(ehl 'peh-rroh 'gee-ah)*
seize (to)	apresar	*(ah-preh-'sahr)*
seizure	ataque, el	*(ehl ah-'tah-keh)*
seldom	casi nunca	*('kah-see 'noon-kah)*
self-defense	autodefensa	*(ow-toh-deh-'fehn-sah)*
sell (to)	vender	*(vehn-'dehr)*
semi-trailer	semirremolque, el	*(ehl seh-mee-rreh-'mohl-keh)*
send (to)	mandar	*(mahn-'dahr)*
sentence	sentencia, la	*(lah sehn-'tehn-see·ah)*

September	septiembre	(sehp-tee-'ehm-breh)
sergeant	sargento, el	(ehl sahr-'hehn-toh)
serial number	número de serie, el	(ehl 'noo-meh-roh deh 'seh-ree-eh)
serious	serio	('seh-ree·oh)
serve (to)	servir	(sehr-'veer)
service	servicio, el	(ehl sehr-'vee-see·oh)
seven	siete	(see-'eh-teh)
seven hundred	setecientos	(seh-teh-see-'ehn-tohs)
seventeen	diecisiete	(dee-ehs-ee-see-'eh-teh)
seventh	séptimo	('sehp-tee-moh)
seventy	setenta	(seh-'tehn-tah)
sewage	desague, el	(ehl dehs-'ah-gweh)
sewing machine	máquina de coser, la	(lah 'mah-kee-nah deh koh-'sehr)
sex	sexo, el	(ehl 'sehk-soh)
sex (to have)	tener relaciones sexuales	(teh-'nehr reh-'lah-see-'oh nehs-sehk-soo-'ah-lehs)
shape	forma, la	(lah 'fohr-mah)
share (to)	repartir	(reh-pahr-'teer)
sharp	filudo	(fee-'loo-doh)
she	ella	('eh-yah)
sheet	sábana, la	(lah 'sah-bah-nah)
shelf	repisa, la	(lah reh-'pee-sah)
shell casing	cartucho, el	(ehl kahr-'too-choh)
shelter	refugio, el	(ehl reh-'foo-hee-oh)
sheriff	alguacil mayor, el	(ehl ahl-gwah-'seel mah-'yohr)
shield	escudo, el	(ehl eh-'skoo-doh)
shirt	camisa, la	(lah kah-'mee-sah)
shock	postración nerviosa, la	(lah poh-strah-see-'ohn nehr-vee-'oh-sah)
shock absorber	amortiguador, el	(ehl ah-mohr-tee-gwah-'dohr)
shoes	zapatos, los	(lohs sah-'pah-tohs)
shoot (to)	disparar	(dees-pah-'rahr)
shooting	disparos, los	(lohs dees-pah-rohs)
shoplifter	ratero de tiendas, el	(ehl rah-'teh-roh deh tee-'ehn-dahs)
shoplifting	ratería en las tiendas, la	(lah rah-teh-'ree-ah ehn lahs tee-'ehn-dahs)
short	corto	('kohr-toh)
shorts	calzoncillos, los	(lohs kahl-sohn-'see-yohs)
shot	balazo, el	(ehl bah-'lah-soh)
shotgun	escopeta, la	(lah eh-skoh-'peh-tah)
shoulder	hombro, el	(ehl 'ohm-broh)
shovel	pala, la	(lah 'pah-lah)
show	espectáculo, el	(ehl eh-spehk-'tah-koo-loh)
shower	ducha, la	(lah 'doo-chah)
sick	enfermo	(ehn-'fehr-moh)
sidewalk	acera, la	(lah ah-'seh-rah)

sign	señal, la	*(lah seh-'nyahl)*
sign (to)	firmar	*(feer-'mahr)*
signal (to)	señalar	*(seh-nyah-'lahr)*
silence	silencio, el	*(ehl see-'lehn-see-oh)*
single	soltero	*(sohl-'teh-roh)*
siren	sirena, la	*(lah see-'reh-nah)*
sister	hermana, la	*(lah ehr-'mah-nah)*
sister-in-law	cuñada, la	*(lah koo-'nyah-dah)*
sit down (to)	sentarse	*(sehn-'tahr-seh)*
site	sitio, el	*(ehl 'see-tee·oh)*
six	seis	*('seh·ees)*
six-pack	paquete de seis, el	*(ehl pah-'keh-teh deh 'seh·ees)*
sixteen	dieciseis	*(dee-ehs-ee-'seh·ees)*
sixth	sexto	*('sehks-toh)*
sixty	sesenta	*(seh-'sehn-tah)*
size	tamaño, el	*(ehl tah-'mah-nyoh)*
skate	patín, el	*(ehl pah-'teen)*
skill	habilidad, la	*(lah ah-bee-lee-'dahd)*
skin	piel, la	*(lah pee-'ehl)*
skirt	falda, la	*(lah 'fahl-dah)*
skyscraper	rascacielos, el	*(ehl rah-skah-see-'eh-lohs)*
sled	trineo, el	*(ehl tree-'neh-oh)*
sleep	sueño	*('sweh-nyoh)*
sleep (to)	dormir	*(dohr-'meer)*
sleeping pill	píldora para dormir, la	*(lah 'peel-doh-'rah 'pah-rah dohr-'meer)*
sleeve	manga, la	*(lah 'mahn-gah)*
slide	resbalador, el	*(ehl rehs-bah-lah-'dohr)*
sling	soporte para el brazo, el	*(ehl soh-'pohr-teh 'pah-rah ehl 'brah-soh)*
slippery	resbaloso	*(rehs-bah-'loh-soh)*
slow	despacio	*(deh-'spah-see·oh)*
slow (person)	lento	*('lehn-toh)*
small	pequeño	*(peh-'keh-nyoh)*
smart	inteligente	*(een-teh-lee-'hehn-teh)*
smell	olor, el	*(ehl oh-'lohr)*
smog device	aparato antismog, el	*(ehl ah-pah-'rah-toh ahn-tee-'smohg)*
smoke	humo, el	*(ehl 'oo-moh)*
smoke alarm	detector de humo, el	*(ehl deh-tehk-'tohr deh 'oo-moh)*
smoke (to)	fumar	*(foo-'mahr)*
smuggler	contrabandista, el	*(ehl kohn-trah-bahn-'dee-stah)*
smuggling	contrabando, el	*(ehl kohn-trah-'bahn-doh)*
snack	merienda, la	*(lah meh-ree-'ehn-dah)*
snake	culebra, la	*(lah koo-'leh-brah)*
sniper	francotirador, el	*(ehl frahn-koh-tee-rah-'dohr)*
snow	nieve, la	*(lah nee-'eh-veh)*

sobriety	sobriedad, la	*(lah soh-bree-eh-'dahd)*
social security	seguro social, el	*(ehl seh-'goo-roh soh-see-'ahl)*
social worker	trabajador social, el	*(ehl trah-bah-hah-'dohr soh-see-'ahl)*
society	sociedad, la	*(lah soh-see-eh-'dahd)*
socks	calcetines, los	*(lohs kahl-seh-'tee-nehs)*
sofa	sofá, el	*(ehl soh-'fah)*
soft	suave	*('swah-veh)*
soft drink	refresco, el	*(ehl reh-'freh-skoh)*
soldier	soldado, el	*(ehl sohl-'dah-doh)*
some	unos; unas	*('oo-nohs, 'oo-nahs)*
someone	alguien	*('ahl-gee-ehn)*
something	algo	*('ahl-goh)*
sometimes	a veces	*(ah-'veh-sehs)*
somewhere	por alguna parte	*(pohr ahl-'goo-nah 'pahr-teh)*
son	hijo, el	*(ehl 'ee-hoh)*
son-in-law	yerno, el	*(ehl 'yehr-noh)*
soon	pronto	*('pron-toh)*
sore	dolorido	*(doh-loh-'ree-doh)*
sore throat	dolor de garganta, el	*(ehl doh-'lohr deh gahr-'gahn-tah)*
sound	sonido, el	*(ehl soh-'nee-doh)*
soup	sopa, la	*(lah 'soh-pah)*
south	sur	*(soor)*
space	espacio, el	*(ehl eh-'spah-see·oh)*
Spanish	español	*(eh-spah-nyohl)*
spare tire	neumático de repuesto, el	*(ehl neh-oo-'mah-tee-koh deh reh-'pweh-stoh)*
spark plug	bujía, la	*(lah boo-'hee-ah)*
speaker	altoparlante, el	*(ehl ahl-toh-pahr-'lahn-teh)*
specialist	especialista, el	*(ehl eh-speh-see·ah-'lee-stah)*
speech	habla, el	*(ehl 'ah-blah)*
speed	velocidad, la	*(lah veh-loh-see-'dahd)*
speed limit	límite de velocidad, el	*(ehl 'lee-mee-teh deh veh-loh-see-'dahd)*
speedometer	indicador de velocidad, el	*(ehl een-dee-kah-'dohr deh veh-loh-see-'dahd)*
spill	derramamiento, el	*(ehl deh-rrah-mah-mee-'ehn-toh)*
spine	columna, la	*(lah koh-'loom-nah)*
splint	cabestrillo, el	*(ehl kah-beh-'stree-yoh)*
sports	deportes, los	*(lohs deh-'pohr-tehs)*
sports car	carro deportivo, el	*(ehl 'kah-rroh deh-pohr-'tee-voh)*
spot	mancha, la	*(lah 'mahn-chah)*
spray	aerosol, el	*(ehl ah-eh-roh-'sohl)*
spring	primavera, la	*(lah pree-mah-'veh-rah)*
sprinkler	rociadora, la	*(lah roh-see·ah-'doh-rah)*
square	cuadrado, el	*(ehl kwah-'drah-doh)*
squirrel	ardilla, la	*(lah ahr-'dee-yah)*
stab (to)	apuñalar	*(ah-poo-nyah-'lahr)*

stabbing	puñalada, la	*(lah poo-nyah-'lah-dah)*
stadium	estadio, el	*(ehl eh-'stah-dee·oh)*
stairs	escaleras, las	*(lahs eh-skah-'leh-rahs)*
stand up (to)	levantarse	*(leh-vahn-'tahr-seh)*
staple	grapa, la	*(lah 'grah-pah)*
star	estrella, la	*(lah eh-'streh-yah)*
start up (to)	arrancar	*(ah-rrahn-'kahr)*
starter	arrancador, el	*(ehl ah-rrahn-kah-'dohr)*
state	estado, el	*(ehl eh-'stah-doh)*
station	estación, la	*(lah eh-stah-see-'ohn)*
station wagon	coche vagón, el	*(ehl 'koh-cheh vah-'gohn)*
statue	estatua, la	*(lah eh-'stah-too-ah)*
stay (to)	quedarse	*(keh-'dahr-seh)*
steak	bistec, el	*(ehl bee-'stehk)*
steal (to)	robar	*(roh-'bahr)*
steel	acero, el	*(ehl ah-'seh-roh)*
steer (to)	dirigir	*(dee-ree-'heer)*
steering wheel	volante, el	*(ehl voh-'lahn-teh)*
step	escalón, el	*(ehl eh-skah-'lohn)*
stepdaughter	hijastra, la	*(lah ee-'hah-strah)*
stepfather	padrastro, el	*(ehl pah-'drah-stroh)*
stepmother	madrastra, la	*(lah mah-'drah-strah)*
stepson	hijastro, el	*(ehl ee-'hah-stroh)*
stereo	estéreo, el	*(ehl eh-'steh-reh-oh)*
stick shift	cambio manual, el	*(ehl 'kahm-bee-oh mah-noo-'ahl)*
sticker	etiqueta, la	*(lah eh-tee-'keh-tah)*
stitches	puntadas, las	*(lahs poon-'tah-dahs)*
stockings	medias, las	*(lahs 'meh-dee·ahs)*
stolen property	propiedad robada, la	*(lah proh-pee-eh-'dahd roh-'bah-dah)*
stomach	estómago, el	*(ehl eh-'stoh-mah-goh)*
stomachache	dolor de estómago, el	*(ehl doh-'lohr deh eh-'stoh-mah-goh)*
stone	piedra, la	*(lah pee-'eh-drah)*
stool	banquillo, el	*(ehl bahn-'kee-yoh)*
stop sign	señal de alto, la	*(lah seh-'nyahl deh 'ahl-toh)*
stop (to)	parar	*(pah-'rahr)*
store	tienda, la	*(lah tee-'ehn-dah)*
storm	tormenta, la	*(lah tohr-'mehn-tah)*
story	cuento, el	*(ehl 'kwehn-toh)*
stove	estufa, la	*(lah eh-'stoo-fah)*
straight	derecho	*(deh-'reh-choh)*
strange	extraño	*(eh-'strah-nyoh)*
stranger	desconocido, el	*(ehl dehs-koh-noh-'see-doh)*
strangulation	estrangulamiento, el	*(ehl eh-strahn-goo-lah-mee-'ehn-toh)*
strawberry	fresa, la	*(lah 'freh-sah)*
stream	arroyo, el	*(ehl ah-'rroh-yoh)*

street	calle, la	*(lah 'kah-yeh)*
streetlight	luz de la calle, la	*(lah loos deh lah 'kah-yeh)*
streetcar	tranvía, el	*(ehl trahn-'vee-ah)*
string	hilo, el	*(ehl 'ee-loh)*
stroller	cochecillo, el	*(ehl koh-cheh-'see-yoh)*
strong	fuerte	*('fwehr-teh)*
student	estudiante, el	*(ehl eh-stoo-dee-'ahn-teh)*
studio	estudio, el	*(ehl eh-'stoo-dee-oh)*
study (to)	estudiar	*(eh-stoo-dee-'ahr)*
style	estilo, el	*(ehl eh-'stee-loh)*
subpoena	apercibimiento, el	*(ehl ah-pehr-see-bee-mee-'ehn-toh)*
subway	metro, el	*(ehl 'meh-troh)*
suddenly	de repente	*(deh reh-'pehn-teh)*
suffer (to)	sufrir	*(soo-'freer)*
suffocation	sofocación, la	*(lah soh-foh-kah-see-'ohn)*
suicide	suicidio, el	*(ehl soo-ee-'see-dee·oh)*
suit	traje, el	*(ehl 'trah-heh)*
summer	verano, el	*(ehl veh-'rah-noh)*
sun	sol, el	*(ehl sohl)*
sunstroke	insolación, la	*(lah een-soh-lah-see-'ohn)*
Sunday	domingo	*(doh-'meen-goh)*
sunglasses	lentes de sol, los	*(lohs 'lehn-tehs deh sohl)*
supermarket	supermercado, el	*(ehl soo-pehr-mehr-'kah-doh)*
suppose (to)	suponer	*(soo-poh-'nehr)*
sure	seguro	*(seh-'goo-roh)*
surgeon	cirujano, el	*(ehl see-roo-'hah-noh)*
surround (to)	rodear	*(roh-deh-'ahr)*
surveillance	vigilancia, la	*(lah vee-hee-'lahn-see·ah)*
survive (to)	sobrevivir	*(soh-breh-vee-'veer)*
survivor	sobreviviente, el	*(ehl soh-breh-vee-vee-'ehn-teh)*
suspect	sospechoso, el	*(ehl soh-speh-'choh-soh)*
suspend (to)	suspender	*(soo-spehn-'dehr)*
swallow (to)	tragar	*(trah-'gahr)*
swamp	pantano, el	*(ehl pahn-'tah-noh)*
sweat (to)	sudar	*(soo-'dahr)*
sweater	suéter, el	*(ehl 'sweh-tehr)*
sweat suit	sudaderas, las	*(lahs soo-dah-'deh-rahs)*
swerve (to)	zigzaguear	*(seeg-sahg-eh-'ahr)*
swimming	natación, la	*(lah nah-tah-see-'ohn)*
swimming pool	piscina, la	*(lah pee-'see-nah)*
sword	espada, la	*(lah eh-'spah-dah)*
syringe	jeringa, la	*(lah heh-'reen-gah)*

T

T-shirt	camiseta, la	*(lah kah-mee-'seh-tah)*
table	mesa, la	*(lah 'meh-sah)*
tablet	tableta, la	*(lah tah-'bleh-tah)*

taillight	faro trasero, el	(ehl 'fah-roh trah-'seh-roh)
tailor	sastre, el	(ehl 'sah-streh)
* Take it easy!	¡Cúidese bien!	('kwee-deh-seh 'bee-ehn)
take out (to)	sacar	(sah-'kahr)
take place (to)	suceder	(soo-seh-'dehr)
take (to)	tomar	(toh-'mahr)
talk (to)	hablar	(ah-'blahr)
tall	alto	('ahl-toh)
tank	tanque, el	(ehl 'tahn-keh)
tape	cinta, la	(lah 'seen-tah)
tape deck	casetera, la	(lah kah-seh-'teh-rah)
tar	brea, la	(lah 'breh-ah)
tattoo	tatuaje, el	(ehl tah-too-'ah-heh)
taxi	taxi, el	(ehl 'tahk-see)
tazer	tázer, el	(ehl 'tah-sehr)
tea	té, el	(ehl teh)
teacher	maestro, el	(ehl mah-'eh-stroh)
team	equipo, el	(ehl eh-'kee-poh)
tear gas	gas lacrimógeno, el	(ehl gahs lah-kree-'moh-heh-noh)
technician	técnico, el	(ehl 'tehk-nee-koh)
teenager	adolescente, el; muchacho, el	(ehl ah-doh-lehs-'sehn-teh; ehl moo-'chah-choh)
telephone	teléfono, el	(ehl teh-'leh-foh-noh)
ten	diez	(dee-'ehs)
tenant	inquilino, el	(ehl een-kee-'lee-noh)
tendon	tendón, el	(ehl tehn-'dohn)
tenth	décimo	('deh-see-moh)
term	término, el	(ehl 'tehr-mee-noh)
terrorism	terrorismo, el	(ehl teh-rroh-'rees-moh)
terrorist	terrorista, el	(ehl teh-rroh-'ree-stah)
testify (to)	testificar	(tehs-tee-fee-'kahr)
testimony	testimonio, el	(ehl teh-stee-'moh-nee·oh)
* Thank you!	¡Gracias!	('grah-see·ahs)
that	ese	('eh-seh)
* That's great!	¡Qué bueno!	(keh 'bweh-noh)
theater	teatro, el	(ehl teh-'ah-troh)
theft	robo	('roh-boh)
their	su	(soo)
theirs	suyo	('soo-yoh)
therapy	terapia, la	(lah teh-'rah-pee·ah)
there	allí	(ah-'yee)
there is, there are	hay	(hi)
thermostat	termostato, el	(ehl tehr-moh-'stah-toh)
these	estos	('eh-stohs)
they (feminine)	ellas	('eh-yahs)
they (masculine)	ellos	('eh-yohs)
they're (qualities, characteristics)	son	(sohn)

they're (temporary state, condition, location)	están	*(eh-'stahn)*
thick	grueso	*(groo-'eh-soh)*
thief	ladrón, el	*(ehl lah-'drohn)*
thigh	muslo, el	*(ehl 'moo-sloh)*
thin	delgado	*(dehl-'gah-doh)*
things	cosas, las	*(lahs 'koh-sahs)*
third	tercero	*(tehr-'seh-roh)*
thirst	sed	*(sehd)*
thirteen	trece	*('treh-seh)*
thirty	treinta	*('treh·een-tah)*
this	este	*('eh-steh)*
those	esos	*('eh-sohs)*
thousand	mil	*(meel)*
threaten (to)	amenazar	*(ah-meh-nah-'sahr)*
three	tres	*(trehs)*
throat	garganta, la	*(lah gahr-'gahn-tah)*
thumb	dedo pulgar, el	*(ehl 'deh-doh pool-'gahr)*
thunder	trueno, el	*(ehl troo-'eh-noh)*
Thursday	jueves	*('hweh-vehs)*
ticket	boleto, el	*(ehl boh-'leh-toh)*
ticket (citation)	boleta, la	*(lah boh-'leh-tah)*
tie	corbata, la	*(lah kohr-'bah-tah)*
tight	apretado	*(ah-preh-'tah-doh)*
time (general)	tiempo, el	*(ehl tee-'ehm-poh)*
time (occurrence)	vez, la	*(lah vehs)*
time (specific)	hora, la	*(lah 'oh-rah)*
tire	neumático, el	*(ehl neh-oo-'mah-tee-koh)*
tire iron	desarmador, el	*(ehl dehs-ahr-mah-'dohr)*
tired	cansado	*(kahn-'sah-doh)*
to	a	*(ah)*
to the	al	*(ahl)*
to the left	a la izquierda	*(ah lah ees-kee-'ehr-dah)*
to the right	a la derecha	*(ah lah deh-'reh-chah)*
toe	dedo del pie, el	*(ehl 'deh-doh dehl 'pee-eh)*
together	juntos	*('hoon-tohs)*
toilet	excusado, el	*(ehl ehks-koo-'sah-doh)*
toilet paper	papel higiénico, el	*(ehl pah-'pehl ee-hee-'eh-nee-koh)*
toll booth	caseta de peaje, la	*(lah kah-'seh-tah deh peh-'ah-heh)*
tomato	tomate, el	*(ehl toh-'mah-teh)*
tongue	lengua, la	*(lah 'lehn-gwah)*
too	también	*(tahm-bee-'ehn)*
too much	demasiado	*(deh-mah-see-'ah-doh)*
tool	herramienta, la	*(lah eh-rrah-mee-'ehn-tah)*
tooth	diente, el	*(ehl dee·ehn-teh)*

toothache	dolor de muela, el	*(ehl doh-'lohr deh 'mweh-lah)*
torch	antorcha, la	*(lah ahn-'tohr-chah)*
tornado	tornado, el	*(ehl tohr-'nah-doh)*
torture	tortura, la	*(lah tohr-'too-rah)*
touch (to)	tocar	*(toh-'kahr)*
tour bus	autobús de turismo, el	*(ehl ow-toh-'boos deh too-'rees-moh)*
tourniquet	torniquete, el	*(ehl tohr-nee-'keh-teh)*
tow bar	barra, la	*(lah 'bah-rrah)*
tow (to)	remolcar	*(reh-mohl-'kahr)*
tow truck	grúa, la	*(lah 'groo-ah)*
towel	toalla, la	*(lah toh-'ah-yah)*
tower	torre, la	*(lah 'toh-rreh)*
towing company	compañía de remolque, la	*(lah kohm-pah-'nyee-ah deh reh-'mohl-keh)*
toy	juguete, el	*(ehl hoo-'geh-teh)*
track	pisada, la	*(lah pee-'sah-dah)*
tractor	tractor, el	*(ehl trahk-'tohr)*
tradition	tradición, la	*(lah trah-dee-see-'ohn)*
traffic	tráfico, el	*(ehl 'trah-fee-koh)*
traffic light	semáforo, el	*(ehl seh-'mah-foh-roh)*
traffic sign	señal de tráfico, la	*(lah seh-'nyahl deh 'trah-fee-koh)*
traffic signal	semáforo, el	*(ehl seh-'mah-foh-roh)*
trail	senda, la	*(lah 'sehn-dah)*
train	tren, el	*(ehl trehn)*
trainer	entrenador, el	*(ehl ehn-treh-nah-'dohr)*
training	entrenamiento, el	*(ehl ehn-treh-nah-mee-'ehn-toh)*
tranfusion	transfusión, la	*(lah trahns-foo-see-'ohn)*
tranquilizer	tranquilizante, el	*(ehl trahn-kee-lee-'sahn-teh)*
translator	traductor, el	*(ehl trah-dook-'tohr)*
transmission	transmisión, la	*(lah trahns-mee-see-'ohn)*
transportation	transporte, el	*(ehl trahns-'pohr-teh)*
trash	basura, la	*(lah bah-'soo-rah)*
trash bin	bote de basura, el	*(ehl 'boh-teh deh bah-'soo-rah)*
travel (to)	viajar	*(vee-ah-'hahr)*
tree	árbol, el	*(ehl 'ahr-bohl)*
trespassing	intrusión, la	*(lah een-troo-see-'ohn)*
trial	juicio, el	*(ehl 'hoo·ee-see·oh)*
triangle	triángulo, el	*(ehl tree-'ahn-goo-loh)*
trick	truco, el	*(ehl 'troo-koh)*
truck	camión, el	*(ehl kah-mee-'ohn)*
truck driver	camionero, el	*(ehl kah-mee·oh-'neh-roh)*
trunk	maletera, la	*(lah mah-leh-'teh-rah)*
trust (to)	confiar	*(kohn-fee-'ahr)*
truth	verdad, la	*(lah vehr-'dahd)*
Tuesday	martes	*('mahr-tehs)*
tunnel	túnel, el	*(ehl 'too-nehl)*
turkey	pavo, el	*(ehl 'pah-voh)*

turn in (to)	entregar	*(ehn-treh-'gahr)*
turn oneself (to)	darse vuelta	*('dahr-seh 'vwehl-tah)*
turn signal	señal de dirección, la	*(lah seh-'nyahl deh dee-rehk-see-'ohn)*
TV	televisor, el	*(ehl teh-leh-vee-'sohr)*
tweezers	pinzas, las	*(lahs 'peen-sahs)*
twelve	doce	*('doh-seh)*
twenty	veinte	*('veh·een-teh)*
twin	gemelo, el	*(ehl heh-'meh-loh)*
twisted	torcido	*(tohr-'see-doh)*
two	dos	*(dohs)*
type	tipo, el	*(ehl 'tee-poh)*

U

ugly	feo	*('feh-oh)*
umbrella (for rain)	paraguas, el	*(ehl pah-'rah-goo-ahs)*
umbrella (for sun)	sombrilla, la	*(lah sohm-'bree-yah)*
uncle	tío, el	*(ehl 'tee-oh)*
uncomfortable	incómodo	*(een-'koh-moh-doh)*
unconscious	inconsciente	*(een-kohn-see-'ehn-teh)*
underpants	calzoncillos, los	*(lohs kahl-sohn-'see-yohs)*
understand (to)	entender	*(ehn-tehn-'dehr)*
underwear	ropa interior, la	*(lah 'roh-pah een-teh-ree-'ohr)*
undocumented	indocumentado	*(een-doh-koo-mehn-'tah-doh)*
unemployment	desempleo, el	*(ehl dehs-ehm-'pleh-oh)*
uneven	desigual	*(dehs-ee-'gwahl)*
uniform	uniforme, el	*(ehl oo-nee-'fohr-meh)*
United States	Estados Unidos, los	*(lohs eh-'stah-dohs oo-'nee-dohs)*
university	universidad, la	*(lah oo-nee-vehr-see-'dahd)*
unleaded	sin plomo	*(seen 'ploh-moh)*
up	arriba	*(ah-'rree-bah)*
upholstery	tapicería, la	*(lah tah-pee-seh-'ree-ah)*
upset	molesto	*(moh-'leh-stoh)*
urgent	urgente	*(oor-'hehn-teh)*
urine	orina, la	*(lah oh-'ree-nah)*
use (to)	usar	*(oo-'sahr)*

V

vaccination	vacunación, la	*(lah vah-koo-nah-see-'ohn)*
vagrant	vagabundo, el	*(ehl vah-gah-'boon-doh)*
valid	válido	*('vah-lee-doh)*
valley	valle, el	*(ehl 'vah-yeh)*
value	valor, el	*(ehl vah-'lohr)*
valve	válvula, la	*(lah 'vahl-voo-lah)*
van	vagoneta, la; furgoneta, la	*(lah vah-goh-'neh-tah; lah foor-goh-'neh-tah)*
vandalism	vandalismo, el	*(ehl vahn-dah-'lees-moh)*

VCR	videocasetera, la	*(lah vee-deh-oh-kah-seh-'teh-rah)*
vehicle	vehículo, el	*(ehl veh-'ee-koo-loh)*
vein	vena, la	*(lah 'veh-nah)*
verdict	veredicto, el	*(ehl veh-reh-'deek-toh)*
* Very well!	¡Muy bien!	*('moo·ee 'bee·ehn)*
veterinarian	veterinario, el	*(ehl veh-teh-ree-'nah-ree·oh)*
vial	frasco, el	*(ehl 'frah-skoh)*
vice	vicio, el	*(ehl 'vee-see·oh)*
victim	víctima, la	*(lah 'veek-tee-mah)*
Vietnamese	vietnamés	*(vee-eht-nah-'mehs)*
violation	violación, la	*(lah vee-oh-lah-see-'ohn)*
violent	violento	*(vee-oh-'lehn-toh)*
visa	visa, la	*(lah 'vee-sah)*
visitor	visitante, el	*(ehl vee-see-'tahn-teh)*
voice	voz, la	*(lah vohs)*
volunteer	voluntario, el	*(ehl voh-loon-'tah-ree·oh)*
vomit (to)	vomitar	*(voh-mee-'tahr)*
vulgarity	vulgaridad, la	*(lah vool-gah-ree-'dahd)*

W

wagon	carretón, el	*(ehl kah-rreh-'tohn)*
wait (to)	esperar	*(eh-speh-'rahr)*
waiter	mesonero, el	*(ehl meh-soh-'neh-roh)*
waiting list	lista de espera, la	*(lah 'lee-stah deh eh-'speh-rah)*
walk (to)	caminar	*(kah-mee-'nahr)*
wall	pared, la	*(lah pah-'rehd)*
wallet	billetera, la	*(lah bee-yeh-'teh-rah)*
want (to)	querer	*(keh-'rehr)*
warden	guardián de la prisión, el	*(ehl gwahr-dee-'ahn deh lah pree-see-'ohn)*
warehouse	almacén, el	*(ehl ahl-mah-'sehn)*
warm	tibio	*('tee-bee·oh)*
warn (to)	advertir	*(ahd-vehr-'teer)*
warning	advertencia, la	*(lah ahd-vehr-'tehn-see·ah)*
warrant	orden de la corte, la	*(lah 'ohr-dehn deh lah 'kohr-teh)*
washing machine	lavadora, la	*(lah lah-vah-'doh-rah)*
watch	reloj, el	*(ehl reh-'loh)*
watchman	vigilante, el	*(ehl vee-hee-'lahn-teh)*
water	agua, el	*(ehl 'ah-gwah)*
we	nosotros	*(noh-'soh-trohs)*
we're (qualities, characteristics)	somos	*('soh-mohs)*
we're (temporary state, location, condition)	estamos	*(eh-'stah-mohs)*
weak	débil	*('deh-beel)*

weapon	arma, el	(ehl 'ahr-mah)
weather	tiempo, el	(ehl tee-'ehm-poh)
wedding	boda, la	(lah 'boh-dah)
Wednesday	miércoles	(mee-'ehr-koh-lehs)
weed	hierba, la	(lah 'yehr-bah)
week	semana, la	(lah seh-'mah-nah)
weekend	fin de semana, el	(ehl feen deh seh-'mah-nah)
weigh (to)	pesar	(peh-'sahr)
weight	peso	('peh-soh)
* Welcome!	¡Bienvenidos!	(bee-ehn-veh-'nee-dohs)
welfare	bienestar social, el	(ehl bee-ehn-eh-'stahr soh-see-'ahl)
west	oeste	(oh-'eh-steh)
wet	mojado	(moh-'hah-doh)
what	qué	(keh)
* What a shame!	¡Qué lástima!	(keh 'lah-stee-mah)
* What happened?	¿Qué pasó?	(keh pah-'soh)
* What time is it?	¿Qué hora es?	(keh 'oh-rah ehs)
* What's happening?	¿Qué pasa?	(keh 'pah-sah)
* What's your name?	¿Cómo se llama?	('koh-moh seh 'yah-mah)
wheel	rueda, la	(lah roo-'eh-dah)
wheelchair	silla de ruedas, la	(lah 'seh-yah deh roo-'eh-dahs)
when	cuándo	('kwahn-doh)
where	dónde	('dohn-deh)
which	cuál	(kwahl)
whip	látigo, el	(ehl 'lah-tee-goh)
whistle	silbato, el	(ehl seel-'bah-toh)
white	blanco, el	('blahn-koh)
who	quién	(kee-'ehn)
whose	de quién	(deh kee-'ehn)
why	por qué	(pohr keh)
wide	ancho	('ahn-choh)
widowed	viudo	(vee-'oo-doh)
wife	esposa, la	(lah eh-'spoh-sah)
wig	peluca, la	(lah peh-'loo-kah)
wild	salvaje	(sahl-'vah-heh)
wind	viento, el	(ehl vee-'ehn-toh)
window	ventana, la	(lah vehn-'tah-nah)
windshield	parabrisas, el	(ehl pah-rah-'bree-sahs)
windshield wiper	limpiaparabrisas, el	(ehl leem-pee·ah-pah-rah-'bree-sahs)
wine	vino, el	(ehl 'vee-noh)
winter	invierno, el	(ehl een-vee-'ehr-noh)
wire	alambre, el	(ehl ah-'lahm-breh)
with	con	(kohn)
within	dentro	('dehn-troh)
without	sin	(seen)
witness	testigo, el	(ehl teh-'stee-goh)

wolf	lobo, el	*(ehl 'loh-boh)*
woman	mujer, la	*(lah moo-'hehr)*
wood	madera, la	*(lah mah-'deh-rah)*
wool	lana, la	*(lah 'lah-nah)*
word	palabra la	*(lah pah-'lah-brah)*
work	trabajo, el	*(ehl trah-'bah-hoh)*
work (to)	trabajar	*(trah-bah-'hahr)*
worker	trabajador, el	*(ehl trah-bah-hah-'dohr)*
worried	preocupado	*(preh-oh-koo-'pah-doh)*
worse	peor	*(peh-'ohr)*
* **Would you like...?**	¿Quisiera...?	*(kee-see-'eh-rah)*
wound (to)	herir	*(eh-'reer)*
* **Wow!**	¡Caramba!	*(kah-'rahm-bah)*
wreck (to)	arruinar	*(ah-rroo-ee-'nahr)*
wrench	llave inglesa, la	*(lah 'yah-veh een-'gleh-sah)*
wrist	muñeca, la	*(lah moo-'nyeh-kah)*
wristwatch	reloj de pulsera, el	*(ehl reh-'loh deh pool-'seh-rah)*
write (to)	escribir	*(eh-skree-'beer)*
wrong	equivocado	*(eh-kee-voh-'kah-doh)*

Y

yard	jardín, el	*(ehl hahr-'deen)*
year	año, el	*(ehl 'ah-nyoh)*
yell (to)	gritar	*(gree-'tahr)*
yellow	amarillo	*(ah-mah-'ree-yoh)*
yield (to)	ceder el paso	*(seh-'dehr ehl 'pah-soh)*
* **You have to...**	Tiene que...	*('tee-'eh-neh keh...)*
you (informal singular)	tú	*(too)*
* **You need to...**	Necesita...	*(neh-seh-'see-tah...)*
you (plural)	ustedes	*(oo-'steh-dehs)*
* **You should...**	Debe...	*('deh-beh...)*
you (singular)	usted	*(oo-'stehd)*
* **You're welcome!**	¡De nada!	*(deh 'nah-dah)*
young	joven	*('hoh-vehn)*
younger	menor	*(meh-'nohr)*
your	su	*(soo)*
youth	juventud, la	*(lah hoo-vehn-'tood)*

Z

zero	cero	*('seh-roh)*
zip code	código postal, el	*(ehl 'koh-dee-goh poh-'stahl)*
zipper	cierre, el	*(ehl see-'eh-rreh)*
zoo	zoológico, el	*(ehl soh-oh-'loh-hee-koh)*

SPANISH-ENGLISH GLOSSARY

Spanish feminine nouns are preceded by the article **la,** and the masculine nouns are preceded by the article **el** (or the plural articles **las** or **los,** respectively). The gender of adjectives and pronouns is masculine in this glossary, but it should be changed to feminine when the sentence requires it. Useful expressions are preceded by an asterisk.

A

a	to
a la derecha	to the right
a la izquierda	to the left
a veces	sometimes
* **¡A ver!**	Let's see!
abajo	down
abandonar	abandon (to)
abierto	open
abogado, el	lawyer
abollado	dented
abrazar	hug (to)
abrigo, el	overcoat
abril	April
abrir	open (to)
abuela, la	grandmother
abuelo, el	grandfather
aburrido	bored
abuso, el	abuse
abuso de las drogas, el	drug abuse
abuso de menores, el	child abuse
abuso sexual, el	molestation
acabar	finish (to)
* **Acabo de...**	I just finished...
accidente, el	accident
acción, la	action
aceite, el	oil
acelerador, el	accelerator
acera, la	sidewalk
acero, el	steel
ácido, el	acid
acondicionador de aire, el	air conditioner
acosamiento, el	harassment
actitud, la	attitude
acusación, la	indictment; charge
acusar	accuse (to)
adentro	inside
adicto, el	addict
* **¡Adiós!**	Good-bye!

adivinar	guess (to)
administrador, el	administrator; manager
adolescente, el	adolescent
adulto, el	adult
advertencia, la	warning
advertir	warn (to)
aeropuerto, el	airport
aerosol, el	spray
afecto, el	affection
afilado	sharp
afroamericano, el	African-American
afuera	outside
afueras, las	outdoors
agencia, la	agency
agente, el	agent
agente funerario, el	mortician
agosto	August
agotado	exhausted
agresión, la	battery
agresor, el	aggressor
agua, el	water
aguja, la	needle
agujero, el	hole
ahora	nowadays
* ¡Ahora vengo!	I'll be right back!
ahorita	right now
aire acondicionado, el	air conditioning
al	to the
al lado de	next to
alambre, el	wire
alarma, la	alarm
alcalde, el	mayor
alcohol, el	alcohol
alcohólico, el	alcoholic
alérgico	allergic
alerto	alert
alfiler, el	pin
alfombra, la	rug
algo	something
algodón, el	cotton
alguacil, el	bailiff; marshal
alguacil mayor, el	sheriff
alguien	someone
alias, el	alias (a.k.a)
aliento, el	breath
alimentar	feed (to)
almacén, el	warehouse

almohada, la	pillow
almuerzo, el	lunch
alquilar	rent (to)
altavoz, el	bullhorn
alterado	altered
alto	high; tall
altoparlante, el	speaker
allá	over there
allí	there
amante, el or la	lover
amarillo	yellow
amarrar	fasten (to)
ambulancia, la	ambulance
amenazar	threaten (to)
americano	American
ametralladora, la	machine gun
amigo, el	friend
amistoso	friendly
amor, el	love
amortiguador, el	shock absorber
año, el	year
anaranjado	orange (color)
anciano, el	elderly
ancho	wide
anglosajón	Anglo-Saxon
aniversario, el	anniversary
ansioso	anxious
antena, la	antenna
anteojos, los	glasses
antes	before
antibiótico, el	antibiotic
antigüedad, la	antique
antorcha, la	flare; torch
aparato antismog, el	smog device
apartamento, el	apartment
apelar	appeal (to)
apellido	last name
apéndice, el	appendix
apercibimiento, el	subpoena
apodo, el	nickname
apostador, el	gambler
apostar	bet (to); gamble (to)
apresar	seize (to)
apretado	tight
aprobación, la	approval
aprobar	approve (to)
aproximadamente	approximately

apuñalar	stab (to)
apurarse	hurry up (to)
aquí	here
árabe, el	Arab
árbol, el	tree
arboleda, la	grove
arbusto, el	bush
archivos, los	files
ardilla, la	squirrel
área, el	area
arena, la	sand
arete, el	earring
arma de fuego, el	firearm
arma, el	weapon
armadura de yeso, la	cast
armario, el	armoire
arrancador, el	starter
arrancar	start up (to)
arreglar	arrange (to)
arrestar	arrest (to)
arriba	up
arroyo, el	stream
arroz, el	rice
arruinar	wreck (to)
artista, el	artist
asaltante, el	assailant
asalto, el	assault
ascensor, el	elevator
asegurar	secure (to)
asesinato, el	murder
asesino, el	killer; murderer
asfalto, el	asphalt
asfixiado	asphyxiated
* ¡Así-así!	Not bad!
asiento, el	seat
asiento trasero, el	back seat
asistencia, la	attendance
asistente, el	assistant
asistir	attend (to)
aspirina, la	aspirin
asunto, el	matter
asustado	afraid
asustar	frighten (to)
ataque al corazón, el	heart attack
ataque, el	seizure
ataúd, el	coffin
atornillador, el	screwdriver

audiencia, la	hearing
ausente	absent
autobús de turismo, el	tour bus
autobús, el	bus
autobús escolar, el	school bus
autodefensa, la	self-defense
autopista, la	freeway; highway
autopsia, la	autopsy
autoridades, las	authorities
avalancha, la	landslide
avenida, la	avenue
avión, el	plane
ayuda, la	assistance; help
ayuda legal, la	legal aid
ayuda para el niño, la	child support
ayudante de camarero, el	busboy
ayudante, el	helper
ayudar	help (to)
azul	blue

B

baile, el	dance
bajo	low
bala, la	bullet
balanza, la	scale
balazo, el	shot
baño, el	bathroom
banco, el	bank
bandera, la	flag
banquillo, el	stool
bar, el	bar
barato	cheap
barba, la	beard
barbilla, la	chin
barra, la	tow bar
barranca, la	gulch
barrera, la	barrier
barricada, la	roadblock (intentional)
barrio, el	neighborhood
básquetbol, el	basketball
basura, la	litter; trash
basural, el	dump
bata de baño, la	bathrobe
bate, el	bat (baseball)
bebé, el	baby
beber	drink (to)
bebida, la	beverage; drink

béisbol, el	baseball
bello	beautiful
beneficioso	beneficial
besar	kiss (to)
biblioteca, la	library
bicicleta, la	bicycle
bicicleta motorizada, la	moped
bien	fine
bienestar social, el	welfare
* **¡Bienvenidos!**	Welcome!
bigote, el	moustache
billete, el	bill (currency)
billetera, la	wallet
bistec, el	steak
blanco, el	white
blusa, la	blouse
boca, la	mouth
bocacalle, la	intersection
bocina, la	horn
boda, la	wedding
bodega, la; almacén, el	grocery store
boleta, la	ticket (citation)
boleto, el	ticket
boliche, el	bowling
bolsa, la	bag
bolsillo, el	pocket
bomba, la	bomb; pump
bombero, el	firefighter
borracho	drunk
borracho, el	drunkard
bosque, el	forest
bota, la	boot
bote, el	boat
bote de basura, el	trash bin
botella, la	bottle
botiquín, el	first aid kit; medicine chest
botón, el	button
boxeo, el	boxing
bragas, las	panties
brazalete, el	bracelet
brazo, el	arm
brea, la	tar
brillante	bright
broche, el	brooch
budista	Buddhist
* **¡Buena idea!**	Good idea!
* **¡Buena suerte!**	Good luck!

* ¡Buenas noches!	Good evening!; Good night!
* ¡Buenas tardes!	Good afternoon!
bueno	good
* ¡Buenos días!	Good morning!
bujía, la	spark plug
bulevar, el	boulevard
burdel, el	brothel
buscar	search (to)
búsqueda, la	search
buzón, el	mailbox

C

caballo, el	horse
cabaña, la	cabin
cabello, el	hair
cabestrillo, el	splint
cabeza, la	head
cable, el	cable
cabo, el	corporal (army)
cadáver, el	cadaver; body (dead)
cadena, la	chain
cadera, la	hip
caer	fall (to)
café	brown
café, el	coffee
cafetería, la	cafeteria
cafiche, el	pimp
caja de fusibles, la	fuse box
caja, la	box
cajero, el	cashier
cajón, el	drawer
calcetines, los	socks
calefacción, la	heating
calendario, el	calendar
calentador, el	heater
calibre, el	caliber
caliente	hot
calificación, la	academic grade
calmado	calm
calmar	calm (to)
calvo	bald
calzoncillos, los	shorts; underpants
calle, la	street
calle sin salida, la	cul-de-sac
callejón, el	alley
cama, la	bed
cámara de comercio, la	chamber of commerce

cámara, la	camera
cambiar	change (to)
cambio, el	change
cambio manual, el	stick shift
caminar	walk (to)
camino, el	road
camión de bomberos, el	fire truck
camión de plataforma, el	flatbed truck
camión de reparto, el	delivery truck
camión, el	truck
camionero, el	truck driver
camioneta, la	pickup
camisa, la	shirt
camiseta, la	T-shirt
campamento, el	campground
campo de recreo, el	playground
campo, el	field
canasta, la	basket
cancelar	cancel (to)
candado, el	padlock
cansado	tired
cantinero, el	bartender
capataz, el	foreman
capellán, el	chaplain
capitán, el	captain
capota, la	hood
cápsula, la	capsule
cara, la	face
carabina, la	carbine
* **¡Caramba!**	Wow!
carburador, el	carburetor
cárcel, la	jail
carga, la	load
cargo, el	charge
carne, la	meat
carnicero, el	butcher
caro	expensive
carpintero, el	carpenter
carretera, la	highway
carretón, el	wagon
carro blindado, el	armored car
carro deportivo, el	sports car
carro, el	car
cartera, la	purse
carterista, el	pickpocket
cartero, el	mail carrier
cartílago, el	cartilage

cartón, el	cardboard
cartucho, el	cartridge; shell casing
casa, la	house
casa de empeños, la	pawnshop
casa prefabricada, la	prefabricated home
casa rodante, la	mobile home
casado	married
cascajo, el	gravel
casco, el	helmet
caseta de peaje, la	toll booth
caseta, la	booth
casete, el	cassette
casetera, la	tape deck
casi nunca	seldom
caso, el	case
castigar	punish (to)
castigo, el	punishment
católico	Catholic
catorce	fourteen
causa, la	cause
cazar	hunt (to)
cebolla, la	onion
ceder el paso	yield (to)
ceja, la	eyebrow
celda, la	cell
celo, el	jealousy
cementerio, el	cemetery
cemento, el	cement
cena, la	dinner
cenicero, el	ashtray
centavo, el	cent
centro, el	downtown
cepillo de pelo, el	hairbrush
cepillo, el	brush
cerca	near
cerca, la	fence
cerdo, el	pig; pork
cerebro, el	brain
cero	zero
cerrado	closed
cerradura, la	lock
cerrajero, el	locksmith
cerrar	close (to)
cerrar con llave	lock (to)
cerro, el	hill
cerrojo, el	latch
certificado, el	certificate

cerveza, la	beer
césped, el	grass; lawn
cicatriz, la	scar
ciclista, el	bicyclist; cyclist
ciego	blind
cielo raso, el	ceiling
cien	one hundred
ciencia forense, la	forensic science
cierre, el	zipper
cigarrillo, el	cigarette
cinco	five
cincuenta	fifty
cine, el	movie theater
cinta, la	tape
cinturón de seguridad, el	safety belt; seat belt
cinturón, el	belt
circo, el	circus
círculo, el	circle
cirujano, el	surgeon
cita, la	appointment
citación, la	citation
ciudad, la	city
ciudadano, el	citizen
cívico	civic
clase, la	class
clasificación, la	classification
clavo, el	nail
cliente, el	client; customer
clima, el	climate
club nocturno, el	nightclub
coartada, la	alibi
cobija, la	blanket
cocaína, la	cocaine
cocina, la	kitchen
cocinero, el	cook
cóctel, el	cocktail
coche habitación, el	house trailer
coche vagón, el	station wagon
cochecillo, el	stroller
código, el	code
código postal, el	zip code
codo, el	elbow
coger	catch (to)
colcha, la	mattress
colección, la	collection
colegio, el	college
color, el	color

columna, la	spine
collar, el	necklace
comedor, el	dining room
comer	eat (to)
comercial	commercial
cometa, la	kite
comida, la	food; meal
cómo	how
* ¿Cómo está?	How are you?
* ¿Cómo puedo ayudarle?	How can I help you?
* ¿Cómo se dice?	How do you say it?
* ¿Cómo se escribe?	How do you write it?
* ¿Cómo se llama?	What's your name?
* ¿Cómo se siente?	How do you feel?
cómodo	comfortable
compañero, el	companion
compañía de remolque, la	towing company
compañía de seguros, la	insurance company
completo	complete
cómplice, el	accomplice
comportamiento, el	behavior
comprar	buy (to)
computadora, la	computer
con	with
* ¡Con permiso!	Excuse me!
concierto, el	concert
condado, el	county
condominio, el	condominium
conejo, el	rabbit
conferencia, la	conference
confesar	confess (to)
confesión, la	confession
confiar	trust (to)
conflicto, el	conflict
confundido	confused
congelador, el	freezer
congelamiento, el	frostbite
congestionado	congested
cono, el	cone
conocer	know someone (to)
conocido, el	acquaintance
consejero, el	counselor
consejo, el	advice
construcción, la	construction
contador, el	accountant
contagioso	contagious
contestar	answer (to)

* ¡Contra la pared!	Against the wall!
contrabandista, el	smuggler
contrabando, el	smuggling
control, el	control
contusión, la	bruise
convicto, el	convict
coordinador, el	coordinator
copia, la	copy
copiadora, la	copier
corazón, el	heart
corbata, la	tie
coronel, el	colonel
corporal	corporal (body)
correa del ventilador, la	fan belt
correa, la	leash
correcto	accurate; right
corrector dental, el	braces
correo, el	mail; post office
correr	run (to)
cortada, la	cut
cortar	cut (to)
corte, la	courthouse
cortés	polite
cortesía, la	courtesy
cortina, la	curtain
corto	short
cosas, las	things
cosecha, la	crop
cosméticos, los	cosmetics
cosmetólogo, el	beautician
costilla, la	rib
costo, el	cost
costumbre, la	custom
crecer	grow (to)
* ¡Creo que sí!	I think so!
crimen, el	crime
criminal, el	criminal
cristiano	Christian
crítico	critical
cruce de peatones, el	crosswalk
Cruz Roja, la	Red Cross
cruzar	cross (to)
cuaderno, el	notebook
cuadra, la	city block
cuadrado, el	square
cuadro, el	painting
cuál	which

cuándo	when
cuánto	how much
cuántos	how many
* ¿Cuántos años tiene?	How old are you?
cuarenta	forty
cuarto	fourth
cuarto, el	quarter; room
cuatro	four
cubano	Cuban
cubrecama, el	bedspread
cuchillo, el	knife
cuello, el	neck
cuenta de banco, la	bank account
cuento, el	story
cuerpo, el	body
cuidado del niño, el	child care
* ¡Cúidese bien!	Take it easy!
culebra, la	snake
culpa la	fault
culpable	guilty
cumpleaños, el	birthday
cuñada, la	sister-in-law
cuñado, el	brother-in-law
cuna, la	crib
cupón, el	coupon
curita, la	Band-Aid
curva, la	curve
custodia, la	custody
chaleco a prueba de bala, el	bullet-proof vest
champaña, la	champagne
chaqueta, la	jacket
charca, la	puddle
cheque de sueldo, el	paycheck
cheque, el	check
chequera, la	checkbook
chimenea, la	chimney; fireplace
chiste, el	joke
chistoso	funny
chocar	crash (to)
chofer, el	driver

D

daga, la	dagger
dañado	damaged
daño, el	damage
dar	give (to)
darse vuelta	turn oneself (to)

de	of, from
* ¡De nada!	You're welcome!
de quién	whose
de repente	suddenly
* Debe...	You should...
débil	weak
décimo	tenth
declaración jurada, la	affidavit
dedo del pie, el	toe
dedo, el	finger
dedo pulgar, el	thumb
defectuoso	defective
defensa, la	defense
defensor público, el	public defender
del	of the, from the
delgado	thin
delincuencia, la	delinquency
delincuencia juvenil, la	juvenile delinquency
delincuente, el	delinquent
delirios, los	delusions
delito mayor, el	felony
delito menor, el	misdemeanor
demandado, el	defendant
demandante, el	plaintiff
demasiado	too much
dentadura postiza, la	dentures
dentista, el	dentist
dentro	within
denunciar	charge (to)
denuncia, la	arraignment
departamento, el	department
departamento de bomberos, el	fire department
departamento de Inmigración, el	Department of Immigration
departamento de vehículos, el	DMV
dependiente, el	clerk
deportación, la	deportation
deportes, los	sports
derecho	straight
derecho de vía, el	right of way
derramamiento, el	spill
desague, el	sewage
desamparado	homeless
desarmador, el	tire iron
desayuno, el	breakfast
descalzo	barefoot
descansar	rest (to)
descapotable, el	convertible

desconocido, el	stranger
descuento, el	discount
descuido, el	negligence
* ¿Desea...?	Do you wish...?
desempleo, el	unemployment
desfalco, el	embezzling
desfile, el	parade
deshidratación, la	dehydration
desierto, el	desert
desigual	uneven
desinflado	flat
desmayarse	faint (to)
desnudo	naked
desodorante, el	deodorant
despacio	slow
despachador, el	dispatcher
despierto	awake
después	after
destruir	destroy (to)
desván, el	attic
desvío, el	detour
detective, el	detective
detector de humo, el	smoke alarm
detener	detain (to)
detenido	detained
detrás	behind
devolver	return something (to)
día de fiesta, el	holiday
día, el	day
diamante, el	diamond
diciembre	December
diecinueve	nineteen
dieciocho	eighteen
dieciseis	sixteen
diecisiete	seventeen
diente, el	tooth
diestro	right-handed
diez	ten
diferente	different
difícil	difficult
dinamita, la	dynamite
dinero al contado, el	cash
dinero, el	money
Dios	God
diputado, el	deputy
dirección, la	address
director, el	principal
dirigir	steer (to)

disciplina, la	discipline
disco compacto, el	compact disc
* ¡Disculpe!	Excuse me!
disfraz, el	costume
disparar	shoot (to)
disparos, los	shooting
disponible	available
disputa, la	dispute
distribuidor, el	distributor
distrito, el	district; precinct
divisoria, la	divider
divorciado	divorced
doblar	bend (to)
doble	double
doce	twelve
docena, la	dozen
documento, el	document
dólar, el	dollar
dolor de cabeza, el	headache
dolor de espalda, el	backache
dolor de estómago, el	stomachache
dolor de garganta, el	sore throat
dolor de muela, el	toothache
dolor, el	pain
dolores de parto, los	labor pains
dolorido	sore
domingo	Sunday
dónde	where
dormido	asleep
dormir	sleep (to)
dormitorio, el	bedroom
dos	two
drenaje, el	drainage
drogadicto, el	drug addict
drogado	drugged, high
droguero, el	dealer (drug)
ducha, la	shower
dueño, el	owner
duro	hard

E

edad, la	age
edificio, el	building
educación, la	education
eje, el	axle
ejecución, la	execution
ejemplo, el	example

él	he
electricidad, la	electricity
electricista, el	electrician
electrodoméstico, el	electric appliance
elegir	choose (to)
ella	she
ellas	they (feminine)
ellos	they (masculine)
embarazada	pregnant
embargar	impound (to)
emblema, el	badge
embrague, el	clutch
emergencia, la	emergency
emigrante, el	emigrant
emocionado	excited
empezar	begin (to)
empleador, el	employee
empleo, el	employment
empresario, el	employer
empujar	push (to)
empujón, el	push
en	at; in; on
* ¡En seguida!	Right away!
encarcelamiento, el	incarceration
encarcelar	incarcerate (to)
encendido, el	ignition
encía, la	gum
encima	above
encontrar	find (to)
enchufe, el	electrical outlet
enero	January
enfermero, el	nurse
enfermo	sick
engranaje, el	gear
enojado	angry
ensalada, la	salad
entender	understand (to)
entrada, la	entrance
entrada para carros, la	driveway
entre	between
entredicho, el	injunction
entregar	turn in (to)
entrenador, el	trainer
entrenamiento, el	training
entrevista, la	interview
epidemia, la	epidemic
equilibrio, el	balance

equipaje, el	equipment; luggage
equipo, el	team
equivocado	wrong
es	is (qualities, characteristics)
* ¡Es la ley!	It's the law!
escalera, la	ladder
escalera mecánica, la	escalator
escaleras, las	stairs
escalón, el	step
escapar	escape (to)
escarcha, la	frost
escena, la	scene
esconder	hide (to)
escopeta, la	shotgun
escribir	write (to)
escritorio, el	desk
escritura de fianza, la	bail bond
escuchar	listen (to)
escudo, el	shield
escuela, la	school
ese	that
esos	those
espacio, el	space
espada, la	sword
espalda, la	back
español	Spanish
especialista, el	specialist
espectáculo, el	show
espectador, el	bystander
espejo, el	mirror
espejo retrovisor, el	rearview mirror
esperar	wait (to)
esposa, la	wife
esposas, las	handcuffs
esposo, el	husband
esquina, la	corner
está	is (temporary state, condition, location)
estación de policía, la	police station
estación, la	station
estacionar	park (to)
estadio, el	stadium
estado civil, el	marital status
estado, el	state
Estados Unidos, los	United States
estamos	we're (temporary state, location, condition)
están	they're (temporary state, condition, location)
estatua, la	statue

estatura	height
este	east; this
estéreo, el	stereo
estilo, el	style
estómago, el	stomach
estos	these
estoy	I'm (temporary state, location, condition)
estrangulamiento, el	strangulation
estrecho	narrow
estrella, la	star
estudiante, el	student
estudiar	study (to)
estudio, el	studio
estufa, la	stove
etiqueta, la	sticker
evidencia, la	evidence
examinador, el	examiner
examinar	examine (to)
excusado, el	toilet
experiencia, la	experience
explicación, la	explanation
explosivo, el	explosive
expresión, la	expression
expuesto	liable
extendido	extended
extensión, la	extension
exterior	exterior
extorsión, la	extortion
extorsionador, el	racketeer
extraño	strange

F

fábrica, la	factory
fácil	easy
factura, la	invoice
falda, la	skirt
falsificación, la	counterfeiting
falsificador, el	forger
falso	fake
faltar	miss (to)
farmacia, la	pharmacy
faro delantero, el	headlight
faro trascro, el	taillight
fatal	fatal
fatiga, la	fatigue
fax, el	fax
febrero	February

fecha, la	date
* ¡Felicitaciones!	Congratulations!
feliz	happy
* ¡Feliz cumpleaños!	Happy Birthday!
feo	ugly
feria, la	fair
feroz	ferocious
ferrocarril, el	railroad
festival, el	festival
fiador, el	bondsman
fianza, la	bail
fiebre, la	fever
fiesta, la	party
filudo	sharp
fin de semana, el	weekend
firmar	sign (to)
fiscal del distrito, el	district attorney
flecha, la	arrow
flojo	loose
flor, la	flower
floristería, la	florist
foco, el	lightbulb
fogón, el	fireplace
follaje, el	foliage
fondo, el	bottom
forma, la	shape
formalidad, la	formality
formulario, el	form
forzar	break in (to)
fósforos, los	matches
fractura, la	fracture
francotirador, el	sniper
frasco, el	vial
fraude, el	fraud
frecuentemente	often
fregadero, el	kitchen sink
freno, el	brake
frente, el	front
fresa, la	strawberry
fresco	cool
frijoles, los	beans
frío	cold
* ¡Fuego!	Fire!
fuego, el	fire
fuegos artificiales, los	fireworks
fuente, la	fountain
fuerte	strong

fugitivo, el	fugitive
fumar	smoke (to)
funda de pistola, la	holster
funeral, el	funeral
funeraria, la	funeral home
furgoneta, la	van
furioso	furious
fusible, el	fuse
fútbol americano, el	football

G

gabinete, el	cabinet
galón, el	gallon
galleta, la	cookie
galleta salada, la	cracker
gancho, el	hook
ganga, la	bargain
garaje, el	garage
garganta, la	throat
garrote, el	billy club
gas, el	gas
gas lacrimógeno, el	tear gas
gasolina, la	gasoline
gasolinera, la	gas station
gata, la	jack
gato, el	cat
gay, el	gay
gemelo, el	twin
gente, la	people
gerente, el	executive
gesto, el	gesture
gimnasio, el	gymnasium
ginebra, la	gin
globo, el	balloon
gobernador, el	governor
gobierno, el	government
goma, la	rubber
gordo	fat
gorra, la	cap
gota, la	drop
gotera, la	leak
grabadora, la	recorder
grabadora telefónica, la	answering machine
grabar	record (to)
* ¡Gracias!	Thank you!
grado, el	grade
grafiti, el; pintadas, las	graffiti
gramo, un	gram (a)

gran jurado, el	grand jury
grande	big
granizo, el	hail
granjero, el	farmer
grapa, la	staple
grava, la	gravel
grifo, el	faucet
gris	gray
gritar	yell (to)
groserías, las	obscenities
grúa, la	tow truck
grueso	thick
guante, el	glove
guantera, la	glove compartment
guapo	handsome
guardabarro, el	fender
guardabosques, el	ranger
guardaespaldas, el	bodyguard
guardería infantil, la	day care center
guardia, el	guard
guardia de seguridad, el	security guard
Guardia Nacional, la	National Guard
guardia salvavidas, el	lifeguard
guardián de la prisión, el	warden

H

habilidad, la	skill
hábito, el	habit
habla, el	speech
hablar	talk (to)
hace	ago
hacer	do (to); make (to)
hacha, el	hatchet
halcón, el	hawk
hambre	hungry
hamburguesa, la	hamburger
hay	there is, there are
* Hay que...	One must...
hebilla, la	buckle
helada, la	ice cream
helicóptero, el	helicopter
herida, la	injury
herir	injure (to); wound (to)
hermana, la	sister
hermano, el	brother
heroína, la	heroin
herramienta, la	tool

hielo, el	ice
hierba, la	weed
hígado, el	liver
hija, la	daughter
hijastra, la	stepdaughter
hijastro, el	stepson
hijo, el	son
hilo, el	string
hogar, el	home
hogar para ancianos, el	nursing home
* ¡Hola!	Hi!
holgazán, el	loiterer
hombre, el	man
hombro, el	shoulder
homicidio, el	homicide
honor, el	honor
honorario, el	fee
hora, la	time (specific)
horario, el	schedule
horno, el	oven
hospital, el	hospital
hostil	hostile
hotel, el	hotel
huérfano, el	orphan
huerta, la	orchard
hueso, el	bone
huevo, el	egg
húmedo	humid
humo, el	smoke
huracán, el	hurricane
hurto, el	larceny

I

identificación, la	identification
idioma, el	language
iglesia, la	church
ilegal	illegal
impermeable, el	raincoat
importante	important
incapacidad, la	disability
incapacitado	disabled
incendio premeditado, el	arson
incendiario, el	arsonist
incesto, el	incest
incómodo	uncomfortable
inconsciente	unconscious
incursión, la	raid
indicador de velocidad, el	speedometer

indicador, el	gauge
indio, el	Indian
indocumentado	undocumented
influenza, la	flu
información, la	information
informante, el	informer
infracción, la	infraction
ingeniero, el	engineer
ingle, la	groin
ingreso, el	income
inhalante, el	inhalant
inhalar	inhale (to)
inmigración	immigration
inmigrante, el	immigrant
inocente	innocent
inofensivo	harmless
inquieto	restless
inquilino, el	occupant; tenant
insolación, la	sunstroke
inspector, el	inspector
instrucción, la	instruction
instrucciones, las	directions
instrumento, el	instrument
insulina, la	insulin
inteligente	bright (person); smart
interior, el	interior
intérprete, el	interpreter
interrogación, la	cross-examination
interruptor, el	light switch
intoxicado	intoxicated
intrusión, la	trespassing
intruso, el	intruder
inundación	flood
investigación, la	inquiry; investigation
investigador, el	investigator
investigar	investigate (to)
invierno, el	winter
inyección, la	injection
inyectar	inject (to)
ir	go (to)
irrigación, la	irrigation
isla, la	island

J

jalar	pull (to)
jamón, el	ham
jardín, el	garden; yard
jardinero, el	gardener

jarra, la	pitcher
jaula, la	cage
jefe, el	chief
jeringa, la	syringe
joven	young
joyas, las	jewelry
judío	Jew
juego de apuestas, el	gambling
juego, el	game
jueves	Thursday
juez, el	judge
jugador, el	player; gambler
jugar	play (to); gamble (to)
jugo, el	juice
juguete, el	toy
juicio, el	trial
julio	July
junio	June
juntos	together
jurado, el	jury
jurisdicción, la	jurisdiction
justicia, la	justice
justo	just
juventud, la	youth

L

labio, el	lip
laboratorio, el	laboratory
ladrillo, el	brick
ladrón, el	thief
lago, el	lake
lámpara, la	lamp
lana, la	wool
lápiz, el	pencil
larga distancia	long distance
largo	long; length
lastimado	hurt
lata, la	can
látigo, el	whip
latino, el	Latin
lavadora, la	washing machine
lavaplatos, el	dishwasher
* ¿Le gusta...?	Do you like...?
leche, la	milk
leer	read (to)
legal	legal
lejos	far
lengua, la	tongue

lentes de contacto, los	contact lenses
lentes del sol, los	sunglasses
lento	slow (person)
lesbiana, la	lesbian
letrero, el	billboard
levantar	lift (to)
levantarse	stand up (to)
ley, la	law
liberar	release (to)
libertad provisional, la	parole; probation
libra, la	pound
libre	free
librero, el	bookshelf
libro, el	book
licencia, la	license
licor, el	liquor
líder, el	leader
ligero	light (not heavy)
lima, la	file (instrument)
límite de velocidad, el	speed limit
limón, el	lemon
limosnero, el	beggar
limpiaparabrisas, el	windshield wiper
limpiar	clean (to)
limpio	clean
línea, la	line
linterna, la	flashlight
líquido, el	liquid
lista de espera, la	waiting list
listo	ready
* ¡Lo siento!	I'm sorry!
lobo, el	wolf
loco	crazy
locura, la	insanity
lodo, el	mud
lote de carros, el	car lot
lote de estacionamiento, el	parking lot
luego	later
lunes	Monday
luz de calle, la	streetlight
luz de parada, la	brake light
luz, la	light

LL

llama, la	flame
llamada, la	call; phone call
llamar	call (to)
llave inglesa, la	wrench

llave, la	key
llave de incendios, la	fire hydrant
llegar	arrive (to)
lleno	full
llevar	carry (to)
llorar	cry (to)
llover	rain (to)
lluvia, la	rain

M

madera, la	lumber; wood
madrastra, la	stepmother
madre, la	mother
maestro, el	teacher
mal	bad
maíz	corn
maletera, la	trunk
maletín, el	briefcase
mancha, la	spot
mandar	send (to)
mandíbula, la	jaw
manejar	drive (to)
manga, la	sleeve
mano, la	hand
manoplas, las; nudillera, la	brass knuckles
* ¡Manos arriba!	Hands up!
mansión, la	mansion
mantener	maintain (to)
manzana, la	apple
mapa, el	map
mapache, el	raccoon
maquillaje, el	makeup
máquina de coser, la	sewing machine
máquina, la	machine
maquinista, el	machinist
mar, el	sea
marca, la	mark
mareado	dizzy
marijuana, la	marijuana
marisco, el	seafood
martes	Tuesday
martillo, el	hammer
marzo	March
más	more
* ¡Más despacio!	More slowly!
* ¡Más o menos!	More or less!
máscara de gas, la	gas mask
matar	kill (to); murder (to)

matrimonio, el	marriage
mayo	May
mayor	older
mecánico, el	mechanic
medianoche, la	midnight
medias, las	stockings
medicina, la	medicine
médico, el	doctor
médico legista, el	coroner
medidas, las	measurements
medio, el	middle
mediodía, el	noon
medir	measure (to)
mejicano	Mexican
mejilla, la	cheek
mejor	better
menor	minor; younger
menor de edad, el	juvenile
menos	less
mentir	lie (to)
mentira, la	lie
mercado, el	market
merienda, la	snack
mes, el	month
mesa de noche, la	nightstand
mesa, la	table
mesonero, el	waiter
metanfetamina, la	methedrine
metro, el	subway
mezclador de cemento, el	cement truck
mi	my
microondas, el	microwave
miedo, el	fear
miércoles	Wednesday
migra, ver Departamento de Inmigración	
mil	thousand
mil millones	billion
milla, la	mile
millas por hora	m.p.h.
millón	million
ministro, el	minister
minusválido, el	handicapped
mío (or mía)	mine (possessive)
miope	nearsighted
mirar	look (to)
misa, la	Mass
mismo	same

mitad, la	half
moción, la	motion
mochila, la	backpack
modelo, el	model
modisto, el	dressmaker
mojado	wet
molestar	bother (to)
molesto	upset
moneda, la	coin
monedero, el	coin case
montaña, la	mountain
morado	purple
moreno	brunette
morgue, la	morgue
morir	die (to)
mortuorio, el	mortuary
mosca, la	fly
motel, el	motel
motivo, el	motive
motocicleta, la	motorcycle
motor, el	engine
muchacho, el	teenager
muchedumbre, la	crowd
mucho	a lot
* **¡Mucho gusto!**	Nice to meet you!
muchos	many
muebles, los	furniture
muelle, el	pier
muerte, la	death
muerto	dead
mujer, la	woman
muleta, la	crutch
multa, la	fine (penalty)
muñeca, la	wrist
municipio, el	city hall
músculo, el	muscle
museo, el	museum
músico, el	musician
muslo, el	thigh
musulmán	Muslim
* **¡Muy bien!**	Very well!

N

nacimiento, el	birth
nacionalidad, la	nationality
nada	nothing
nalga, la	buttock

naranja, la	orange
narcóticos, los	narcotics
narcotráfico, el	drug traffic
nariz, la	nose
natación, la	swimming
navaja, la	razor
navegación a vela, la	sailing
navegar	sail (to)
navidad, la	Christmas
neblina, la	fog
necesario	necessary
* Necesita...	You need to...
negar	deny (to)
negocio, el	business
negro, el	black
nervio, el	nerve
nervioso	nervous
neumático de repuesto, el	spare tire
neumático, el	tire
nieta, la	granddaughter
nieto, el	grandson
nieve, la	snow
niña, la	girl
niñero, el	babysitter
niñez, la	childhood
niño, el	boy; child
ninguno	none
niveladora, la	bulldozer
* ¡No entiendo!	I don't understand!
* ¡No sé!	I don't know!
* ¡No se preocupe!	Don't worry!
nombre	name
norte	north
nosotros	we
notario, el	notary public
noticia, la	notice
novecientos	nine hundred
noveno	ninth
noventa	ninety
noviembre	November
nube, la	cloud
nublado	cloudy
nuera, la	daughter-in-law
nuestro	our
nueve	nine
nuevo año, el	New Year's
número de tiros, el	round (number of bullets)

número de serie, el	serial number
número, el	number
nunca	never

O

o	or
obedecer	obey (to)
obrero, el	worker; laborer
obsceno	obscene
obstáculo, el	roadblock (natural)
obstruir	obstruct (to)
octavo	eighth
octubre	October
ocupación, la	occupation
ocupado	busy
ocupar	occupy (to)
ocurrir	occur (to)
ochenta	eighty
ocho	eight
odio, el	hate
odómetro, el	odometer
oeste	west
ofensa, la	offense
oferta, la	offer
oficial a cargo de la libertad provisional, el	probation officer
oficial, el	officer; official
oficina, la	office
oír	hear (to)
* ¡Ojalá!	I hope so!
ojo, el	eye
olor, el	smell
once	eleven
onza, la	ounce
operador, el	operator
órden de la corte, la	warrant
orden de restricción, la	restraining order
orden, el	order
orden, la	command
oreja, la	ear
oriental, el	Oriental
orilla, la	curb
orina, la	urine
oso, el	bear
otoño, el	autumn
otra vez	again
óvalo, el	oval
oxígeno, el	oxygen

P

paciencia, la	patience
paciente, el	patient (sick person)
padrastro, el	stepfather
padre, el	father
padrinos, los	godparents
pagar	pay (to)
página, la	page
pago, el	payment
país, el	country
pala, la	shovel
palabra la	word
paño, el	diaper
panadero, el	baker
pandilla, la	gang
pandillero, el	gang member
pantalones, los	pants
pantano, el	swamp
papa, la	potato
papel, el	paper
papel higiénico, el	toilet paper
papeleo, el	paperwork
paquete de seis, el	six-pack
par, el	pair
para	for
parabrisas, el	windshield
parachoques, el	bumper
parada de autobús, la	bus stop
paraguas, el	umbrella (for rain)
paramédico, el	paramedic
parar	stop (to)
pared, la	wall
parentezco, el	relationship
pariente, el	relative
parque de diversiones, el	amusement park
parque, el	park
parquímetro, el	parking meter
pasajero, el	passenger
pasaporte, el	passport
pasar	happen (to); pass (to)
Pascua, la	Easter
* ¡Pase!	Go ahead!
pasillo, el	hallway
pastel, el	pie
patín, el	skate
patio, el	backyard; courtyard
patrulla, la	patrol
patrullera, la	patrol car

411

patrullero, el	patrolman
pavimento, el	pavement
pavo, el	turkey
peatón, el	pedestrian
pecho, el	chest
pedal, el	pedal
pedazo, el	piece
pegamento, el	glue
pegar	hit (to)
peine, el	comb
pelea, la	fight
pelear	fight (to)
* ¡Peligro!	Danger!
peligro, el	danger
peligroso	dangerous
pelota, la	ball
peluca, la	wig
peluquero, el	hairdresser
pendiente, el	pendant
penicilina, la	penicillin
penitenciaría, la	penitentiary
pensión para el ex-cónyugue, la	alimony
peor	worse
pequeño	small
pera, la	pear
perder	lose (to)
* ¡Perdón!	Excuse me!
perezoso	lazy
periódico, el	newspaper
perjurio, el	perjury
perjuro, el	perjurer
permiso, el	consent; permit
pero	but
perrera, la	doghouse
perro de la policía, el	police dog
perro, el	dog
perro guía, el	seeing eye dog
perseguir	chase (to)
persona, la	person
pesado	heavy
pesar	weigh (to)
pescado, el	fish
pescador, el	fisherman
pescar	fish (to)
peso	weight
pestaña, la	eyelash
pestillo, el	dead bolt
petición, la	claim; request

piano, el	piano
pie, el	foot
piedra, la	stone; rock (small)
piel, la	skin
pierna, la	leg
piezas de auto, las	auto parts
pilas, las	batteries
píldora, la	pill
píldora para dormir, la	sleeping pill
piloto, el	pilot
piña, la	pineapple
pintar	paint (to)
pintor, el	painter
pintura, la	paint
pinzas, las	pliers; tweezers
pisada, la	track
piscina, la	swimming pool
piso, el	floor
pista, la	lane
pistola, la	pistol
placas, las	plates
planta, la	plant
plástico, el	plastic
plátano, el	banana
plato, el	plate
playa, la	beach
pleito, el	lawsuit
plomero, el	plumber
pluma, la; bolígrafo, el	pen
población, la	population
pobre	poor
pobreza, la	poverty
poco	a little
pocos	few
poder	be able (to)
policía, el	police officer
policía, la	police (general)
póliza, la	policy
polvo, el	dust
pólvora, la	powder
pollo, el	chicken
poner	put (to)
por	by
por alguna parte	somewhere
por ciento, el	percent
* ¡Por favor!	Please!
por ninguna parte	nowhere
por qué	why

por todas partes	everywhere
porche, el	porch
pornografía, la	pornography
porque	because
portarse	behave (to)
portillo, el	hatch
portón, el	gate
poste, el	post
postración nerviosa, la	shock
postre, el	dessert
práctica, la	practice
practicar	practice (to)
precio, el	price
preferir	prefer (to)
pregunta, la	question
preguntar	ask (to)
preocupado	worried
présbita	farsighted
presidente, el	president
preso, el	inmate
prestar	lend (to)
presupuesto, el	budget
prevención, la	prevention
primavera, la	spring
primero	first
primeros auxilios, los	first aid
primo, el	cousin
prisión, la	prison
prisionero, el	prisoner
privado	private
probar	prove (to)
problema, el	problem
procedimiento, el	procedure
producto químico, el	chemical
prometer	promise (to)
pronto	soon
pronunciar	pronounce (to)
propiedad, la	property
propiedad robada, la	stolen property
propósito, el	purpose
prostitución, la	prostitution
prostituta, la	prostitute
proteger	protect (to)
protestante	Protestant
proveer	provide (to)
próximo	next
prueba, la	proof
psicólogo, el	psychologist

pubertad, la	puberty
público, el	public
* **¿Puedo ayudarle?**	May I help you?
puente, el	bridge
puerta, la	door
puerto, el	port
puertorriqueño	Puerto Rican
pulgada, la	inch
pulmón, el	lung
puma, el	mountain lion
puñalada, la	stabbing
puño, el	fist
punta, la	end
puntadas, las	stitches
puntual	punctual
puro, el	cigar

Q

qué	what
* **¡Qué bueno!**	That's great!
* **¿Qué hora es?**	What time is it?
* **¡Qué lástima!**	What a shame!
* **¿Qué pasa?**	What's happening?
* **¿Qué pasó?**	What happened?
* **¡Qué tenga un buen día!**	Have a nice day!
quebrar	break (to)
quedarse	stay (to)
queja, la	complaint
quemadura, la	burn
querer	want (to)
queso, el	cheese
quién	who
quieto	quiet
quince	fifteen
quinientos	five hundred
quinto	fifth
* **¿Quisiera...?**	Would you like...?
quizás	maybe

R

racismo, el	racism
radar, el	radar
radiador, el	radiator
radio, el	radio
radio transmisor, el	radio transmitter
rampa, la	ramp
rápidamente	rapidly
rápido	fast

rascacielos, el	skyscraper
rata, la	rat
ratería en las tiendas, la	shoplifting
ratero de tiendas, el	shoplifter
rato, el	awhile
ratón, el	mouse
raza, la	race
razón, la	reason
reacción, la	reaction
recepcionista, el	receptionist
receta, la	prescription
recibo, el	receipt
recompensa, la	reward
reconocer	recognize (to)
recordar	remember (to)
rectángulo, el	rectangle
recuperar	recover (to)
recurso, el	resource
redondo	round (shape)
reemplazar	replace (to)
reflector, el	floodlight
refresco, el	soft drink
refrigerador, el	refrigerator
refugiado, el	refugee
refugio, el	shelter
refugio de animales, el	animal shelter
regalo, el	gift
regañar	scold (to)
región, la	region
registrar	frisk (to)
registro, el	registration
regla, la	rule
reglamento, el	regulation
rehabilitación, la	rehabilitation
rehén, el	hostage
rehusar	refuse (to)
reír	laugh (to)
relaciones sexuales, tener	have sex (to)
relajado	relaxed
relámpago, el	lightning
relampagueante	flashing
religión, la	religion
reloj dc pulsera, el	wristwatch
reloj, el	clock; watch
remolcar	tow (to)
renovar	renew (to)
repartir	share (to)

repetir	repeat (to)
repisa, la	shelf
reportar	report (to)
represa, la	dam
requisito, el	requirement
resbalador, el	slide
resbaloso	slippery
rescate, el	ransom
Reserva, la	Reserve (Army)
reservar	reserve (to)
reservista, el	reservist
resfrío, el	cold (illness)
residencia, la	residence
residente, el	resident
respeto, el	respect
respiración artificial, la	CPR
respirar	breathe (to)
responder	respond (to)
responsable	responsible
respuesta, la	response
restaurante, el	restaurant
restricción, la	restriction
resultado, el	result
retrato, el	picture
retroceder	back up (to)
reunión, la	meeting
revista, la	magazine
revólver, el	revolver
rezar	pray (to)
rezo, el	prayer
rico	rich
rifle, el	rifle
riñón, el	kidney
rincón, el	nook
río, el	river
robar	rob (to); steal (to)
robo de mayor cuantía, el	grand theft
robo, el	robbery
robo en tránsito, el	hijacking
robo mayor, el	grand theft
rociadora, la	sprinkler
rodear	surround (to)
rodilla, la	knee
rojo	red
romo	dull
rompecabezas, el	puzzle
ropa interior, la	underwear

ropero, el	closet
roto	broken
rubio	blonde
rueda, la	wheel
ruidoso	loud
ruta, la	route
rutina, la	routine

S

sábado	Saturday
sábana, la	sheet
saber	know something (to)
sacar	take out (to)
sacerdote, el	priest
sala de billar, la	pool hall
sala de masajes, la	massage parlor
sala, la	living room
salida, la	exit
salir	leave (to)
salón de belleza, el	beauty salon
salón, el	lobby
saltamontes, el	grasshopper
* **¡Salud!**	Bless you!
saludar	greet (to)
salvaje	wild
salvamento, el	rescue
salvar	save (to)
sangrar	bleed (to)
sangre, la	blood
sangriento	bloody
sargento, el	sergeant
sastre, el	tailor
* **¿Se puede?**	May I come in?
secador de pelo, el	hair dryer
secadora, la	clothes dryer
secar	dry (to)
sección, la	section
seco	dry
secretario, el	secretary
secreto, el	secret
secuestrador, el	kidnapper
secuestro, el	kidnapping
sed	thirst
sedán, el	sedan
seguir	continue (to); follow (to)
segundo	second
seguro	safe; secure; sure

seguro, el	insurance
seguro social, el	social security
seis	six
selva, la	jungle
semáforo, el	traffic light; traffic signal
semana, la	week
semirremolque, el	semi-trailer
señal de alto, la	stop sign
señal de dirección, la	turn signal
señal de tráfico, la	traffic sign
señal, la	sign
señalar	signal (to)
señor (Sr.)	Mr.
señora (Sra.)	Mrs.
señorita (Srta.)	Miss
senda, la	path; trail
seno, el	breast
sentarse	sit down (to)
sentencia, la	sentence
septiembre	September
séptimo	seventh
serio	serious
serrucho, el	saw
servicio, el	service
servicios sanitarios, los	restrooms
servir	serve (to)
sesenta	sixty
setecientos	seven hundred
setenta	seventy
sexo, el	sex
sexto	sixth
SIDA, el	AIDS
siempre	always
siete	seven
siguiente, el	following
silbato, el	whistle
silenciador, el	muffler
* ¡Silencio!	Quiet!
silencio, el	silence
silla de ruedas, la	wheelchair
silla, la	chair
sillón, el	armchair
simpático	nice
sin	without
sin plomo	unleaded
sirena, la	siren
sistema de seguridad, el	security system

sitio, el	place; site
sobre, el	envelope
sobredosis, la	overdose
sobrevencido	overdue
sobreviviente, el	survivor
sobrevivir	survive (to)
sobriedad, la	sobriety
sobrina, la	niece
sobrino, el	nephew
sociedad, la	society
socio, el	partner
* ¡Socorro!	Help!
sofá, el	sofa
sofocación, la	suffocation
soga, la	rope
sol, el	sun
soldado, el	soldier
solo	alone
soltero	single
soltero, el	bachelor
sombrero, el	hat
sombrilla, la	umbrella (for sun)
somos	we're (qualities, characteristics)
son	they're (qualities, characteristics)
sonido, el	sound
sopa, la	soup
soplar	blow (to)
soporte para el brazo, el	sling
sordo	deaf
sospechoso, el	suspect
sostén, el	brassiere
sótano, el	basement
soy	I'm (qualities, characteristics)
su	her; his; its; their; your
suave	soft
suceder	take place (to)
sucio	dirty
sudaderas, las	sweat suit
sudar	sweat (to)
suegra, la	mother-in-law
suegro, el	father-in-law
suelo, el	ground
sueño	sleep
suéter, el	sweater
suficiente	enough
sufrir	suffer (to)
suicidio, el	suicide

supermercado, el	supermarket
suponer	suppose (to)
sur	south
suspender	suspend (to)
suya	his; hers; yours
suyo	his; her; theirs

T

tabla, la	board
tablero de instrumentos, el	dashboard
tableta, la	tablet
talega, la	duffel bag
tamaño, el	size
también	too
tanque, el	tank
tapacubo, el	hubcap
tapicería, la	upholstery
tapón del tanque, el	gas cap
tardanza, la	delay
tarde	late
tarea, la	homework
tarjeta de crédito, la	credit card
tarjeta, la	card
tarjeta postal, la	postcard
tatuaje, el	tattoo
taxi, el	taxi
tázer, el	tazer
té, el	tea
teatro, el	theater
técnico, el	technician
techo, el	roof
teléfono, el	telephone
televisor, el	TV
temerario	reckless
temprano	early
tendón, el	tendon
tener	have (to)
teniente, el	lieutenant
terapia, la	therapy
tercero	third
terminar	end (to)
término, el	term
termostato, el	thermostat
terremoto, el	earthquake
terreno, el	land
terrorismo, el	terrorism
terrorista, el	terrorist

testificar	testify (to)
testigo, el	witness
testimonio, el	testimony
tía, la	aunt
tibio	warm
tiempo, el	time (general); weather
tienda, la	store
* Tiene que...	You have to...
tierra, la	dirt
tijeras, las	scissors
tina, la	bathtub
tío, el	uncle
tipo, el	type; guy
tirador, el	handle
toalla, la	towel
tobillo, el	ankle
tocadiscos, el	record player
tocador, el	dresser
tocar	touch (to)
* ¡Todavía no!	Not yet!
todo	all; everything
* ¡Todos hacia atrás!	Everyone get back!
tomar	consume (to); take (to)
tomate, el	tomato
toque de queda, el	curfew
torcido	twisted
tormenta, la	storm
tornado, el	tornado
tornillo, el	screw
torniquete, el	tourniquet
torre, la	tower
torta, la	cake
tortura, la	torture
tos, la	cough
trabajador, el	worker
trabajador social, el	social worker
trabajar	work (to)
trabajo, el	job; work
tractor, el	tractor
tradición, la	tradition
traductor, el	translator
tráfico, el	traffic
tragar	swallow (to)
traje de baño, el	bathing suit
traje, el	suit
tranquilizante, el	tranquilizer
transfusión, la	transfusion

transmisión, la	transmission
transporte, el	transportation
tranvía, el	streetcar
trapo, el	rag
travesura, la	mischief
trece	thirteen
treinta	thirty
tren, el	train
tres	three
triángulo, el	triangle
tribunal, el	court
trineo, el	sled
triste	sad
truco, el	trick
trueno, el	thunder
tu	your (informal singular)
tú	you (informal singular)
tubería, la	plumbing
tubo de escape, el	exhaust
tubo, el	pipe
tuerca, la	nut
tumbar	knock down (to)
tumulto, el	riot
túnel, el	tunnel
tutor, el	legal guardian

U

un	a, an
uniforme, el	uniform
universidad, la	university
uno	one
unos, unas	some
urgente	urgent
usar	use (to)
usted	you (singular)
ustedes	you (plural)
uva, la	grape

V

vaca, la	cow
vaciar	empty (to)
vacío	empty
vacunación, la	vaccination
vagabundo, el	vagrant
vagoneta, la; furgoneta, la	van
válido	valid
valor, el	value

válvula, la	valve
valle, el	valley
*¡Vamos!	Let's go!
vandalismo, el	vandalism
vaso, el	glass (drinking)
*¡Vaya con Dios!	Go with God!
vecino, el	neighbor
vehículo de recreo, el	recreation vehicle
vehículo, el	vehicle
veinte	twenty
vejiga, la	bladder
velocidad, la	speed
vena, la	vein
vendaje, el	bandage
vendedor de drogas, el	drug dealer
vendedor, el	salesman
vender	sell (to)
veneno, el	poison
venganza, la	revenge
venta, la	sale
ventana, la	window
ventilador, el	fan
ver	see (to)
verano, el	summer
verdad, la	truth
verde	green
veredicto, el	verdict
verificar	check (to)
vesícula, la	gallbladder
vestido, el	dress
veterinario, el	veterinarian
vez, la	time (occurrence)
viajar	travel (to)
vicio, el	vice
víctima, la	victim
vida, la	life
videocasetera, la	VCR
vidrio, el	glass
viejo	old
viento, el	wind
viernes	Friday
vietnamés	Vietnamese
vigilancia, la	surveillance
vigilante, el	watchman
vino, el	wine
violación, la	rape; violation
violador, el	rapist

violar	rape (to)
violencia doméstica, la	domestic violence
violento	violent
visa, la	visa
visitante, el	visitor
viudo	widowed; widower
vivienda, la	housing
vivir	live (to)
vivo	alive
volante, el	steering wheel
volquete, el	dump truck
voluntario, el	volunteer
vomitar	vomit (to)
* **Voy a...**	I'm going to...
voz, la	voice
vuelo, el	flight
vulgaridad, la	vulgarity

Y

y	and
yerno, el	son-in-law
yo	I

Z

zanahoria, la	carrot
zancudo, el	mosquito
zanja, la	ditch
zapatos, los	shoes
zigzaguear	swerve (to)
zoológico, el	zoo
zurdo, el	left-handed

Made in the USA
Middletown, DE
25 January 2023

23121844R00243